# 攻坚“最后一公里”

## 中国普惠金融发展报告（2018）

THE REPORT OF FINANCIAL INCLUSION DEVELOPMENT IN CHINA (2018)

主　　编　贝多广
执行主编　莫秀根

中国金融出版社

责任编辑：贾　真
责任校对：张志文
责任印制：张也男

**图书在版编目（CIP）数据**

攻坚“最后一公里”：中国普惠金融发展报告. 2018/贝多广主编 .—北京：中国金融出版社，2018. 10
ISBN 978—7—5049—9789—0

Ⅰ. ①攻…　Ⅱ. ①贝…　Ⅲ. ①金融业—经济发展—研究报告—中国—2018　Ⅳ. ①F832

中国版本图书馆 CIP 数据核字（2018）第 226016 号

出版发行　中国金融出版社
社址　北京市丰台区益泽路 2 号
市场开发部　(010)63266347，63805472，63439533（传真）
网上书店　http：//www. chinafph. com
　(010)63286832，63365686（传真）
读者服务部　(010)66070833，62568380
邮编　100071
经销　新华书店
印刷　北京侨友印刷有限公司
尺寸　185 毫米×260 毫米
印张　16. 75
字数　326 千
版次　2018 年 10 月第 1 版
印次　2018 年 10 月第 1 次印刷
定价　148. 00 元
ISBN 978—7—5049—9789—0

# 2018 中国普惠金融国际论坛

## 中国 · 北京

## 发　布


主　　编：贝多广

执行主编：莫秀根

课题主要成员（按姓氏首字母拼音顺序排列）：

贝多广　邓　鹏　顾　雷　黄媚媚　赖丹妮

刘　琰　莫秀根　熊德平　徐默莅　余新平

曾恋云　张晓峰　张亦辰　朱晓莉

课题参与人员（按姓氏首字母拼音顺序排列）：

刘澄清　鲁　梅　陆俊宇　吴跃华

鸣　　谢

资助单位及机构：

民生银行

Visa 公司

宜信普惠

美团金融

浙江省农村信用社联合社

北京信托与普惠金融研究中心

# 前言

中国普惠金融研究院每年出版一本年度中国普惠金融发展报告，已经成为我们的例行任务。每年的报告都会推出一个主题：第一年我们讨论“好金融、好社会”，先树立我们想要追求的未来愿景。第二年我们讨论“普惠金融国家发展战略”，在远大愿景的前提下，国家需要有迈向目标的规划和战略，其中不乏值得推敲的选择和难以回避的挑战。第三年，我们讨论“普惠金融与能力建设”，这源于我们的深刻认识：普惠金融好比一艘航船，船上的人能否顺利抵达彼岸，取决于他们能力的高低。今年已是第四个年头，我们把主题定为攻坚“最后一公里”，一方面，全球普惠金融面临的最大难题就是所谓金融服务的“最后一公里”；另一方面，我国正在实施厘定年度目标的扶贫攻坚战略，普惠金融的“最后一公里”与扶贫攻坚的“最后一公里”有相当程度的契合。

“最后一公里”这一说法源自英文“the last mile”，直译是“最后一英里”。国人足够智慧，入乡随俗，把它译成“最后一公里”，以符合国人的阅读语境。台湾人更讨巧，把它译成“最后一里地”，两面不得罪。

说到金融服务的“最后一公里”，人们首先想到的是那些身处边疆海角、深山戈壁的弱势人群，于是出现了马背银行和大篷车银行的艰难跋涉。近些年，我国在推进普惠金融进程中，不少商业银行、农村信用合作社将金融服务物理触达点——比如助农取款服务点——延伸到最后一公里，基本上在全国农村地区实现了行政村全覆盖。毫无疑问，这是让世人惊艳的成绩。

不过，“最后一公里”问题是普惠金融面临的一项全球性难题。它的难点有物理距离上的原因，但远不止于此。今年我们对此进行了比较深入的研究，发现至少可以从四个方面来剖析“最后一公里”的内涵。首先，最容易理解的是，从物理位置上直观地表现为金融服务商与“最后一公里”客户之间的距离。其次，从成本角度看，为了服务客户，金融服务商需要付出相对较高的交通成本和时间成本，即便存在固定或临时服务网点，金融服务商提供服务的方式效率相对较低，难以保持商业可持续。再次，从供应方金融能力来看，金融服务商服务“最后一公里”客户多是产品导向，如此提供的产品往往也就难以适应客户的生产生活需求。最后，从需求方金融能力来看，客户使用金融服务的经验相对较少，金融素养和技能不足，金融态度和行为更容易与其最佳金融利益相悖。由此可见，“最后一公里”只是一个形象的比喻，用比较学术的语言来表述，实际上就是金融服务的“缺口”。

令人欣喜的是，人们并不乏解决“最后一公里”问题的探索。我们在报告中归纳了直营模式、代理模式、互助模式、数字模式和供应链金融模式五种模式以及诸多国际上的经验案例。但任何一种单一模式似乎都无法从根本上解决“最后一公里”问题。比如，我们观察到一方面助农取款服务点全覆盖，另一方面不少服务点流于形式，客户并不解渴，而金融服务商也为服务点的商业可持续性头疼。2017 年，全球普惠金融的先驱穆罕默德·尤努斯教授参加了在人民大学举办的一场对话。当有人提到商业银行对服务下沉颇感吃力时，尤努斯教授的回答是：“我们没有‘最后一公里’的困扰，因为我们 from the bottom up（意指自下而上）。当我们把最底层的人群都服务好了，往上服务就没有问题。”在尤努斯教授眼里，最贫穷的人群压根不是“最后一公里”，而恰恰是他服务的“第一公里”或者“最先一公里”。早在 20 世纪 70 年代，当尤努斯教授掏出 27 美元借给 42 位最贫困的村妇时，他就是从这“第一公里”开始的——从观察最贫困群体的需求出发，为她们设计缓解生活所难的金融服务。

尤努斯精神是震撼人心的。“最后一公里”问题的解决，首先应该是思想认识上的头脑风暴，即回归初心、服务实体，真正把“最后一公里”客户当作服务本体，也就是“第一公里”的思维。从产品导向转变为客户导向，以客户为中心，由此出发来寻找解决久悬难题的答案。

为了攻坚“最后一公里”，我们需要探索能够更好地适应“最后一公里”金融服务的交易流量和成本结构的服务模式，更高效率地填补市场空缺。数字技术为我们带来了这样的机会。举例而言，尤努斯教授创建的格莱珉银行，采用信贷员挨家挨户上门拜访的方式，在 40 年里服务了 900 万名客户。而我国的一家金融科技公司通过数字化手段，3 年就能建立 3000 万名客户。通过对比可以发现，数字金融服务在金融“最后一公里”的优势是显而易见的。我们需要持续推动数字金融服务发展，充分发挥其触达范围广、边际成本低、交易效率高等优势。

当然，我们在赞美数字红利的同时，也要清醒地看到数字鸿沟的存在。有趣的是，许多数字鸿沟问题还需要通过线下服务来解决。就像我们观察到的，目前银行越来越多的业务可以通过人机对话完成，但是复杂业务、复杂问题还是离不开人工服务。无论是从国际还是国内经验来看，解决金融服务的“最后一公里”问题，线下服务依旧扮演着重要的角色。即使建立了线上线下相结合的服务模式，“最后一公里”客群需求稀疏、量小的特征仍然是金融服务商头疼的问题。以我国银行体系的助农取款服务点为例，在部分乡村地区，曾经出现单个行政村中有多家银行分别布放POS机具的情况。由于不同银行布放的POS机具不能互通使用，而村民持有银行卡的发卡行又不尽相同，最终导致一些银行布放的POS机具逐渐荒废，部分村民的基础金融服务需求仍未得到满足。由此可见，要实现“最后一公里”金融服务可持续、高效率、功能全的发展目标，突破规模瓶颈是关键。

根据国际经验和我国实际情况，我们认为组建超越机构的“最后一公里”金融服务聚合供应商（简称聚合器，即英文aggregator）是当前解决我国金融“最后一公里”问题、突破规模瓶颈的重要途径。聚合器聚合多种类、多渠道的金融服务，比单家供应商更容易实现规模效应，可以为“最后一公里”客户提供一站式解决方案。本报告第二部分对此展开了较为详尽的探讨。

最后，我们将今年的主题定为“攻坚最后一公里”，也是经过了反复斟酌，颇费了一番心思。起初，我们考虑用“决胜最后一公里”或“打通最后一公里”。但听上去，前者过于自信，仿佛胜利在望；后者又过于轻松，没有表达出其难其艰。选定“攻坚”一词，重在表达“最后一公里”问题是全球现象、是长期现象，未必能毕其功于一役、一蹴而就。首先要反映其难，要久久为功，就像国家正在推动的扶贫攻坚战一样。其次，“最后一公里”问题是一个动态的概念。金融服务初级阶段是解决人们的存汇兑困难，但随着整体金融事业的提升以及人民收入水平的提高，人们对金融服务的需求也会随之持续增加，如对贷款的需求、对保险的需求等。不排除在不久的将来，广大农民想要投资基金股票等各种理财产品。因此，“攻坚”既是一场阵地战，又是一场持久战。

古人云：“富贵难义合，困穷易感恩。”我们每年的发展报告，就是对自己的一份压力、一场挑战。好在冥冥之中总有力量在支持我们，让我们从开题时的困顿走到终稿时的喜悦。我们的研究团队在这一过程中也获得了明显的升华。每当此时，我的内心总是洋溢着暖暖的感恩之情。当然，我还要向所有支持和帮助完成这一报告的合作伙伴和各位同仁送上真诚的谢忱。

贝多广

2018年9月19日于北京宣武门

# Preface

Every year, Chinese Academy of Financial Inclusion (CAFI) publishes a report on China's financial inclusion development. This has become a routine for us. Every report has a theme of the year. In the first report, our theme was "Good Finance, Good Society" to state our grand vision for this industry. The second report focused on discussion of "National Development Strategy of Financial Inclusion" . Under the grand vision, we need to consider strategies and plans on a national level, discussing controversial choices and unavoidable challenges. For the third year, we talked about "Financial Inclusion and Capacity Building" . This choice of topic came from our profound insight: whether financial inclusion services could actually help the disadvantaged groups greatly depends on their financial capability. In this fourth year, we set the theme to "Conquering the Last Mile" . On one hand, on a global scale, the "Last Mile" issue has become the biggest problem of international financial inclusion industry. On the other hand, China is at the last stage of implementing the poverty alleviation strategy; the "Last Mile" of financial inclusion and the "Last Mile" of poverty alleviation overlap to a great extent.

Talking about the "Last Mile", people tend to think about the disadvantaged groups of people living in remote mountainous villages. So the first attempt of solving the "Last Mile" issue was inventing "banks on horseback" and "banks on wagons" . In recent years, a number of commercial banks and rural cooperatives have extended physical existence of financial services — such as farmer-assistance cash withdraw facilities — to the "last mile", achieving a full coverage of all administrative villages in China. Undoubtedly, this is an astonishing achievement.

However, the issue of "Last Mile" is a global challenge, and physical distance is only one of its many difficulties. This year, based on our in-depth research, we found that the difficulty comes from four aspects. First and the most apparent reason is the physical distance between financial service providers and the end clients. Secondly, from a cost point of view, financial providers would bear high commuting cost and time cost in serving the end clients along the “Last Mile” . Even with physical existence, the efficiency of service provision would still be very low, making it very hard to achieve commercial sustainability. Thirdly, some financial service providers have low financial capability to provide client-oriented products. Lastly, from the clients' point of view, end consumers along the “Last Mile” have little experience, financial literacy and capability, and their financial attitude and behaviors are not suited for best interest. It can be said that, the “Last Mile” is just a vivid analogy, and a more formal terminology should be a “shortfall” of financial services.

Delightfully, the attempt to solve the “Last Mile” issue has never stopped. In this report, we introduce the direct chain model, agency model, cooperative model, digital model and supply-chain financing model, and a number of international experiences and examples. Any single model is insufficient to fundamentally solve the “Last Mile” issue. For example, despite of the full coverage of farmer-assistance cash withdraw facilities, a lot of them are “form over substance”: the real needs of end clients left unmet and financial service providers are struggling with the commercial sustainability of their attempts. Last year, the pioneer of global financial inclusion, Professor Muhammad Yunus attended a forum in Renmin University of China. When asked whether they have had difficulty in lowering their banking services to the bottom clients, that is, as Professor Yunus put it “the poorest of the poor”, he responded that, they never had the “Last Mile” issue, because their services had been “bottom-up”; if the bottom clients were served well, going up was never a problem. Professor Yunus regard the bottom clients not the “Last Mile”, but the “First Mile” . In the 1970s, when Professor Yunus lent 27 Dollars to 42 poor village women, he started from the “First Mile” — by observing the needs of the poorest and designing financial products best to meet their needs.

The Yunus Spirit is heartshaking. Solving the “Last Mile” issue calls for transforming our mindset, that is to return to *Shoshin* (beginners' mind), serve the real economy, and treating the real “Last Mile” clients as the “First Mile” . A true answer to the unsolved problem would be found if we can have a mindset of client-orientation instead of product orientation.

To conquer the "Last Mile" issue, we need to explore a service model that can better suit the transaction volume and cost structure of the "Last Mile", in order to fill the market gap more effectively. In this regard, digital technology has equipped us with powerful tools. The Grameen Bank established by Professor Yunus took the in-person visits model, and served 9 million clients in about 40 years. Using digital means, however, a FinTech company had established a client base of over 30 million in only 3 years. We can also see that, digital financial services have obvious advantages along the "Last Mile" . We need to keep promoting the development of digital financial services, to maximize its advantages of broader reach, lower marginal cost, and higher transaction efficiency.

However, while we appreciate the benefits brought about by digital technology, we should also be aware of the problem of the digital gap. The funny thing is, many of digital gap problems need to be solved off-line. Just like what we see, that although more and more banking services can be completed on a machine, more complex businesses still need assistance by person. Based on international and domestic experiences, online and offline services are equally important in solving the "Last Mile" issue. Although both online and offline service models had been established, the low transaction volume is still a major headache for financial service providers. Again let's take the farmer-assistance cash withdraw services for an example. It was once seen that POS terminals from different financial institutions had been set up in a single village. As a POS terminal can only be used in conjunction with the bank card from the same financial institution, and not all banks set up the facilities, therefore some of the POS machines were rarely used and some villagers' needs were still unmet. Therefore, in order to achieve the goals of high sustainability, high efficiency, and fully functionality, the key might be volume breakthrough.

Based on international experience and China's particular circumstances, we believe that building financial service aggregators might be an essential key to achieve the volume breakthrough. By aggregating multi-type and multi-channel financial services, the financial aggregators can realize scale economies compared to single providers, and provide one-stop solution for clients along the last mile. The Part II of this book discusses "Financial Aggregators" in more detail.

We set the theme of this year to "Conquering the Last Mile" after careful and repeated debates and discussions. We also considered "Winning the Last Mile" or "Getting through the Last Mile" . But we then decided that the former sounded a bit overconfident and the latter made the task seem too easy. Finally we chose "Conquering" to indicate that the "Last Mile" issue is a global, long-term problem. Winning a single battle is not winning the war. We need to appreciate the difficulties and challenges, and prepare ourselves for a long-term fight, just like the nation's tough fight against poverty. In addition, the "Last Mile" issue is a dynamic concept. Initially, we would aim at solving people's difficulties in basic banking services such as saving, remitting, and cashing, etc. But with the development of the financial industry and people's living standard, demand for other financial services such as loan and insurance would increase as well. It might be possible that in the near future farmers might also have needs to invest in funds and equities. Therefore, we are "conquering" both a positional battle and a protracted war.

An old saying in China says "The rich and wealthy hardly gather for morality and justice, while the poor and troubled appreciate every piece of assistance." Our yearly report is a challenge and pressure for us. Luckily, we feel like having a secret power behind us, raising us from confusion in the beginning to joy at the end. Maybe this power is the sense of social consciousness and responsibility. Our research team has improved and matured during the process as well. Every time we finish a report, I am flooded with a warm sense of appreciation and inspiration. I would like to express my sincere gratitude for our colleagues and cooperative partners who have put in so much effort in this report.

Bei Duoguang
Written in Xuanwumen, Beijing
19th September 2018

# 目录

概要 / 1

绪论　攻坚金融服务的“最后一公里” / 1

一、什么是金融服务的“最后一公里”问题 / 1

二、触达“最后一公里”的服务模式 / 2

三、“最后一公里”问题存在的原因 / 7

四、解决金融“最后一公里”问题的国际经验 / 9

五、金融“最后一公里”问题的解决思路 / 20

第一部分　面向“中小微弱”的金融服务

第一章　农村金融服务机构的改革与实践 / 27

一、中国普惠金融事业版图 / 27

二、政策性银行普惠金融改革与实践 / 31

三、中国农业银行普惠金融的改革与实践 / 35

四、中国邮政储蓄银行普惠金融改革与实践 / 38

五、农村信用社普惠金融改革与实践 / 42

六、新型农村金融服务机构 / 46

七、互联网金融企业在普惠金融发展中的作用 / 53

第二章　新型金融机构的崛起和困境 / 55

一、互联网和金融科技正在重构金融服务体系 / 55

二、主要新型金融企业的创新实践现状考察 / 58

三、主要新型金融机构金融服务因基因而不同 / 62

四、主要新型金融企业在普惠金融方面的服务困境 / 65

**第三章　国际机构与中国普惠金融发展 / 67**

一、国际机构在中国的三个阶段 / 68
二、国际机构的类别和投资方式 / 72
三、解决金融“最后一公里”问题的成效 / 82
四、成败经验 / 88

## 第二部分　跨越“最后一公里”的桥梁

**第四章　金融聚合器与“最后一公里” / 93**

一、“最后一公里”问题现状 / 93
二、农村金融聚合器的类型 / 110
三、金融聚合器的应用模式 / 114
四、问题及建议 / 126

**案　例　善用金融聚合器　锻造多方共赢普惠金融服务 / 128**

**第五章　超级数字金融平台与“最后一公里” / 132**

一、超级数字金融平台的发展现状 / 132
二、超级数字金融平台解决“最后一公里”问题的难点与建议 / 136
三、超级数字金融平台的业务发展逻辑、优势与趋势 / 137

## 第三部分　穿越“最后一公里”的环境条件

**第六章　金融科技与“最后一公里” / 145**

一、金融科技中的关键技术 / 145
二、金融科技的应用 / 149
三、金融科技在降低成本中的作用 / 155
四、金融科技在风险控制中的作用 / 156

五、金融科技当前的问题所在 / 158

第七章 穿越金融“最后一公里”的基础设施 / 164

一、建设现状 / 164

二、仍然存在的问题 / 180

三、改善建议 / 181

第八章 打通“最后一公里”问题的适度监管 / 184

一、当前金融监管对“最后一公里”问题造成实际影响 / 184

二、解决“最后一公里”问题适度监管原则调整 / 186

三、解决“最后一公里”问题适度监管若干建议 / 189

四、穿越“最后一公里”宏观制度环境与政策支持 / 192

第四部分 决胜“最后一公里”的社会效果

第九章 指标监测结果对解决“最后一公里”问题的启示 / 199

一、中国普惠金融发展指数的构建 / 199

二、指数应用之一：浙江省普惠金融发展现状分析 / 201

三、指数应用之二：浙江丽水市金融改革效果分析 / 205

第十章 银行服务促进小微企业发展 / 211

一、引言 / 211

二、银行账户超越财务管理功能 / 212

三、银行账户的普惠金融价值 / 214

四、员工收入水平偏低 / 215

五、证实模型 / 219

六、结论 / 225

参考文献 / 227

# Contents

Summary / 1

INTRODUCTION Conquering the "Last Mile" Issue of Financial Services / 1

1. Define the "Last Mile" Issue / 1
2. Service Models for the "Last Mile" / 2
3. Reasons Behind the "Last Mile" Issue / 7
4. International Experiences in Solving the "Last Mile" Issue / 9
5. Possible Solutions for the "Last Mile" Issue / 20

## PART Ⅰ FINANCIAL SERVICES TO THE DISADVANTAGED

Chapter 1 Reforms and Practices of Rural Area Financial Service Institutions / 27

1. Current Landscape of Financial Inclusion in China / 27
2. Reforms and Practices of Financial Inclusion by Policy Banks / 31
3. Reforms and Practices of Financial Inclusion by Agricultural Bank of China / 35
4. Reforms and Practices of Financial Inclusion

by Postal Savings Bank of China / 38
5. Reforms and Practices of Rural Cooperatives / 42
6. New Type Financial Service Institutions / 46
7. Roles of Internet Financial Companies in the Financial Inclusion Industry / 53

Chapter 2 Rise and Dilemmas of New Type Financial Institutions / 55
1. Internet and FinTech Reshaping the Financial Service System / 55
2. Reviewing the Innovative Practices of Major New Type Financial Companies / 58
3. Differences between Major New Type Financial Institutions / 62
4. Dilemmas Faced by Major New Type Financial Institutions in Financial Inclusion Services / 65

Chapter 3 International Institutions and China's Financial Inclusion Development / 67
1. Three Phases in International Institutions' Practice in China / 68
2. Types and Investment Methods of International Institutions / 72
3. Results Accomplished by International Institutions / 82
4. Lessons and Experiences / 88

PART Ⅱ PASSING THE "LAST MILE"

Chapter 4 Financial Aggregators and the "Last Mile" / 93
1. Current Conditions of the "Last Mile" Issue / 93
2. Types of Rural Area Financial Aggregators / 110
3. Application Models of the Financial Aggregators / 114
4. Problems and Suggestions / 126

Case Study Using Financial Aggregators to Provide All-winning Inclusive Financial Services / 128

Chapter 5 Super Digital Financial Platforms and the "Last Mile" / 132

1. Current Conditions of the Super Digital Financial Platforms / 132
2. Difficulties Faced by Super Digital Platforms and Our Suggestions / 136
3. Logics, Advantages, and Trends Behind Super Digital Financial Platforms / 137

PART Ⅲ ENVIRONMENT OF PASSING THE "LAST MILE"

Chapter 6 FinTech and the "Last Mile" / 145

1. Key Technologies in FinTech / 145
2. Application of FinTech / 149
3. FinTech in Cost Reduction / 155
4. FinTech in Risk Control / 156
5. Current Problems of FinTech / 158

Chapter 7 Infrastructure for the "Last Mile" / 164

1. Current Status of the Infrastructure / 164
2. Existing Problems of the Infrastructure / 180
3. Suggestions for Improvement / 181

Chapter 8 Moderate Regulation along the "Last Mile" / 184

1. Actual Implications of Current Regulation on the "Last Mile" Issue / 184
2. Adjusting the Regulation Principles on the "Last Mile" Issue / 186
3. Regulatory Suggestions / 189

4. Macro Environment and Regulatory Support Along the "Last Mile" / 192

## PART Ⅳ SOCIAL IMPACT OF CONQUERING THE "LAST MILE" ISSUE

Chapter 9 Implications of Indicator Monitoring Results on Solving the "Last Mile" Issue / 199
1. Constructing the China Financial Inclusion Index / 199
2. Index Application Case 1：Study on Zhejiang Financial Inclusion Development / 201
3. Index application Case 2：Effect of financial Reforms Based on a Lishui study / 205

Chapter 10 Banking Services Promotes Development of Small and Micro Enterprises / 211
1. Introduction / 211
2. Bank Accounts：Beyond the Financial Management Function / 212
3. Bank Accounts' Value in Financial Inclusion / 214
4. Low Employee Income Level / 215
5. Empirical Model / 219
6. Conclusions / 225

Bibliography / 227

# 概要

金融服务难以突破最后一段距离而触达边缘群体的现象，通常被称为金融服务的“最后一公里”问题，反映了在现有金融体系条件下，最边缘客户获得金融服务的难度远远超过其他客户的现象。本书研究了“最后一公里”问题的背景，金融服务机构与金融科技等在解决“最后一公里”问题中的探索与实践，并且总结了现有成果与相关问题思考。

“最后一公里”问题是一个动态复杂的概念。服务成本高、可负担高利息的能力比较低、风险高，是阻碍金融机构为最边缘客户提供服务最主要的原因。而对于边缘群体，金融能力不高、金融素养和技能不足、对金融服务不信任的态度也阻碍了他们获得和使用金融服务；金融“最后一公里”问题，还与政策环境有关，不合理的财政政策和金融政策，缺乏客户保护，都可能导致中小微企业和弱势群体难以获得金融服务。

目前能够触达边缘客户的金融服务包含直营模式、代理模式、互助模式、数字模式以及供应链金融模式。其中，前三种模式主要是直接接触客户服务模式；数字模式包含各类金融机构、准金融机构提供的数字金融服务，主要指无直接接触的服务模式；供应链金融模式在实践中既可能是纯线上、纯线下的，也可能是线上、线下相结合的，由于其具有独特的风控模型，所以将其划分为一种独立的服务模式。

国际上已经存在许多解决“最后一公里”问题的经验，如肯尼亚的M－PESA手机银行、巴西国家邮政银行代理网点等模式。它们在金融科技服务供应商如何有效获取边缘客户，政府和业界如何合作，对待金融服务的竞争以及边缘客户保护的经验，对中国在解决“最后一公里”问题上都有借鉴意义。

在普惠金融的“最后一公里”问题解决过程中，需要引导金融供应商以客户为中心，通过持续推动数字金融服务发展构建线上与线下融合的金融服务体系，同时探索跨机构金融服务聚合供应模式并持续优化金融生态系统等，才能为最边缘客户提供与其需求相匹配的金融服务，在改善客户福祉的同时推动经济社会包容性发展。

农村金融服务机构的发展对中国普惠金融发展战略与精准扶贫战略的推进，以及攻坚金融“最有一公里”问题的成效，具有决定性影响（第一章）。目前，我国涉农金融机构既包括传统金融机构、新型农村金融机构，也包括近年兴起的互联网金融企业，以及其他非银行业金融机构与行业龙头企业等延伸的金融服务机构。

近年来，国家开发银行和中国农业发展银行两大涉农政策性银行在解决金融服务“最后一公里”方面作出了积极贡献。例如，国家开发银行通过支持易地扶贫搬迁、支持贫困地区特色产业发展等一系列活动针对贫困户加大了金融服务；中国农业发展银行为易地扶贫搬迁提供贴息贷款与金融扶贫实验示范区建设，与地方政府联合构建产业扶贫合作模式，探索投贷结合融资和两权抵押贷款等。这些措施都引导了资金投向边缘地区和贫困户，发挥了政策性的导向作用。

农村信用社（农村商业银行）、农业银行、邮储银行等，是解决“最后一公里”问题参与程度比较深的传统银行。它们通过金融科技数字技术进行产品创新，建立了农户的信用评级体系并开发出各种适合以当地客户的信用产品，并在农村社区建立金融综合服务站为当地农民提供了基本的金融服务。这三家机构建立的金融综合服务站，已经形成了中国分布最密集的技术金融服务网络，基本实现了金融服务的全覆盖。而村镇银行、农村资金互助社等新型农村金融机构，也增加了农村金融供给的总量。与此同时，互联网企业也凭借强大的金融技术能力，将金融服务送达边远客户群并发挥了积极作用。

快速发展的新型金融机构在帮助解决“最后一公里”问题的过程中也面临着独特的挑战与困境（第二章）。信息科技的快速迭代和发展对金融服务业起到深刻的变革和推进作用。我们在分析新型金融机构发展的同时，也了解到了它们在解决“最后一公里”问题中所起到的作用与遇到的挑战。

新型金融机构在攻坚普惠金融“最后一公里”中发挥了很大的作用。其在金融服务深度和效率方面具有明显的优势，这些机构能够让边缘群体较为便捷地使用服务，在保护了客户隐私的同时也提升了社会金融服务质量与普惠服务能力。例如，网商银行依托蚂蚁金服和阿里平台的技术积累，给小微企业和个人创业者提供的金融服务，切实弥补了传统金融机构过去未服务和不服务的用户空白。截至2018年6月底，网商银行累计向1000万小微企业和个人经营者提供了超过1万亿元的经营性贷款；网商银行面向农村市场推出的“旺农贷”产品服务近400万家农村小微企业，农村个体工商户，农村种植、养殖户。

新型金融机构通过将新技术引入金融领域而大幅提高可以获得金融服务的受众面同时，也要认识到鉴于金融服务的基础是信用，交易的核心是信任和安全，被传统金融机构排除在外的小微企业和个人所能够获得或实际获得的金融服务仍有欠缺，新型金融对于企业的普惠金融服务还存在诸多挑战。

国际机构在中国开展的普惠金融业务对中国的普惠金融发展提供了有价值的实践经验（第三章）。国际机构参与中国普惠金融发展与中国改革开放国策密切相关。四十多年来，国际机构通过将普惠金融发展需要的资源引进中国，推动了中国普惠金融发展。它们参与中国普惠金融发展可分为发展援助阶段、捐赠投资阶段与社会影响力投资阶段。参与中国普惠金融发展的国际机构包含多边/双边发展机构、非营利组织、跨国公司与境外金融机构。

国际机构在中国的实践经验，对中国普惠金融发展有三个方面的启示。第一，由于普惠金融的重点服务对象是“中小微弱”群体，天然地决定了普惠金融供应方要平衡财务绩效和社会绩效，因此，双目标平衡机制对普惠金融供应方的可持续发展起着决定性的作用。第二，本土化创新对国际普惠金融服务模式能否适应与扎根中国市场有着重要影响。第三，管理模式的建构对普惠金融项目成败或机构可持续发展有着重要的影响。

国际机构对中国普惠金融事业的发展，在模式借鉴、资金支持、技术支持等方面，有过不可磨灭的贡献。特别是在小额信贷方面，国际机构的支持起到非常重要的促进作用。

了解普惠金融“最后一公里”的主要服务对象与地区特征有利于寻找最有效的解决办法（第四章）。中国普惠金融研究院（CAFI）发布的浙江省普惠金融综合指数，为我们识别边缘群体提供了数字依据。

我们了解到边缘群体的特征包括家庭劳动力供养负担重，就业比例低，收入不稳定，经济负担大；较低的家庭教育程度与收入进而降低对金融服务的需求；边缘家庭的消费支出比例大，没有自信能够获得社会帮助。以上因素会导致边缘人群受到金融排斥的程度比较高。此外，我国的东西部地区在普惠金融发展上的差异明显，西部城市普惠金融发展的可得性、使用情况、质量及满意度等方面均处于排斥度相对较大的位置。总体而言，我国普惠金融未来发展与扶持政策重点应该向西部地区有一定程度的倾斜。

金融服务的“最后一公里”问题，往往出现在农村地区。农村作为基础金融服务的薄弱地区，发展潜力巨大且有一定的后发优势。比如，与“三农”相关的保险产品会有较大的市场空间。另外，农村市场的融资难与融资贵问题，一定程度上是由于征信体系建设不完全导致的。解决融资问题是解决农村产业发展，从而提高农村居民收入的关键推动力。

农村金融中，聚合器在现阶段有其存在的必要性。由于中国农村社会、经济、文化、人群的发展能力与城市差别非常大，农村金融服务与城市金融服务有很大的不同，很多金融服务必须要通过连接供给、需求双方的聚合器来完成。聚合器在服务对象与金融服务提供商（FSP）之间发挥重要的“桥梁”作用。一方面，聚合器赋能于金融服务商，帮助其进行服务能力传导到农村居民；另一方面，聚合器也赋能于农村居民，在与金融服务商的沟通中获取更多、更好的金融服务。比较典型的农村金融聚合器的类型包含村级金融服务站、农村地区的金融服务代理商、农村合作组织、农村基层组织、农业龙头企业、农村平台企业与金融监管机构搭建的平台等。

农村金融服务的实现形式大部分都要依赖于某种或几种聚合器。在商业实践中，农村金融服务的实现所依赖的聚合器类型会产生不同的商业模式。打通农村金融“最后一公里”的各种模式在实践中也并非是绝对独立的，多数机构是运用几种模式而非单一模式综合提供金融服务的。如直营+代理+数字模式、线上平台+线下机构、互联网金融+公益小额贷款机构/农村信用社+农户、G2B2C数字模式（监管机构与金融机构合作为农村居民提供服务）与互助模式。我们通过分析聚合器的模式与效果发现其中的问题与提出了具体的建议。

在善用金融聚合器的讨论中，我们加入了宜信的案例。宜信通过锻造多方共赢的普惠金融服务，积累了需要攻坚“最后一公里”的宝贵经验。

超级数字金融平台对于解决“最后一公里”问题也发挥着重要的作用（第五章）。超级数字金融平台具备综合化、数字化、平台化、客户群规模化等特征。其既能为目标客户提供生活工作等在线平台服务，还能提供金融服务。在中国，众多“最后一公里”的“中小微弱”群体并未触网是超级数字金融平台触达“最后一公里”的困难所在。我们把金融聚合器称为为“中小微弱”群体提供链接服务的金融代理。它扎根“中小微弱”群体聚集的村/社区或乡镇，通过互联网与智能设备，持续为“中小微弱”群体提供各类服务，直接触达“中小微弱”群体。

金融聚合器作为可以直接接触“最后一公里”的“中小微弱”群体的个人或机构，在这个链条中起到代理作用。超级数字金融平台触达“最后一公里”的难点在于解决与“不触网客户”链接的问题，它与金融聚合器建立合作，看中的正是金融聚合器与“中小微弱”群体的紧密关系。为解决金融“最后一公里”的问题，超级数字金融平台与金融聚合器的合作方式包括业务加载形式、业务混合形式与业务拓展形式。

目前，超级数字金融平台参与解决金融“最后一公里”问题仍面临不少难题，如超级数字金融平台的合规发展、金融聚合器的发展程度、“中小微弱”群体的金融能力等。作为解决办法，首先，超级数字金融平台需在合规的基础上摸索并打造成熟而可持续的业务模式，真正发挥互联网金融技术优势。其次，要丰富超级数字金融平台与金融聚合器的合作模式，注重“中小微弱”群体金融能力的提升与为“中小微弱”群体提供更多元丰富的产品与服务。最后，超级数字金融平台应积极融入国家信用体系建设。

金融科技可以在解决“最后一公里”问题中发挥了重要作用（第六章）。云计算、大数据、人工智能和区块链，构成了当今金融科技的核心技术。金融科技的发展离不开硬件设备的快速发展，无论是服务器的计算能力，还是存储资源和网络资源，随着工业技术的成熟度越来越高，硬件设备的成本逐渐降低，这保证了云计算平台的实现时间与空间灵活度的可能性，同时为后续的大数据、人工智能等技术打下基础。

由金融科技的广泛应用而形成的数字金融产品，均有利于解决普惠金融“最后一公里”问题。以支付服务为基础，大数据信用评分服务作为其他业务的依据和支撑，信贷业务作为提供普惠金融服务的有效手段，配合理财和保险服务，达到为用户提供全方位的金融服务。而金融科技在其中扮演重要的工具角色，帮助服务提供商降低获客成本，提高风控和定价能力，降低享受金融服务的门槛，真正体现了普惠金融高可得性、可负担、产品丰富、商业可持续的特点。

金融技术可以大幅度降低金融服务成本，在大幅度减少一线服务人员数量、减少人员费用开支的同时也减少了金融机构的物理网点与开销。另外，金融技术也可以降低风险管理的成本，提高效率与风控能力。风控能力决定了普惠金融业务的成本和可持续性，通过金融科技解决分控能力是解决普惠金融“最后一公里”问题中的重要一环。

金融技术可以在解决普惠金融“最后一公里”问题中发挥着至关重要的作用，随着智能手机在农村的普及，农村地区及弱势群体享受普惠金融产品的成本大大降低。但由于农村地区用户对金融知识了解普遍较少，金融科技在解决“最后一公里”问题当中可能遇到一些挑战，如金融诈骗、数据安全、数字鸿沟与排斥等问题，也可能对监管范围和方式产生挑战。

解决“最后一公里”问题需要考虑到其中存在的监管问题（第七章）。金融监管体系中的一些问题妨碍了“最后一公里”问题的解决。第一，金融监管体系尚未成熟，农村金融监管资源不足，非正规农村金融机构游离于监管之外，难以形成有效监管。金融机构没有按原来的使命为农村最贫困人群提供及时、可得和负担得起的金融服务，产生“最后一公里”问题在所难免。第二，个别监管政策过于刚性，导致农村金融机构的发展长期受阻，金融服务资源难以覆盖到边缘地区从而导致普惠金融资源有效供给明显不足。第三，过于严苛的利率管制导致资金价格扭曲。第四，对农村普惠金融消费者保护有待提高。第五，部分监管指标过于理想化。

结合我国实际情况，采取更为包容的监管政策适合我国普惠金融初创阶段的发展。在原有金融监管原则的基础上，可以对审慎监管原则审慎使用，增加“适度性监管原则”“包容性监管原则”和“差异性监管原则”，有效避免穿透式监管、机构监管对普惠金融带来的负面影响，这有利于促进普惠金融行业有效竞争和公平发展。我们建议对现行抵押担保监管方式进行调整，加强普惠金融教育对当前利率监管政策适度调整，完善普惠金融消费者保护体系并利用科技创新驱动普惠金融快速发展。

解决“最后一公里”问题离不开相关基础设施的建设（第八章）。改革开放以来，普惠金融基础设施建设得到稳步发展，支付结算系统、征信系统、评估系统、支持性系统的建设不断满足普惠金融普及与惠及的目标。首先，支付基础设施得到了明显的改善。农村地区无网点银行与设备的覆盖稳步发展，尤其助农取款服务点实现了村级行政区的覆盖，并且随着金融科技的发展，使支付结算业务对网点的依赖下降。其次，形成了传统征信与大数据信用评分并存，且以公共征信为主、商业征信为辅的征信系统。大数据信用评分机构在数据源上也对传统征信进行了有益补充。再次，国内也开始讨论普惠金融社会影响力评估指标的建设，以期形成财务绩效和社会影响力绩效两套指标。最后，支持系统也为攻坚“最后一公里”的普惠金融服务提供发展环境、资源拓展、人才培养等各种支持。

但是，目前农村地区的支付结算系统整体建设水平仍低于城镇地区，征信系统仍存在城乡差距、失信惩戒效用低、信息安全等问题，评估系统仍未实现高效的行业预测和风险预警，也未形成普惠金融全行业的支持系统。下一轮普惠金融的发展浪潮在于代理商、互联网和其他无网点银行渠道。在这样的趋势与背景之下，中国农村地区金融基础设施建设，要更多地从“中小微弱”群体的需求与习惯出发。

CAFI 普惠金融发展指标监测体系对于“最后一公里”的解决提供了数据支持（第九章）。作为普惠金融发展的重要基础设施建设之一，指标与监测体系在精准度量、动态监测、适时评估其发展程度上会起到重要作用。CAFI 的“数字普惠金融指标与监测体系建设”项目通过与浙江省农村信用社联合社合作开展的调研与分析收集到的数据，建立了一个衡量普惠金融发展指标的动态监测体系。应用上述普惠金融发展指数分析浙江省的普惠金融发展情况，结果显示，浙江省普惠金融发展水平较高。这体现了普惠金融服务水平较高，受排斥程度较低，地理分较为均匀，各样本区县普惠金融综合指数均值差异并不显著。

浙江省金融能力和使用情况是普惠金融发展的短板。金融能力和使用情况维度的排斥程度最高，是最具改善空间的两个维度。数据还表明了低收入跟高年龄受金融排斥的可能性较大。提高受教育程度可以减少排斥度的特征。除了可得性、使用情况等构成指数的维度和指标外，受访人年龄、所在家庭户主学历、所在家庭人均收入、金融服务使用障碍以及数字化程度指标均对普惠金融综合指数具有显著影响。此外，数据显示更低金融排斥程度对应更佳未来预期。

我们还使用该体系评价了丽水市 2006 年以来实施的农村金融改革对普惠金融发展的效果。结果显示，丽水金融改革显著降低了丽水普惠金融服务的排斥率并显著提高金融服务的总体包容性。丽水市农村金融改革增加了金融的包容性与改革的内容有紧密的关系。改革在金融组织、金融产品、惠农政策、金融市场、信用、服务平台、支付服务、金融生态八大体系着力，最主要的目的就是增加客户端的体验。显然，改革对客户端产生显著的良好效果。

银行通过提升服务可以有效促进小微企业发展（第十章）。普惠金融强调要为中小微企业提供银行服务，促进社会的均衡发展，是基于中小微企业的发展可以为中低收入阶层提供大量的就业机会，增加他们的收入水平，改善他们的生活前提。这也是为中小微企业提供金融服务的社会效果。本书通过实证研究证明了为小微企业提供金融服务与中低收入人群的收入水平提高的关系。

分析发现，银行账户的多少与小微企业的合同工人数以及员工工资有显著的关系。企业的银行账户数目，实际上反映了企业资金的流动性的大小，并可以增加企业获得信贷资金从而增加流动资金总量的机会，增加了企业生产服务的稳定性，提高了企业的效率，促进了企业的可持续发展。其具体表现为增加企业的合同制员工人数和员工工资。我们得出的结论：通过改善小微企业账户服务，提高服务的便利性，可以促进小微企业发展，增加就业机会，改善低端就业人群的收入水平，促进社会均衡发展。

本书介绍了在解决金融服务“最后一公里”问题过程中的中国实践。我们希望本书的研究与发现可以有助于为服务不足的群体提供更好的金融服务，提升机构的服务水平，并最终成为一个金融健康的社会。

# Summary

The "Last Mile" issue often refers to the difficulty of financial services to reach the marginalized population, reflecting the higher cost of marginalized groups in obtaining financial services compared to other clients in current financial system conditions. This Report studies the background of the "Last Mile" issue, and the explorations and practices on the "Last Mile" issue by financial institutions and FinTech companies. This report also summaries existing accomplishments and reflections on related issues.

The "Last Mile" issue is a complex and dynamic concept. The main factors preventing financial institutions from serving marginalized clients include high service costs and high risk to be borne by the institutions, and low affordable interest rates by clients. The lack of financial capability, knowledge and skills, and the distrust of financial institutions by those marginalized groups further hinder their use of financial services. The "Last Mile" issue is also related to the policy environment. Inappropriate fiscal and financial policy and the lack of consumer protection are all negative factors affecting the popularization of financial services among small and micro enterprises and the disadvantaged individuals.

Currently, the financial service models reachable to marginalized clients include the direct chain model, agency model, cooperative model, digital model and supply-chain financing model. Among them, the first three allow direct interaction with end clients. Digital model is found in digital financial services provided by all types of financial institutions and quasi-financial institutions, and often involves indirect interactions with clients. Supply-chain model can be online, offline, or a hybrid of both. It is regarded as a different service model due to its unique risk-control method.

Examples of international experiences on solving the "Last Mile" issue include M-PESA mobile banking in Kenya and the Agency Network Model of Banco Postal in Brazil. They provide valuable experiences on solving the "Last Mile" issue in China in areas of acquiring marginalized clients by FinTech service providers, cooperation between government and the industry, competition in financial services, and consumer protection, etc. .

In the attempt to solve the "Last Mile" issue, financial service providers should focus on the needs of end clients, promote the development of digital financial services to construct online-offline hybrid service system, explore on the cross-institution aggregated service model and optimize the whole financial ecosystem, so as to provide financial services that are best matched to the needs of end clients, improve client welfare and at the same time promote the inclusive development of economic society.

Rural financial service institutions play a vital role in promoting the development of financial inclusion in China, achieving targeted poverty alleviation, and conquering the "Last Mile" issue (Chapter 1) . Currently, agriculture-related financial institutions include traditional financial institutions, new type rural financial institutions, newly-emerged internet financial companies, and other non-bank financial institutions and some leading conglomerates with financial divisions.

In recent years, the two agriculture-related development banks, i. e. China Development Bank and Agricultural Development Bank of China, have made positive contributions to solving the issue of the "Last Mile" . For example, China Development Bank supported the demolition and relocation of poverty areas and provided funds for characteristic industries in poverty areas. Agricultural Development Bank of China provided interest-subsidy loans, participated in construction of poverty alleviation experimental demonstration areas, established cooperative models on industrial poverty alleviation with local governments, made attempts on Equity-Loan Combined Financing and Dual-Right① Collateralized Loans. Such measures all directed funds towards marginalized areas and poverty households, playing a leading political role.

Rural Credit Cooperatives (Rural Commercial Banks), Agricultural Banks, Postal Banks are traditional banks deeply involved in solving the "Last Mile" issue. These institutions made innovations on FinTech digital technology, built a rural household credit rating system, and developed credit products suitable for local clients, and set up comprehensive financial service station to provide basic financial services to local residents. The comprehensive financial service stations set up by these three institutions have formed the most concentrated technological financial services network, achieving a full coverage of all village residents. At the same time, rural banks, rural mutual cooperatives and other new type rural financial institutions have increased the overall sup-

① The two rights are: operating rights on the contracted land by farmers, and property right of rural housing.

ply of rural financial services. Also, internet companies, taking advantages of their FinTech skills, are playing a constructive role in delivering financial services to rural area clients.

Fast developing new type financial institutions are facing unique challenges and dilemmas in solving the "Last Mile" issue (Chapter 2) . The speedy development and iteration of information technology are playing a profound revolutionary role in the financial industry. In Chapter 2 we will discuss the development of new type financial institutions and introduce their contributions and challenges in solving the "Last Mile" issue.

New type financial institutions are essential in conquering the "Last Mile" issue in financial inclusion. They offer deep and efficient services for rural clients, enhancing financial service quality and financial inclusion capability while protecting consumer privacy. As an example, based on Ant Financial and the IT skills of Alibaba, MyBank provides financial services to small and micro companies as well as individual entrepreneurs, filling the un-serviced and under-serviced market gap left open by traditional financial institutions. By the end of June 2018, the accumulated loan issuance had amounted to over 1 trillion RMB, and 10 million small and micro companies had benefited from such services. The loan product facing the rural market, "Wang Nong Dai", had served almost 4 million clients, including small and micro enterprises and farming households.

While new type financial companies increased the audience scope of financial services through improved new technology, we should be aware that the foundation of all financial services is credit, and the core of all transaction is trust and safety. For the previously excluded small and micro companies and entrepreneurs, the available financial services are still rather limited. There are yet mounting difficulties and challenges in the inclusive finance business faced by new type financial institutions.

International institutions undertook financial inclusion practices in China, providing valuable experiences (Chapter 3) . The participation by international institutions in China's inclusive finance market is closely related to China's national policy of reform and opening up. In almost 40 years, international institutions introduced resources necessary in the development of financial inclusion into China, stimulating its development. Their involvement in China's financial inclusion industry can be divided into the following three phases: the development assistance phase, endowment investment phase, and social impact investment phase. International participants in China's financial inclusion include multilateral/bilateral development institutions, non-profit institutions, cross-border companies and oversea financial institutions.

The implications of international institutions' practices in China can be three-fold. Firstly, as the targeted audiences of financial inclusion are mainly small and micro sized companies and disadvantaged individuals, there is a natural trade-off between economic impact and social impact in determining the effectiveness of such practices. Therefore, a dual-purpose balancing mechanism should play a decisive role in the sustainable development of financial inclusion. Secondly, localized innovations determine the successfulness of implementing international experiences in China. Thirdly, the imported advanced management models are also very influential for financial inclusion projects and the sustainable development of institutions.

In summary, international institutions have made significant contributions on financial inclusion development in China, especially in business modes, fund support, and technical support for micro loans.

A clear understanding of the target audience and local characteristics helps to find the best solution in solving the "Last Mile" issue (Chapter 4) . The Chinese Academy of Financial Inclusion (CAFI) Financial Inclusion Index provides data evidence on the characteristics of marginalized clients based on a Zhejiang sample.

Their characteristics include: heavy household labor burdens, low employment ratio, unstable income, and heavy economic burdens; low education level and income level resulting in low financial service demands; high expenditure ratio and lack of confidence in obtaining social assistance. All above factors contribute to relatively high exclusiveness in receiving financial services. Besides, there are distinct differences in the level of financial inclusion between the east and west side of the country. In the west provinces, the accessibility, usage, quality, and consumer satisfactory level are relatively at the left side of the distribution (more excluded) . Overall, the development and policy assistance should be tilted towards the west in China.

The occurrences of the "Last Mile" issue are mostly likely to happen in the rural areas in China. Although naturally disadvantaged, rural areas have huge development potential. For example, insurance products related to "San Nong" (agriculture, villages, and farmers) have large development potential. Besides, the difficult and costly financing problem is partly due to the incomplete credit referencing system. Solving the financing problem is the key impetus to the development of agricultural industry and improving personal income in rural areas.

In rural finance, a financial aggregator has an important role to play. As the social conditions, economic conditions, culture, and growth potential of the residence of rural areas differ significantly from that of cities, financial services should differ too among the two regions. In rural areas, completion of financial services requires the facilitation from an aggregator, which is connected to both demand side and supply side. The aggregator plays an important "bridging" role between the audience and financial service providers (FSP). On the one hand, the aggregator enables financial service providers to reach potential clients in the rural areas; on the other hand, the aggregator also helps rural residence to better communicate their needs with FSP in order to receive more and better financial services. Typical financial aggregators include: village-level financial service stations, financial service agents in rural areas, rural cooperative organizations, local basic-level government organizations, leading enterprises in rural areas, and platforms jointly established by rural platform companies and financial regulators, etc..

The realization of financial services in rural areas relies heavily on one or more forms of aggregators. In commercial practice, the type of aggregators has profound effect on the choice of the business models. All business model types are not isolated either, and are often used jointly by most institutions, such as Direct Chain + Agency + Digital Model, Online + 2B2C + 2G2C Model, Internet Finance + Non-Profit Micro Loan Institution/Rural Cooperatives + Farming Households Model, G2B2C Digital Model (regulator together with financial institutions provide services to rural households) and Mutual Cooperative Model. This chapter reviews different financial aggregator models, discusses their problems and provides corresponding suggestions.

During the discussion of financial aggregators, we also included a case study of a company which successfully established an all-winning financial inclusion business model making use of the financial aggregators, which provided valuable experience in tackling the "Last Mile" issue.

Super Digital Financial Platforms also plays a crucial role in solving the "Last Mile" issue (Chapter 5). Super Digital Financial Platforms show characteristics of being comprehensive, digital, platform-based, and large client based etc.. They can provide financial services as well as other life-style services. The biggest challenge for such platforms to solve the "Last Mile" issue is that large amount of marginalized clients are not online clients yet. In such cases, the above mentioned financial aggregators are required to link the platforms to end clients. Such aggregators are deeply rooted in villages, and thus are able to channel direct financial services provided by the platforms to end marginalized clients.

As financial aggregators can directly interact with institutions and individuals along the "Last Mile", they act on an agency role. The effectiveness of cooperation between super digital financial platforms and financial aggregators relies largely on the close relationship between the aggregators and end marginalized clients. Their cooperation models include: “Business Add-on Model”, “Business Hybrid Model” and “Business Extension Model” .

Other challenges faced by super digital platforms in solving the “Last Mile” issue include: regulation and compliance, development level of financial aggregators, and financial capability of marginalized client, etc.. To solve these problems, firstly, super digital financial platforms should try to develop sustainable business models, play their IT strengths to the maximum. Secondly, we should explore more cooperative methods between super digital financial platforms and financial aggregators; enhance marginalized clients' financial capability, in order to provide more diversified products and services to these clients. Thirdly, super digital financial platforms should be actively involved in the credit system construction.

FinTech is an influential contributor in solving the “Last Mile” issue (Chapter 6). Cloud Computing, Big Data, Artificial Intelligence and Blockchain are the core technologies used in the financial industry. The development of FinTech relies heavily on the hardware technology advances. Computing power, storage and internet resources will become more cost efficient with technology advances, ensuring flexibility in time and space in cloud computing by the platforms. This builds solid foundation for technologies such as Big Data and Artificial Intelligence.

Digital financial products based on the wide applications of FinTech skills can facilitate solving the “Last Mile” issue. Based on payment services, credit information collection and credit referencing services can provide basis for other products. Loan provision is an essential product. Wealth management and insurance are also important supplements to the complete product line. For all of the above products and services, FinTech plays an important role, helping to reduce client acquisition cost, enhance the risk management and pricing abilities, lowering the entry requirements for end clients. These are all consistent with the high accessibility, affordability, abundance, and sustainability of financial inclusion. Some closely relevant technologies such as machine learning and biological identification are also introduced in this chapter.

Service costs can also be greatly reduced by FinTech. The large cut in front-line personnel can reduce both HR costs and costs related to physical branches. Besides, FinTech also reduces costs related to risk management, enhancing efficiency and risk control ability. Risk control ability determines operational cost and sustainability of financial inclusion businesses. Therefore, improving risk control ability through advancing FinTech skills is crucial for operational efficiency in the industry.

We should also be aware that, with enhanced cost efficiency and accessibility of inclusive finance products and services, challenges started to accumulate due to lack of financial education and capability. Problems such as financial fraud, digital safety, digital gap and exclusion, etc.. may further threaten the healthy development of the industry.

Regulation requires particular attention in solving the "Last Mile" issue (Chapter 7). Problems in the regulation system, firstly less developed financial regulation system, lack of regulation resources in rural areas, informal rural financial institutions are excluded in the regulation system, all hinder effective regulation. It is inevitable for the "Last Mile" problem to occur when financial institutions are not providing timely, accessible and affordable financial services. Secondly, the lack of flexibility of some regulatory rules may have caused a long term negative effect on the development of rural financial institutions, leading to lack of inclusive financial service supply as financial service resources could not cover the marginalized areas. Thirdly, over-regulated interest rates are leading to mispriced financial assets. Fourthly, consumer protection in rural inclusive finance consumption needs to be improved. Fifthly, some regulatory indicators might be overly idealistic.

Based on practical circumstances, a more "inclusive" regulation regime should be adopted during the early phases of financial inclusion in China. On the basis of existing regulatory principles, prudential regulatory principles shall be used more "prudently"; and other regulatory principles such as "moderateness" "inclusiveness", and "differentiation" shall be applied as well. This can promote the effective competition and fair development, and avoid negative effect brought about by penetrative regulation and institutional regulation. We also recommend adjusting the current collateral guarantee regulation and strengthen financial inclusion education, adjust regulation regarding interest rate, improve the consumer protection system, and take advantage of technological innovations to promote the speedy development of financial inclusion in China.

Financial infrastructure is the foundation for solving the "Last Mile" issue (Chapter 8). Since the reform and opening up in China, financial infrastructure has made steady improvements in areas of payment and settlement system, credit reference system, evaluation system, and the supporting system. Firstly, in terms of payment infrastructure, branch-less and terminal-less banking services have been established; farmer-assisting cash withdraw services have reached the village level. And with the development of technology, the reliance on bank branches has been dramatically reduced. Secondly, the credit referencing system has seen the co-existing of traditional credit referencing and new Big Data referencing. The traditional public sector credit referencing service is supplemented with Big Data commercial credit referencing services which provide a new data source. Next, the evaluation of financial inclusion industry has also evolved. Social impact evaluation indicators are being discussed together with economic and financial indicators. Thirdly, the industry-wide supporting system is also providing environment, resources, and talents for the better development of the industry.

However, the overall condition of payment and settlement system in rural areas is generally less developed, large urban-rural gap exists in the credit reference system, punishments to dishonest behaviors are inefficient, evaluation system is unable to make industry forecast and risk alert, and the supporting system for industry-wide financial inclusion has not yet been established. With this background, the construction of financial infrastructure needs to start from the organic needs and demands from the disadvantaged clients.

The CAFI Financial Inclusion Indicator and Monitoring System provide data support for the “Last Mile” issue (Chapter 9) . As a major component of the financial inclusion infrastructure, the precise measurement, dynamic monitoring, and timely evaluation of the financial inclusion development using an indicator and monitoring system is of great significance. CAFI developed a “Digital Financial Inclusion Indicator and Monitoring System” . Using a sample of 14 counties in Zhejiang based on the cooperating with Zhejiang Rural Credit Cooperatives, CAFI finds that Zhejiang Province has a relatively high financial inclusion development level. Evidences include high service level, low exclusion level, a relatively small difference between different geographic regions in the sample.

Financial capability and usage of inclusive financial services are the two less satisfactory sub-indices and thus have larger improvement potential. Data also shows that, lower income, lower educational level, and higher age groups are more likely to be “excluded” . Determinants such as age, educational level of household head, difficulties in using financial services, and level of digitization not only significantly affect the above two sub-indices, but also significantly affect the comprehensive index of financial indication (proxied using different variables) . Moreover, data shows that low financial exclusion level is significantly associated with better future prospects.

CAFI also conducted a survey in Lishui City, Zhejiang Province to examine the effect of the rural financial reforms started in 2006. Results show that the financial reform in Lishui significantly reduced the exclusiveness of financial services. The reform targeted at eight areas such as financial organizations, financial products, farmer-benefiting policies, financial markets, credit, service platforms, payment services, financial ecosystems etc.. The main objective was to enhance client experience. And based on the study, we can conclude that such financial reforms have produced satisfactory effects.

Banks can effectively promote the development of small and micro enterprises (Chapter 10). As small and micro enterprises make extensive contribution in providing jobs and improving people's income level and life quality, inclusive finance emphasizes on providing banking services to these enterprises to promote the balanced development of the society. This chapter shows that providing financing to small and micro enterprises significantly increases people's income level.

Study shows that, the number of bank accounts owned by an enterprise in the sample is significantly associated with the number of contracted employees and the level of employee salary. The number of bank accounts for a company is used as a proxy for its cash liquidity, which increases the probability of the company receiving loan credit and thus further increase liquid asset size. Company's liquidity is an important factor contributing to the operational stability, efficiency, and sustainable development of the company. And the latter effects are proxied using two variables: number of contracted employees and salary level of employees. Therefore, it can be concluded that, improving banking services for small and micro enterprises has positive social implications.

This report describes China's experiences in addressing the 'last mile' issue in financial inclusion practices. We wish our findings could assist in providing financial services to the underserviced, promoting financial services and eventually making our society a one with sound financial health.

# 绪　论　攻坚金融服务的“最后一公里”

绪论主要结合金融“最后一公里”的案例梳理出其关键特征，并以此引出对金融“最后一公里”问题的定义；总结了金融“最后一公里”的服务模式；探讨了金融“最后一公里”问题的原因；基于国际经验，对金融“最后一公里”的几个核心问题进行了讨论；最后结合我国实际情况，提出了金融“最后一公里”问题的解决思路。

## 一、什么是金融服务的“最后一公里”问题

长期以来，由于居民居住密度较低、金融服务需求分散，草原地区通常并非每个乡镇都有银行营业网点。为了触达零星散落在广袤草原上的各个家庭，草原上的银行业务员骑着马，顶着风雪烈日，将金融服务送到离旗县较远的牧民家门口，被人们亲切地称为“马背银行”。

类似的故事不止发生在草原的马背上。在我国辽阔的边疆、险峻的山区和宽广的水域，“大篷车银行”穿越戈壁大漠，“集市银行”追赶人流潮汐，“水上银行”从最初的舢板升级到了如今的摩托艇上。虽然这些“银行”是流动的，通常若干天才巡回一次，但如果没有“流动银行”，边缘客户不得不跋山涉水，为了办理一笔简单的业务花费不少财力和时间，还有可能因为证件材料不齐全、错过银行上班时间等原因一而再、再而三地无功折返，最后在蹉跎中失去了使用金融服务的信心。距离的横亘，使得一部分居民可能一辈子都不会享受到可以改变其人生的金融服务。

除了“流动银行”外，还有长期亏损却坚持驻扎海岛或边陲的银行营业网点、五年前欲下乡赶“蓝海”而如今面临“清退回收”境地的 ATM 自助服务、时常被记忆力不好或不理解电子交易流程的客户误会责骂的金融服务代理商，以及摩拳擦掌、频频试错的电商和金融科技平台等。

人们常把以上这些例子中金融服务难以突破最后一段距离触达边缘群体的现象，

称为金融服务的“最后一公里”问题。这种表述似乎把普惠金融的问题当成空间距离的问题。在国际讨论中，“最后一公里”问题常被归结为金融服务的触达问题。实际上它包含很复杂的内容。本书中的“最后一公里”问题指，在现有金融体系条件下，最边缘客户获得金融服务的难度远远超过其他客户的现象。从空间位置来看，它直接表现为金融基础设施的布局问题，即金融服务网点与边缘客户的距离比较远，阻碍了客户获得适当的金融服务。但是，距离往往不是问题的全部。一方面，金融机构不能够提供成本可负担的实用的金融产品和服务、不能满足客户生产生活需求、服务不便捷等供给方的因素也可以成为妨碍客户获得金融服务的重要原因；另一方面，需求方的能力不足也阻碍了他们获得金融服务，包括金融素养和技能不足、对金融服务不信任的态度、不正确的行为等。此外，金融“最后一公里”问题，还可能与政策环境有关，不合理的财政政策和金融政策、缺乏客户保护等，都可能导致中小微企业和弱势群体难以获得金融服务。

需要注意的是，金融“最后一公里”问题是一个动态的概念。相较我国银行体系建立初期，当前我国金融体系能够有效触达的范围已经有了天壤之别。因此，伴随着相关基础设施的完善、产品和制度的创新，“最后一公里”客户能够享受到的应该不止于存贷汇等基础服务，而是与其需求相适应的，可持续、高效率、功能全面的金融服务，这正是本书尝试引导和推动的。

## 二、触达“最后一公里”的服务模式

有些金融服务的模式并不是为了触达边缘客户而设计的，大多数传统的大型金融机构在管理、风控和交易模式等方面，主要是针对大型企业和高端的客户。目前，从实际情况来看，有五种模式在触达边缘客户方面发挥了一定的作用：直营模式、代理模式、互助模式、数字模式和供应链金融模式（见表1）。其中，前三类主要是直接接触客户服务模式，由于触达客户的形式不同，其所能服务的客户群体也就有所区别；数字模式包含各类金融机构、准金融机构提供的数字金融服务，主要指无直接接触的服务模式；供应链金融模式在实践中既可能是纯线上或纯线下的，也可能是线上、线下相结合的，由于其具有独特的风控模型，所以将其划分为一种独立的服务模式。

### （一）直营模式

直营模式是指金融机构或准金融机构以开设直营物理网点或提供流动服务的形式提供金融服务。在金融“最后一公里”服务中，供应商通常包括农村信用社、邮储银行、商业银行、村镇银行、微型金融机构和小额贷款公司等。从所服务的行政区域来看，金融机构或准金融机构有从业人员值守的直营网点通常最低设在乡镇，极少数村镇银行在村一级设有营业网点，少数村或社区有ATM等自助服务网点。延伸物理服务网点触角，或者至少延伸自助服务网点服务范围，可能是金融体系在服务“最后一公里”客户方面最早的，也是最先经历挑战和挫折的尝试。维持物理服务网点所需的成本决定了其所服务的客户交易必须达到一定的密度和规模，否则即使是只有ATM的自助服务网点也可能持续亏损。持续亏损的网点只能依靠政策扶持，商业可持续性需要进一步探索。

在直营物理网点触达能力有限的情况下，许多流动服务形式被创造出来，于是才有了上面提到的策马穿山、乘风破浪的金融服务故事。虽然流动服务创造的价值是值得肯定的，但在技术迅速发展的今天，似乎已经可以对“最后一公里”金融服务的连续性和多样性提出更高的要求。为了实现连续的、多样化的金融服务，需要对各种服务模式形成更为清晰的认识，并对过去未能实现有效服务的原因进行反思和总结，才能整合出适合我国国情的金融“最后一公里”问题的解决思路。

### （二）代理模式

代理模式是指通过村或社区内的代理人代为提供金融服务的模式。在金融服务中，供应方通常包括农村信用社、邮储银行、商业银行、村镇银行等银行类机构，也包括电商集团和保险公司等。代理模式是真正根植于村或社区范围内的服务模式。其常见形式包括农村基层组织以基层民委或党支部成员为代理人，运用以财政资金为基础设立的扶贫基金，向村内有脱贫意愿的贫困群体发放扶贫贷款；银行类机构通常以村或社区内居民熟悉的零售商户为代理人，办理存取款、转账汇款、代缴代取社保等基础服务，以及贷款等其他业务的信息服务；电商集团以村或社区内居民熟悉的零售商户为“村淘”代理人，在提供代理网购、代领物流包裹等电商服务的同时，附带推广金融服务；保险公司在村或社区内的代理人则通常没有固定经营场所，依靠上门主动获客达成交易。

代理模式的优势体现在两个层面：一是在“触达”层面，由于代理人本身就在村或社区内开展其他非金融业务，因此除了安装和更新所需简易设备产生费用，通常不需要为实现“触达”花费较高的固定成本，在手续佣金之外，也不需要机构或客户花费额外的交通费等变动成本；二是在“信任”层面，代理人是与村或社区内居民相熟的基层组织代表、零售商户等，更容易取得社区内客户的信任。虽然目前代理人主要代理一些较为基础的银行业务，在发展过程中也遇到了诸多问题，但由于其具有天然的成本和信息优势，未来还可以进一步拓展服务内容，并探索与之相适应的监管规则和基础设施支持体系。

（三）互助模式

互助模式是指通过设置风险分担和制衡机制，互助组织利用会费、会员储蓄以及外部资金轮流向会员提供贷款，并由此实现理财和平滑消费功能的金融服务模式，主要包括农村资金互助社和农民合作社等形式。在实践中，互助模式的外部资金可能来自政府、金融机构、非政府组织（NGO）或互联网平台等渠道。从服务的范围来看，互助模式是与参与者生产生活联系最为紧密的一种金融服务模式。由于会员通常在生产生活上具有一定的联系，互助模式在提供信用、理财等服务时往往更符合会员的收入现金流规律。在理性发展的状态下，其在风险控制方面也具备了一些金融机构所不具备的内部信息优势。从监管和可持续发展的角度，目前尚需对类似组织的法律身份和会员权责关系等加以明确。规模小、金融经营管理能力和风控能力等是这类模式需要加强的方面。

（四）数字模式

数字模式是指各类金融机构或准金融机构以数字技术、通信技术和生物识别等技术为基础，以手机或电脑等数字设备的界面为窗口，提供金融服务的模式。无论是网上银行、手机银行，还是银行或第三方机构提供的移动支付服务，或是目前各类机构正在不断探索的移动信贷、综合理财、众筹等金融服务，数字模式以其无须物理网点固定成本、边际人工成本趋近于零的优势天生契合了“最后一公里”金融服务距离较远、密度较低、需求规模小的特征。尤其是在我国通信基础设施不断改善、智能手机普及率不断提高的趋势下，通过数字模式提供金融服务应该是解决我国金融“最后一公里”问题的重要手段。然而，通过近年来的实践和观察，我们认为即使在相关技术持续发展的假设下，各种金融服务中，人工参与部分服务依旧是必要的，因此，未来金融服务更有可能是线上与线下相结合的模式。

（五）供应链金融模式

供应链金融需求的一个重要特征是为生产需求服务。无论是农户贷款购买种子、化肥、农机，还是小微企业经营者以存货和应收账款等为抵押进行融资，与核心企业相联系的供应链金融服务都是一种高效便捷的选择。供应商通常包括核心企业、电商、商业银行、小额贷款公司和 P2P 平台等。供应链金融模式由于完全基于供应链上的交易，相较于一般贷款业务其风险控制更多地依赖于大数据技术。

**表 1　金融“最后一公里”服务模式**

| 模式 | 供应商 | 主要股东/资金来源 | 一线服务者 | 主要服务内容 | 触达客户范围 | 成本 | 效率 | “最后一公里”持续性 | 质量和风险 |
|---|---|---|---|---|---|---|---|---|---|
| 直营模式 | 农村信用社 | 民营 | 网点柜员<br>信贷员 | 账户、存款、汇款转账、贷款、代售保险 | 通常营业网点设置到乡镇，自助服务设置到部分村/社区；流动服务 | 较高 | 较低 | 难以持续 | 标准化服务 |
| | 邮储银行 | 国有 | | | | | | | |
| | 商业银行 | 国有/民营 | | | | | | | |
| | 村镇银行 | 发起行 | | | | | | | |
| | 微型金融机构 | 可能有战略股东 | 信贷员 | 贷款 | | | | | |
| | 小额贷款公司 | 民营 | | | | | | | |
| 代理模式 | 农村基层组织 | 财政 | 基层民委和党支部成员 | 扶贫滚动基金贷款 | 村内有脱贫意愿的贫困群体 | 较低 | 较高 | 易持续，但也有规模效应挑战 | 可能出现纠纷 |
| | 农村信用社 | 民营 | 零售商户<br>售货员 | 存取款、汇款转账、代缴代取社保、其他业务的信息服务 | 村民 | | | | |
| | 邮储银行 | 国有 | | | | | | | |
| | 商业银行 | 国有/民营 | | | | | | | |
| | 电商+金融 | 电商集团 | 村级代理 | 代理网购、物流代领、推广支付产品及其他金融服务 | | | | | |
| | 保险公司 | 国有/民营/外资 | 保险经纪人 | 保险产品 | | | | | |
| 互助模式 | 农村资金互助社 | 会员费、扶贫基金 | 村民委和党支部成员 | 贷款（兼具理财功能） | 互助社会员 | 较低 | 较高 | 视项目而定 | 可能隐藏、积聚风险 |
| | 农民合作社 | 会员费或储蓄、金融机构、NGO、互联网平台 | 农民中的能人 | 贷款（兼具理财功能）、众筹团购农资、团销农产品 | 合作社会员 | | | | |

续表

| 模式 | 供应商 | 主要股东/资金来源 | 一线服务者 | 主要服务内容 | 触达客户范围 | 成本 | 效率 | “最后一公里”持续性 | 质量和风险 |
|---|---|---|---|---|---|---|---|---|---|
| 数字模式 | 农村信用社 | 民营 | 以线上为主，可能有短期推广员 | 以网上银行、手机银行为平台的转账汇款、查询、贷款、信用卡、理财、保险等服务 | 在地域/年龄层面存在数字鸿沟，贷款等服务需要数据积累过程 | 低 | 高 | 持续，但存在获客挑战 | 标准化服务 |
| | 商业银行 | 国有/民营 | | | | | | | |
| | 第三方支付机构主导的综合金融平台 | 民营/间接外资 | | 支付、理财、贷款、信用评分、保险 | | | | | |
| | P2P 网贷平台 | 民营/风投/国资/银行等 | 以线上为主；使用服务时，部分平台有实地考察员 | 贷款、理财 | | | | | |
| | 网络小贷 | 电商等 | | 贷款 | | | | | |
| | 众筹平台 | 民营/风投/国资/银行/电商等 | | 以商品、服务、收益权、股权为回报的众筹服务，互助型类保险服务 | | | | | |
| 供应链金融模式 | 核心企业 | 国有/民营 | 通常为约定好的非常驻工作人员，部分为纯线上服务 | 基于供应链交易的商业信用贷款 | 村内参与供应链生产的农户或小微企业经营者 | 较低 | 较高 | 视项目而定 | 通常较好 |
| | 电商 | 民营 | | | | | | | |
| | 银行 | 国有/民营 | | | | | | | |
| | 小额贷款公司 | 民营 | | | | | | | |
| | P2P 网贷平台 | 民营/风投/国资/银行等 | | | | | | | |

不难发现，以上五种模式并不以供应商或者资金提供方作为划分标准，而是五种几乎所有具有相关资质的金融机构、准金融机构都可以涉足的模式。在国家普惠金融发展战略的推动下，不仅农村信用社等传统农村金融服务机构积极寻求改革，大型商业银行更是纷纷成立普惠金融事业部并尝试与金融科技企业联手推动创新，深耕多年的国际 NGO 主导的微型金融机构继续在成败中总结经验教训，以服务小微、服务“三农”为定位发端的小额贷款公司、村镇银行也在探索差异化发展。然而，金融“最后一公里”的服务现状仍然不尽如人意。既然已经有了服务金融“最后一公里”的热情和方法，为什么还是做不好呢？下面将对金融“最后一公里”问题的原因进行讨论。

## 三、“最后一公里”问题存在的原因

实践经验告诉我们，服务“最后一公里”金融需求知易行难：从表面上看，触达目标对象一次、两次或者是短时期内保持触达似乎并不是大难题。本质而言，金融“最后一公里”的真正挑战是，如何以成本可负担的方式，可持续、高效率地提供功能全面的金融服务。以下将从客户、供给商和监管方三个层面剖析金融“最后一公里”问题的原因。

### （一）难以形成规模效应

客户分散、需求额度小、能力低形成客户端的“最后一公里”问题。这些特征造成部分客户与其他客户相比受到金融排斥的程度更大。

一是地理分布遥远、分散。之所以会出现“马背银行”“摩托车银行”“集市银行”等流动银行形式，正是由于部分客户通常距离银行营业网点较为遥远且分散。金融机构网点的运行需要一定的固定成本和变动成本。虽然没有必要要求每一笔金融交易都是盈利的，但对于网点和从业人员的可持续运转，从金融交易获取的收益必须达到一定规模才有可能实现。当一定时期内区域内金融需求的总额度较低、总次数较少时，金融机构物理网点将难以在该区域实现商业可持续。

二是现金流额度小、不规律。在金融机构物理网点难以触及的区域，需求方主体更有可能是中低收入甚至是赤贫者，他们可以用于消费（支付）、存款和理财的资金额度相对较少。此外，不规律性是其收入另一重要特征。Collins 等（2009）列举了许多生动的案例：他们可能是种植农户，收入是季节性的；也可能是临时工，不具备稳定的雇用关系。当面临疾病、意外或是自然灾害时，他们的生活很可能面临难以持续的窘境。

三是金融经验少、金融能力不足。由于缺乏金融交易的基本条件及交易经验，金融"最后一公里"的需求方主体缺少"干中学"的机会，与此同时，来自本地亲友经验的外溢影响小，更有可能面临金融能力不足的问题。

### （二）缺乏创新服务的动力和能力

从供应商的角度来看，不了解客户特征和需求、缺乏解决问题和创新服务的能力是其难以服务好"最后一公里"客户的深层次原因。主要表现在如下两个维度。

一是提供服务以产品为导向，不了解客户特征和需求。正如前面所探讨的，边缘客户群体存在特有的地理分布特征、现金流特征及金融能力特征。如果供应商以产品为导向，直接用既有的产品服务边缘客户，其结果将不仅难以满足客户需求，更会因为成本高、收益低而难以实现商业可持续，最后很可能白白浪费掉前期的各项投入。例如，阿里系电商和金融平台曾经尝试通过"村淘"代理服务站的形式在农村地区推广淘宝购物和支付宝交易，并借此积累今后可服务于金融业务的交易数据。然而，目前"村淘"取得的进展有限。农村地区的人口密度相对更低，物流体系远不如城市地区发达，此外，农村居民的购物习惯和需求也与城市居民存在区别，他们不仅有一部分食物和日用品可以自给自足，还有一部分农产品需要售出，而很多农村地区的物流体系还不足以支持新鲜农产品快速配送售出。于是，"村淘"的发展大抵远不及最初规划的速度。

在探索"最后一公里"金融服务的历程中，以产品为导向的例子不胜枚举。例如，在解决金融"最后一公里"问题的号召下，不少银行都曾满怀热情地在农村地区增开营业网点；又如，在 2013 年，曾有创业者试图掀起一场 ATM"下乡"热，他们认为为每个村配备 ATM 是"极富想象力的生意"。然而，网点和设备荒废、大笔投资亏损的教训却一次又一次地证明，了解客户特征和需求是金融供应商所应完成的第一要务。

二是解决问题和创新服务的动力和能力不足。边缘客户在地理分布上难以形成规模效应，是长期以来金融机构服务边缘客户动力不足的重要原因。虽然随着技术的进步，许多金融机构逐渐意识到这部分客户的价值，但即使在有了各种技术和商业模式的今天，要服务好边缘客户似乎依旧困难重重。究其原因，普惠金融服务供应商不仅需要了解客户特征和需求，还需要不断以业务实践为基础测试，改进产品和服务，不断提升解决问题和创新服务的能力。

### （三）金融基础设施和客户保护薄弱

从监管方的角度来看，基础设施建设不足、客户保护体系不健全以及对解决"最后一公里"问题缺乏统筹规划，是金融"最后一公里"问题持续存在的重要原因。主要表现在如下两个维度。

一是金融基础设施薄弱。近年来，我国道路交通等物理层面和信息通信等技术层面的基础设施得到了飞速发展，但以征信体系为代表的金融基础设施还存在不足。以个人征信为例，一方面是个人有效征信覆盖率还较低；另一方面是准金融机构在使用征信系统、将交易记录共享到征信系统等方面还存在种种障碍。由于绝大部分边缘客户是没有征信记录的，这意味着这部分客户获取贷款首先面临着更高的初始门槛。

二是客户保护体系不健全。目前，我国金融客户保护体系仍有待改进。例如，在当前金融混业愈加深入的趋势下，金融消费者保护属于多部门责任范围，许多金融业务落入监管交错的空白之中，导致部分客户在权益受到侵害的同时陷入投诉无门的煎熬境地；又如，在2017年发生的若干“现金贷”事件中，由于多头责任导致无人监管，许多借款人因为恶意甚至是暴力催收而在亲朋好友中身败名裂。由于边缘客户金融经验相对较少、金融能力相对不足，且易接触到非持牌机构提供的良莠不齐的金融服务，在尝试进行金融交易的过程中更容易受到权益侵害，因此，边缘客户应该是金融消费者保护工作的重点服务对象。

通过上述讨论，不难发现解决金融“最后一公里”问题的确不能一蹴而就。客户群体的特点决定了金融“最后一公里”问题需要特殊的商业模式，也需要监管部门在巩固基础设施和优化客户保护的同时，发挥适当的统筹协调功能。下面将基于国际经验，对金融“最后一公里”的几个核心问题进行总结和讨论，尝试探索“他山之石”。

## 四、解决金融“最后一公里”问题的国际经验

在前面的讨论中，我们已经总结了解决金融“最后一公里”问题的五大模式，以及在客户、供应商、监管方三个层面存在的问题，以下尝试以“他山之石”，介绍解决金融“最后一公里”问题的国际经验，着重探讨如下四个问题：金融科技服务供应商如何有效获取边缘客户；政府和业界如何共同维持代理商网络，提升代理商生存能力；如何看待金融服务的竞争问题；以及边缘客户保护问题。

### （一）M-Pesa的“客户第一”策略

成本是解决金融“最后一公里”问题的最大障碍因素。以边际成本极低的金融科技服务触达目标客户群体，是许多供应商频频试错却依旧跃跃欲试的领域。然而，目前，获取边缘客户依旧让不少供应商感到困难重重，尤其是在面对金融素养不足、数字技术接受度低的客户时更是如此。

M-Pesa 的“客户第一”（Customer First）策略也许能够提供一些启示。成立于2007年的M-Pesa几乎是普惠金融领域最为家喻户晓的移动钱包（Mobile Money）服务提供商，目前在肯尼亚占据超过70%的市场份额。就是这样一家一路高歌猛进的公司，在其母公司Safaricom 2017年年报中，依旧提到了如何以“客户第一”策略不断增强能力，“区域团队被赋予亲近客户、了解客户的任务，如此其获取新客户、维持客户活跃度的能力不断增强，通过更快的决策过程，区域团队持续地通过优化服务网络和服务质量为客户带来价值。”在了解客户的基础上，M-Pesa还为获取不同地区的新客户采用了符合区域特征的促销方式，并通过超过13万家代理商来确保M-Pesa的服务与需求的同步。

M-Pesa所提供的移动钱包服务与我国移动支付服务的最大区别在于其提供存取现金的服务，因此也就必须仰仗于物理网络。截至2017年Safaricom年报报告期，M-Pesa的代理商网络已经壮大至136000家代理商，平均约200名客户就有一家代理商为其服务。然而，不容忽视的是，M-Pesa的代理商并非仅仅具备提供存取款服务的功能。通过强大的代理商网络，M-Pesa可以向其客户及潜在客户提供看得见、摸得着的关心和支持，这对于金融素养不足、数字技术接受度低的“最后一公里”客户而言更为重要。

需要阐明的是，我们并非就此建议所有供应商都去铺设代理商网络，而是强调亲近和了解对于获取和维护“最后一公里”客户的特殊意义。至于通过何种方式亲近和了解客户，则是关于市场策略以及竞争与合作的进一步议题。

### （二）提升代理商生存能力

我国银行体系在提升基础金融服务可得性的实践中，较为普遍地使用了代理模式。在操作上主要由银行业金融机构在营业网点难以触达的地区，选择当地村民熟悉、具有良好声誉的零售商铺布放POS机具，充当“助农取款服务点”，代理银行提供取款、汇款、代理缴费及综合金融信息咨询服务。然而，从平均业务量来看，全年农村助农取款服务点所办理支付业务的平均笔数为493笔，平均金额约为40万元。即使按照2%的比例计算银行可以收取的手续费，平均8000元的手续费入账也需要精打细算地去应对各项成本支出，更不用说目前助农取款服务点面向需求方几乎都是免费提供服务。因此，如何维持全面覆盖的代理商网络和提升代理商生存能力，是持续做好基础金融服务不得不面对和解决的问题。

由于国际上大部分移动钱包代理商都兼营存取款服务，他们也面临着我国银行“助农取款服务点”所面临的几乎同样的挑战。因此，以下我们尝试通过来自巴西、墨西哥、坦桑尼亚和印度的四家银行及移动钱包服务提供商的代理网络案例来探讨如何提升代理商的生存能力[①]。同时，也可以对我国移动支付服务解决“最后一公里”问题提供参考。

### 巴西：公共政策干预提供激励

巴西早在1973年就允许银行雇用代理商为其提供支付交易服务，并于2010年实现了所有自治市银行代理商全覆盖。回顾巴西代理银行业务1973年至今的发展历程，其公共政策干预所发挥的作用是值得关注的，包括有时间限制的、逐渐减少的政府补贴，调动国有资产，以及设置金融服务全覆盖基金等。

1973—2010年：将全覆盖作为明确的政策目标

两家国有银行充分调动资源实现目标：自2001年起，国家邮政银行将每一个邮局都变为一个银行代理网点；自2000年起，国家储蓄银行让其已有的彩票网点兼营银行代理网点，并通过经办政府转移支付（G2P）来提升代理网络的交易量。

2011年至今：修正运营模型，平衡包容与风险

自2011年起，为了平衡前期激进扩张代理网络过程中可能潜藏的风险，巴西中央银行开始要求提供代理服务的必须是企业（而非个人），并强制监督和审计所有代理网络。自2013年起，巴西的银行代理商数量开始下降，主要源自部分地区代理商饱和、监管趋严以及移动支付渠道流量的增长。随着巴西代理银行体系进入巩固阶段，为了防止覆盖率下降，聚合代理和分层部署等方法可能带来益处（借鉴下述坦桑尼亚和印度的经验）。

通过上述分析可以看出，巴西代理银行体系经历了激进扩张阶段，实现了全面覆盖的代理网络。目前正处在风险平衡阶段，需要合理地处理全覆盖目标与风险控制、支付业态转型（更多的移动支付）的关系，并积极学习新的“最后一公里”金融服务经验。由于巴西代理银行体系与我国银行“助农取款服务点”有相似之处，因此其经验教训尤其值得我国借鉴。

---

① PABLO GARCIA ARABEHETY，CLAUDIA MCKAY，and PETER ZETTERLI. Proximity Matters：Five Case Studies in Closing the CICO Gap [M]. CGAP Publication，2018.

**OxxO（墨西哥）：数据分析帮助代理商优化服务、管理风险和增加收入**

OxxO公司是墨西哥最大的街角零售连锁店和银行代理商网络，为墨西哥国内外11家银行提供代理服务。借鉴其自身的零售专长，OxxO从一开始就将严密的数据分析用于其代理银行业务，尤其是在客户体验、风险管理、销售和运营成本节约层面。

在客户体验层面，OxxO通过数据分析办理不同业务的最佳时间，以缩短等待时间。例如，OxxO分析发现，为了优化客户的等待体验，代理银行业务的服务时间最好在40秒到1分钟之间，开设账户的时间最好在3.5分钟内。针对类似研究结果，OxxO还会每6个月进行更新评估，并依此对服务人员进行培训、对系统流程进行简化。

在风险管理层面，OxxO设置了一系列监测指标，一方面，可以为代理商提供及时的现金管理指导；另一方面，当代理商的行为偏离设定的运营范围时，会触发敏感的系统响应。

在销售和运营成本节约层面，OxxO深入分析直接和间接的销售收入，以及相关联的消费者行为特征。基于对这些指标的灵敏洞见推动其零售主业和代理银行业务的共同增长。

**Selcom（坦桑尼亚）：聚合代理缓解运营成本问题**

Selcom是坦桑尼亚市场占有率25%的聚合代理商，在前端拥有超过17000家零售代理网点，后端为超过35家移动网络运营商、银行和公用事业公司提供共享代理服务。Selcom的聚合功能既体现在前端，也体现在后端。

在前端，Selcom不断拓展零售商加盟为代理网点，以最大化交易量和总效率。代理网点可以使用手机或POS机具设备来为客户办理联结众多后端公司的交易业务。

在后端，Selcom的聚合功能重点体现在以下两个层面：

一是支付聚合。Selcom将支付工具供应商（如银行、移动网络运营商）与第三方公司（如公共事业公司）聚合起来，减少支付障碍。

二是账户聚合。Selcom实现了让终端客户可以在移动钱包和银行账户之间转账；为数字支付提供无缝的取现、支付服务。账户聚合的成本部分由银行吸收，部分由终端客户承担。

通过聚合代理，在收入方，Selcom实现了单个代理商可处理业务量的最大化，提升了它们的生存能力；在支出方，由于单个账户即可覆盖众多服务提供商，Selcom的代理商在启动和运营方面的成本都得以降低。

### Oxigen（印度）：分层部署模型适应地区特色

Oxigen公司管理多达20万家独立代理商的网络，并对其设置了初始成本（主要包括加盟、培训及硬件费用）从8美元至385美元不等的7层部署模型，便于代理商选择最适合当地供需的类型。在交易量小且不确定性大的地区，代理商可以从最低成本的模型开始，并可以随着交易量的增长启用具有更丰富功能的模型。其中，94%的代理商都采用了轻模型（见下表前5类模型），它们完成了Oxigen网络中77%的交易量。重模型则适用于需要包括银行服务在内的多样化服务的地区。

**表　Oxigen的7层部署模型**

| 部署模型 | 终端 | 初始成本 | 主要交易类型 | 纸质收据 | 生物识别 |
|---|---|---|---|---|---|
| 移动代理 | 手机（代理商自有） | 8美元 | 支付，点对点交易 | 无 | 无 |
| 网页APP | 个人电脑和打印机（代理商自有） | 15美元 | 支付，点对点交易 | 有 | 无 |
| 基础POS | 基础POS机 | 75美元 | 支付，点对点交易 | 有 | 无 |
| 微型ATM | 生物识别POS机 | 155美元 | 支付，点对点交易，银行业务 | 有 | 有 |
| 银行门户 | 个人电脑和打印机（代理商自有），生物识别设备 | 385美元 | 支付，点对点交易，银行业务 | 有 | 有 |
| 公司直营连锁 | 收银员（零售商自有） | 无 | 支付，点对点交易 | 有 | 无 |
| 客户移动钱包 | 手机（客户自有） | 无 | 支付，点对点交易 | 无 | 无 |

注：以上初始成本为2016年9月价格。

上述来自四个国家的案例给予我们若干重要启示：为了提升金融服务代理商的生存能力，适当的政策干预和市场创新都是不可或缺的，既要充分运用数字技术的成本效率优势，也要通过巧妙的机制设计（如聚合代理）实现金融服务的规模效应，并根据当地社会经济实际情况调整业务模式（如分层部署），防止盲目地以产品为导向进行市场推广。

### （三）有效竞争优化服务

早在2010年发布的《G20创新性普惠金融原则》中，第二条即指出了市场竞争对于普惠金融长远发展的重要性，“发展多样性，实施促进竞争的政策办法，提供以市场为基础的激励，既推动服务供应商的多样化，又推进可持续的普惠金融可得性以及可负担的、功能广泛的服务（储蓄、信贷、支付、转移和保险）”。为了更形象地说明不同层面的市场竞争问题，我们以非洲移动金融服务发展相对成熟的两个市场肯尼亚和坦桑尼亚为例，比较不同的竞争环境所带来的不同影响①。

**畅通的市场进入渠道使竞争成为可能**

肯尼亚和坦桑尼亚的移动金融服务提供商既包括银行、第三方机构，也包括移动通信运营商，且服务普遍经由移动通信运营商处理无结构辅助服务数据（USSD）实现。由于后者掌控着USSD的技术渠道，且有足够的动机去限制竞争者，那么这样的市场就存在着市场进入渠道的基本矛盾——可能导致具备创新潜力、可为客户带来高价值的企业难以进入市场，市场产品种类受限于渠道控制商，或竞争者将高渠道成本通过价格上涨的形式转嫁给消费者等问题。

这样的问题在肯尼亚尤其严重，因为肯尼亚的移动通信运营商一家独大，其向合作伙伴实施0费率优惠，而向银行和第三方机构收取相对高得多的USSD费率，结果必然显著地影响竞争格局。针对这种差别定价，一种解决方法是由银行或第三方机构自己申请移动通信牌照。不过，这种方法在坦桑尼亚和肯尼亚很可能面临着不同的结局——虽然两国都是由电信监管当局发放牌照，但只有坦桑尼亚的监管当局才提供了实际代码，而在肯尼亚，代码实际上直接由最大的移动通信运营商发放的，那些向其申请代码的移动金融服务提供商就处在讨价还价的劣势地位。

在面临类似情况时，监管当局需要采取恰当的干预措施，包括保证市场进入渠道的基本畅通、监督渠道服务商的服务质量、关注并在谨慎前提下调控过高的渠道价格等。

---

① MAZER, R., ROWAN, P. Competition in Mobile Financial Services: Lessons from Kenya and Tanzania [M]. CGAP Publications, 2016.

### 透明的产品和服务降低搜索成本、提升产品可比性

产品和服务的透明度通常被视为客户保护和行为规范问题，但其同样会通过增加搜索成本、降低产品可比性来影响有效竞争。当客户在搜索替代产品时面临着过高成本时，销售者在定价或设计产品质量时就可以无视竞争问题。

例如，在坦桑尼亚，M-Pawa 是一种兼有申请贷款和付息储蓄功能的账户，客户可以使用手机通过 M-PESA 移动钱包平台获取。然而，当客户通过手机申请贷款时，在被要求接受服务条款前，他们并没有被服务界面告知利率和展期费用。而查看服务条款不仅需要花费相当的精力，还必须前往供应商的网页才能看到，这也就意味着查看服务条款的前提是既有智能手机又有数据网络。最后，很多客户在并没有弄清楚服务条款的情况下获取了贷款。

为了推动金融服务（尤其是触达范围更加广泛的移动金融服务）的透明度，相关监管当局应该制定价格披露标准，优化披露信息内容及形式，提升产品和服务的可比性，推动更有效的竞争。在制定披露规则的基础上，监管当局还需要推动规则执行、监测市场行为并惩罚不合规的供应商。

### 互通性进一步优化市场竞争

金融服务的互通性是指面向终端客户的渠道（如第三方支付平台、线下代理商网络）与不同金融服务供应商的互通连接。基于良好的互通性，客户可根据服务的质量和价格自由地转换服务获取渠道，提升使用体验；代理商可降低排他性，在增加服务内容的同时，提升业务流量和生存能力，这对“最后一公里”金融服务而言尤为重要；金融服务供应商不再受限于服务渠道，同时也有更大的动力提升产品和服务的质量。

虽然互通性能从诸多层面提升竞争的有效性，但真正实现了互通性的移动金融服务市场寥寥无几。例如，在肯尼亚，虽然早在 2014 年国家支付系统法案就已经将互通性作为一项市场目标，但由于市场份额第一的移动金融服务供应商占据绝对的市场流量优势，实现互通性目标的进展十分缓慢。相较而言，坦桑尼亚可能是一个例外，该国移动金融服务虽然也主要由移动通信运营商占有市场，但市场集中度相对更低。在移动通信市场份额排名第二位至第四位的供应商 Airtel、Tigo 和 Zantel 于 2014 年率先达成互通协议后，市场份额排名第一的供应商 Vodacom 也于 2015 年加入了互通协议。

值得关注的是，坦桑尼亚移动金融服务的互通性在城市和农村并不是均衡的。以代理商排他性为例，在坦桑尼亚最大的城市达累斯萨拉姆，代理商非排他比例是84%，而在农村地区，代理商的非排他比例仅为38%。同一时期城市与农村金融服务互通性的不同很可能源自市场发展阶段的差异。

互通性的实现需要考虑市场发展阶段。在移动金融服务发展的初期，强制推动互通性可能会打击先试渠道开拓者的积极性，因为他们需要在开拓市场、建立代理商网络、完善平台等方面花费大量的成本。但从长远来看，为了促进市场的有效竞争，监管层需要逐步推动实现互通性。互通性的实现是一个市场竞争优化的过程，其中非常重要的一个环节是要求供应商保持金融服务背后的技术互通性。在此基础上，一旦在商业层面达成互通协议，技术互通才可以保证协议的实现。

以上三个层面的竞争问题给予我们的启示在于，在推动金融服务发展的过程中，我们需要观察市场所处的发展阶段。随着市场的逐步成熟，有效竞争对于持续做好普惠金融服务将愈加重要，需要及时的政策和制度支持以及有效的执行来推动市场竞争，并通过市场规则来不断优化金融服务。

### （四）更有效的客户保护

数字信贷触达范围广泛、借款额度门槛低、服务便捷，很好地契合了边缘客户所处地理位置偏远、借款额度低、非计划性借款需求多等特征。然而，也正是数字信贷的这些特质导致了不同于传统信贷的客户保护风险，包括客户对贷款成本和逾期后果理解不足，这种风险可能因交互界面的限制而加剧；对贷款的用途、成本、还款来源考虑不充分；以及过分容易地实现高成本贷款的展期。这些风险可能导致消费者在不知情、考虑不充分甚至没有实际需求的情况下借入高成本贷款，而后面临难以按时偿还、留下失信记录的后果。除此之外，在数据共享规则不明确的情况下，数字信贷消费者对于自身借款记录的使用缺乏控制权，也很可能因为数据共享渠道不畅通而难以享受正面信用记录的好处。

Mazer 和 Mckee（2017）对非洲多国数字信贷客户保护的研究成果进行了整理。为了推动更有效的数字信贷客户保护实践，下面结合非洲多国的经验，介绍有助于优化客户保护的不同层面的方法和机制。

## 有效披露服务条款

为了促进数字信贷消费者理性贷款和按约还款，监管当局和行业需要共同研究和推广提升服务条款披露有效性的规则。除了强调签约前披露外，还应制定最低披露标准，并不断探索更高效的披露形式。

最低披露标准应该包括：

（1）贷款的所有费用，包括以金额和年化利率方式表示的所有费用，以及绑定产品（如理财、保险产品）的成本费用。

（2）偿付时间表、逾期费用及其他逾期后果，包括偿还的时间点和额度、逾期不同期限（天/月/年）的费用、逾期的信用记录后果和法律后果。

（3）客户数据的使用和处理规则。明确告知客户数据将被如何使用和处理。

（4）服务条款的其他关键项目。服务条款通常是冗长且复杂的，大部分客户不会查阅全文，或看不懂条款内容。除了关于价格、偿还要求、客户数据的条款外，也应该单列出其他关键项目。

在此基础上，通过设计更有效的内容披露形式，可以显著促进客户理性贷款和按约还款行为。这些披露形式包括：

（1）突出成本。在一次模拟实验中，通过将本金和息费分开展示，例如，将“偿还228”改为“偿还200+28”，违约率从29.1%下降到20%（Mazer、Vancel和Keyman 2016）。

（2）将“查看服务条款”选项和关键事项小结分页置顶。通过将“查看服务条款”选项从页面底端转移到一个新的界面，并添加对关键事项的小结，上述实验客户“查看服务条款”的比例从9.5%上升到23.8%，而那些查看了服务条款的实验客户的绝对拖欠率降低了7%。

（3）事前告知客户获取数据类别和处理方式。例如，服务于新兴市场贷款供应商的数据分析和信用评分公司FirstAccess最初在征求客户数据使用授权时，仅仅询问客户是否同意将其“手机记录”用于贷款申请。通过调查了解到客户对“手机记录”所包含的内容存有疑问后，FirstAccess补充解释了“手机记录是在手机使用过程中获取的信息，包括电话、短信、充值或移动钱包账户”，还向客户澄清了“手机记录仅被FirstAccess用于作出贷款推荐，不会向任何人分享客户个人信息”，并留下电话接受客户咨询。除此之外，FirstAccess还在每一次获取客户手机记录时重新询求客户授权，让客户了解他们的数据是何时、如何被使用的。

## 负责任地营销

在由供给方驱动的信贷市场中，主动贷款供给可能会造成一些行为偏误，包括过分重视贷款可以带来的短期利益的“存在偏误”，害怕失去贷款机会的“损失厌恶”，以及在无实际需求的情况下受好奇心影响而尝试高风险贷款产品，受营销信息影响而申请超过实际需求的贷款额度，或为了提高授信额度而短时间重复借贷的种种非理性行为。

负责任营销的核心是促进客户理性借贷，一是要有实际需求，二是要有理性的偿还计划和资金来源。一种主要的解决思路是在借贷实现过程增加一点阻力，创造“理性”得以被唤醒的时间余地。例如，南非的非存款放贷机构的经验是，年轻人容易冲动消费，给他们贷款不能太容易，拿到贷款合同之后要考虑3天才能再签订合同。此外，Mazer和Mckee（2017）还提出了让消费者主动申请贷款而不是被动接受贷款供给的建议。供给方可以通过媒体、互联网、应用市场广告甚至营销代理等形式吸引消费者，但消费者必须主动提出和完成贷款申请过程。

## 遵循消费者适当性原则

数字信贷消费者适当性原则的核心是供应商应该将适应消费者需求和境况的贷款产品销售给相应的客户群体。为了实现这个目标，数字信贷供应商首先需要明确目标客群及分类；其次要尽责评估客户的还款能力；最后还需要不断优化产品设计，让产品更好地契合客户的需求。

例如，非洲最早的数字信贷供应商之一仍然在向其客户提供与多年前定价和服务条款一样的产品。实际上，凭借多年来积累的数据，该供应商完全可以更好地划分客群，并依靠数据进行更低成本的定价和多样化产品的供给。举例而言，一位已经按时或提前归还了10次贷款的客户，是否应该在第11次贷款时支付与第1次贷款时一样的利率？遵循消费者适当性原则意味着不断追求更适合的产品和服务，而由于大量采用了最为先进的数字技术，数字信贷是最应该发挥表率作用的金融服务领域之一。

## 探索适应客户特征的公平催收方法

每一个供应商都应该致力于探索更有效的、适应客户特征的公平催收方法，融合软硬兼施的影响力，通过测试选取出最高效的方法组成具有机构特色的催收体系。以下是一些来自非洲国家的实验结果，也许可以为我国的数字信贷供应商带来启发。

（1）提到出借方的姓名可能带来“同伴效应”。肯尼亚P2P网贷平台Pesa Zetu测试发现，在偿还提醒短信中提到出借个人的姓名或出借平台的名字可以有效提升偿还率，这可能源自出借方姓名给借款人带来的情感上的“同伴效应”。

（2）傍晚提醒比早上提醒更有效。数字信贷供应商Jumo在肯尼亚的田野实验发现，傍晚时发送偿还提醒的响应率比早上高出8%。

（3）信用记录的积极暗示可能优于消极威胁。肯尼亚离网能源供应商M-Kopa与信用服务商TransUnion和Credit Information Sharing Kenya合作测试了一个可以学习信用知识、查询信用记录及更正错误信用信息的短信平台。短信平台的内容采用了积极的暗示，将信用记录与按约还款和帮助实现未来的贷款联系在一起。测试结果显示，主动使用这个短信平台的用户申请和获批了更多的贷款，也更有可能全额还款。相较而言，消极信用记录的威胁是被更经常采用的偿还提醒内容，部分供应商规律性地，甚至每天向拖欠者发送威胁短信。然而，“黑历史”的威胁有可能收效甚微，因为消极的描述可能造成抵触情绪和隧道效应，而对信用记录的描述也可能因为不够具体而不足以唤起拖欠者对后果的重视。

（4）尝试提供有偿重组逾期贷款的服务。许多贷款供应商都对逾期贷款收取提前设置好的高额罚息，并在核销贷款和汇报至征信局前延长一段时间的还款期限（如90天或180天）。然而，考虑到数字信贷收取客户偿还贷款的边际成本是极低的，针对逾期贷款的一种解决思路是提供有偿重组逾期贷款的服务，相当于客户为自己购买更多的时间来偿还贷款，可能有利于减少贷款核销以及增加客户忠诚度。目前世界银行扶贫协商小组正在与非洲一家供应商合作测试提供有偿重组逾期贷款服务的效果。

**推动实现消费者主导的数据共享机制**

实现公平的数据共享机制是数字信贷飞速发展过程中一个待解决的问题。消费者缺乏对自身数据的控制权可能会带来诸多问题。他们不仅受到隐私侵犯，还不能从自身的数据记录中获得最大化效用，甚至因为部分供应商只向征信局汇报消极记录而不汇报正面借贷记录，或向征信局汇报了错误的信用记录，而遭受不公平待遇。

例如，尽管肯尼亚征信局早在2013年就要求汇报全面的征信记录，但是肯尼亚最大的数字信贷供应商直到2016年才开始汇报正面借贷记录。此外，一项在内罗毕开展的数字信贷客户调查显示，查看了信用记录的420位受访者中，92位（22%）指出信用记录中存在错误，并且许多错误都来自数字信贷记录。以上现象都表明数字信贷消费者需要更多地参与到信用记录的使用和处理过程中，逐步成为数据共享机制的主导角色。

以上来自非洲多国的研究及实践经验表明，客户保护需要真正从客户出发。尤其是就数字金融服务而言，应该充分运用数字交易记录的即时性、便捷性，了解和刻画不同客户群体的行为习惯，探索符合其行为特征的、更高效的客户保护方法和机制。

通过以上介绍的国际经验我们已经发现，金融“最后一公里”问题并非仅仅是可得性问题，也并非让受排斥客户使用上金融服务就可以了。在解决金融“最后一公里”问题的过程中，还需要关注市场竞争和客户保护问题，归根结底是关注客户福祉（well-being）以及落实包容性发展目标。

## 五、金融“最后一公里”问题的解决思路

### （一）引导金融供应商走向以客户为中心之通途

“最后一公里”问题的解决，首先应该是思想认识上的颠覆，即回归初心，服务实体，真正把边缘客户当作服务本体，也就是“第一公里”的思维。以客户为中心，以此出发来寻找探索长期未解决的问题的答案。

实际上，早在20世纪70年代，尤努斯教授掏出27美元借给42位最贫困的村妇时，他就是从“第一公里”开始做的——从观察最贫困群体的需求出发，为他们设计缓解生活困难的金融服务。这也体现在格莱珉银行的业务方针上——从底层做起（from the bottom up），在解决客户问题的同时成就业务的发展。

更进一步地，我们还需要认识到，将“最后一公里”当作“第一公里”并非道德上的观点问题，也并非只是他国的个案，而是供应商面对市场压力作出的明智决策。当前市场供需格局、信息生产和传播方式已经发生了重大变化，供应商需要主动重塑金融服务的思维和业务模式。

从市场供需来看，金融机构“躺着赚钱”的时代已然过去。在以创新追逐“痛点”的行业发展特征下，曾经被称作“末端”的需求已毫无疑问地成为许多新业态产生的“第一公里”，市场正在迅速向买方市场转变，客户才是中心。

从信息生产和传播方式来看，自 Web 2.0 时代起，信息传播即进入了中心逐渐弱化、分布式信息爆发积聚的时期。尤其是近几年，信息成为金融行业愈加重要的生产资料，处于核心地位的定价和营销流程都已大量地采用了源于潜在客户的信息。也就是说，客户是信息这种重要生产资料的源头。如果不从“第一公里”的客户出发，供应商很容易走向以产品为导向，甚至走上“使命漂移”的歧途。

在明确以客户为中心的方向之后，供应商还需掌握向以客户为中心转变的方法，因为这并非是能够一蹴而就的——从制定方案策略，到争取战略支持；从建立了解客户的长期有效渠道，到对员工进行投资和赋能，甚至要专门为此选拔合适的领导者，通常是一个需要若干年才能完成的组织全面变革过程（Burritt 和 Coetzee，2016）。幸运的是，这个看似不易的过程，恰恰是攻坚金融“最后一公里”的通途。

### （二）持续推动数字金融服务发展

当我们谈到以客户为中心，首先应该充分认识到边缘客户遥远、分散、交易额度相对小等根本特征。也正是由于这些特征，发展四十余年的微型金融实践还远远无法满足日益增长且迫切的金融需求。虽然微型金融已经在世界各个角落实现了许多伟大的成就，为众多无征信记录可查询、无资产可抵押、在非正式经济部门工作的人提供融资服务，甚至帮助他们发展生存技能，共同抗击贫困、灾祸等生存压力。正如微型金融实践先驱、哈佛商学院 Michael Chu 先生所言，“很少有其他人道主义工作能够宣称有如此大规模的、持续的触达力”。然而，尽管成绩斐然，在四十年后的今天，全世界仍然有 17 亿名成年人甚至没有账户，无法享受到最基础的金融服务。而从融资服务来看，在荷兰、挪威、瑞典等发达国家超过 50%的成年人持有贷款余额的同时，发展中国家成年人的贷款持有率通常不超过 10%[①]。从以上数据可以看出，解决金融“最后一公里”问题的任务依旧十分艰巨。

为了攻坚“最后一公里”，我们需要探索更好地适应“最后一公里”金融服务交易

---

① 资料来源：世界银行发布的 2017 年 Global Findex 报告。

流量和成本结构的服务模式，更高效率地填补市场空缺。数字技术为我们带来了这样的机会。举例而言，诺贝尔和平奖获得者、“穷人的银行家”尤努斯教授，采用信贷员挨家挨户上门拜访的办法，在四十年里服务了900万名客户。而现在大的金融科技公司通过数字化手段，三年就能建立3000万名客户。通过对比可以发现，数字金融服务在解决“最后一公里”问题的优势是显而易见的。我们需要持续推动数字金融服务发展，充分发挥数字金融服务触达范围广、边际成本极低的、交易效率高等优势。

### （三）构建线上与线下融合的金融服务体系

无论是从国际还是从国内经验来看，线下服务的份额逐渐减少，但是依旧扮演着重要的角色。在过去的5年里，越来越多的证据表明，金融服务的使用情况与线下物理网点的亲近程度是强相关的（Arabehety、McKay和Zetterli，2018）。此外，2018年CAFI团队针对浙江省丽水市基础金融服务体系的调查研究还发现，居民收入与银行柜台网点的距离显著负相关，但通过更多地使用POS机等替代性服务，可以在一定程度上抵消银行柜台网点距离遥远的负面影响。

构建线上与线下融合的金融服务体系的必要性，一方面源于存取现服务的刚性需求，即使在移动支付迅速渗透的今天，存取现服务依旧是必不可少的基础金融服务；另一方面源于金融服务供应商在“最后一公里”与潜在客户建立联结、为现存客户提供人性化服务的需要。无论是通过直营还是代理的模式，线下服务网点可以即时地为潜在或现存客户提供更为人性化的关怀和帮助，有助于树立产品和服务的亲切感和信誉度。而由于边缘客户通常缺乏金融服务经验，数字技术接受程度也相对更弱，这种让金融服务存在于客户身边的机制设计对于获取和培养客户尤为重要。对于线下金融服务，我们需要认识到的是，物理服务网点不仅仅为边缘客户带来了服务的可得性，也不仅仅为他们使用金融服务提供方便，线下服务网点的存在本身就为客户带来了金融认知的影响，身边亲友使用网点服务的经验也可以给原本受排斥的群体带来金融素养、态度和行为的启发。

### （四）探索跨机构金融服务聚合供应模式

在明确融合线上与线下服务的目标之后，我们还需要直面金融服务（尤其是线下服务）的可持续问题，探索有助于实现高效率、功能全面的金融服务的方法和机制。这也是在前面国际经验的介绍中重点讨论的如何提升代理商生存能力的原因——即使采用相对低成本的代理模式，也并非所有代理商都能轻易实现持续经营。

以我国银行体系的助农取款服务点为例，在部分乡村地区，曾经出现的单个行政村中有多家银行分别布放POS机具的情况。由于不同银行布放的POS机具不能互通使用，而村民所持有的银行卡各不相同，最后，不仅一些银行布放的POS机具逐渐被荒废，部分村民的基础金融服务仍旧得不到满足。上述例子再次引出了金融服务需求稀疏、少量的特征。在此基础上，要实现金融服务可持续、高效率、功能全面的发展目标，突破金融服务的规模“瓶颈”应该是解决问题的关键。

根据国际经验和我国实际情况，我们认为跨机构的金融服务聚合供应模式（aggregators）可能是当前解决我国金融“最后一公里”问题、突破规模“瓶颈”的潜在途径。通过聚合多种类、多渠道的金融服务以及第三方产品和服务，它们比单家供应商更容易实现规模效应，可以为边缘客户提供一站式服务。其中，最常见的是以支付服务为核心的聚合供应商，如前面提到的坦桑尼亚聚合代理商Selcom。这一类聚合供应商通常在金融服务端聚合了银行、移动支付等多种支付结算渠道，终端客户可以通过它们灵活选用支付渠道，办理金融业务或购买第三方产品和服务。为了组建超越机构的金融服务聚合供应商，政策制定者需要与业界沟通合作，一方面要突破一些各自为战的藩篱，另一方面要为聚合状态下的市场竞争提供制度支持。

### （五）持续优化金融生态系统

为了解决金融“最后一公里”问题，我们还需要持续优化金融生态系统。首先，要不断优化宏观政策安排，活跃农村金融市场供给和需求，为超越金融机构的竞争与合作提供政策支持。其次，要着重加强农村消费者保护，提供有利于解决“最后一公里”问题的适度监管，强化监管政策在农村的执行效力。再次，要从通信、网络、征信和法制等方面着手，持续改善金融“最后一公里”基础设施，不断提升金融服务可得性。最后，还要推动金融技术在解决“最后一公里”问题中发挥作用，充分发挥金融技术的效率优势。宏观政策支持、适度监管安排、完善的基础设施以及深入的金融技术应用，将与供应商一起组成良性的金融生态系统。

值得强调的是，金融“最后一公里”问题是一个动态的概念。我们期待各界共同努力，攻坚普惠金融的“最后一公里”问题，为最边缘的客户提供与其需求相匹配的金融服务，在改善客户福祉的同时推动经济社会包容性发展。

# 第一部分

# 面向“中小微弱”的金融服务

解决“最后一公里”问题，金融服务机构是主力军。传统金融机构，在国家普惠金融战略指引下，纷纷着手建立普惠金融部，它们的表现拭目以待。部分传统金融机构，例如，信用合作社，一直扎根农村，服务在“最后一公里”的第一线。新兴金融机构以其金融科技优势迅速崛起，已经成为不可或缺的力量。国际机构以其丰富的实践经验推动中国普惠金融发展。

# 第一章　农村金融服务机构的改革与实践

【摘要】农村是中低收入人口和贫困人口集中的地区。农村金融服务机构的发展程度对中国普惠金融发展战略与扶贫战略的推进，以及金融“最后一公里”问题攻坚工作的成效，具有决定性影响。目前，我国涉农金融机构既包括传统金融机构、新型农村金融机构，也包括近年兴起的互联网金融企业，以及其他非银行业金融机构与行业龙头企业等延伸的金融服务机构。

## 一、中国普惠金融事业版图

自2016年1月国务院发布《推进普惠金融发展规划（2016—2020年）》以来，发展普惠金融成为国家发展战略，中国普惠金融事业版图（见图1-1）得以迅速扩大。除了传统金融机构、新型农村金融机构以外，近年兴起的互联网金融企业，以及其他非银行业金融机构与行业龙头企业等延伸的金融服务机构，都属于普惠金融范畴。中国已经进入全金融行业协力发展普惠金融事业的时代。

农村是中低收入人口和贫困人口集中的地区。农村金融服务机构的发展程度对中国普惠金融战略与精准扶贫战略的推进，以及“最后一公里”问题攻坚工作的成效，具有决定性影响。目前，中国银保监会数据显示（见图1-2），截至2016年末，我国主要的涉农金融机构包括2家政策性银行（国家开发银行和中国农业发展银行），1家大型商业银行（中国农业银行），1家邮政系统银行机构（中国邮政储蓄银行），农村信用社系统银行机构的1114家农村商业银行、40家农村合作银行、1125家农村信用社，新型农村金融机构中的1443家村镇银行、13家贷款公司和48家农村资金互助社，以及非银行业金融机构的8673家小额贷款公司。截至2017年末，我国银行业金融机构涉农贷款余额达到30.95万亿元，其中，农户贷款余额8.11万亿元，农村企业及各类组织贷款余额17.03万亿元，城市涉农贷款余额5.81万亿元；小微企业贷款余额30.74万亿元，小微企业贷款户数达到1520.92万户。

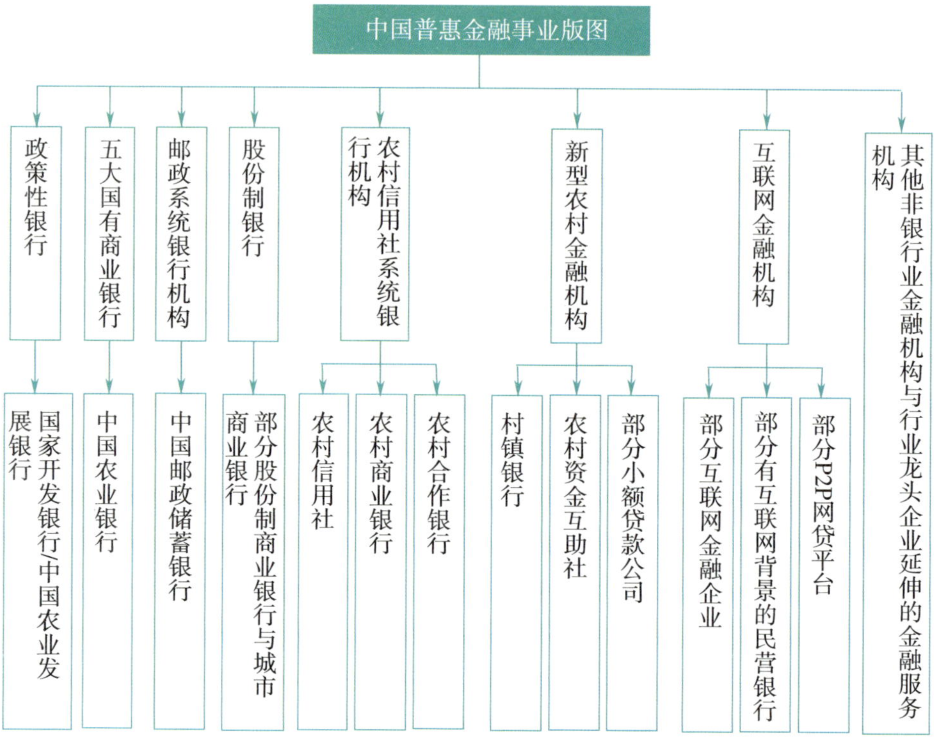


**图 1-1 中国普惠金融事业版图与涉农金融机构**

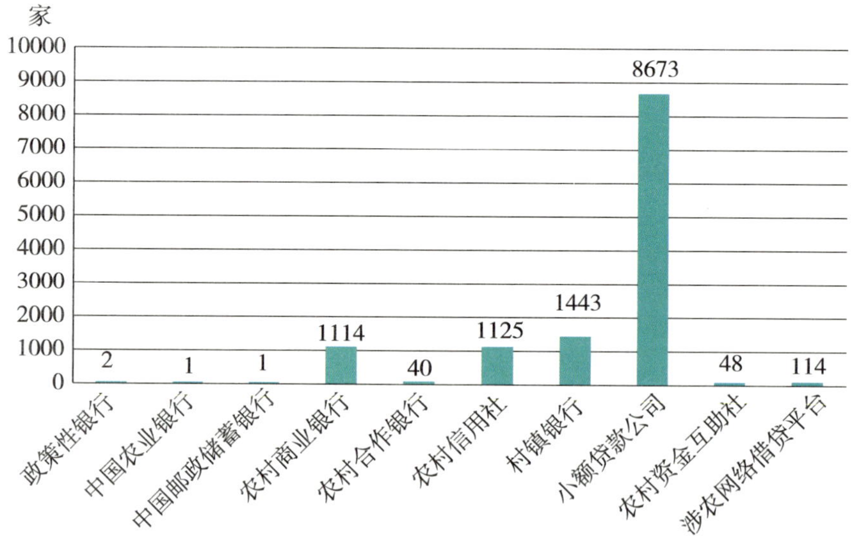


**图 1-2 2016 年中国提供农村金融服务的机构数**

如表 1-1 所示，目前，传统金融机构、新型农村金融机构、互联网金融企业、非银行业金融机构与其他行业龙头企业等无不着力分设普惠金融业务板块，部分涉农金融机构更是专注于为“三农”、中小微型企业等提供金融服务。值得强调的是，由于近

**表 1-1　中国普惠金融事业版图与国际机构的关系**

| 中国普惠金融事业版图 | 受资方（中国普惠金融标的机构/普惠金融供应方） | 案例、贷款标准、服务模式 | | 投资方（国际机构）类型 | 投资方（国际机构）投资方式 |
|---|---|---|---|---|---|
| 传统金融机构 | 服务于农业、农村、农民的政策性银行 | 中国农业发展银行：扶贫资金，多数单笔超过500万元 | 直营模式、数字模式 | — | — |
| | 已成立普惠金融事业部并聚焦“三农”和中小微企业的五大行 | 中国农业银行：“惠农e贷”产品，户均贷款额度约10万元 | 直营模式、数字模式 | — | — |
| | 积极开展普惠金融业务的商业银行 | 招商银行：中小企业贷款，笔均余额31万元左右 | 直营模式、数字模式 | — | — |
| | 专注“三农”与中小微企业的邮储行 | 中国邮政储蓄银行：涉农贷款，笔均6万余元 | 直营模式、数字模式、供应链模式 | — | — |
| | 部分为城市小微企业、个体工商户等提供金融服务的城商行 | 包商银行：小微企业贷款，户均余额不到10万元 | 直营模式、数字模式 | | — |
| | 专注“三农”和中小微企业的农村信用社系统银行机构 | 中国农村信用社：农户贷款，户均贷款余额8万元 | 直营模式、数字模式、供应链模式 | 国外金融机构/投资机构 | 社会影响力投资、商业投资 |
| | 外资银行 | 汇丰银行：汇丰村镇银行的农户与小微企业的贷款 | 直营模式、合作社联保模式 | 国外金融机构/投资机构 | 社会影响力投资、商业投资 |

续表

| 中国普惠金融事业版图 | 受资方（中国普惠金融标的机构/普惠金融供应方） | 案例、贷款标准、服务模式 | | 投资方（国际机构）类型 | 投资方（国际机构）投资方式 |
|---|---|---|---|---|---|
| 新型农村金融机构与小额贷款公司 | 扎根村镇的村镇银行 | 中银富登村镇银行：涉农信贷产品，户均贷款余额25万元 | 直营模式、数字模式 | 国外金融机构/投资机构 | 社会影响力投资、商业投资 |
| | 部分为“三农”、中小微企业等提供金融服务的小贷公司 | 中和农信：小额农户贷款，笔均不到2万元<br>南充美兴小额贷款有限责任公司：小微企业贷款，笔均约5.4万元 | 直营模式、数字模式 | 国际多边/双边机构、国际非营利组织、跨国公司、国外金融机构/投资机构 | 发展援助、慈善捐赠、社会影响力投资、商业投资 |
| 互联网金融企业 | 利用大数据技术服务最广泛群体的民营银行 | 蚂蚁金服旗下网商银行：小微企业信贷产品，户均余额1.5万元 | 数字模式、供应链模式 | 国外金融机构/投资机构 | 社会影响力投资、商业投资 |
| | 部分具有公益目标，且服务于“三农”、中小微企业、社会低收入人群的P2P网贷平台 | 宜信惠民：人均余额7.3万元<br>中和农信：乡信产品，户均借款金额1.92万元 | 宜信惠民：数字模式、批发贷款模式<br>乡信：数字模式 | 国外金融机构/投资机构 | 社会影响力投资、商业投资 |
| 非银行业金融机构与其他行业龙头企业 | 非银行机构延伸多种金融服务 | 中国平安的互联网金融平台：陆金所，人均余额12万元 | 数字模式 | — | — |
| | 其他行业龙头企业延伸多种金融服务 | 温州民商银行：小微企业贷款 | 直营模式、数字模式 | — | — |

续表

| 中国普惠金融事业版图 | 受资方（中国普惠金融标的机构/普惠金融供应方） | 案例、贷款标准、服务模式 | | 投资方（国际机构）类型 | 投资方（国际机构）投资方式 |
|---|---|---|---|---|---|
| 其他 | 援助项目、慈善项目、NGO 机构等延伸的普惠金融服务 | 仪陇县乡村发展协会：互助小额贷款 | 资金转贷模式、互助模式、非营利模式 | 国际多边/双边机构、国际非营利组织、跨国公司 | 发展援助、慈善捐赠 |

年来互联网金融企业发展迅速，包括大型综合互联网金融企业和涉农网络借贷平台，在获客、信用评估、风险防控等方面体现了数字化模式服务“三农”的优势。一方面，大型综合互联网金融企业包括蚂蚁金服、京东金融、腾讯金融业务、百度金融、苏宁金融、小米金融等多家多牌照互联网金融机构，具备雄厚互联网产业背景和庞大客户资源；另一方面，据零壹财经统计，截至 2016 年末，以农村金融为重要业务的网贷平台至少 114 家。此外，其他非银行业金融机构与行业龙头企业也以“三农”为服务对象，延伸出相应的涉农金融服务，如中国平安的互联网金融平台平安口袋银行与陆金所，以及森马集团、奥康鞋业等当地行业龙头企业发起的温州民商行。

普惠金融是一个具有多样性和探索性的新领域，其基本概念在过去几十年中不断地变化和演进。不同的主体从不同的维度对普惠金融进行阐述，导致普惠金融的内涵及其强调的金融产品或服务也不尽一致。在综合国际组织及各国专家学者等研究经验的基础上，结合中国的实际情况，中国普惠金融研究院将普惠金融定义为：立足于机会平等和商业可持续原则。在成本可负担的前提下，面向“三农”、中小微型企业、个体工商户、社会低收入人群、创业和失业人群、特殊群体（如残疾人）等在内的需要金融服务的群体（也就是“中小微弱”），通过合理的价格，有效、全方位、可持续地提供及时的、方便的、差别化的金融服务，以实现金融资源供求平衡，缩小贫富两极分化推动社会和谐发展的金融体系。基于该定义，以及中国政府推进全金融行业发展普惠金融事业的雄心，只要符合金融权力公平性、服务对象包容性、服务群体可变性、服务产品全面性等普惠金融特征的，不管是传统金融机构，还是新型农村金融机构、小额贷款公司、互联网金融机构，又或者非银行业金融机构与其他行业龙头企业等，只要它们为“中小微弱”群体提供的金融服务，就都符合国际、国内对于普惠金融的界定标准。

## 二、政策性银行普惠金融改革与实践

近年来，国家开发银行和中国农业发展银行认真贯彻落实党中央、国务院关于推进普惠金融发展的战略部署，主动服务农业供给侧结构性改革，积极推进体制机制创新和产品服务创新，在解决金融服务“最后一公里”方面作出了积极贡献。

### （一）国家开发银行的改革与实践

国家开发银行坚持精准扶贫、精准脱贫，切实加大脱贫攻坚工作力度，同时围绕农村土地制度改革，积极推进“两权”抵押贷款试点。

1. 构建开发性金融精准扶贫新机制

第一，组建脱贫攻坚“集团军”。按照《中共中央国务院关于打赢脱贫攻坚战的决定》（中发〔2015〕34号）关于“国家开发银行、中国农业发展银行分别设立扶贫金融事业部”的要求，国家开发银行高效率组建扶贫金融事业部，以专门机构、专业队伍，为开发性金融支持脱贫攻坚提供有力保障。第二，研究制定脱贫攻坚“路线图”。提出“易地扶贫搬迁到省，基础设施到县，产业发展到村（户），教育资助到户（人）”的工作思路和方法，确定了“十三五”期间发放脱贫攻坚贷款1.5万亿元的工作目标。第三，签订脱贫攻坚“军令状”。坚持党建引领，强化责任担当，总行党委与25家有脱贫攻坚任务的分行党委签订脱贫攻坚责任书，全面落实脱贫攻坚任务目标，形成全行上下齐抓共管的脱贫攻坚工作局面。第四，强化脱贫攻坚政策研究。加强与中农办、人民银行、国家发展改革委、国务院扶贫办、银监会、国家卫计委、水利部、交通部、教育部等部委沟通联络，积极开展脱贫攻坚政策研究，共同推动重点领域、重点行业的扶贫开发工作。第五，与地方政府建立脱贫攻坚合作机制。先后与贵州、甘肃、云南等21个省份签订开发性金融支持脱贫攻坚合作协议，为合力推进脱贫攻坚奠定坚实基础。通过与地方政府共同建立省、市、县三级“开发性金融脱贫攻坚合作办公室”，搭建金融精准扶贫工作机制和银政合作平台。第六，构建信贷风险补偿机制。创新扶贫捐赠资金使用方式，将捐赠资金注入贫困县信贷风险补偿金，重点支持贫困地区特色产业发展，有效缓解产业项目风险高、融资难的瓶颈制约。

2. 力争开发性金融精准扶贫新突破

第一，大力支持易地扶贫搬迁，打好脱贫攻坚首仗。按照中央“省负总责，市县抓落实”的易地搬迁工作要求，协助22个省（自治区、直辖市）政府建立省级扶贫投融资主体，研究建立省、市、县三级资金管理体系，畅通资金运作渠道，严格规范资金借、用、管、还各环节，切实加大评审承诺和资金投放力度。第二，创新融资模式，支持贫困地区特色产业发展。充分发挥产业化龙头企业和新型农业经营主体对贫困农户的组织带动作用，完善推广“四台一会”融资机制，以批发的方式融资支持贫困地区群众发展生产，有效促进建档立卡贫困户就业增收，在河南、甘肃、陕西、贵州等贫困地区探索形成了可推广、可复制、可借鉴的产业扶贫好做法、好经验。例如，以村级互助资金协会为核心的甘肃“双联”贷款模式、陕西商洛“政府＋开发银行＋供销集团＋龙头企业（合作社）＋贫困户”产业扶贫模式、贵州小额农贷模式等。第三，立足薄弱环节，加大对教育医疗卫生领域的支持力度。要实现脱贫目标，教育和医疗是需要解决的突出“短板”。国家开发银行发挥助学贷款主力银行优势，进一步扩大助学贷款覆盖面，并开展贫困助学贷款试点。在云南，以“省级统贷”的模式支持“云南省现代职业教育和县级公立医院及妇女儿童医院扶贫工程”实施，有效改善和提升了云南贫困地区教育医疗基础设施条件，为金融支持教育扶贫和健康扶贫工程作出了试验示范。

3. 积极稳妥推进“两权”抵押贷款试点

自人民银行会同银监会、保监会等六个部门发布《农民住房财产权抵押贷款试点暂行办法》（银发〔2016〕78号）和《农村承包土地的经营权抵押贷款试点暂行办法》（银发〔2016〕79号）的文件后，国家开发银行积极贯彻落实有关要求，在条件相对成熟的黑龙江、吉林、内蒙古、四川等粮食主产省率先开展农村承包土地经营权抵押贷款试点工作，融资支持新型经营主体开展农业项目建设，取得了初步成效。2016年，全行新增发放“两权”抵押贷款1.1亿元。在黑龙江，国家开发银行以庆安县农村土地经营权流转服务中心为融资平台，以农村承包土地经营权流转合同项下全部权益和收益提供质押担保发放13年期共4914万元贷款，有效促进了土地规模化经营，达到了土地增产节支和农户创业增收的目的，实现了多方共赢；在吉林，国家开发银行创新模式，由政策性担保公司提供保证担保，以承包土地经营权提供反担保，引入保险公司建立风险保障机制，引入粮食收储企业解决农户卖粮难和还款资金难落实问题，发放贷款3660万元，支持榆林、九台、四平等5个市县、30余家农业合作社的土地流转和规模化种植融资需求，惠及1148户农户，有效缓解了新型农业经营主体信用能力不足的融资难题，有力推动了现代农业的发展。

## （二）中国农业发展银行的改革与实践

中国农业发展银行认真落实精准扶贫、精准脱贫方略，同时进一步加大创新力度支持我国农业现代化建设。

1. 全力支持易地扶贫搬迁

成立服务脱贫攻坚工作领导小组，率先在全国金融系统成立扶贫金融事业部，下设5个一级部门，对全行扶贫业务进行指导、管理和监督。在22个扶贫重点省份设立扶贫业务处，二级分行设立扶贫业务部，在839个国家贫困县设立“扶贫金融事业部”或派驻扶贫工作组，率先实现贫困地区政策性金融服务机构全覆盖，努力构建全行全力扶贫工作格局。率先编制政策性金融扶贫五年规划，为做好服务脱贫和攻坚工作提供行动指南。

积极参与国家及地方政府政策规划研究，迅速研发专项贷款产品，率先投放首笔易地扶贫搬迁贷款。2016 年累放易地扶贫搬迁贷款 1202 亿元，余额 1921 亿元，支持搬迁项目 624 个，惠及 414.2 万名建档立卡贫困人口。在国家下达的易地扶贫搬迁贴息贷款、专项建设基金规模中，中国农业发展银行占比均超过 50%，发挥了金融服务主力军的作用。

2. 探索推进政策性金融扶贫试验示范区建设

第一，加强与发展改革委、农业部、交通部、住建部等相关部门合作，签署合作协议，发布支持政策，共同推进网络扶贫、特色产业扶贫、交通扶贫、小城镇建设等专项扶贫行动。积极参与地方政府扶贫规划及政策制定，已与 22 个省级政府或扶贫开发主管部门签订合作协议。第二，开展合作扶贫。各级分支机构通过与当地财政局、发展改革委、农业局等产业主管部门对接，成立本级行动领导小组，联合构建产业扶贫合作支持模式。对领导小组推荐的符合条件的企业或项目，中国农业发展银行优先保证信贷规模，优先受理调查评估，加快贷款审批速度，给予适度利率优惠。第三，支持东西部扶贫协作。制定《关于支持东西部扶贫协作的指导意见》，东西部地区各级行主动对接地方政府，建立合作机制，切实发挥在东西部扶贫协作中的支持和引导作用。向四个协作帮扶项目发放贷款 4.3 亿元，带动建档立卡贫困人口 4 万余人。第四，支持“万企帮万村”精准扶贫。与全国工商联、国务院扶贫办、中国光彩会共同签署《政策性金融支持“万企帮万村”精准扶贫行动战略合作协议》，制定实施意见，以“万企帮万村”精准扶贫行动为抓手，建立项目库，构建支持产业扶贫新模式。湖北分行已率先与当地有关部门签订了合作协议，搭建了四方合作平台。

会同国务院扶贫办，在广西百色、河北保定、贵州毕节、陕西安康相继创建四个政策性金融扶贫实验示范区，同时与贵州、重庆等省级政府合作创建省级试验示范区，将试验示范区作为先行先试平台，积极探索财政资金与政策性金融合力扶贫的有效模式，加强财政扶贫、金融扶贫、社会扶贫的协同合作，引领各方资源形成扶贫合力。

3. 促进农村一、二、三产业融合

（1）积极支持农村土地有序流转和适度规模经营。第一，围绕破解“谁来种地”问题，支持地方政府牵头搭建农村土地流转经营服务平台，探索出“临颍土地银行模式”，有效解决流转双方信息不对称、相互不信任和流转不规范等问题。第二，围绕破解新型农业经营主体融资难、融资贵问题，探索推进“江苏沛县统贷统还”模式，统筹解决从基础设施投入到农业生产全过程的融资难题。第三，围绕破解“如何种地”问题，通过“政、银、社、企”密切合作，探索推出“山东土地托管”模式，较好地破解了基层“为农服务中心”因小、弱、散而难以获得银行融资支持等问题，有力地支持了农业生产全程化社会服务体系建设。第四，围绕支持优势区域率先实现农业现代化，不断探索完善安徽整建制推进现代农业示范园区建设的“宣城模式”。

（2）全力推进投融资模式创新。第一，探索“投贷结合”融资模式。通过中国农业发展银行专项建设基金投入，引导社会资金和商业银行资金进入国家重点项目，实现投贷联动。江苏泰州创新推出“债贷投”组合推进高标准农田建设模式，得到国务院领导的肯定。第二，发展供应链金融模式。整合农业全产业链核心企业与上下游企业资源，设计金融产品，提供全链条服务，促进一、二、三产业融合发展。第三，探索开展“政银担”“政银保”合作模式。通过与地方政府、担保和保险等机构的合作，建立风险分担补偿机制，加大对新型农业经营主体的支持力度。第四，探索“两权”抵押贷款业务，研究出台制度办法指导分行探索开展农村承包土地的经营权抵押贷款业务。

## 三、中国农业银行普惠金融的改革与实践

近年来，中国农业银行认真贯彻落实党中央、国务院“三农”工作决策部署，积极应对宏观经济减速降挡、县域有效金融需求不足的影响，主动适应和服务经济新常态，加大改革创新力度，着力打通金融服务“最后一公里”。

### （一）普惠金融改革

1.“三农金融事业部”改革

为探索大型商业银行服务“三农”有效模式，实现面向“三农”与商业运作的有机结合，农业银行从2008年起启动实施了“三农金融事业部”改革。“三农金融事业部”实施农业银行总行、试点省分行、地（市）分行管理部门“三级督导”，县域支行“一级经营”的事业部管理架构，对纳入改革试点的县域支行实行“六个单独”（单独的资本管理、单独的现代管理、单独的会计核算、单独的风险拨备与核销、单独的资金平衡、单独的绩效考核）的运行机制，并给予财税优惠、差别化存款准备金率和监管费减免等扶持政策。试点经国务院批准，在2011年9月、2013年11月和2015年4月先后三次扩大范围后，推广至农业银行全部县域支行。

2016年，农业银行制定出台了《关于进一步深化三农金融事业部改革的意见》，以完善“三农金融事业部”组织架构、下沉经营管理和决策重心、改革“三农”和县域业务考核政策、探索放权搞活县支行有效路径等为重点，深入推进“三农金融事业部”改革工作，强化事业部对“三农”和县域业务的支持保障能力。农业银行按照“三级督导、一级经营”的改革要求，在总行层面成立了“三农”金融部，在省、市分

行层面成立了“三农”金融分部，将所有县域支行改造成为“三农金融事业部”的基本经营单元，不断强化面向“三农”的经营主体地位。以地域为界，将所有县域机构的全部业务纳入“三农金融事业部”核算和管理范围。按照高于全行平均水平的原则，倾斜配置“三农金融事业部”经营资源。

2. 推进互联网金融服务“三农”

2017 年，农业银行将互联网金融服务“三农”作为“三农”金融服务工作的一号工程。全面推进惠农通工程与互联网金融的融合升级，做好县域普惠金融服务；积极开展农村电商金融服务，建立适合农村商贸流通特点的电子商务金融服务体系；创新开展县域互联网融资服务，重点推进农户贷款业务线上化改造，实现农户贷款线上申贷、线上办贷、线上放贷，推动农户贷款向批量化、线上化、自动化作业方式转变。

按照国家推进普惠金融发展规划要求，农业银行依托传统网点、渠道，积极引入互联网新技术，大力发展农户贷款业务，努力缓解农户贷款难、贷款贵问题，提升贷款可得性和可负担性；着力优化网点布局，将城区低效网点迁至乡镇在农村地区加快建设自助银行，扩大网点服务覆盖范围；深入开展“金穗惠农通”工程提质增效工作，改造升级惠农通电子机具，对接农业部信息进村入户工程，扩大服务覆盖面，增加服务内容，提升服务质量，让广大农民足不出村就能享受现代金融服务。

3. 积极开展金融扶贫

在全国，农业银行有 1 万多个机构分布在县域，有 21 万名员工长期工作在县域和农村及边缘地区。其中，边境线 2 公里以内的网点有 82 家，海拔 3500 米以上的网点有 483 家，海拔 4800 米以上的网点有 18 家。截至 2017 年末，农业银行实现对所有贫困县的物理网点覆盖，网点无法覆盖的贫困村，则以“惠农通”工程实现普惠金融服务的触达。截至 2017 年末，农业银行推动 24.5 万个“惠农通”服务点实现互联网升级，“惠农通”电子机具行政村覆盖率达 74.4%，767 个国家级贫困县的 17.6 万名农企农户实现“触网”。

此外，农业银行立足自身资金实力强、机构网点多、经营范围广的优势，积极服务好以农业农村大企业、大项目、大市场为代表的“大三农”，以新产业、新业态、新主体为中心的“新三农”，以及以特色农业、乡村旅游业、传统手工业为重点的“特色三农”，助推现代农业农村加快发展。截至 2017 年末，农业银行发放的涉农贷款余额为 30762 亿元，小微企业贷款余额 13638 亿元。其中，农业产业化龙头企业贷款余额 1517.48 亿元，农民专业合作社及社员贷款余额 228.96 亿元；农户贷款余额 2060.44 亿元，专业大户（家庭农场）贷款余额 656 亿元；“农民安家贷”1820.2 亿元；扶贫贷款 3718 亿元，支持和带动建档立卡贫困人口 665 万人。

### （二）强化普惠金融服务创新

1. 创新“三农”信贷政策和互联网金融产品

2016 年，农业银行继续出台年度《“三农”信贷政策指引》，研究制定《食品制造行业信贷政策》等涉农行业信贷政策，对江西赣南、广西、新疆、浙江宁波等地区出台有针对性的区域信贷政策，进一步完善了“以年度信贷政策指引为引领、以涉农产行业政策为基础、以差异化的区域信贷政策为重点”的“三农”差异化信贷政策体系。针对“三农”发展新需求，制定下发《中国农业银行林果贷款管理办法》《集体经营性建设用地使用权抵押管理办法》《农户养老贷款业务管理办法》等专项信贷管理办法；研究制定“三农”独立价值评估模型，规范特色押品管理，形成覆盖包括林权、海域使用权、土地经营权、集体经营性建设用地、渔船、农机具等常见“三农”特色押品管理体系，进一步加强了“三农”信贷制度建设。

针对农业农村新产业、新业态、新要素、新市场、新需求，2016 年农业银行先后研发推出农民住房“安家贷”、政府购买服务贷款、“三权”抵押贷款、金穗快农贷等 10 个全行性新产品，财政风险补偿基金担保农户贷款、美丽乡村贷款、光伏扶贫贷、“金穗甜蜜贷”农户贷款等 120 项区域特色“三农”产品，有效满足了新时期“三农”发展的金融服务需求。截至 2016 年末，农业银行“三农”专属金融产品数量已达 193 个，其中全行性“三农”金融产品 43 个，区域特色“三农”金融产品 150 个，“三农”金融产品体系更加完备。

**专栏 1-1　立足服务“三农”，中国农业银行创新产品和服务**①

中国农业银行作为中国最大的商业银行之一，自 2007 年起在落实服务农业、农村和农民（“三农”）这项政策方面一直处于领先地位。近几年，农业银行在产品与服务创新方面更进一步，更好地服务了“三农”。

动产融资创新。鉴于全国人大仅授权部分试点地区采用农村承包土地的经营权和农民住房财产权作为贷款抵押物，农业银行开发了各种非土地相关抵质押物，如农机具、库存农产品、粮食直补资金等，借此促进农村抵（质）押贷款融资。

“三农”产品创新。综合性品牌“金益农”整合了农业银行近年来开发的 149 种“三农”专属金融产品，为农户、农村居民和企业家提供了众多金融服务。针对农业龙头企业生产的季节性特点，农业银行开发了粮贷通、化肥淡季商业储备等特色产品。为促进城镇化，农业银行还开发了城镇化建设贷款、农村新民居贷款等产品。

① 资料来源：中国农业银行。

2. 创新“三农”金融服务模式和农村金融服务渠道

近年来，农业银行根据自身发展战略及市场定位，利用辖内“三农”有利环境和资源禀赋，按照“服务到位、风险可控、发展可持续”原则探索形成了较为完备的金融服务模式体系。探索推广了江苏分行、甘肃分行的政府增信模式，重庆分行、内蒙古分行的特定融资主体带动模式，江西分行、福建分行的特色产业链带动模式，河北分行、湖北分行的专业市场带动模式，四川分行的旅游带动模式等，构建起一系列有特色、能复制、可持续的金融服务“三农”好模式，破解当前“三农”服务成本高、风险大、收益低的难题。

全面推动“金穗惠农通”工程与互联网金融融合升级，与移动通信公司合作，加大网上银行、掌上银行推广力度，为农村居民提供基础金融服务；对接农业部“信息进村入户工程”，推动农村信息化进程，为农村居民提供信息服务。农业银行在2017年全面启动互联网金融服务“三农”的“一号工程”，在685个国家扶贫重点县上线“惠农e通”电商平台，打造“农银惠农e贷”“农银惠农e付”“农银惠农e商”三大业务。截至2017年末，“农银惠农e贷”服务了15.1万户农户，贷款余额达151.8亿元；“农银惠农e付”以互联网化的惠农通服务点为依托，提供24.5万个使用场景和支付产品的服务；“农银惠农e商”为156万户上线商户，提供2491.5亿元交易金额的服务。

## 四、中国邮政储蓄银行普惠金融改革与实践

中国邮政储蓄银行自2007年成立以来，始终坚持服务“三农”战略定位，不断探索农村金融服务创新，持续加大对“三农”领域的金融支持力度，助力解决金融服务“最后一公里”。

### （一）普惠金融改革

1. “三农金融事业部”改革

按照2016年中共中央 国务院《关于落实发展新理念 加快农业现代化 实现全面小康目标的若干意见》（2016年中央一号文件）“支持中国邮政储蓄银行建立‘三农金融事业部’，打造专业化为农服务体系”的要求，中国邮政储蓄银行于2016年9月8日成立“三农金融事业部”，通过整合全行资源，加大“三农”金融业务资源倾斜力度，扩宽“三农”金融业务服务领域，提升“三农”金融业务专业化运作水平，实现“三农”金融业务统筹协调发展。

第一，由“三农金融事业部”统筹全行“三农”金融服务，通过内设小额贷款部（扶贫业务部）、农业产业化部、农村项目部三个专业营销部门，在做好农户服务的基

础上，将原“三农”金融业务范围扩展为对农户、新型农业经营主体、农业产业化、农业农村基础设施等全部涉农领域，使其更加适应农业现代化发展趋势和农村社会经济转型需求。第二，整合全行资源，形成“三农”金融业务管理与营销有效融合。一方面，将贷款审查审批、信贷风险管理和政策及业务创新职能嵌入事业部，实现单笔贷款全流程管理，提高“三农”服务效率；另一方面，成立人力资源、财务管理、风险管理和资产负债管理四个后台支撑服务中心，增强中后台管理策略与前台经营需求的匹配度，有效解决前台、中台、后台信息不对称问题，提高内部管理运行效率。此外，构建“三农金融事业部”“总部—省级分部—市级分部—县级营业部”垂直的四级组织架构，并在县级营业部成立专业化支农的小额贷款人员队伍。在资源配置方面，对人力、物力等方面给予适度倾斜，在信贷资金紧张的情况下，给予“三农”金融业务专项的信贷规模额度支持。截至2016年末，广东、吉林、内蒙古、河南、安徽5家分行实施了“三农金融事业部”改革试点。

2. 助推农村金融服务机构全覆盖

从网点分布来看，截至2017年末，邮储银行有近4万家网点、14.3万个助农取款点、近12万台自助设备在内的实体网络，服务个人客户达5.53亿人。此外，邮储银行电子银行客户规模突破2.34亿户，其中手机银行客户规模达1.75亿户。

从服务对象来看，邮储银行的小微信贷专属产品接近60个，户均年贷款不足百万元，处同业最低水平，远低于全国平均280万元的水平。此外，涉农小额贷款笔均6万余元。

从业务进展来看，截至2017年末，邮储银行的消费信贷余额达到1.41万亿元，当年累计发放小微企业贷款7607.52亿元，涉农贷款余额是1.05万亿元。此外，截至2017年9月底，邮储银行金融精准扶贫贷款余额是421亿元。

**专栏1－2　邮储银行宁波市分行“扶贫贷”带动扶贫路**

近年来，邮储银行宁波市分行根据党中央、国务院精准扶贫、精准脱贫基本方略，以金融助推脱贫攻坚为己任，积极构建绿色金融体系，发展普惠金融。该行通过完善网络服务体系，创新金融产品、服务与技术手段，撬动更多的社会资本，以使金融力量助推精准扶贫。目前，邮储银行宁波市分行拥有邮政金融网点317个，其中县及以下网点281个，网点覆盖所有乡镇，真正实现了农村邮政金融服务“最后一公里”全覆盖。在不断完善物理网络的同时，该银行进一步加快产品创新，稳步推进扶贫小额贷款产品的推广。

邮储银行扶贫小额贷款是指为低收入农户，以及带动低收入农户发展的农业龙头企业、农民专业合作社、家庭农场、种养大户、来料加工企业（经纪人）、乡村旅游“农家乐”等发展特色优势产业的经营组织提供的贷款。借款对象为低收入农户的，最高贷款10万元；借款对象为农村经营主体的，根据带动低收入农户户数，单笔贷款授信最高可达200万元的贷款。

该行根据授信对象的特殊性，以宁海支行为试点，积极调研，积极走访，统筹各方，通过拜访宁波市委农村工作办公室，加强和保险公司合作等方式最终协调采取“财政＋银行＋保险”三方联动模式，构建新型农业经营主体与贫困户的紧密利益联结机制，实现“资金流向企业，企业发展产业、产业致富农民”的利益传导。经过前期反复调研，不断调整，2016年9月28日实现首笔放款，金额200万元，该贷款落地以后，该行依旧没有放弃努力，调研，优化，加强合作，倾听客户心声，截至2018年3月底，小额扶贫贷款累计放款101笔，金额8200万元，贷款结余60笔，金额5170万元，让众多低收入农户增收致富，普惠金融再一次照亮了其他金融资本望而却步的领域。据悉，该行2017年下半年与宁波市委农村工作办公室签订了《扶贫战略合作协议》，接下来将在宁波区域重推，持续加大金融助推脱贫攻坚力度。

据悉，下一步，该行将坚持把开展“精准扶贫”和发展普惠金融紧密结合起来，以“金融扶贫”取得的成果作为新的起点，坚持服务“三农”，把普惠金融服务送到田间地头，支持县域农村地区经济发展，努力把邮储银行打造成为普惠金融的“中国样本”。

3. 创新“三农”金融服务模式

邮储银行深化银政、银协、银企、银担和银保五大平台合作，强化和拓宽“总对总”战略合作范围，创新贷款增信要素，丰富抵（质）押担保措施，加大了依托五大平台的产品及服务方式创新力度，开发了依托合作平台的对应产品及服务，形成了从“总对总”战略合作框架到产品创新、市场拓展、业务监测、风险管理和绩效评估等系统化建设模式。特别是加强了同国家农业信贷担保联盟的合作，强化了各层级的高效对接、友好合作。目前，邮储银行已有31家一级分行与对应省级农担机构进行了对接，累计发放贷款13.45亿元。

邮储银行在全国积极推广农村手机金融服务，发展手机银行万能版，积极推广便捷版手机银行，还在有条件的农村网点实现WIFI无线网络覆盖，通过电子银行渠道改善农村地区金融服务条件。同时，邮储银行积极推进农村地区电子渠道的使用。

## （二）普惠金融业务创新

1. 创新“三农”金融服务产品

邮储银行已经形成了农户贷款、新型农业经营主体贷款、涉农商户贷款、县域涉农小微企业贷款、农业龙头企业贷款五大产品体系，每个产品线下又细分为多个贷款品种，基本上实现了涉农经营主体全覆盖。同时，按照“一县一业、一行一品”的发展思路，结合本地实际，针对各地优势特色农业产业开发各类产品。例如，在江西推出“财政惠农信贷通”、在江苏试行“小额流水贷”、在浙江试点开办“掌柜贷”等特色信贷产品，有效服务了当地现代农业发展。其中，“掌柜贷”业务结合了互联网思维和邮政农村电商两方面的优势。

结合城镇化农民的住房、医疗、养老、教育需求，通过加强银政合作，开展代发养老金及农民拆迁款、金融社保 IC 卡、助学贷款住房贷款等产品；结合城镇化农民的消费升级需求，积极发展信用卡、POS 机收单等产品；结合城镇化农民的资产保值增值需求，发展保本理财、国债、货币基金等低风险产品。对尚未开始城镇化或处于城镇化建设初期的区域，开展“新农保”“新农合”、助农取款、绿卡村镇建设等服务，带动新型城镇化建设的发展。邮储银行稳妥推进新型城镇化消费贷款服务产品，同步在深圳、海南、内蒙古等地探索面向中低收入阶层的个人保障房贷款服务，为改善农村地区居住和消费环境贡献力量。

2. 优化贷款业务流程

邮储银行积极开展依托移动终端的移动展业信贷办理模式，利用移动电子设备，实现贷款客户调查的位置定位、拍照上传、录音、调查内容记录等功能。信贷员仅需一台移动智能终端，就可以完成现场调查，实现当日申请、次日放款。该服务 2014 年开始在福建、河北等地试点，目前已在邮储银行 36 家一级分行全面推广使用范围覆盖农户保证贷款、商户保证贷款、农户联保贷款、商户联保贷款等多个业务品种，已累计受理并实现放款 7.1 亿元。

邮储银行推出了小额贷款业务优势行业调查报告模板、小额贷款业务合同打印功能和零售信贷辅助营销系统等优化业务流程的应用。小额贷款业务优势行业调查报告模板目前主要服务种植、养殖、收购、生产加工四个优势行业，有效提升了小额贷款作业效率，进一步促进了前台、中台的有效沟通。小额贷款业务合同打印功能，减少了合同填写环节的疏漏，减少了信贷人员合同填写工作量，提升了客户贷款服务体验度。零售信贷辅助营销系统实现了对零售信贷客户信息的 360 度标准化覆盖，为充分挖掘丰富的客户资源，实现精准服务、精准管理、精准风控、精准学习提供了数据支撑。

3. 创新抵（质）押担保方式

邮储银行积极推进“林权”及“农村承包土地的经营权、农民住房财产权”（简称“两权”）抵押贷款业务。截至2016年末，21家分行开办了林权抵押贷款，36家分行均已开办“两权”抵押贷款业务。农村承包土地的经营权抵押贷款已在30家分行实现放款，贷款结余超过12.4亿元，其中，吉林、黑龙江、新疆、四川4家分行贷款结余均已超过1亿元。农民住房财产权抵押贷款已在浙江、湖南、辽宁、江西和江苏5家分行实现放款，贷款结余超过16亿元。同时，邮储银行积极引入政策性担保公司和保险公司，与人保财险、诚泰财险等公司合作，共同开展了保证保险贷款业务。

## 五、农村信用社普惠金融改革与实践

农村信用社历史上是中国农村地区机构网点分布最广的金融服务提供者，因此也是实现中国普惠金融目标、解决金融服务“最后一公里”的关键机构。

### （一）改革发展历程

中国农村信用合作社（现在一般称为农村信用社）成立于20世纪50年代初期，成立时是按农户自愿入股组成，其服务对象是本社社员，基本上体现了自愿、合作的特点，这使农村信用社在1949—1957年得到健康快速发展。成立之初，农村信用社是内生于农村的合作性金融组织，主要是为了调剂农村地区内部的资金余缺，曾一度为国家经济恢复作出了巨大贡献。但后来由于政治原因，合作社逐渐失去了其合作性质。

从1984年开始到1996年，国家曾两次试图恢复农村信用社的合作性质，但均以失败告终。1979年初，国务院决定由中国农业银行对农村信用社进行管理。1984年，由于经营不善、财务状况不佳等原因，农村信用社仍未能实现有效服务“三农”的目标，因此国务院提出对农村信用社股权设置、组织管理等进行全面改革，以恢复农村信用社的合作金融性质，更好地服务农村和县域经济。此后，农村信用社主要以村、镇法人机构为主要组织形式。这一阶段的改革壮大了农村信用社的资金实力，有效地促进了其业务发展，但也出现了农村信用社自主经营权受地方干预等新问题，影响了农村信用社普惠金融潜能的发挥。

1996年，国务院发布《关于农村金融体制改革的决定》，明确农村信用社与中国农业银行脱离行政隶属关系，按合作制原则加以规范。为了增强农村信用社的风险防范能力和运营管理水平，国务院办公厅1997年转发了《中国人民银行关于进一步做好农村信用社管理体制改革工作的意见》，重申要按合作制原则改革农信社管理体制。此次改革总体上较好地改善了农村信用社的管理体制。随着国有商业银行纷纷撤回县域内分支机构，农村信用社更多承担起服务“三农”的重担。然而，由于历史包袱重、资产质量差、经营不善，农村信用社之后出现了大面积亏损。到1999年末，全国信用社系统的所有者权益为负值，农村信用社服务“三农”的能力受到了较大影响。

2003年6月，中央政府启动对农村信用社的深化改革。农村信用合作社在组织形式上基本实现了由合作制向商业化的转变；在产权结构上实现了由乡级法人—县乡两级法人—县级统一法人（甚至省级统一法人）的转变；并且，组织规模不断扩大（见表1-2）。在这次改革中，不再强调坚持农信社在股权结构、管理和业务经营上的“合作”属性，并创造了两个新型的组织形式——农村商业银行和农村合作银行。许多农村信用社因而被改制成农村商业银行或农村合作银行，以提升其治理水平，并将其调整为商业可持续的经营模式。地方政府被赋予进一步改革的权力，地方政府随后出台并实施了配套政策，帮助减少不良贷款和进行产权改革。截至2016年末，全国共有1114家农村商业银行和40家农村合作银行。

**表1-2　2003年以来有关农村信用社改革的文件①**

| 日期 | 文件 | 主要内容 |
|---|---|---|
| 2003年6月27日 | 《深化农村信用社改革试点方案》 | 以法人为单位改革信用社产权制度，允许不同的产权形式；将信用社的管理交由地方政府负责 |
| 2003年9月15日 | 《关于农村信用社以县（市）为单位统一法人工作的指导意见》 | 对农村信用社以县（市）为单位统一法人提出具体操作意见 |
| 2004年8月17日 | 《关于进一步深化农村信用社改革试点的意见》 | 在首批8省（市）试点的基础上增加21个省（自治区、直辖市）作为试点地区，加强信用社的产权制度和管理体制改革，同时明确提出信用社要加大金融支农力度 |
| 2005年8月9日 | 《县（市）农村信用合作联社组建审批工作指引》 | 对县（市）农村信用合作联社的组建程序、审核要求、股权结构、法人治理结构等提出要求与指导意见 |
| 2006年6月8日 | 《关于推进农村信用社以县（市）为单位统一法人工作的通知》 | 提出具体工作要求，争取在三年内基本实现农村信用社以县（市）为单位的一级法人制 |
| 2008年6月27日 | 《中国银行业监督管理委员会农村中小金融机构行政许可事项实施办法》 | 对包括农村信用社、农村商业银行和农村合作银行在内的农村中小金融机构进行行政规范 |

① 资料来源：根据农村信用社改革各年文件整理。

归纳起来，我国农村信用合作社的发展大致经历了七个阶段：（1）1949—1953年，在推行合作化运动中试办信用合作组织；（2）1954—1957年，农村信用合作社逐步普及，实现了一乡一社，并以“信用合作社”的名称统一不同类型合作金融组织；（3）1958—1977年，农村信用合作社先后被下放给人民公社、生产大队和贫下中农组织管理，这一时期各地的农村信用社都是以乡镇为单位，相互独立，彼此之间没有协作和制衡关系；（4）1979—1984年在国有银行管理体制下扩大自主权改革阶段；（5）1984—1996年试图恢复合作金融组织“三性”阶段；（6）1996—2003年农村信用社与农业银行脱钩后按合作制规范阶段；（7）2003年后逐步“去合作化”、商业化的阶段。

2003年的改革助推农村信用社稳健发展。截至2009年3月，农村信用社资产质量和收益大幅改善，在业务经营、股权结构和公司治理等方面也取得很大进展。由此，农村信用社进入了历史上发展最快的时期，总体经营持续向好，服务实体经济能力不断增强。2016年，全国农村信用社系统实现净收益519亿元；2016年末，不良贷款率为7.3%，资本充足率为8.4%；截至2017年末，我国农村信用社各项存贷款余额分别为27.2万亿元和15.0万亿元。其中，涉农贷款余额为9.0万亿元，占全部银行业金融机构涉农贷款余额30.95万亿元的29%；农户贷款余额为4.4万亿元，占全部农户贷款余额8.11万亿元的54%。

### （二）改革对农户信贷可得性的影响

如上所述，六十多年来，中国农村信用社从乡级法人合作性质的金融机构发展到县级法人的农村信用社，在一定程度上失去了合作的性质；尤其是自2008年以来，无论是政策上还是实务上，所有农村信用社都有发展为农村商业银行的趋势（有县级、市级和省级多种类型）。那么，农村信用社商业化改革对农户信贷可得性的影响如何呢？

根据吴本健、马九杰和臧萌（2017）对浙江、山西、甘肃三省农户调查数据的研究表明，经过一系列改革，农村信用社在产权结构和法人治理结构、内部管理制度、资产质量方面都取得了明显改善，但也带来了一些问题。

一方面，县联社对基层社贷款审批权限的上收，拉长了贷款审批链条，增加了贷款审批的难度，农户小额贷款产品的推出和信用评级的广泛开展，增加了贫困农户取得贷款的比例，提高了普通农户从信用社获取贷款的可能性。随着县乡两级法人变成以县为单位统一法人，甚至更高级别法人，信用社的服务与社员的性质发生了改变，信用社与客户之间的“距离”在拉长，审贷过程中的信息不对称程度更严重。规模化、复杂化的组织管理、信贷管理制度，使针对小农户、小企业的信贷审批周期更长、对小农户提供信贷服务的交易成本更大，从而限制了小农户特别是经济不发达地区小农户信贷的获取。调查中，发现以县为单位统一法人的改革之后，资金从欠发达乡镇向县城集中的倾向是非常明显的。县城网点的存贷比显著高于偏远乡镇网点。

另一方面，信用社有提高法人级别的强烈愿望，满足改革条件的信用社在争取改革，未满足改革条件的信用社也在尽力改造和创造条件，县社制度信用社所在地区的经济环境明显好于乡社制度信用社。但是，以县（市）为单位统一法人改革并未改变信用社的法人治理现状，产权主体依然缺位，三会制度流于形式，缺乏有效的激励约束机制。

此外，从支农力度的提高这一角度来说，农村信用社统一法人改革是把“双刃剑”。

（1）农村信用社以县（市）为单位统一法人改革后，信用社基层网点的撤并破坏了农信社固有的“地缘”和“人缘”优势，导致信息搜寻成本增加，抑制了对小农户的信贷供给，但信息技术的采用（如信用评级的开展、联络员制度的实施等）缓解了这一问题。

（2）农村信用社以县（市）为单位统一法人改革后，贷款审批制度更加规范和严格，乡镇信用社的贷款决策权明显降低，审批权限的上收、审批链条的拉长合理引导了贷款投向资金需求额小的普通贫困农户，降低了支农政策的代理成本，强化了对小农户的信贷供给。

（3）农村信用社以县（市）为单位统一法人改革后，资金可在更大范围内调度，一方面提高了信用社资金的流动性，解决了基层社资金实力不足的弊端；另一方面导致资金从经济条件差的地区流向经济条件好的地区，降低了贫困农户的信贷可得。

（4）农村信用社以县（市）为单位统一法人改革对农户正规信贷可得并无显著影响，既不能明显缓解农户面临的正规信贷约束，也绝不会增加农户正规信贷约束的限度。

事实上，在推动普惠金融发展过程中，许多农村信用社仍面临着一些挑战，治理不善、客户群规模小以及地方政府过度干预等问题仍困扰着一些农村信用社。农村信用社总体创新能力有限，尤其是在利用数字技术改进产品设计及优化交付方式方面显得力不从心，它们因而也面临着来自新市场参与主体的激烈竞争。

随着改革的不断深化，期待农村信用社在服务“三农”和推进普惠金融方面能够发挥更大作用。相关政策含义如下。

（1）加快创建社会征信系统，完善信用社对农户的信用评级体系，提高农户信用意识。伴随着农村信用社改革所带来的法人级别的不断提高，农村信用社的信贷决策集权程度增加，其在软信息方面所拥有的成本优势逐步丧失。为了实现硬信息和软信息之间的转换，农村信用社对农户的信用评级工作还必须继续落实。由于农村信用社法人级别提高后，资金实力得到加强，农村信用社可以通过对电子信息系统的投入来建立农户电子档案，把原本掌握的农户软信息进行标准化，并对今后农户的信贷记录进行电子归档，从而在该农户再次申请贷款时因了解其之前的信贷违约记录而减少不良贷款的发放并降低了信息搜寻成本。

（2）健全农村信用社支农激励机制，尽快出台并实施相关强制性政策。在农村信用社改革的双目标中，商业目标是具有内在激励的，它是农村信用社进行商业经营的原动力，而支农目标则必须通过设计科学合理的激励和约束机制，甚至出台并实施相关强制性政策措施，才能使农村信用社保证对弱势贫困农户保有一定的放贷比例。

（3）尽量保持农村信用社以县为单位统一法人的格局长期稳定。由前述对调研数据的分析可知，资金调度范围的扩大只会让信贷资金在更大的范围内“嫌贫爱富”。因此，在缺乏科学合理的农村信用社支农激励机制的当下，农村信用社的法人级别不宜盲目提高，作为总组织成本最低的县级法人格局应是当前信用社发展的长期选择。

（4）明晰信用社的产权主体，建立有效的法人治理制衡机制。农村信用社产权主体缺位生长于长久的历史背景之中，要改变这一现状不是一朝一夕就能实现的。目前允许多种产权形式的改革已在推行，优化农村信用社股权结构、让农村信用社的股东能够主张自身权利应是首先要实现的目标。这一目标的实现需要依靠对“三会”的整顿和监督，如对“三会”进行职责设定并实施责任追究；分设理事长与信用社主任，解决信用社主任被架空的问题；强化监事长权力，以增强内部监督等。

## 六、新型农村金融服务机构

2006—2008 年，中国政府出台了若干制度以规范新型农村金融服务提供者的设立，其中既包括村镇银行、农村资金互助社等新型农村金融机构，也包括小额贷款公司（新型贷款机构）。这些政策旨在提升传统上服务缺失和不足群体金融服务的普惠性。从某种意义上说，设立新型农村金融服务提供者可以看作提升农村信用社服务“三农”能力所作努力的延伸和补充，同时也可被视为增强农村金融服务竞争性的一项机制。

新型农村金融服务提供者存在着一些共同特征，如服务对象明确、设立条件相对宽松等（见表 1－3）。就服务对象而言，这些机构服务的目标群体包括农村居民和中小微企业。在设立条件方面，监管机构对各类新型农村金融服务提供者在注册资本、组织结构和股权结构等方面的要求各有不同，但都要宽松得多。涉及新型农村金融服务提供者的一些灵活规定允许符合条件的个人参与设立具有独立法人性质但运营限于一定区域的新型机构。村镇银行和小额贷款公司可以设立分支机构，而农村资金互助社则不允许设立分支机构。这种模式有利于增强新型农村金融服务提供者管理的灵活性和对本地目标服务群体的适应能力。自 2010 年以来，政府向满足定条件（如贷款余额增长达到一定水平或涉农贷款和小微企业贷款达到一定比例）的村镇银行和农村资金互助社提供补贴（不超过平均贷款余额的 2%）①。2015 年，中央财政部门为此拨付 29 亿元作为专项补贴资金。

**表 1-3　新型农村金融服务提供者基本情况对比**

| | 村镇银行 | 小额贷款公司 | 农村资金互助社 |
|---|---|---|---|
| 数量（家）（截至 2016 年末） | 1519 | 8673 | 48 |
| 试点年份 | 2006 | 2005 | 2006 |
| 监管部门 | 银监会 | 省级政府金融办或相关部门 | 银监会 |
| 规范性文件 | — | 2008 年 5 月 4 日，银监会和人民银行联合发布《关于小额贷款公司试点的指导意见》，各省以此为依据，相继出台了小额贷款公司管理办法 | 2007 年 1 月 22 日，银监会发布《农村资金互助社管理暂行规定》 |
| 主要特征 | 独立企业法人，最大股东或唯一股东必须是银行业金融机构，且持股比例不得低于村镇银行股本总额的 15% | 独立企业法人，不吸收公众存款，经营小额贷款；主要资金来源为股东缴纳的资本金、捐赠资金等；从银行业金融机构融入资金的余额不得超过资本净额的 50% | 独立企业法人，由乡（镇）、行政村农民和农村小企业自愿入股组成，仅面向社员提供存款、贷款、结算等业务的社区互助性银行业金融机构 |

资料来源：中国银监会。本书凡是选取的事件及法律文件发生在机构改革前的，银行、保险监管机构名称仍用银监会、保监会。

### （一）村镇银行

2006 年 12 月，全国村镇银行试点工作正式启动。2007 年 1 月，银监会发布《村镇银行管理暂行规定》。按照国家有关规定，村镇银行可经营的业务包括吸收公众存款；发放短期、中期和长期贷款；办理国内结算；办理票据承兑与贴现；从事同业拆

① 根据财政部 2016 年发布的《普惠金融发展专项资金管理办法》，这些补贴资金由中央和地方财政部门分担，如东部、中部和西部地区的资金分担比例分别为 30/70、50/50 和 70/30。

借；从事银行卡业务承销政府债券，代理收付款项及代理保险业务等。就治理结构而言，村镇银行的性质是独立的企业法人，但村镇银行实行发起人制度必须有一家符合监管条件的商业银行作为主要发起银行。发起银行持股比例不得低于村镇银行股本总额的15%，并且具有一定程度的监督职责。截至2015年末，五家大型商业银行和约40%的股份制银行设立了村镇银行；此外，约15%的农村商业银行和76%的城市商业银行也设立了村镇银行，村镇银行为这些银行提供了获取农村新客户群体的宝贵机遇。

根据相关法律规定，村镇银行对同一借款人的贷款余额与村镇银行资本余额的比例不得超过10%（与传统商业银行一样）。由于村镇银行总体经营规模较小，在正常情况下，其对单个客户的贷款余额通常不会太大。截至2016年末，村镇银行户均贷款余额仅为41万元。截至2016年末，中国已成立村镇银行1519家，其中65%设立在中西部地区村镇银行总资产12380亿元，总贷款余额7020亿元，其中涉农贷款和小微企业贷款余额总计6.530亿元，占各项贷款余额的93%，村镇银行80%的贷款低于500万元。

**专栏1-3　温岭联合村镇银行"仟禾福"惠农工程案例**

在滨海葡萄种植行业内，王冬青是位远近闻名的"葡萄种植能手"。他能通过观察葡萄叶的状态准确判断葡萄树的生长情况，还经常被种植户邀请到全国各地给葡萄树"治病"。他种的葡萄颗粒饱满、大小匀称，收益比别人种植的每亩要多出好几百斤，"我盘算着筹点钱再承包点土地，新增些树苗，但商业银行贷款利息高，手续麻烦"。正当老王为钱犯愁时，听说温岭联合村镇银行支农贷款利率优惠、手续简便，决定向温岭联合村镇银行申请贷款。银行了解了老王的实际情况后，快速放款15万元，解了他的燃眉之急。

温岭联合村镇银行滨海支行针对葡萄种植的行业特点，推出灵活分期、按季度结息等还款方式以及随借随还、利率优惠等措施，让村民享受到了简单、方便、快捷的金融服务。

### （二）小额贷款公司

小额贷款公司是由自然人企业法人与其他社会组织投资设立、不吸收公众存款经营小额贷款业务的有限责任公司或股份有限公司，有独立的法人财产，以全部财产对其债务承担民事责任。小额贷款公司股东依法享有获得资产收益、参与重大决策和选择管理者等权利，以其认缴的出资额或认购的股份为限对公司承担责任。小额贷款公司法人治理结构相对独立，实行所有权和经营权分离的经营模式。小额贷款公司按照市场化原则进行经营，但面临着某些融资限制。2005 年，人民银行启动小额贷款公司试点。2008 年 5 月，银监会、人民银行联合发布《关于小额贷款公司试点的指导意见》。

小额贷款公司只贷不存，不能吸收公众存款，主要为“三农”及小微企业提供服务。与村镇银行类似，一些省份规定，小额贷款公司应以金融服务不足群体为目标客户。例如，小额贷款公司 70%的贷款必须发放给贷款余额不超过 50 万元的小额借款人，其余 30%的贷款可发放给单户贷款余额不超过小额贷款公司资本净额 5%的借款人。根据银保监会发布的数据显示，截至 2017 年末，全国小额贷款公司达到 8551 家，实收资本是 8270.33 亿元，贷款余额是 9799.49 亿元。

**专栏 1-4　南充美兴小额贷款公司　坚持服务小微客户**

南充美兴成立于 2007 年 9 月，属于中国人民银行发起的首批小额信贷试点项目之一，也是中国第一家外资小额贷款公司。南充美兴于 2007 年 10 月发放首批贷款，目前拥有 3 家分公司和 11 个服务网点，公司员工 268 人，其中客户经理 184 人。

自成立以来，南充美兴始终坚持为农民、个体工商户及小微企业等缺少融资途径、规模较小的群体提供贷款服务。南充美兴具有以下四个经营特色：（1）重信用，轻抵押。与更倚重担保和抵押品的传统信贷模式不同，南充美兴的贷款业务更注重客户现金流分析，重视客户的经营稳定性和业务前景。南充美兴 90%的贷款是无担保贷款。（2）坚持“额小（单笔）、量大（总额）、分散、短期”的贷款原则。截至 2018 年，南充美兴累计投放贷款 12 万多笔，累计贷款金额超过 60 亿元。目前，南充美兴拥有客户 1.6 万多户，单笔 10 万元以内的贷款占比为 90%。（3）坚持“快速决策快速投放”原则。南充美兴建立了标准化的贷款决策流程，采用高效的信用审核流程，并实现了信息系统管理与远程贷款审批。贷款从申请到发放平均只需要 23 天，老客户申请贷款基本可以实现当天批准当天发放。（4）坚持商业可持续和社会效益双重目标。自 2011 年起，南充美兴开始实施企业社会绩效管理，开展客户保护工作。因此，南充美兴获得国际组织 Smart Campaign 的客户保护认证，是中国首家获此认证的小额贷款公司。

从网点分布看，中国小额贷款公司协会发布的《中国小额贷款公司行业发展报告（2005—2016）》指出，我国还有 100 多家公益性的扶贫小额信贷组织，分布于国家级与省级的重点扶贫县。从服务对象来看，小额贷款公司设立的前提，是要坚持“小额、分散”的原则，面向农户和微型企业提供信贷服务。如图 1－3 所示，四川、内蒙古、河北的小额贷款公司户均贷款额在 40 万～100 万元；浙江、江西、河南、山东的小额贷款公司户均贷款额在 100 万～200 万元；重庆的小额贷款公司户均贷款额是 4.11 万元，部分原因是重庆市集中了全国最多的网络小额贷款公司，如蚂蚁金服的花呗等网络小额贷款产品的户均贷款额比较低。

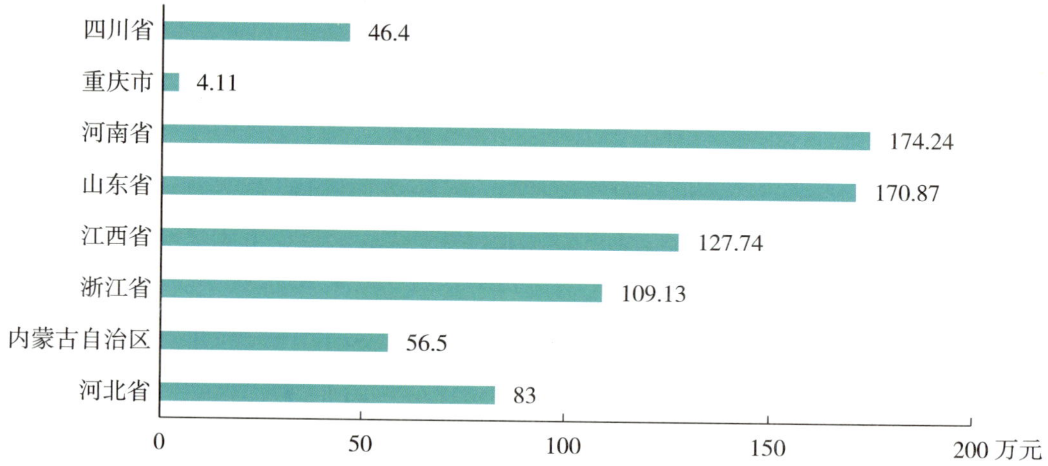


资料来源：中国小额贷款公司协会发布的《中国小额贷款公司行业发展报告（2005—2016）》，2016 年 9 月版。

**图 1－3　2015 年中国部分省市小额贷款公司户均贷款额**

## （三）农村资金互助社

2007 年，中国银监会发布《农村资金互助社管理暂行规定》，促进农村资金互助社发展。农村资金互助社依托行政村或者农民专业合作社设立，面向社员开展存款、贷款和结算、买卖政府债券和金融债券等业务。成立农村资金互助社的目的在于将农民联合起来，弥补农村地区（特别是经济发展落后的贫困地区）金融服务空白，解决农村金融服务落后等不足，以资金合作的模式来谋求农民的自我发展。

2007 年，中国首家由农民自愿入股组建的农村资金互助社——吉林省梨树县闫家村百信农村资金互助社正式挂牌营业。截至 2016 年末，全国共组建农村资金互助社 48 家，分布在 16 个省份，主要集中在浙江、黑龙江、山西等地，服务社员 6 万人，存款余额 27 亿元，贷款余额近 19 亿元，其中农户贷款余额 18 亿元，占贷款总额的 96.8%。2012 年，农村资金互助社模式并未实现预期目标。为了将精力集中于其他政策措施上，银监会暂缓发放新的农村资金互助社牌照。阻碍农村资金互助社发展的主要原因是内部管理不善和经营规模过小。此外，还出现了多起假借互助社名义进行非法集资或非法吸收公众存款的事件，对互助社的声誉造成了负面影响。

### （四）积极作用

新型农村金融服务提供者自成立以来，利用自身的特点和独特优势积极服务普惠金融目标群体，弥补了传统金融机构的不足。具体而言，其独特优势体现在以下三个方面。

第一，新型农村金融服务提供者具有为目标群体服务的区位优势。大多数村镇银行设立在县城或者乡镇，农村资金互助社设在农村地区，许多小额贷款公司则设在小微企业聚集的地区或社区，这些机构距离服务目标群体非常近。

第二，新型农村金融服务提供者具有清晰的市场定位和明确的目标客户群体。在一定程度上，基于监管对目标客户的规定，村镇银行、小额贷款公司主要服务于小微企业和农户，资金互助社则服务于社员。

第三，新型农村金融服务提供者在管理和信息方面的优势使其能够更好地服务于目标客户。相比于传统银行，新型农村金融服务提供者经营管理层级较少，贷款审批更为方便快捷，能更好地契合农户、小微企业融资“短、小、频、急”的特点。在很大程度上，新型农村金融服务提供者的运转建立在“熟人社会”的基础上。如同传统上的微型金融机构，这类机构对客户知根知底，信息不对称程度相对较低，因而降低了交易成本，而农民、小微企业在农村和社区内的信誉意识也克服了缺乏抵押物带来的风险。此外，就村镇银行而言，其主发起行在村镇银行的硬件开发建设、人才培养以及风险防控等方面起到了重要作用。

因此，新型农村金融服务提供者起到了许多积极作用，它们为获取农村金融服务提供了便利，弥补了农村金融服务的空白，降低了农民和小微企业对民间金融的依赖，因而在一定程度上有助于改善农村金融环境。

### （五）问题和挑战

新型农村金融服务提供者的设立无疑是中国在推进普惠金融发展中的一项重要尝试，对于解决金融服务“最后一公里”问题非常重要。但同时金融服务提供者在现阶段也存在一些问题，这些问题有些具有共性（如创新能力不足），有些是某类机构特有的问题。

村镇银行面临的主要是管理成本、经营灵活性和产品创新能力等方面的问题。一是村镇银行发起人面临较高管理成本。根据中国银监会的规定，村镇银行网点的设立必须在发达和欠发达地区之间进行搭配。如果发起人银行在某个省份还没有设立分支机构，那么村镇银行往往由发起人银行总行管理。这不仅提高了管理成本，还降低了村镇银行的经营灵活性。二是村镇银行创新能力相对较弱。由于规模小等原因，村镇银行产品和服务创新能力不强，同时因受发起人银行影响较大（相对于其他潜在投资者者的影响而言），村镇银行的经营模式容易成为发起人银行的翻版，常常出现产品和服务与传统银行同质化的现象，由此限制了政策制定者最初设定的村镇银行向目标群体提供更有针对性的合适产品的能力。过高的管理成本、有限的经营灵活性，以及同质化的产品不但导致了较低的利润率，也给持续向更多目标群体提供创新产品造成了困难。

小额贷款公司发展面临的主要问题包括市场定位与商业银行雷同、风险防控薄弱、资金来源渠道狭窄、税收负担较重，以及经营区域限制等。具体如下：

一是部分小额贷款公司运营偏离了服务普惠金融目标群体的市场定位，未能有效填补普惠金融空白。现实中，许多小额贷款公司在经营上与传统金融机构类似，没有将服务小微放在重要地位①。

二是风险防控成为阻碍小额贷款公司可持续发展的核心问题。有些小额贷款公司的客户处于监管政策所限制的行业，或是负债率较高、不具备财务可持续性的企业；还有一些小额贷款公司存在担保形式单一、程序不完善、内部管理和风险防控能力弱等问题，从而加大了经营风险。

三是在只贷不存制度框架下，小额贷款公司必须以股东投入的资本金放贷。2008年银监会和人民银行《关于小额贷款公司试点的指导意见》的规定限制了小额贷款公司获取资金的能力，相应限制了其贷款业务的运作空间。各省的监管要求各不相同，有的省份通过设置较高的初始最低资本来提高准入门槛。之前，小额贷款公司的税率一般会比那些典型的金融机构高，同时也未能享受国家颁布的支持农村地区和小微企业发展的税收优惠政策。这一状况在 2017 年初得以改变，小额贷款公司从此也可以享受到税收优惠政策。

四是小额贷款公司的经营范围通常限于一县之内，向邻县扩展业务需要重新申请，并需新设一个独立的公司，这限制了经营的拓展及有效扩张。由于在风险管理、融资、地理限制等方面存在一系列挑战，小额贷款公司在扩大规模和实现商业可持续上面临一定困难，许多小额贷款公司还存在财务困难。为使小额贷款公司能够在发展普惠金融中扮演更重要的角色，还须解决法律和监管环境上面临的挑战。

在暂缓发放农村资金互助社牌照后，银监会亟待解决的问题是明确此类机构（或类似机构）在推动农村地区为农户服务的合作性金融中的角色定位。

---

① 根据张睿等（2015）的调查结果显示，样本小额贷款公司的平均贷款额是 190 万元，中位数是 127 万元。单笔小于或等于 5 万元的贷款笔数占比仅为 11.7%，金额只占 1.5%；相比之下，单笔 100 万元以上的贷款笔数占比为 38.3%，金额占比高达 67.9%。

## 七、互联网金融企业在普惠金融发展中的作用

近年来，“互联网＋金融”的创新与实践在中国经历了野蛮生长到合规经营的历程。

### （一）互联网金融企业从快速生长到合规经营的历程

一是网络借贷方面。2007 年 6 月，中国第一家 P2P 网络借贷平台拍拍贷成立；2013—2015 年，网络小额贷款发展迅猛；在现金贷风险爆发之后，2017 年 11 月 21 日，互联网金融风险专项整治工作领导小组办公室发布了《关于立即暂停批设网络小额贷款公司的通知》，收紧对网络小额贷款牌照的管理，据网贷天眼不完全统计，截至 2017 年 11 月 21 日，市场上共有网络小额贷款牌照 249 张（含已过公示期但尚未完成工商注册的网络小额贷款牌照）；截至 2017 年 11 月 20 日，全国有 648 家正常运营的网贷平台上线银行资金存管系统①。

二是网络支付方面。2010 年《非金融机构支付服务管理办法》颁布后，2011 年 5 月 18 日，第一批第三方支付牌照发放；2017 年 8 月，非银行支付机构网络支付清算平台的运营机构网联清算有限公司获批成立，处理非银行支付机构发起的涉及银行账户的网络支付业务，实现非银行支付机构及商业银行一点接入；2017 年，中国人民银行对第三方支付领域开启强监管，截至 2017 年末，第三方支付牌照从 271 张减少至 218 张②。

三是网络众筹方面。2011 年 7 月，中国第一家众筹网站点名时间上线；同年，第一批股权众筹网站天使汇等也正式成立；2014 年《私募股权众筹融资管理办法（试行）》发布，2014 年被称为众筹元年。

四是互联网保险方面。2013 年，阿里巴巴、腾讯和中国平安联手成立了众安保险，拿到国内第一张互联网保险牌照；2015 年《互联网保险业务监管暂行办法》出台，2016 年《互联网保险风险专项整治工作实施方案》印发，2017 年《中国保监会关于进一步加强保险业风险防控工作的通知》发布，互联网保险监管日益规范；截至 2017 年上半年，有 129 家保险机构经营互联网保险业务③。

目前，在互联网金融监管日趋严格的情况下，一批劣质的互联网金融平台被淘汰出局，一批大型的综合互联网金融企业通过完善牌照和业务，日益明确其金融服务的

---

① 资料来源：http://www.sohu.com/a/214698593_802420。
② 资料来源：中国支付清算协会发布的《中国支付清算行业运行报告（2018）》，2018 年 4 月。
③ 资料来源：https://news.p2peye.com/article-505706-1.html。

内容，并细化服务对象，积极将数字金融服务下沉到农村地区。

### （二）渗透“三农”的生产与生活

目前，大型综合互联网金融企业是数字普惠金融服务的重要供应方，包括蚂蚁金服、京东金融、腾讯金融、苏宁金融、小米金融、百度金融等多家机构。

在业务总量上，短短几年间，大型综合互联网金融企业提供的涉农贷款与其他服务，逐步追上了中国农业发展银行、中国农业银行、中国邮政储蓄银行、农村信用社等传统金融机构，而且它们最重要的优势还在于，互联网产业背景为数字普惠金融服务提供了多元化的场景，深入浸透农村地区的产业，以及中低收入人口和贫困人口生产与生活。也正因为如此，大型综合互联网金融企业提供的数字普惠金融服务多与产业链、供应链、生活消费息息相关，为农村地区提供脱贫与致富的机会。

以京东金融为例，截至 2017 年末，京东金融的农村金融，为贫困地区销售商品 200 亿元，服务了 1700 个县、30 万个行政村，覆盖了 832 个国家级贫困县，超过 30 万名农户获益；众创众筹为 12000 多个项目累计融资 54 亿元，扶持创业创新企业近 9000 家；企业金融累计服务 20 万家中小企业，发放贷款近 5000 亿元；京东闪付服务了 800 多万家线下商家。

以蚂蚁金服为例，截至 2018 年 3 月，网商银行为 277 万家小微企业累计发放 879 亿元贷款；支付宝为 6 亿名用户和 4000 万家小商家提供支付服务；余额宝规模超过 1.5 万亿元，为 6 亿多名支付宝用户提供互联网理财服务；芝麻信用记录了农村地区超过 1.63 亿名农村消费者的支付、保险、信贷服务等数据。

# 第二章　新型金融机构的崛起和困境

**【摘要】**本章讨论了金融行业的信息科技发展过程、新型金融机构的创新实践现状、各大新型金融机构的差异以及它们在服务普惠金融中遇到的困境。新型金融机构各有优势且均利用金融科技手段打破传统金融服务壁垒，但仍面临需求困境和监管等一系列难题。

## 一、互联网和金融科技正在重构金融服务体系

如果说信息技术是金融现代化和效率提升的重要支柱，那么信息科技的快速迭代和发展同样对金融服务业起到深刻的变革和推进作用。

金融行业的信息科技应用可以分为三个阶段：第一阶段是金融电子化，第二阶段是互联网金融，第三阶段是金融科技①。随着人工智能、区块链、云计算、大数据等新兴技术的发展与应用，互联网和金融科技正在重塑金融服务体系，“无科技不金融”已逐渐成为行业共识。

在第一阶段的金融电子化时期，金融机构主要是尝试以现代通信网络和数据库技术为基础，将业务数据逐步集中汇总，利用信息化软硬件实现办公的电子化，提升业务处理效率。代表性应用包括核心交易系统、账务系统、信贷系统等。

第二阶段是互联网金融发展期，主要是互联网技术和金融业务深入融合，金融机构利用互联网对接金融的资产端—交易端—支付端—资金端，实现渠道网络化，并催生出大量创新的业务模式和业务形态。代表性应用包括网上银行、互联网基金销售、P2P、移动支付等。

第三阶段以金融科技应用发展为代表，主要是金融机构利用大数据、云计算、人工智能和区块链等前沿技术进行业务革新，将传统的银行业务、证券业务、保险业务进行分解，

---

① 中国信息通信研究院、云计算与大数据研究所发布的《中国金融科技产业生态分析报告》，2018 年 1 月。

提供更加精准、高效的金融服务。通过自动化、精细化和智能化业务运营，有效降低交易成本，提升运营效率。代表性应用包括大数据征信、智能投顾、风险定价、量化投资等。

科技手段是打破传统金融服务壁垒的工具，但将金融服务全面通过科技手段来提供和实施还面临诸多挑战，尤其是产品创新与监管合规方面的碰撞，是新型金融机构崛起必须克服的挑战和必将持续面对的问题。从传统金融服务的含金量来看，信贷、理财、交易和支付是核心业务线，而在这些业务领域，新型金融机构首先从支付寻找突破口，且这个突破口是相对最容易被科技解决和做好风险管理的部分。

以第三方支付为例，2004 年支付宝的成立是互联网第三方支付的元年。互联网第三方支付经历了两个爆发期，第一个是 PC 时代，第二个是移动时代。互联网第三方支付的真正爆发来自智能手机使用量的增长和移动支付的推广。

2013 年后，移动支付随着移动互联网的兴起大幅增长，交易规模年度增速一直保持在 100%以上，2017 年中国移动支付规模已超越 100 万亿元①。而这一成果的取得是建立在信息技术和大数据处理能力和系统稳定性持续快速提升的基础上的（见图 2－1）。以支付宝为例，通过不断完善的运维平台（IAAS）、技术平台（PAAS）、数据平台（DAAS）和业务平台（SAAS）四层架构实现系统平台的稳定，弹性资源分配与访问管理，提高海量数据处理与计算的技能，使得用户可以随时随地使用安全支付服务。在 2017 年“双 11”，支付宝的新支付峰值诞生：25.6 万笔/秒，比 2016 年增长超 1.1 倍，再次刷新全球纪录。同时诞生的还有数据库处理峰值，为 4200 万次/秒。

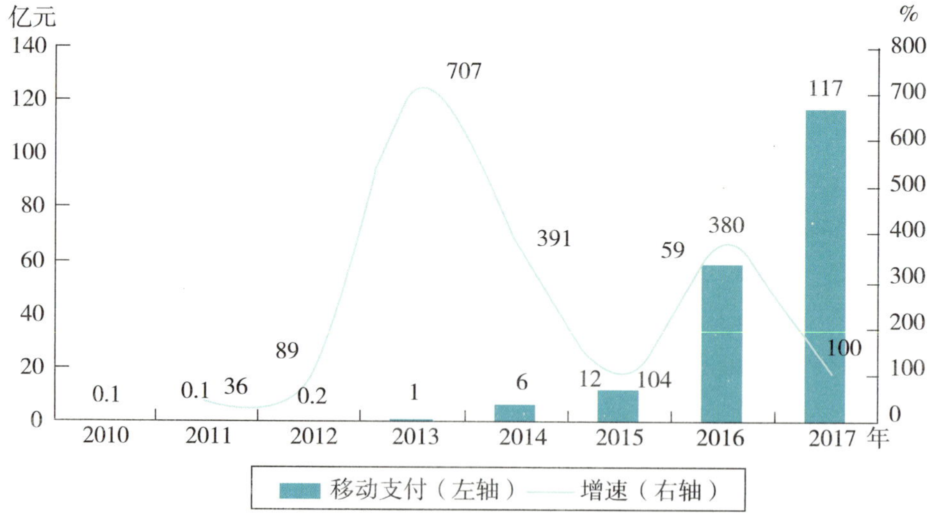


资料来源：艾瑞咨询。

**图 2－1　移动支付的规模及增速**

① 中国信息通信研究院发布的《中国信息消费发展态势暨综合指数报告（2018 年）》，2018 年 1 月。

与此同时，移动支付的便捷和技术能力保障加之硬件移动端设备的普及，使支付服务真正惠及中国的大多数个体。图 2－2 显示的是中国 O2O 市场近年来的规模和增速。

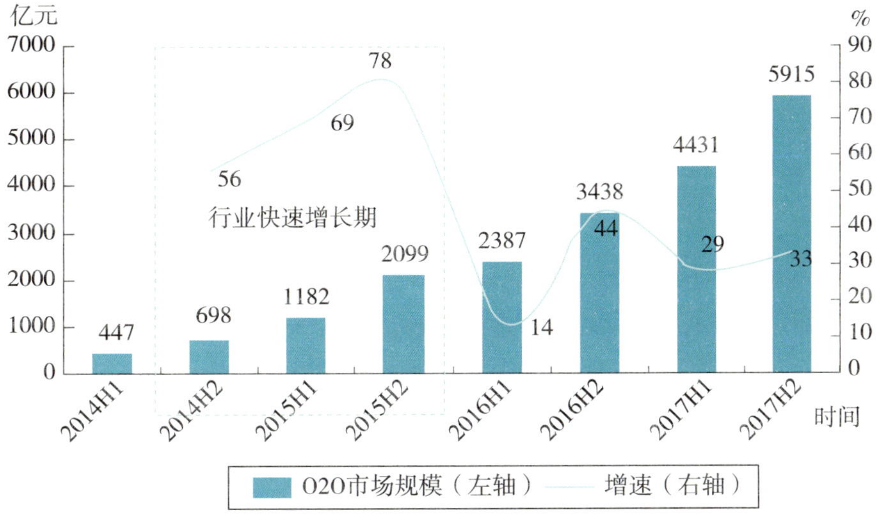


资料来源：易观国际。

**图 2－2　O2O 市场规模及增速**

而同样基于中国巨大的人口基数，科技的应用实际上可以实现中国市场的全球独一无二的巨大潜力，同时也使中国市场成为真正有可能通过科技实现普惠服务的市场。由 2017 年 12 月中美移动支付代表产品的月度活跃用户数（MAU）对比可以看到，中美用户已不在一个数量级上（见图 2－3）。

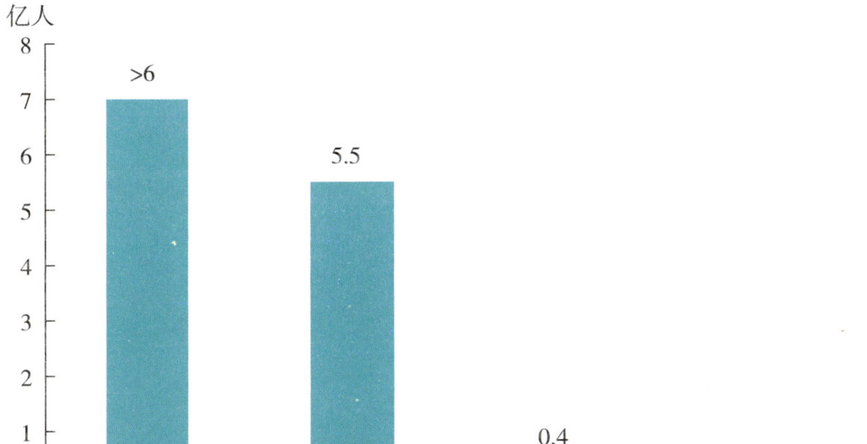


资料来源：Quest Mobile，App Annie。

**图 2－3　2017 年 12 月中美移动支付代表产品 MAU 对比**

综上，新型金融机构或者说金融服务借助金融科技有了更多的使用场景和获客手段，零售、餐饮、出行、快递服务都成为新型金融机构服务和获客的手段，但是在支付业务之外的信贷、理财和资产交易方面如何突破现有的服务模式和触及普惠金融业务则需要进一步创新业务模式和服务手段，并实现新的数字化赋能。

## 二、主要新型金融企业的创新实践现状考察

### （一）新型金融机构的分类和特点

新型金融企业包罗万象，但一个基本特点是不以传统模式开展线下业务，即不是通过传统的扩张资本金规模、广布实体营业网点的形式去触及最终的需求群体。与此同时，与终端用户非实际接触也对了解客户（KYC）、确认交易的真实性、实现交易的全程跟踪和最终履行相关还款或其他兑付责任提出了更高的要求，无论是征信、风控还是资产溯源均需要多重管理和印证。

因此，我们也可以看到，新型金融机构要实现上述功能的全覆盖是非常困难的，且对自身的信息管理和数据挖掘、技术实现能力有极高的要求，不同机构之间的合作共赢成为必然，且即使通过新技术手段来解决各个环节的问题，也需要不断地试错和调整数据处理模型和总结实际经验。我们把新型金融企业简要分为以下类型，具体详见表 2-1。

**表 2-1　新型金融企业简要分类**

| 类型 | 特点 | 典型企业 |
|---|---|---|
| 支付 | 支付处理、转账、移动支付、外汇、信用卡、预付费卡、奖励计划 | 支付宝、财付通、汇付天下、易宝支付等 |
| 保险 | 经纪、承保、理赔、风险管理 | 众安、保盒科技等 |
| 规划管理（金融赋能） | 业务管理自动化、客户关系管理、合规、供应链管理、个人理财工具 | 萨摩耶金服、挖财、通联数据、鼎复数据等 |
| 借贷/众筹 | 众筹平台、社交借贷等 | 借贷宝、51 信用卡、京东众筹等 |
| 交易/投资 | 交易管理、机器人咨询、交易算法、交易平台、经纪、清算 | 摩羯智投、富途证券、老虎证券等 |
| 安全 | 数字身份、欺诈管理、网络安全、数据加密 | 同盾科技、算话征信、天创信用等 |
| 区块链结合产品 | 数字货币、智能合约、资产/身份管理 | 趣链科技等 |

从上述分类及各类型企业业务特点可以看到，新金融企业开展金融类业务的核心是通过技术手段实现过去需要人工或者交易双方直接沟通商议完成的工作。一方面，科技手段提升了交易效率，并降低了人为干预或者人固有的执行效率波动变化的缺陷；另一方面，科技手段是否能触及我们所重点考察的普惠金融服务对象，则需要区别分析。

### （二）新型金融机构提供普惠金融服务的创新

中国普惠金融研究院将普惠金融定义为：立足于机会平等和商业可持续原则，在成本可负担的前提下，面向“三农”、中小微型企业、个体工商户、社会低收入人群、创业和失业人群、特殊群体（如残疾人）等在内的需要金融服务的群体（也就是“中小微弱”），通过合理的价格，有效、全方位、可持续地提供及时的、方便的、差别化的金融服务，以实现金融资源供求平衡，缩小贫富两极分化并推动社会和谐发展的金融体系。然而，随着科技的发展和实践的深入，国际上对于普惠金融的理解也在不断深化和完善。虽然目前关于普惠金融仍无统一的明确定义，但是关于普惠金融的几条原则已经被大多数国家和国际组织接受：（1）普惠金融的服务对象是社会各个类别的人群，且主要是被传统金融体系排斥在外的群体；（2）负责任的普惠金融服务：提供普惠金融应当采取负责任的方式来开展业务，同时有效地保护普惠金融服务对象的权益；（3）正规金融服务提供者来从事普惠金融：普惠金融服务的提供者必须合法，并且作为一个经济实体存在。

因此，我们考察新型金融机构的普惠金融服务，实质上是要考察在新工具和新技术背景下，各类新型金融机构是否在合法的前提下，通过新的服务模式和手段覆盖或者触及了传统金融机构未能触及也不愿意服务的群体。例如，网商银行筹建时就提出要让传统金融机构没有提供服务的80%的人群和小企业群体获得金融服务，但这一愿景通过什么方式去实现并且做到商业可持续也是新型金融机构需要去实践和破解的难题。

1. 新业务

金融服务的核心是支付和资金的跨期配置，从这个角度讲，新型金融机构的业务类型并不会发生根本变化，但由于新技术的应用，原有的业务体量可以发生变化，即原来从成本收益上看传统金融机构无法执行的业务具备了可操作性。例如，截至2018年6月底，网商银行及前身阿里小贷累计为超过1000万小微企业和个人经营者提供了超过1万亿元的经营性贷款。其中，近400万户“三农”用户获得了贷款支持。这样的业务量和频次如果通过传统商业银行线下客户拜访和贷审流程来做，将是完全不经济的，且这些小微客户也一直不是传统商业银行的目标客群，可以说是我们上述定义下被传统金融体系排斥在外的群体。因此，新型金融机构的业务类型并非从无到有，但其覆盖客群和交易频次却可以填补传统金融服务从未涉足的领域。

2. 新模式

传统金融机构对客户的信息是严格保密的，除了依托人民银行征信平台进行客户的信用背景和历史贷款情况查询外，很难在金融机构之间或外部获得更多的信息支持和数据，以衡量客户信用情况和实施差别化定价。因此，传统金融机构也很难对小微客户提供无抵押的信用贷款。而在新型金融机构的服务模式下，完全可以通过安全的方式对客户信息进行分类和交叉比对：包括实际商品交易数据、频次、物流情况、货物品类变化和定价周期等；与此同时，客户的不同行为也可以进行交叉验证，即客户的企业行为和个人行为，以及作为不同业务角色时的交易特征都可以进行混合排序和打分，能够在非线下接触的情况下作出用户画像和信用评价，并通过多频次、连续性的服务数据即时调整放款条件和加强催收提醒等，实际上有效降低了交易风险和信贷风险，同时也降低了社会整体的交易成本，从而使原来无法获得金融服务的客群成为商业可持续金融服务的接受主体。

3. 新产品

如果说支付是金融的基本功能，那么从普惠金融的角度看，让被排斥在金融体系外的群体有可获得、可承受、可持续的信贷服务是普惠金融覆盖面的重要指标。在众多新型金融机构的产品中，纯信用贷款且贷款利率在借贷客户可接受范围内的移动信贷产品就是极具代表性的金融产品创新。在灵活还款方式和期限的同时，还可以做到根据用户非信贷以外的行为情况为贷款进行综合定价，如果能够在更广的区域和用户类型中推广，将极大限度地弥补普惠人群信贷供给不足的现状。

传统银行普惠金融服务不足的很大原因在于提供产品的成本过高，服务小微和边远地区个人及农户不具备商业可持续性。而通过信息科技手段和大数据挖掘的信用评价方式，新型金融机构可以极大限度地降低服务的单位成本，在实现新产品提供的同时保持金融服务供给的可持续性。

以小额、快速的网商银行为例，网商银行平均单笔贷款不足 1 万元，单笔信贷成本 2.3 元，而一般银行的单笔信贷成本则在 2000 元左右。

4. 新技术的现状

第一，大数据技术。以网商银行为例，多年来通过大数据模型来发放贷款，形成了网络贷款的"310"模式，即"3 分钟申请、1 秒钟到账、0 人工干预"的服务标准①。

① 廉薇，边慧，苏向辉，蒋鹏程．蚂蚁金服：从支付宝到新金融生态圈［M］．北京：中国人民大学出版社，2017.

第二，人脸识别技术。人脸识别技术的几项核心算法分别是活体检测算法、图像脱敏算法以及人脸比对算法。移动端采用高准确率的人脸识别技术是用技术实现了解客户的重要手段，也是防控金融风险的一个重要关口。

第三，云计算技术。互联网金融中的云平台可以助力金融创新、助力金融机构的IT架构实现升级，构建更加稳健安全、低成本、敏捷创新的金融级应用，使金融机构可以更好地服务自己的客户。目前，国内领先金融云已经具备如下特点：高可用容灾、资金安全管理、高并发交易、实时安全控制、低成本交易。

第四，智能风控技术。线上风控系统利用历史交易数据进行个性化的验证，提高账户安全性。80%左右的风险事件在智能风控环节就能解决。除了事后审核外，事前预防、事中监控也非常重要——事前，将账户的风险分级，不同账户对应不同风险等级；事中，对新上线的产品进行风险评审以及监控策略方案评审。

第五，人工智能技术。人工智能技术目前集中表现在“智能客服”，通过大数据挖掘和语义分析技术来实现问题的自动判断和预测。比如，识别到用户的身份信息并了解用户的行为逻辑，就可以知道用户是在哪个环节遇到障碍，并且通过更新系统知识库提升智能客服的服务能力和响应速度。

从新技术运用到对传统金融功能的全覆盖，以蚂蚁金服为例，其一方面起到了推动传统金融行业革新的鲇鱼作用；另一方面其与传统金融机构进行合作和提供数字化服务也提升了行业整体的普惠金融服务能力（尽管“最后一公里”的普惠金融服务并不要求新型金融机构去完成）。

### （二）新型金融机构普惠金融服务的深度和效率

在考量新型金融机构的金融服务深度和效率方面，需要考量几个方面：首先是产品的可获得性，即是否能够让被传统金融排除在外的人群较为便捷地知悉和申请该项服务；其次是风控模型的实际效果，如果风控模型完备，但数据或者客户真实准确的信息实际很难获得（如在不同新型个人服务平台之间共享），就会使得产品创新失去意义；再次是可以通过大数据的运营和管理能力来检验机构的业务广度、执行能力以及对客户信息的完整性、准确性和隐私性的保护能力；最后是社会影响力，即新型服务模式和产品对社会金融服务质量、普惠服务能力提升以及推广应用的支持度，从而能够更快速地实现广覆盖和商业可持续化。

图2-4体现了新型金融机构在数据和信息优势前提下如何利用信息共享和技术输出为传统金融业务实现赋能，从而提高服务深度和广度，使踏入普惠金融服务、触及被传统金融排斥的客群成为可能。

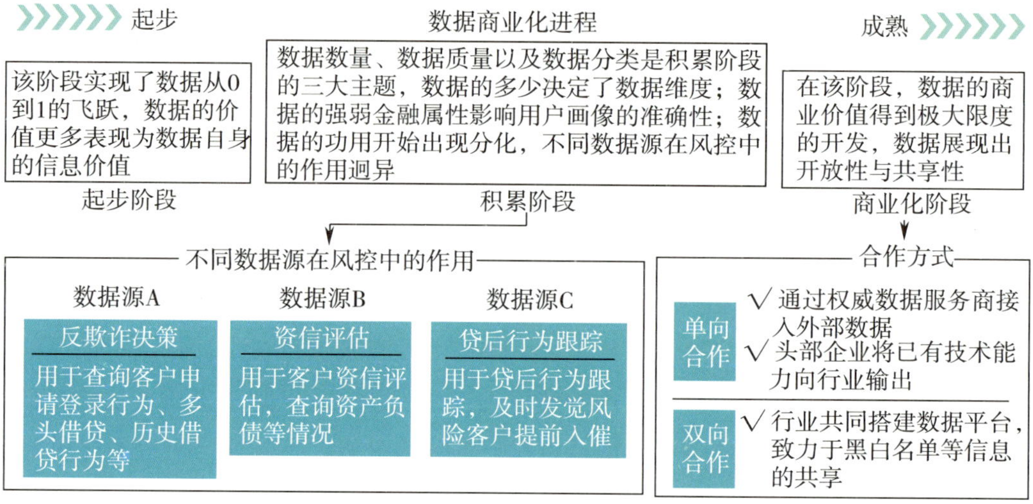


**图 2-4　新型金融机构的数据商业化进程**

## 三、主要新型金融机构金融服务因基因而不同

金融信息化离不开互联网，我国的大型互联网公司也是最早将业务延伸到金融服务的新型金融机构。从 BATJ（百度、阿里巴巴、腾讯、京东）来看，各自互联网业务模式的不同（基因的不同），造就了主要新型金融机构平台在切入金融服务时的方式和发展战略的差异，也演化出当前各自金融服务的路径和规模差异，而在普惠金融服务方面，也当然形成不同的业务模式探索和成效。

### （一）BATJ 的金融版图

**表 2-2　BATJ 金融版图**

| | 百度 | 蚂蚁金服 | 腾讯 | 京东金融 |
|---|---|---|---|---|
| 支付 | 百度钱包 | 支付宝 | 微信支付、财付通 | 网银在线、京东支付 |
| 信贷 | 百度小贷、百度财富、百度有钱 | 蚂蚁小贷（花呗、借呗） | 人人贷、微粒贷 | 京保贝、京小贷、京东白条 |
| 理财 | 百度金融、百度财富 | 蚂蚁财富（余额宝、招财宝、基金、股票等理财平台） | 理财通 | 小金库 |
| 银行 | 百信银行 | 网商银行 | 微众银行 | |
| 保险 | 百安保险（筹） | 众安保险、信美人寿 | 众安保险 | |
| 证券、基金 | 百发 100 指数基金 | 天弘基金 | 富途证券、好买基金 | |
| 众筹 | 影视产品众筹 | 蚂蚁达客 | 腾讯乐捐 | 京东众筹 |

注：百度从 2015 年开始全面进入金融领域后，百安保险并未最终成立。2018 年 4 月，百度宣布旗下金融服务事业群组正式完成拆分融资协议签署，拆分后百度金融将启用全新品牌“度小满金融”，实现独立运营。

从 BATJ 这些大型互联网平台切入金融领域的角度看，时间有先后，出发点也各不相同。

最早的蚂蚁金融服务起步于 2004 年成立的支付宝。2013 年 3 月 7 日，阿里小微金融服务集团宣布筹建，小微金服（筹）成为蚂蚁金服的前身。2014 年 10 月，蚂蚁金服正式成立。显然，作为电商平台的阿里巴巴的发展离不开交易和信用，而创新性地解决交易信用问题的支付宝成为中国互联网金融乃至新的大型金融服务平台的旗帜，也成为全球最大的支付平台。由于支付宝积累的用户数据和交易数据天然与中小企业信用具有紧密的关联度，并能够成为数字金融服务的底层可靠数据来源，蚂蚁金服将业务延伸到小微贷和大数据信用及理财领域就变得顺理成章。

以社交和游戏为核心业务的腾讯最早是从游戏币角度涉及交易和支付，但对金融业的整体布局与其核心业务的发展轨迹类似，即边学习边建设，微信支付通过社交场景迅速崛起，但将各金融板块业务整合形成合力和清晰的战略布局尚有待时日。

百度以搜索业务为核心，在拓展金融版图时首先入手的是理财产品，并期望加快在金融全领域的布局，但互联网平台企业在缺乏核心业务抓手的情况下以技术切入传统金融实为不易。2018 年，百度金融事业部的重组是期望在金融领域再次通过金融科技的技术手段，实现从金融业务切入向科技赋能，利用智能的技术、数据支撑所有金融机构，并减少探索中带来的不确定的冲击。从导流转向争取实现一种共赢的、良性的生态，人工智能所具备的图像技术、语音技术、识别技术等，也为未来金融科技、智能金融的走向提供了更多探索场景。

相较于 BAT（百度、阿里巴巴、腾讯），由于电商平台、自建物流的基因，京东金融在落地金融领域时首先选择了供应链和消费金融。因此，“京保贝”和“京东白条”成为重要的核心产品。京东众筹以产品众筹为主要模式，也是互联网平台众筹业务中较为持续和活跃的平台。随着金融业务的深入，大数据指数、供应链金融业务的资产证券化、设立小额贷款公司、整合金融相关产品进入移动用户端、将京东金融重组独立发展等一系列举动都显示了京东在金融领域战略的日益成熟和聚焦。

综上，成长路径不同造就了大型互联网企业在进军金融领域时的落地差异和业务进展差异，而不同的互联网基因也给这些大型新型金融机构的普惠金融服务打下了烙印。

### （二）BATJ 的普惠金融业务

近年来，以蚂蚁金服为代表的中国科技企业运用数字技术解决农村居民融资难的问题，让上亿名农村居民和数百万家小微企业获得平等、便捷的普惠金融服务。在实践中，蚂蚁金服对农村客户群体进行分层，并运用大数据技术提供多元化的信贷服务：

一是通过“数据化预授信模式”满足农村消费者和小型经营者的碎片化信贷需求；二是通过“数据化产融模式”打通农村经济价值链，解决规模种植、养殖户在资金与销售上的后顾之忧。蚂蚁金服的服务对象分为以下三种类型。

一是小微客户。线上利用阿里巴巴在 B2B、淘宝、天猫等电子商务平台，线下通过“码商计划”，不断积累客户的信用数据及行为数据，向这些通常无法在传统金融渠道获得贷款的小微客户发放“金额小、期限短”的纯信用小额贷款。截至 2018 年 6 月底，网商银行及前身阿里小贷累计为超过 1000 万小微企业和个人经营者提供了超过 1 万亿元的经营性贷款。

二是农村市场。结合阿里巴巴集团“千县万村”计划，利用“村淘合伙人”模式，结合消费品下乡、农产品上行以及农村生态圈等信贷场景，推进农资农具购买以及农产品上行等特定金融服务。同时，为农业龙头企业的大型种养殖户提供包括信贷、保险、支付在内的供应链金融综合服务。2015 年 11 月推出“旺农贷”产品，分别为农村种养殖户和农村经营者提供信贷支持，最高额度 50 万元，无须抵押物、无须担保，从贷款申请到贷款发放最快只需要半个小时。截至 2018 年 6 月底，蚂蚁金服的支付业务服务的“三农”用户数为 2.4 亿户，保险业务服务的“三农”用户数为 2 亿户，信贷类业务服务的“三农”用户数超过 1 亿户。另外，蚂蚁金服还服务近 400 万农村小微企业、农村个体工商户及农村种植、养殖户。

三是服务中小金融机构。依托自身的互联网风险识别能力、科技系统能力和数据分析能力，为各类中小金融机构提供风险管理能力和技术、信息系统、产品开发能力等整合服务，帮助它们更好地服务用户。

再如，腾讯旗下的微众银行，于 2014 年 12 月 16 日正式开业，以线上互联网金融业务为核心，主要产品为消费信贷产品“微粒贷”。截至 2016 年末，“微粒贷”主动授信超过 7000 万人，开通用户超过 1500 万人，覆盖全国 31 个省（自治区、直辖市）、567 座城市；累计发放贷款 1987 亿元，管理贷款余额 517 亿元，笔均放款约 8000 元。微众银行通过建立同业合作模式下的“联贷平台”，与 25 家金融机构合作，尽力满足大众的小额资金需求。

又如，京东金融，于 2013 年 10 月开始独立运营，目前包括九大业务板块——供应链金融、消费金融、众筹、财富管理、支付、保险、证券、农村金融和金融科技。截至 2017 年 6 月 18 日，京东金融已合作 400 余家银行、55 家保险公司、近百家基金公司以及 50 万线上、线下商户，共同为 1.5 亿户京东金融用户提供服务。

京东金融从自营金融业务起步，以供应链金融和消费金融为主要产品，利用京东集团的客户优势和数据积累，提供互联网金融产品。“京保贝”为京东平台上自营供应商提供融资，已累计服务超过 10 万家中小微企业，“京小贷”为京东平台上的入驻商户融资。在消费金融端，京东金融的“小白条”为传统电商客户提供消费贷款，而后续推出的“大白条”跨出京东体系，与旅游、租房、装修、教育、汽车等更多消费场景结合。截至2016年末，京东金融消费信贷、企业融资和供应链融资的期末余额分别为253亿元、7亿元和116亿元，同比增速分别为153%、40%和90%。

从2016年开始，京东金融已经在原有自营金融的基础上，探索金融科技输出的新模式，尝试将自身大数据、人工智能、风险定价、风控管理等金融科技核心技术对外合作，与大型金融机构构筑新的业务和战略合作关系。

京东金融的整体战略是更好地发挥金融科技的作用，而其农村金融事业部也在对农村种养殖供应链进行深入了解的基础上进行数字化转型，“京农贷”产品从2016年下半年开始转型为“数字农贷”。“数字农贷”是全新的微供应链金融模式。“数字农贷”以农业生产过程的数据模型和农民的历史生产数据为基础，对未来生产结果作出预测，再以预测的统计学结果产生信用；进而对生产过程进行全程的、高频次的、多方面的监管，以资金管理和风险管理辅助农业生产管理。京东“数字农贷”尝试用量化手段解决农业生产中的信用产生问题，不用传统的抵押担保模式来进行信用风险控制，而是通过对农业生产过程的全程量化评估来确定资金流使用和信贷投放。以目前已经介入的肉禽养殖板块为例，数字农贷做到以下几点：（1）“数字农贷”是做资金管理，不是贷款。“数字农贷”深入学习养殖技术，对养殖程序、过程中农资的需求有精准的把握。以此为基础，把资金精准匹配到成产过程中。同时，对养殖厂未来的现金流作出预测，辅助养殖户作出合理的资金计划。（2）“数字农贷”追求资金效率，而不是利率。实现了资金与养殖需求的精准匹配，避免了闲置资金，最大化资金的使用效率。效率的提升带来了农民支付利息的大大降低。（3）指定场景，专款专用。“数字农贷”实现了四定：定时、定点、定向、定量，即在贷款过程中，在特定的时间，把资金打到特定的地点，用来购买特定的农资，按照特定的数量，真正解决了贷款过程中的“定向支付、专款专用”的问题。“数字农贷”可以把饲料的用量精确到天、到克，并据此匹配贷款资金，其结果是农民只需为养殖中实际使用到的资金支付利息，而不会为任何闲置资金支付任何利息。以山东牧族生态农业有限公司的蛋鸡养殖为例，使用数据化“京农贷”养鸡，覆盖养鸡过程中需要的12元饲料款，总共只需支付利息6分钱。这对于农民一只鸡大约2元的利润来说，是完全承担得起的。目前，“数字农贷”业务覆盖了山东、河南、河北、辽宁、江苏、山西、安徽、四川、重庆等省份，借款主体100余家，受益养殖户2000～3000户，预计规模短期将迅速上升到数十亿元。

## 四、主要新型金融企业在普惠金融方面的服务困境

新型金融企业通过信息科技以及将新技术和算法引入金融领域无疑大幅提高了可

以获得金融服务的受众面，但鉴于金融服务的基础是信用，交易的核心是信任和安全，对于被传统金融机构排除在外的小微企业和个人，其能够获得或实际获得的金融服务仍有欠缺，新型金融企业的普惠金融服务还存在诸多困难。

第一，普惠金融目标人群面临需求困境。从某种程度上看，从移动支付到手机理财和交易需求完美遵循了互联网行业的逻辑，即供给催生需求，而并非是需求推动供给。科技和网络的应用实际上是把原先的需求的满意度阈值提升了，交易速度、服务响应频次和随时随地可交易成为默认需求，过去能够通过线下网点、柜面服务人员完成的人工服务迁移到了线上，但这些并没有改善金融知识和利用金融服务意识匮乏的情况。因此，网络和各种新型媒体无法覆盖的人群依然游离于金融服务之外，或者说即使是新型金融机构也未能将其定位为目标用户。

第二，在新的科技服务手段下，即使新型金融机构提供面向小微金融客群的产品，很多普惠金融目标人群在不需要提供担保物的情况下依然无法满足风控信息提供的要求，因为它们并没有相应的社交和其他可数字化交易信息作为授信评价的支持基础。相应地，普惠金融服务的任务不应局限于相关工具和操作交易便捷性的提升，基础认知普及和能力建设的工作依然重要。

第三，金融恐惧（金融诈骗和民间高利贷的影响），无法理解新事物和金融产品同样构成新型金融机构的服务障碍。从这一环节上看，技术和能力不是问题，但基础认知和全社会的金融安全成为触达普惠金融“最后一公里”的难点。

第四，从供给方，即新型金融机构的角度看，如何真正落地普惠金融服务也依然面临一些障碍和问题，包括为了覆盖信贷风险和实现商业利润核算得出的高贷款利率会吓退接触信贷服务的小微客户；新型金融企业的数字化赋能业务在与传统金融机构合作时常常面临的兜底要求；新型金融机构自身缺乏相对低成本可持续的资金来源；新技术的应用还有一个试验、验证和调整的过程等，信用评价、风控的实际操作也是一个经验积累和模型调试的过程，新技术并非一试即灵；另外，新型金融机构为了吸引客户设置的较高平台利率和潜在的刚性兑付责任一直是制约新型金融机构普惠金融业务的最大障碍，对合理定价和可持续运营均构成实质威胁。

综上，新型金融机构在普惠金融服务中已经取得了很大的成绩，并切实扩大了用户群体，但面临的诸多技术和实际操作问题仍有待解决。

# 第三章 国际机构与中国普惠金融发展

【摘要】中国普惠金融事业已经进入全金融行业规模化发展普惠金融业务的阶段。国际机构进入中国普惠金融市场的发展进程可分为三个阶段：发展援助阶段（20世纪80年代到90年代初期）、慈善捐赠与商业投资并进阶段（1993—2004年）、社会影响力投资阶段（2005年以来）。进入中国普惠金融市场的国际机构主要可分为四大类，包括国际多边/双边机构、国际非营利组织、跨国公司、国外金融机构和投资机构；它们的投资方式可以分为四大类，包括发展援助、慈善捐赠、社会影响力投资、商业投资。国际机构支持或投资的中国普惠金融供应方，解决“最后一公里”问题的成效各有差异，积累了宝贵经验。

2015年9月25日，联合国第七十届会议发布了《变革我们的世界：2030年可持续发展议程》，为人类、地球与繁荣制订了一个行动计划，提出了17个可持续发展目标和169个具体目标。其中，“在全世界消除一切形式的贫困”是可持续发展目标的首要目标，到2030年要在世界所有人口中消除极端贫穷。可喜的是，可持续发展目标现已成为各国政府以及民间社会制订计划、开展行动、研发产品等的指导性目标。

消除贫困和普惠金融是相关性很强的领域，因为贫困人口就是普惠金融的服务对象之一。从资本市场的反应来看，微型金融投资是实现可持续发展目标的重要投资类别之一，已经受到越来越广泛的认可，尤其投资界已经介入超过10年。根据全球影响力投资网络对影响力投资者的调查，2006—2016年，有超过百亿美元的资金投入微型金融领域，其所占比例仅次于住房供给与能源两个领域。

国际机构参与中国普惠金融事业，与全球化进程密切相关，也与中国改革开放国策密切相关。目前，全球有超过100000家多国企业[①]，以及超过67000家的国际组织

① 根据联合国贸易和发展会议发布的《2017世界投资报告》数据计算。

（包括政府间组织）[1]。这些机构在全球范围内积极推动跨国协定、国际投资、国际贸易、跨国慈善项目等。虽然参与中国普惠金融事业的国际多边/双边机构、国际非营利组织、跨国公司、国外金融机构和投资机构只占全球多国企业和国际组织的极小部分，但它们为中国普惠金融市场带来了大量的资金、技术、经验、理念、人才等资源，帮助中国实现经济发展和社会进步。可以这么说，中国普惠金融事业的发展，离不开国际机构的投入与贡献。

## 一、国际机构在中国的三个阶段

国际机构能否在中国提供普惠金融服务，与国家政策、市场环境、行业成熟度等密切相关。虽说 1951 年中国人民银行下发乡镇建立农村信用合作社的政策[2]之后，就已隐约可见普惠金融的初始萌芽状态，但国际机构真正进入中国普惠金融市场还要从改革开放国策全面推行之后说起。

如图 3－1 所示，国际机构参与中国普惠金融事业的发展进程可分为三个阶段：发展援助阶段（20 世纪 80 年代到 90 年代初）、慈善捐赠与商业投资并进阶段（1993—2004 年）、社会影响力投资阶段（2005 年以来）。

### （一）发展援助阶段（20 世纪 80 年代到 90 年代初期）

改革开放初期，中国有巨大的建设资金需求，主动寻求向国际机构引入援助项目。20 世纪 80 年代，中国处于改革开放初期，百废待兴，有巨大的建设资金需求。中国政府从援助资金着手，开始积极与各类国际多边/双边机构接触，引入各种类型的援助项目。随即，为了支持中国扶贫事业、农村发展、社会进步，国际农业发展基金、联合国妇女发展基金会、联合国人口基金会等开始以发展援助的形式为中国提供建设资金，其中有一部分资金进入小额信贷领域，这也是中国小额信贷的最早探索。除各类国际多边/双边机构之外，少数国际非营利组织也在中国农村开展各类慈善项目，如宣明会、乐施会等。

---

① 资料来源：https://uia.org/ybio。

② 资料来源：皮特·斯帕布姆、艾瑞克·迪弗罗．（2012）：世界银行扶贫协商小组（CGAP）和中国普惠金融工作组联合发表的《中华人民共和国的金融普惠状况——对现有研究和公开数据的分析》，中国普惠金融第 7 号论文。

中国人民银行要求每个乡镇建立农村信用合作社，为中国 80%生活在农村地区的人口提供储蓄和信贷服务。尽管农村信用合作社的所有权和管理权经历数次改革，但其农村合作金融的特质与普惠金融为"中小微弱"群体提供金融服务的本质是一致的。

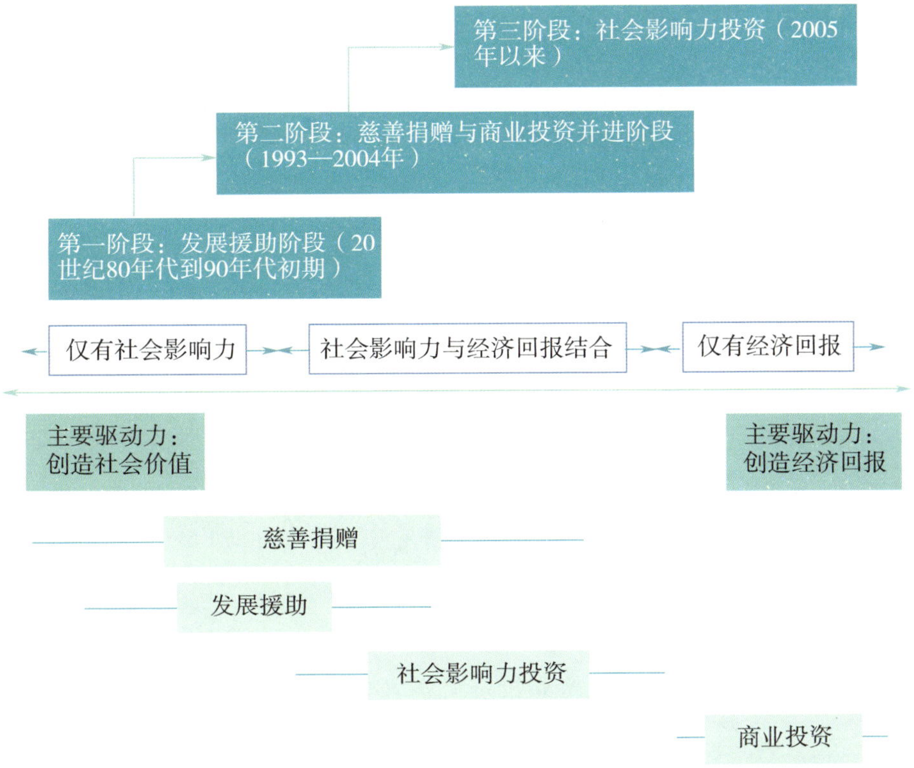


**图 3-1　国际机构参与中国普惠金融事业发展进程及其投资方式的光谱**

创造社会价值是国际机构在这一阶段进入中国的主要驱动力。在发展援助阶段，无论是国际多边/双边机构，还是国际非营利组织，它们在中国运作的小额信贷项目的主要驱动力是创造社会价值，力求对中国的经济发展、社区建设、生态环境改善、社会稳定、能力建设产生积极正面的影响。可以说，这些国际机构一开始都有着比较纯粹的公益慈善目标。

援助项目对资金的使用可分为赠与援助与非赠与援助两种方式。发展援助与慈善捐赠的区别不在于社会目标，而在于对资金的使用有两种方式，即赠与援助与非赠与援助。赠与援助与慈善捐赠相类似，不要求收回援助款，甚至是服务费或利息；而非赠与援助则恰恰相反，要求收回援助款，可能还要加收服务费或利息，以便援助款可以用于下一个援助项目或支持其他国家的发展。所有基本的操作原则，都会在多边/双边机构成立或项目执行过程中，通过多边/双边协商而达成一致。

许多援助项目随着项目周期的结束而结束，而小额信贷实践还处于探索实验期。在发展援助阶段，援助项目的在地管理与执行通常会依托于地方项目办公室。因为援助项目在设计之初就已经做了详尽的调研与细致的目标设定，地方项目办公室的首要职责是确保项目目标的达成，项目的可持续性或可复制性反而不是最重要的。此外，地方项目办公室或执行层面的工作人员一般都由地方政府部门、地方农村信用社、地方妇联等的派出代表组成，他们没有绝对的压力要确保项目可持续。实际上，发展援助阶段的小额信贷实践还处于探索实验期。许多项目随着项目周期的结束而结束，是符合当时的现实情境的。

### （二）慈善捐赠与商业投资并进阶段（1993—2004 年）

1993 年外国小额信贷模式进入中国。中国普惠金融自 20 世纪 90 年代初才开启其发展进程①，作为起点的代表性事件是 1993 年中国社会科学院农村发展研究所最早引入孟加拉格莱珉银行模式，成立了扶贫经济合作社，外国小额信贷模式正式进入中国。

1993—2004 年②，中国迎来国际机构大规模进入小额信贷领域的一次高峰。它们为中国带来了资金、技术、解决方案等重要资源，项目数量一度超过 260 个③。在这一时期，国际多边/双边机构继续各种援助项目的扩张，新的国际非营利组织继续在各地开出新的慈善项目，跨国公司在企业社会责任的框架下为小额信贷机构或项目提供慈善捐赠，国外金融机构和投资机构开始探索种子基金、股权投资等新投资形式。

社会影响力和经济回报是这一阶段国际机构支持或投资小额信贷发展的双重动力。在这个阶段，国际机构在中国运作各种小额信贷项目，甚至是尝试投资，其原因和动力在于，一方面，孟加拉格莱珉银行模式得到实践验证，既实现机构的可持续发展，又产生积极的社会效应；另一方面，世界银行等国际机构对中国国情进行研究之后认为中国有巨大的小额信贷需求，是一个很有潜力的小额信贷市场。也就是说，在这个阶段，国际机构投入中国普惠金融事业有社会影响力和经济回报的双重动力，社会影响力是慈善捐赠看重的，而经济回报是商业投资看重的。

这一阶段形成了援助资金、慈善捐赠资金、投资资金的资金结构。在这个阶段，国际机构带入的资金，除了国际多边/双边机构的赠与援助和非赠与援助资金之外，还有国际非营利组织和跨国公司的慈善捐赠资金，以及国外金融机构和投资机构的投资资金。国际机构在中国落地小额信贷项目的方式更趋丰富，除了依托于地方项目办公

① 焦瑾璞，黄亭亭，汪天都，张韶华，王瑱．中国普惠金融发展进程及实证研究［D］．北京：中国人民银行工作论文，No. 2015/2.

② 杜晓山在《我国小额信贷发展报告》中，将中国小额信贷发展分成四个阶段：小额信贷项目或机构试验的初期阶段（1993 年至 1996 年 9 月）；项目的扩展阶段（1996 年 9 月至 2000 年）；农村正规金融机构全面介入和各类项目可能进入制度化建设阶段（2000 年至 2005 年）；中央管理部门鼓励民营和海外资本进入，试行商业性小额信贷机构活动（2005 年至今）。

③ Planet Finance，the Micro-finance Platform. China Country Overview，2004.

室之外，还可以选择在项目地成立非营利性的非政府组织，或者与当地非营利性的社团组织或非政府组织形成合作关系。这也就形成了当时被热烈讨论的“公益性小额信贷”。在这个阶段，国际机构与当地项目合作方越来越关注项目的可持续性。由于服务的对象是“中小微弱”群体，小额信贷由于成本高、风险大、回报率低，仍然面临生存之困。

### （三）社会影响力投资阶段（2005 年以来）

2005 年以来，中国小额信贷的政策环境、市场环境、行业成熟度已经上了一个新台阶。政策环境方面，2005 年，中国人民银行在山西、四川、贵州、陕西等省份进行“只贷不存”的商业性小额信贷组织试点工作，探索民间资本进入小额信贷市场的可行性。2006 年，《中共中央　国务院关于推进社会主义新农村建设的若干意见》（2006 年中央一号文件）明确提出，在保证资本金充足、严格金融监管和建立合理有效地退出机制的前提下，鼓励在县域内设立多种所有制的社区金融机构，允许私有资本、外资等参股。市场环境方面，2001 年 12 月 11 日中国正式加入世界贸易组织（WTO）后，中国银行业、证券业、保险业、外汇管理等有计划、有步骤地加大金融业对外开放。2006 年 12 月 11 日，中国取消对外资金融机构的限制，实现金融业的全面对外开放。行业成熟度方面，2005 年联合国大会提出“普惠金融”的概念，强调通过完善金融基础设施，以可负担的成本将金融服务扩展到欠发达地区和社会低收入人群，向他们提供价格合理、方便快捷的金融服务，不断提高金融服务的可获得性。中国为“中小微弱”群体提供金融服务的实践，从小额信贷服务开始，发展到各种类型的微型金融服务，在经验、机构实体等方面都取得了一定进展。

2005 年以来，中国迎来国际机构大规模投资小额信贷供应方的又一次高峰，国外金融机构和投资机构成为主力军，进入中国的渠道、方式更加多元了。外资可以入股农村金融机构，如农村商业银行、农村合作银行、小额贷款公司等；也可以独资或合资组建农村金融机构，如城镇银行、小额贷款公司、网络贷款平台等。这些主体所提供的普惠金融产品也愈发多样，如小额信贷、小额保险、汇款、支付、结算、网上银行、手机银行等。

之所以把 2005 年以来国际机构对中国普惠金融市场的投资称为“社会影响力投资”，原因在于，第一，2005 年联合国提出的“普惠金融体系”有非常明确的社会目标；第二，2007 年提出“社会影响力投资”类别之后，投资界把对微型金融机构的投资视为社会影响力投资的重要组成部分。“社会影响力投资”是一种既注重社会绩效，又注重财务绩效的投资方式，进一步促进了微型金融机构对社会目标和机构可持续目标的双重管理。

## 二、国际机构的类别和投资方式

进入中国金融市场的国际机构主要可分为四大类（参见第一章表1-1）。一是多个或两个国家之间为了共同目标通过协议规定权利与义务而产生的国际多边/双边机构；二是在各国开展非营利、公益型项目的国际非营利组织；三是在世界各地设立分支机构或子公司以从事国际化生产与经营活动的跨国公司；四是境外的金融机构和投资机构。

国际机构的投资方式也可以分为四大类（参见第一章表1-1）：一是以受援助国经济和社会发展为目标的发展援助方式，有赠与援助和非赠与援助两种资金使用方式；二是以创造社会价值为主要目标的慈善捐赠方式；三是社会绩效和财务绩效并重的社会影响力投资方式；四是以创造经济价值为主要目标的商业投资方式。

为解决金融“最后一公里”问题，国际机构支持或投资的中国普惠金融标的机构，其选择的服务模式各不相同（参见第一章表1-1），包括资金转贷模式、直营模式、互助模式、非营利项目模式、批发贷款模式、供应链金融模式、数字模式等。其中，资金转贷模式是国际多边/双边机构早期采用的方式；非营利项目模式是国际非营利组织选择的比较特殊的方式，对普惠金融服务的流程设计有一套独特的逻辑。

可以这么说，国际机构对中国小额信贷行业乃至普惠金融事业的发展，在模式借鉴、资金支持、技术支持等方面，有过不可磨灭的贡献。正如程恩江、徐忠（2006）[①] 所言，中国的小额信贷以国际机构资助的项目为主，基本是属于引进的，而非本土成长起来的。

### （一）国际多边/双边机构

20世纪80年代到90年代，国际多边/双边机构（见表3-1）多以资金援助者的身份，在中国开展赠与援助（包括方案援助、计划援助、技术合作、粮食援助、紧急灾害救助、债务减免）和非赠与援助（长期低息优惠贷款），部分援助项目以小额信贷形式开展。国际多边/双边机构协助中国政府解决改革开放初期建设资金不足的问题，为我国农村金融体制改革提供了宝贵经验。

由于援助项目有项目期限，为了项目的可持续，部分项目选择向机构转化，注册成立了社会团体、民办非企业等，继续为当地贫困人口提供小额信贷服务。不过，国际多边/双边机构开展的小额信贷项目多数因为对捐赠的依赖、社区基础薄弱、本地化程度不足、政策环境不友好、贷款利率与扶贫舆论的悖论等困难而关闭。目前，表3-1统计的150多个项目中，真正实现财务可持续的可谓屈指可数。

---

① 程恩江，徐忠．中国小额信贷发展报告［J］．财经杂志，2006（10）．

**表 3-1　国际多边/双边机构在中国开展普惠金融服务不完全统计**

| 序号 | 名称 | 开始年份 | 投资方式 | 受资方 | 主要服务模式 |
|---|---|---|---|---|---|
| 1 | 联合国人口基金会 | 20 世纪 80 年代后期 | 提供贷款资本金 | 15 个项目 | 资金转贷模式 |
| 2 | 国际农业发展基金 | 1981 | 低息贷款 | 28 个项目 | 资金转贷模式、直营模式 |
| 3 | 联合国妇女发展基金会 | 1982 | | | |
| 4 | 联合国开发计划署（UNDP） | 1994 | 提供贷款资本金 | 32 个项目 | 直营模式、互助模式 |
| 5 | 联合国儿童基金会：SPPA 项目和 LPAC 项目 | 1996 | 提供贷款资本金 | 68 个项目 | 直营模式 |
| 6 | 世界银行 | 1996 | 低息贷款 | 5 个项目 | 转贷模式 |
| 7 | 澳大利亚发展署 | 1996 | 提供贷款资本金 | 1 个项目 | |
| 8 | 加拿大发展署 | 1996 | 捐赠 | 1 个项目 | |
| 9 | 国际劳工组织 | 1997 | | | |
| 10 | 新发署社区基金 | 2005 | 提供贷款资本金 | 1 个项目 | |
| 11 | 欧盟 | 2007 | 捐赠 | 中和农信① | 直营模式 |
| 12 | 德国技术合作机构 GTZ | | 技术援助 | 1 个项目 | 直营模式 |
| 13 | 国际复兴开发银行 | | | | |
| 14 | 国际开发协会 | | | | |
| 15 | 亚洲开发银行 | | | | |
| 16 | 日本 | | | | |
| 17 | 荷兰社区发展基金 | | | | |
| 18 | 英国国际发展署 | | | | |

资料来源：Planet Finance，the Micro-finance Platform. China Country Overview，2004；Planet Finance，the Micro-finance Platform. China Country Overview，2008；程恩江，徐忠．中国小额信贷发展报告［J］．财经杂志，2006（10）；吴国宝．小额信贷在中国——艰难前行的公益小额信贷［M］．北京：中国财政经济出版社，2013；中国财政科学研究院和联合国开发计划署驻华代表处联合发布的《中国扶贫可持续筹资报告》，2016 年；http://hope. huanqiu. com/。

国际多边/双边机构在早期采用过资金转贷模式来操作小额信贷项目，如国际农业发展基金和世界银行。资金转贷模式是国内上级政府部门与国际多边/双边机构签订资金借贷协议，上级政府部门再将资金按协议条件贷给下属政府机构或非政府组织。资金转贷模式的主要特点包括：（1）协议：转贷的每个层级之间以协议约定项目周期、服务区域、涉及产业、贷款类别（高度优惠贷款、中等优惠贷款、普通贷款）、贷款期限、小额贷款额度、目标群体等要素；（2）利差：转贷的每个层级之间存在利差，农

① 中和农信由 1996 年启动的世界银行扶贫项目发展而来，2001—2007 年，资金接收方还是中国扶贫基金会。2008 年之后，中和农信项目管理有限公司成立。本书将资金接收方统一列为中和农信。

户获得贷款时的实际利息高于从国际多边/双边机构借入时的水平；（3）转贷模式[①]：分为政府主导型、正规金融部门社会低收入人群主导型、非政府组织辅助型；（4）不同项目选择不同的农户贷款条件：还款能力、个人信用、担保、抵押、小组联保等；（5）不同项目选择不同的农户还款方式：一次性还款、分期还款、不定期还款。

国际多边/双边机构也采用过直营模式来操作小额信贷项目，如联合国开发计划署和世界银行支持当地农村金融机构或非政府组织借鉴格莱珉模式为当地农户提供金融服务。格莱珉模式的主要特点是：（1）小组联保：一般是5人一个小组，5～6个小组组成一个中心，定期召开小组会；（2）贷款资格：不需要实物抵押和担保；（3）贷款额度：小额贷款；（4）贷款期限：一般是1年；（5）分期还款：每周、每两周、每月还款；（6）以妇女为主要服务对象；（7）续贷激励机制：小组全体成员按时还款后，可获得更大额度的后续贷款；（8）当项目进行机构转制之后，如要实现机构的财务可持续，利率设计一般以实现微利为出发点。

### （二）国际非营利组织

与国际多边/双边机构在中国活跃的时期差不多，国际非营利组织（见表3-2）在中国开展小额信贷项目也多集中于20世纪90年代到21世纪10年代初，主要分为两类组织：一类是资助型组织（包括资助型基金会），另一类是操作型组织（包括操作型基金会）。资助型组织主要为执行小额信贷项目的机构提供资金支持，方式多为捐赠。操作型组织一般直接参与项目，即直接进入社区或面对服务对象，提供借贷、赋能、社区建设等有明显非营利项目特色的服务。

**表3-2 国际非营利组织在中国开展普惠金融服务不完全统计**

| 序号 | 名称 | 开始年份 | 投资方式 | 受资方 | 主要服务模式 |
|---|---|---|---|---|---|
| 1 | 世界宣明会 | 1982 | 捐赠 | 中国西南部项目 | 非营利项目模式 |
| 2 | 香港乐施会 | 1992 | 捐赠 | 中国西南部项目 | 非营利项目模式、互助模式、直营模式 |
| 3 | 福特基金会 | 1993 | 捐赠 | 中国社会科学院农村发展研究所项目 | 直营模式 |
| 4 | 国际鹤类组织 | 1994 | 提供贷款资本金 | 1个项目 | |

① 王云魁．国际农业发展基金（IFAD）中国农村金融项目转贷模式研究［M］．乌鲁木齐：新疆农业大学，2009.

续表

| 序号 | 名称 | 开始年份 | 投资方式 | 受资方 | 主要服务模式 |
|---|---|---|---|---|---|
| 5 | 国际计划 | 1995 | 捐赠 | 河北项目、陕西妇女联合会 | 直营模式 |
| 6 | 四川农村发展项目（DORS） | 1996 | 捐赠 | 四川项目 | |
| 7 | 国际小母牛项目组织 | 1996 | 捐赠（家畜） | 12省项目 | 非营利项目模式、互助模式 |
| 8 | 西藏扶贫基金（TPAF） | 1998 | 捐赠 | 西藏项目 | |
| 9 | 希望国际 | 2000 | 捐赠 | 建华基金会 | |
| 10 | 国际美慈组织 | 2001 | 捐赠 | 中和农信 | 直营模式 |
| 11 | 机会国际 | 2003 | 提供贷款资本金 | 安徽、江西、江苏项目 | 直营模式 |
| 12 | 法国沛丰中国 | 2004 | 咨询与技术服务 | 中和农信等20多个省市项目 | 直营模式 |
| 13 | 香港嘉道理基金会 | 2006 | 捐赠/无息贷款 | 西藏项目、中和农信 | 直营模式 |
| 14 | 壳牌基金会 | 2006 | 捐赠 | 中和农信 | 直营模式 |
| 15 | WOKAI | 2007 | 投资 | WOKAI in China（已停止运营） | 数字模式 |
| 16 | 施永青基金会 | 2008 | 直接提供免息、低息、市场化利息贷款 | 小额信贷项目 | 直营模式 |
| 17 | 赠与亚洲 | 2008 | 捐赠 | 扶贫与经济发展项目、中和农信 | 直营模式 |
| 18 | Accion Microfinance China | 2009 | 提供借贷服务 | 赤峰市元宝山区高信隆小额贷款有限公司 | 直营模式 |
| 19 | 全球基金会 | 2011 | | | |
| 20 | 高盛基金会 | 2015 | 提供融资贷款服务 | 高盛“巾帼圆梦”万名女性创业助学计划 | 非营利项目模式 |

续表

| 序号 | 名称 | 开始年份 | 投资方式 | 受资方 | 主要服务模式 |
|---|---|---|---|---|---|
| 21 | 香港救世军 | | 捐赠 | 云南项目 | |
| 22 | CARE | | 捐赠 | 中国西南地区项目 | |
| 23 | 花旗集团基金会 | | 捐赠 | 中国小额信贷协会 | |
| 24 | 美国 KIVA 基金会 | | | 宁夏东方惠民小额贷款股份有限公司 | 直营模式 |
| 25 | 比尔及梅琳达·盖茨基金会 | | | | |
| 26 | Unitus | | | | |
| 27 | 社区伙伴 | | | | |

资料来源：Planet Finance，the Micro-finance Platform. China Country Overview，2004；Planet Finance，the Micro-finance Platform. China Country Overview，2008；程恩江，徐忠．中国小额信贷发展报告［J］．财经杂志，2006（10）；吴国宝．小额信贷在中国——艰难前行的公益小额信贷［M］．北京：中国财政经济出版社，2013；http://hope.huanqiu.com/。

非营利项目模式是国际非营利组织在中国操作小额信贷项目的一种较为特殊的方式，其主要特点是不以盈利为目标、服务于贫困人口或贫困社区、规模受项目选址和资助金额等限制、有项目期限等。国际非营利组织在设计小额信贷项目的时候，更多的是基于项目当地的农户、社区、经济水平等条件，适当调整小额信贷的贷款期限、还款方式、风控模式等。

以国际小母牛组织为例，它们秉持"传递礼物"的理念，把"礼物"从家畜变为无息小额贷款，其项目操作模式是资金互助模式和礼物传递模式的结合体。（1）组建村级互助基金，国际小母牛项目组织通过当地合作机构为基金提供基本资金；（2）村民出资，加上政府配套资金，形成村民的完整股权，村民享有分红权、选举权、决策权、贷款权；（3）村民提出贷款申请，获得无息贷款之后，购买家畜进行饲养，售卖家畜之后获得营利，除盈余之外，还能偿还贷款；（4）设计一定的贷款偿还期限，按月还款；（5）村级互助基金将还款提供给新的贷款申请者，实现"礼物"的传递。

## （三）跨国公司

21 世纪初期，中国掀起了新一轮的企业社会责任潮流，"生产守则""社会条款"、联合国的“全球协议”、SA8000等是世界企业社会责任运动产生的一些准则和标准，深刻影响了企业的管理模式。在这个背景下，一些进入中国市场的跨国公司主动通过公益慈善项目来赢取当地政府和消费者的好感，其中有一部分善款就进入小额信贷扶贫领域。如表3-3所示，微软（中国）、拜耳公司、康宁公司、壳牌公司、达能集团、耐克、如新集团等通过中国扶贫基金会支持小额信贷项目（2008年注册成为中和农信项目管理有限公司），为其提供捐赠资金支持。

**表3-3　跨国公司在中国开展普惠金融服务不完全统计**

| 序号 | 名称 | 开始年份 | 投资方式 | 受资方 | 主要服务模式 |
|---|---|---|---|---|---|
| 1 | 微软（中国） | 2006 | 捐赠 | 中和农信 | 直营模式 |
| 2 | 拜耳公司 | 2006 | 捐赠 | 中和农信 | 直营模式 |
| 3 | 康宁公司 | 2006 | 捐赠 | 中和农信 | 直营模式 |
| 4 | 壳牌公司 | 2006 | 捐赠 | 中和农信 | 直营模式 |
| 5 | 法国达能集团 | 2008 | 无息贷款 | 中和农信 | 直营模式 |
| 6 | 耐克 | 2008 | 捐赠 | 中和农信 | 直营模式 |
| 7 | 如新集团 | 2008 | 捐赠 | 中和农信 | 直营模式 |
| 8 | 摩托罗拉 | 2008 | 捐赠 | 中和农信 | 直营模式 |
| 9 | 英国富尔德律师事务所 | 2008 | 捐赠 | 中和农信 | 直营模式 |
| 10 | Empower | | | | |
| 11 | Oikocredit | | | | |
| 12 | Areva | | | | |
| 13 | Visa | | | | |
| 14 | 万事达卡 | | | | |
| 11 | 沃尔玛 | | | | |

资料来源：Planet Finance，the Micro-finance Platform. China Country Overview，2004；Planet Finance，the Micro-finance Platform. China Country Overview，2008；程恩江，徐忠．中国小额信贷发展报告［J］. 财经杂志，2006（10）；吴国宝．小额信贷在中国——艰难前行的公益小额信贷［M］. 北京：中国财政经济出版社，2013；中和农信历年年报。

跨国公司支持小额信贷的慈善捐赠项目，一般不会把经济回报置于首位，会更关注捐赠项目本身是否带来更全面、更广泛的社会影响力，以及项目本身的可持续性和可复制性。

### （四）国外金融机构/投资机构

经历过20世纪90年代的扶贫金融和21世纪初期的微型金融发展阶段，2005年之后，中国进入普惠金融阶段[①]，小额贷款公司、村镇银行、商业银行、网络贷款平台等多种金融主体为“最后一公里”的“中小微弱”群体提供了更加丰富的金融产品。

如表3-4所示，外资对中国金融供应方的投资在2006—2007年和2014—2016年形成了两次小高潮。形成第一次小高潮的原因在于，2005年的商业性小额信贷组织试点、2006年中央一号文件、2007年金融业全面对外开放等利好政策促使外资大量涌入中国农村金融市场；第二次小高潮的原因在于，2014—2016年是中国的互联网金融或数字金融发展最迅猛的阶段[②]。

**表3-4 国外金融机构/投资机构在中国开展普惠金融服务不完全统计**

| 序号 | 名称 | 开始年份 | 投资方式 | 受资方 | 主要服务模式 |
|---|---|---|---|---|---|
| 1 | 孟加拉格莱珉银行信托 | 1993 | 种子基金、低息贷款 | 中国社会科学院农村发展研究所项目、格莱珉中国 | 直营模式 |
| 2 | 国际金融公司 | 2000 | 项目资助、股权投资 | 中和农信、南充美兴服务有限责任公司（第一家外资小额贷款公司）、杭州农村合作社、杭州联合农村商业银行等 | 直营模式 |
| 3 | HORUS Development Finance | 2001 | 微型金融投资基金 | La Fayette Participations | |
| 4 | 德国复兴银行 | 2005 | 低息贷款、技术支持 | 内蒙古赤峰项目、南充美兴服务有限责任公司及中国的数家商业银行 | 直营模式 |
| 5 | Northwater Capital | 2005 | 投资 | 信而富 | 数字模式 |

① 贝多广，李焰．好金融 好社会——中国普惠金融发展报告（2015）[M]．北京：经济管理出版社，2016.

② 不过，自进入2016年互联网金融监管元年以后，不少互联网金融企业开始整顿P2P网贷平台业务。在这一轮整顿过程中，大批P2P网贷平台相继“爆雷”，淘汰滥竽充数的平台、留下资质良好的平台成为这一轮整顿的“主旋律”。

续表

| 序号 | 名称 | 开始年份 | 投资方式 | 受资方 | 主要服务模式 |
|---|---|---|---|---|---|
| 6 | Broadline Capital | 2005 | 投资 | 信而富 | 数字模式 |
| 7 | Hewlett-Packard | 2005 | 投资 | 信而富 | 数字模式 |
| 8 | 荷兰合作银行 | 2006 | 股权投资 | 杭州联合农村商业银行 | 直营模式 |
| 9 | 澳大利亚和新西兰银行集团有限公司 | 2006 | 股权投资 | 上海农村商业银行股份有限公司 | 直营模式 |
| 10 | 荷兰农业合作银行 | 2007 | 股权投资 | 杭州农村合作社 | 直营模式 |
| 11 | 德意志 Investitionsund Entwicklungesellschaft Sparkassen 国际发展信托公司 | 2007 | 股权投资 | 杭州农村合作社 | 直营模式 |
| 12 | 法国美信集团（MicroCred S. A） | 2007 | 股权投资 | 南充美兴服务有限责任公司 | 直营模式 |
| 13 | 美国国际集团 | 2007 | 股权投资 | 南充美兴服务有限责任公司 | 直营模式 |
| 14 | 渣打银行 | 2007 | 批发贷款 | 中和农信 | 直营模式 |
| 15 | 摩根大通 | 2007 | 捐赠 | 中和农信 | 直营模式 |
| 16 | QED Investors | 2007 | 投资 | 信而富 | 数字模式 |
| 17 | Northwater Capital | 2007 | 投资 | 信而富 | 数字模式 |
| 18 | DLB Capital | 2007 | 投资 | 信而富 | 数字模式 |
| 19 | 红杉资本 | 2010 | 股权投资 | 中和农信、拍拍贷、简普科技、融 360 | 直营模式、数字模式 |
| 20 | 瑞士蓝色果园基金 | 2010 | 批发贷款 | 中国微金融发展投资基金（筹） | 批发贷款模式 |
| 21 | 美国凯鹏华盈 | 2010 | 投资 | 简普科技 | 数字模式 |
| 22 | Kleiner Perkins Caufield & Byers | 2011 | 投资 | 宜信、融 360 | 数字模式 |
| 23 | 美国 Sagamore Investments | 2012 | 投资 | Accion Microfinance China 的中国赤峰项目 | 直营模式 |

续表

| 序号 | 名称 | 开始年份 | 投资方式 | 受资方 | 主要服务模式 |
|---|---|---|---|---|---|
| 24 | 新加坡淡马锡集团 | 2014 | 投资 | 中银富登村镇银行、富登信贷、简普科技、积木盒子、融360 | 直营模式、数字模式 |
| 25 | 法国 Ventech | 2014 | 股权投资 | 积木盒子 | 数字模式 |
| 26 | 经纬中国 | 2014 | 股权投资 | 积木盒子、91旺财 | 数字模式 |
| 27 | 英国天达集团 | 2014 | 股权投资 | 积木盒子 | 数字模式 |
| 28 | 狮桥资本 | 2014 | 投资 | 融租E投 | 数字模式 |
| 29 | 嘉御基金 | 2015 | 投资 | 宜农科技 | 数字模式 |
| 30 | 美国海纳亚洲创投基金 | 2015 | 股权投资 | 拍拍贷 | 数字模式 |
| 31 | 老虎环球基金 | 2015 | 投资 | 点融网 | 数字模式 |
| 32 | 渣打直接投资有限公司 | 2015 | 投资 | 点融网 | 数字模式 |
| 33 | 香港鼎珮投资集团 | 2015 | 股权投资 | 拍拍贷 | 数字模式 |
| 34 | 香港天天向上基金 | 2016 | 股权投资 | 中和农信 | 直营模式 |
| 35 | 韩国 Simone 投资管理公司 | 2017 | 投资 | 点融网 | 数字模式 |
| 36 | 新加坡政府投资公司（GIC） | 2017 | 投资 | 点融网 | 数字模式 |
| 37 | 欧力士亚洲资本有限公司 | 2018 | 投资 | 点融网 | 数字模式 |

资料来源：Planet Finance，the Micro-finance Platform. China Country Overview，2004；Planet Finance，the Micro-finance Platform. China Country Overview，2008；程恩江，徐忠．中国小额信贷发展报告［J］. 财经杂志，2006（10）；吴国宝．小额信贷在中国——艰难前行的公益小额信贷［M］. 北京：中国财政经济出版社，2013；中和农信历年年报；毕马威历年中国银行业发展报告；https://www.crunchbase.com/；http://zdb.pedaily.cn/；https://www.wdzj.com/。

在这个阶段，有两种需求在不断碰撞。一是国内微型金融机构对资金的需求。正如世界银行高级顾问 Fred D. Levy 所认为的，几乎在所有的国家，捐赠资金和政府资金都不会大到或者持久到保证小额信贷服务可以持续地满足数量庞大贫困群体的需求。因此，微型金融机构不能过度依赖捐赠资金或政府资金，能否获得商业融资，是微型金融机构长期发展的重要条件之一。二是国外资本对中国市场的投资需求。2005 年之后，国家鼓励商业性小额信贷试点、鼓励民营和海外资本参股微型金融机构、开放民营和海外资本进入金融业等政策信号，使对中国市场分外敏感的国外金融机构与投资机构跃跃欲试。

社会影响力投资的概念于 2007 年①被首次提出，指介于慈善捐赠与商业投资之间的，同时兼顾财务回报和社会影响力回报的投资类别。由于普惠金融的服务对象是“最后一公里”的“中小微弱”群体，其业务天然地具有社会效应，全球影响力投资网络认为，微型金融是社会影响力投资的重要投资领域之一。如图 3－2 所示，2016 年全球 208 个社会影响力投资者（含微型金融投资基金管理者）管理着 1137 亿美元的总资产，其中约 136.4 亿美元投入微型金融领域，占总资产的 12%。②

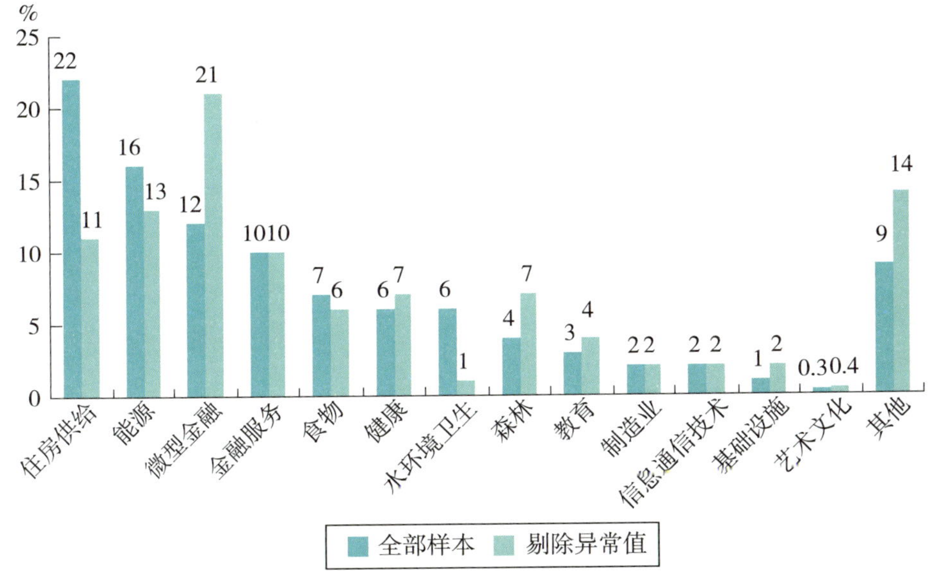


资料来源：Global Impact Investing Network. Annual Impact Investor Survey 2017，2017.

**图 3－2　2016 年全球社会影响力投资数据**

微型金融投资基金的实践早于社会影响力投资概念的提出，最早的一只微型金融投资基金出现在 1975 年。单个或多个投资者将资金集合于微型金融投资基金，由资产管理者进行投资组合管理和提供投资建议。微型金融投资基金主要分成三种类别：固定收益基金（85%以上非现金资产以债权形式投资）、股票基金（65%以上非现金资产以股权形式投资）、混合基金（债权与股权相结合，且 15%～65%的非现金资产以股权形式投资）。据 Syminvest 数据库的统计，有少数几只微型金融投资基金关注中国市

① 中国发展研究基金会和友成企业家扶贫基金会发布的《中国社会价值投资报告》，2016 年。

② 资料来源：Global Impact Investing Network. Annual Impact Investor Survey 2017，2017.

场，如 HORUS Development Finance 管理的 La Fayette Participations（见表 3-4）。

随着中国小额贷款公司、网络贷款平台等的快速发展，2005 年以来，国外投资机构积极地在中国遴选优秀的投资标的，以股权投资、战略投资等形式进行投资。目前，这样的投资并未全部纳入全球影响力投资网络的统计。以小额贷款公司为例，中国普惠金融研究院 2018 年开展了全国小额贷款公司运营情况调查，收回有效问卷 400 份，其中 47 家小额贷款公司有 1～3 家外资机构入股，占比为 11.75%。

虽然，并不是所有的小额贷款公司和 P2P 网贷平台都可以称作普惠金融供应方，因为不排除资本投资设立小额贷款公司和 P2P 网贷平台的目的是为了牟利。但是，部分投资客观上解决了“中小微弱”群体的金融服务问题，产生了普惠金融的效果。当然也有不少小额贷款公司和 P2P 网贷平台明确将“三农”、中小微企业、个体工商户、社会低收入人群、创业和失业人群、特殊群体等“中小微弱”群体定位为服务对象，有意识地为他们提供普惠金融服务，如小额贷款公司中的中和农信、南充美兴服务有限责任公司等，P2P 网贷平台中的信而富、宜信、积木盒子、宜农科技等，也都可以被当作普惠金融的供应方。因此，国外投资机构对这些小额贷款公司、P2P 网贷平台、互联网金融企业，以及村镇银行、农村商业银行等普惠金融供应方的投资，也都可以认为是社会影响力投资。

## 三、解决金融“最后一公里”问题的成效

本书共选取了国际农业发展基金、格莱珉中国、云南省富滇银行·富滇—格莱珉扶贫贷款项目、海南省农信联社·格莱珉模式小额信贷试点项目、中和农信、仪陇县乡村发展协会、汇丰村镇银行、中银富登村镇银行、南充美兴小额贷款有限责任公司、赤峰市元宝山区高信隆小额贷款有限公司、拍拍贷 11 个机构，从服务广度、服务深度、社会目标、机构可持续等几个方面进行比较，分析它们解决金融“最后一公里”问题的成效（见表 3-5）。

第一，同为小额贷款公司的中和农信、南充美兴和高信隆小贷三者中，中和农信的社会绩效最优，并保持较为稳定的财务绩效。

（1）三个机构都不可以吸收存款。

（2）服务模式都是直营模式。中和农信有 258 个分支机构和 2729 位信贷员，南充美兴有 43 个网点和 570 多位信贷员。

（3）中和农信的社会绩效最好。首先，中和农信网点覆盖贫困县 180 个，占所有网点的 70%以上，累计受益人数超过 400 万户农户；其次，中和农信的单笔贷款额为 1.34 万元，明显低于南充美兴的 5.4 万元和高信隆小贷的 9.4 万元，说明在服务深度

**表 3－5　国际机构的投资与解决金融“最后一公里”问题的成效**

| 指标 | 案例 | 地方项目管理办公室、地方农信社、地方妇联等NGO | 格莱珉中国 | 云南省富滇银行·富滇—格莱珉扶贫贷款项目 | 海南省农信联社·格莱珉模式小额信贷试点项目 | 中和农信 | 仪陇县乡村发展协会 | 汇丰村镇银行 | 中银富登村镇银行 | 南充美兴小额贷款有限责任公司 | 赤峰市元宝山区高信隆小额贷款有限公司 | 拍拍贷 |
|---|---|---|---|---|---|---|---|---|---|---|---|---|
| 投资情况 | 国际机构投资方 | 国际农业发展基金 | 格莱珉信托等 | 格莱珉模式合作（完全复制） | 格莱珉模式合作（本土化） | 世界银行、国际金融公司、红杉资本等 | 联合国开发计划署 | 香港上海汇丰银行有限公司 | 新加坡淡马锡旗下富登金融控股有限公司 | 法国美兴集团、国际金融公司等 | 美国安信永 | 美国上市 |
| | 投资总额 | 21.92亿美元 | | | | | | | | | | |
| | 投资方式 | 发展援助 | 社会影响力投资 | 社会影响力投资 | 社会影响力投资 | 社会影响力投资 | 社会影响力投资 | 社会影响力投资 | 社会影响力投资 | 社会影响力投资 | 社会影响力投资 | 商业投资 |
| 投资情况 | 受资方机构类型 | 政府与非营利民间组织 | | 银行 | 农信联社 | 小额贷款公司 | 非营利民间组织 | 村镇银行 | 村镇银行 | 小额贷款公司 | 小额贷款公司 | P2P贷款平台 |
| | 储蓄业务 | | 不可吸储 | 可吸储 | 可吸储 | 不可吸储 | 不可吸储 | 可吸储 | 可吸储 | 不可吸储 | 不可吸储 | 资金撮合 |

续表

| 指标 \ 案例 | | 地方项目管理办公室、地方农信社、地方妇联等NGO | 格莱珉中国 | 云南省富滇银行·富滇—格莱珉扶贫贷款项目 | 海南省农信联社·格莱珉模式小额信贷试点项目 | 中和农信 | 仪陇县乡村发展协会 | 汇丰村镇银行 | 中银富登村镇银行 | 南充美兴小额贷款有限责任公司 | 赤峰市元宝山区高信隆小额贷款有限公司 | 拍拍贷 |
|---|---|---|---|---|---|---|---|---|---|---|---|---|
| 机构情况 | 服务模式 | 资金转贷模式 | 直营模式 | 直营模式 | 直营模式 | 直营模式 | 直营模式、互助模式 | 直营模式、供应链金融模式 | 直营模式 | 直营模式 | 直营模式 | 数字模式 |
| | 数据截止时间 | 2018年4月 | 2015年6月 | 2017年 | 2014年 | 2017年末 | 2011年末 | 2017年末 | 2017年末 | 2017年 | 2016年末 | 2018年1月 |
| | 起始年 | 1981年 | 2014年 | 2016年 | 2007年 | 1996年 | 1999年 | 2007年 | 2011年 | 2007年 | 2009年 | 2011年 |
| | 经营年限 | | 5年 | 2年 | 12年 | 22年 | | 11年 | 8年 | 11年 | 9年 | 7年 |
| | 网点/分支机构数 | | 8个 | | | 258个 | 6个分会 | 26个 | 213个 | 43个 | 6个 | |
| | 员工人数 | | | | | 4071人 | | | | 570多人 | | |
| | 信贷员人数 | | | | | 2729人 | | | | | | |

续表

| 指标 | 案例 | 地方项目管理办公室、地方农信社、地方妇联等NGO | 格莱珉中国 | 云南省富滇银行·富滇—格莱珉扶贫贷款项目 | 海南省农信联社·格莱珉模式小额信贷试点项目 | 中和农信 | 仪陇县乡村发展协会 | 汇丰村镇银行 | 中银富登村镇银行 | 南充美兴小额贷款有限责任公司 | 赤峰市元宝山区高信隆小额贷款有限公司 | 拍拍贷 |
|---|---|---|---|---|---|---|---|---|---|---|---|---|
| 服务广度 | 累计贷款总额/交易总额 | | 92万元 | 235.2万元 | 130亿元 | 278亿元 | 近亿元 | 220亿元 | 274亿元 | 84.5亿元 | 12.67亿元 | 966亿元 |
| | 累计贷款笔数/交易笔数 | | | 142笔 | 63万笔 | 207万笔 | | | | 15.7万笔 | 1.35万笔 | 3600万笔 |
| | 贷款余额 | | | | | 59.41亿元 | 314万元 | 12亿元 | | | | 191亿元 |
| | 有效客户数 | | 50人 | | | 38.2万人 | | | | 25000人 | | |
| 服务深度 | 人均贷款额 | | 1.8万元 | | | | | | | | | |
| | 单笔贷款额 | | | 1.66万元 | 2.06万元 | 1.34万元 | | | | 5.4万元 | 9.4万元 | |
| | 户均贷款余额 | | | | | 1.56万元 | | | 25万元 | | 5.5万元 | 0.35万元 |

续表

| 指标 | 案例 | 地方项目管理办公室、地方农信社、地方妇联等NGO | 格莱珉中国 | 云南省富滇银行·富滇—格莱珉扶贫贷款项目 | 海南省农信联社·格莱珉模式小额信贷试点项目 | 中和农信 | 仪陇县乡村发展协会 | 汇丰村镇银行 | 中银富登村镇银行 | 南充美兴小额贷款有限责任公司 | 赤峰市元宝山区高信隆小额贷款有限公司 | 拍拍贷 |
|---|---|---|---|---|---|---|---|---|---|---|---|---|
| 社会目标 | 受益人数 | 439.33万户 | | 167名 | 51.8万户 | 超过400万户 | 15万贫困户 | 百万人 | 百万户 | 25万人以上 | | 超过1056万人 |
| | 网点覆盖面 | 项目地以欠发达地区为主 | | 覆盖2018年已脱贫贫困乡镇1个 | 覆盖贫困县1个 | 覆盖贫困县180个 | 覆盖贫困县1个 | | | | | |
| 机构可持续 | 风险贷款率（>30 days）/贷款拖欠率 | | | | | 0.94% | 9.77% | | 3.23% | | | 2.4% |
| | 年利润 | | | | | | 40万元 | | 4.57亿元 | | | |
| | 机构目前运营情况 | | 2016年后无公开数据 | | | 可持续运营 | 目前无公开数据 | 可持续运营 | 可持续运营 | 可持续运营 | | 2018年2月后无公开数据 |

资料来源：各机构官网或年报、Mixmarket数据库，以及相关新闻报道。

和贫困识别方面，中和农信做得更好一些，其目标市场集中于中低收入农户；最后，中和农信的有效客户数 38.2 万人，明显多于南充美兴的 2.5 万人，说明在服务广度方面，中和农信也好于南充美兴和高信隆小贷。

（4）中和农信和南充美兴都已实现机构的可持续运营，虽然中和农信的盈利水平不高，但保持较为稳定的财务绩效。据中和农信发布的历年财务绩效指标来看，从 2009 年开始持续盈利，总资产回报率多年保持在 3%以下，贷款总额回报率多年保持 2%以下，证明其盈利水平虽不高①，但财务绩效比较平稳。

第二，对比同是银行类金融机构的云南富滇银行项目、海南农信联社项目、汇丰村镇银行、中银富登村镇银行，从财务绩效和社会绩效的表现来看，村镇银行的优势较大。

（1）四个机构都可以吸收存款。

（2）服务模式都是直营模式。中银富登村镇银行的网点机构数最多，有 213 个。

（3）从服务广度来看，海南农信联社项目、汇丰村镇银行和中银富登村镇银行的累计贷款总额都超过 100 亿元。其中，中银富登村镇银行的最多，有 274 亿元；其次是汇丰村镇银行，有 220 亿元；云南富滇银行项目的累计贷款总额最少，有 235.2 万元。

（4）汇丰村镇银行、中银富登村镇银行、海南农信联社项目的社会绩效明显好于云南富滇银行项目，其中，汇丰村镇银行和中银富登村镇银行的受益人数都超过了百万人。

（5）汇丰村镇银行与中银富登村镇银行实现了可持续发展。

第三，对以不同的服务模式触达“最后一公里”的“中小微弱”群体的 11 个机构而言，数字模式在服务广度和服务深度方面占优，直营模式和数字模式在社会绩效和机构可持续方面各有千秋。

（1）从服务广度来说，数字模式的绩效表现明显优于直营模式。数字模式的拍拍贷，其累计交易总额是 966 亿元，累计交易笔数 3600 万笔；直营模式中，中和农信的累计贷款总额是 278 亿元，汇丰村镇银行的是 220 亿元，中银富登村镇银行的是 272 亿元，海南农信联社项目的是 130 亿元，南充美兴的是 84.5 亿元，高信隆小贷的是 12.67 亿元，仪陇县乡村发展协会和云南富滇银行项目的绩效表现平平，分别是近亿元和 235.2 万元。数字模式的拍拍贷在经营 7 年之后，其服务广度的绩效表现超过了直营模式中表现最好的中和农信（22 年）、汇丰村镇银行（11 年）、中银富登村镇银行（8 年）、海南农信联社项目（12 年）。

① 深圳国际公益学院公益金融与社会创新中心发布的《植根农村与服务低收入农户的小微金融典范——中和农信小额信贷案例研究》，2017 年。

（2）从服务深度来说，数字模式的绩效表现也优于直营模式。数字模式的拍拍贷，其户均贷款余额仅有 0.35 万元；直营模式中，中和农信的单笔贷款额和户均贷款余额分别是 1.34 万元和 1.56 万元，云南富滇银行项目的单笔贷款额是 1.66 万元，海南农信联社项目的单笔贷款额是 2.06 万元，南充美兴的单笔贷款额是 5.4 万元，高信隆小贷的单笔贷款额和户均贷款余额分别是 9.4 万元和 5.5 万元，中银富登村镇银行的户均贷款余额是 25 万元。可见，数字模式使单笔业务最小化成为可能。

（3）从社会目标来说，资金转贷模式、直营模式、数字模式的绩效表现各有千秋。国际农业发展基金项目属于发展援助类型的投资，其项目目标锁定各类有利于社会发展的指标，比专注普惠金融服务的指标更全面。直营模式的中和农信、南充美兴、高信隆小贷、汇丰村镇银行、中银富登村镇银行、海南农信联社项目、云南富滇银行项目等通过信贷员直接触达“最后一公里”的“中小微弱”群体，切实帮助他们获得发展机会。数字模式的拍拍贷受益人群最大，已超过千万人，证明数字技术确实有助于提升解决“最后一公里”问题的效率。

（4）从机构可持续发展来说，直营模式和数字模式的绩效表现也各有优势。直营模式的中和农信、汇丰村镇银行、中银富登村镇银行、南充美兴都基本实现了财务可持续和规模化发展，在管理模式、产品设计、风控模式等方面都相对成熟。2011 年，部分国际机构开始撤出中国，非营利民间组织类型的仪陇县乡村发展协会对国际援助或捐赠资金有一定依赖，其机构可持续发展面临较大困难。数字模式的拍拍贷，在《互联网金融风险专项整治工作实施方案》等监管政策出台之前，其财务运营情况良好，并于 2017 年在美国上市成功；不过，受监管政策影响较大，内部调整的过程一定程度上影响了业务运营情况。

## 四、成败经验

第一，由于普惠金融的重点服务对象是“中小微弱”群体，天然地决定了普惠金融供应方要均衡地实现财务绩效和社会绩效，因此，双目标平衡机制对普惠金融供应方的可持续发展起着决定性的作用。以南充美兴为例（见图 3－3），其社会绩效与财务绩效的双重目标平衡机制实现了三组平衡：服务深度和服务广度的平衡通过平衡信贷额度配给、平衡信贷产品类型、平衡信贷环境效益来实现；管理效率和生产效率的平衡通过平衡人员配置与风险控制、平衡流程设置与风险控制来实现；对弱势群体的覆盖面和盈利能力的平衡通过平衡贷款价格（人工成本、资金成本、风险成本等）与弱势群体对利率定价接受度来实现。以上三组平衡关系决定了社会绩效管理与财务绩效管理的平衡是否能够顺利实现，也决定了机构是否能顺利完成社会使命。

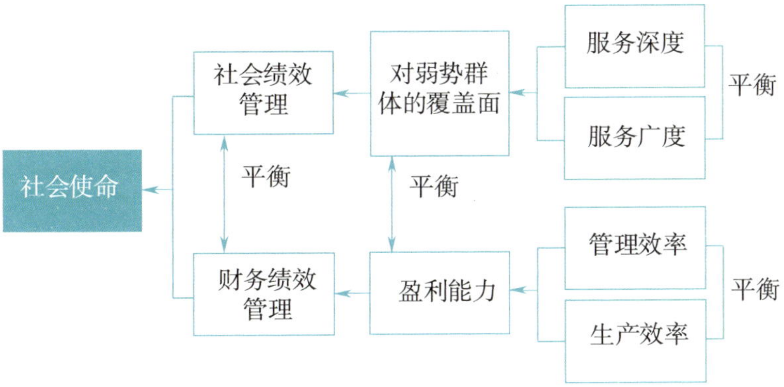


资料来源：贝多广，李焰．好金融　好社会——中国普惠金融发展报告［M］．北京：经济管理出版社，2016.

**图 3-3　南充美兴的双重目标平衡机制**

第二，本土化创新对国际普惠金融模式能否适应与扎根中国市场有着重要影响。以格莱珉模式为例，格莱珉中国和云南富滇银行项目代表的是对格莱珉模式的完整复制，中和农信和海南农信联社项目代表的是对格莱珉模式的本土化创新。格莱珉中国遭遇的最大困难是不能通过吸储来获得低成本的本金，而同样是不能吸储的中和农信，却通过本土化创新，实现了机构的可持续发展。中和农信模式最重要的突破包括公司化改制破除了“两张皮”双重管理困难，市场化运营引入了市场资本而突破了资金“瓶颈”，保持业务的增长速度又坚持业务模式的普惠性、规模化、专业化。目前，中和农信模式在中低收入农户这个细分市场中，已经形成了一套经过实践检验的“最后一公里”问题解决方案，具备一定的市场竞争力，尤其是其产品设计、连锁经营、风控模式等，符合中国农村业务的需求。

第三，管理模式的建构对普惠金融项目的成败或机构的可持续发展有着重要的影响。以国际农业发展基金对中国的援助项目为例（见图 3-4），国际农业发展基金有一套完善的项目管理制度，包括项目管理架构、项目执行的管理流程、项目评估方法等，有助于理顺国际农业发展基金与中国政府、中国基层执行机构的关系，也有利于按时间线与资源投入量来控制项目目标的完成，以及及时调整突发问题的应对策略。实际上，国际机构的管理经验对中国普惠金融供应方来说，是一笔宝贵的财富。

又如，国内村镇银行中机构数量最多、业务范围最广的中银富登村镇银行（见图 3-5），中国银行和富登金控合作建立起了一套“批量化”“规模化”“标准化”“集约化”管理模式与商业模式，极大地保障了机构财务绩效和社会绩效，还有效地解决了小微企业和“三农”客户业务规模普遍较小、抗风险能力相对较弱、贷款风险大、成本高等经营难题。

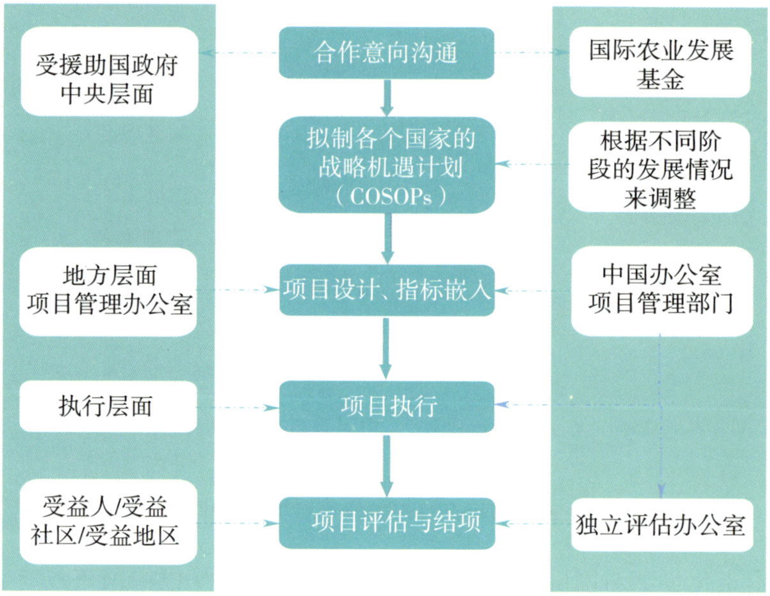


**图 3－4　国际农业发展基金项目执行的管理流程**

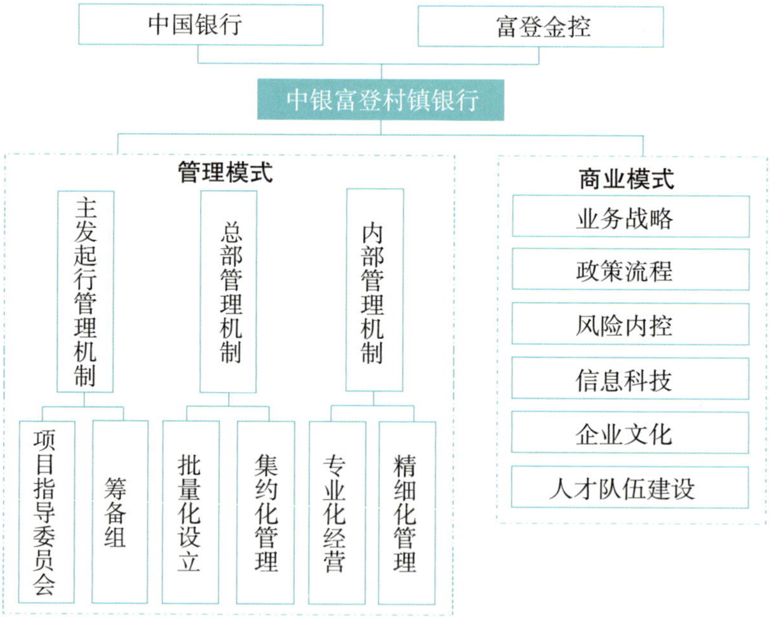


资料来源：中银富登村镇银行发布的《中银富登村镇银行的可持续发展和对中国银行的影响》。

**图 3－5　中银富登的管理模式和商业模式**

# 第二部分

# 跨越“最后一公里”的桥梁

金融服务存在繁荣超级平台和缺位于“最后一公里”两个极端现实。架起一座有效的中间桥梁，是解决“最后一公里”问题的关键所在。我们引进金融聚合器的概念，它可以在金融超级平台和中小微弱之间发挥桥梁作用。

# 第四章　金融聚合器与“最后一公里”

**【摘要】**“最后一公里”普惠金融服务的主要服务对象与地区是什么？这些服务对象有何特征？与较易获得金融服务的人群有何区别？本章将利用中国普惠金融研究院在全国的调研数据及其他统计数据尝试回答以上问题。由于普惠金融重点服务对象与较易获得金融服务的人群与地区的差异，聚合器将在服务对象与金融服务提供商（FSP）之间发挥重要的“桥梁”作用。本章重点探讨聚合器存在的必要性与主要的类型，分析聚合器如何在各种金融服务模式中发挥“桥梁”作用，并通过对比各种模式指出各自存在的问题与未来的发展趋势。

在绪论中，我们将金融服务的“最后一公里”问题定义为，在现有金融体系条件下，最边缘客户获得金融服务的难度远远超过其他客户的现象。这个问题可能是由于空间距离的障碍，也可能是成本的障碍、能力的障碍、制度的障碍、产品的障碍等造成的。一方面是在现有的金融服务体系内，已经存在很多金融机构和农产品，在市场经济原则下顺利地为一部分人提供服务。另一方面是“中小微弱”群体在同样的金融体系内不能获得服务。是否存在某一种可以打通现有服务的平台和最边缘群体的服务通道的金融服务模式，是本章要讨论的问题。

## 一、“最后一公里”问题现状

### （一）“最后一公里”的边缘群体

了解处于“最后一公里”的边缘群体，有利于根据他们的特点，寻找有效的解决办法。中国普惠金融研究院（CAFI）发布的浙江省普惠金融综合指数，为我们识别边缘群体提供了数字依据。浙江省的综合金融排斥指数为 0.4198（0 表示没有任何排斥，1 表示完全被排斥），还有 11.9%家庭的金融排斥指数大于 0.5，2.1%的家庭排斥数大于0.55。浙江省代表普惠金融发展比较好的地区，但是这个结果告诉我们即使是在比较发达的地区，“最后一公里”问题一样存在。如果将排斥指数大于0.5的人群视作金融服务“最后一公里”的边缘人群，单独对他们进行分析，可以了解这部分人群的主要特征。

1. 边缘家庭劳动力供养负担重

按照排斥指数大于0.5作为边缘群体划分标准并对他们分组进行比较，我们发现边缘群体有如下特征。

第一，边缘群体中户主为女性的比例比较高，对金融服务使用比较保守。表4-1边缘群体中，户主为男性的比例比女性低了1.7%，也就是说，边缘家庭中多为女性当家。女性在家庭管理、经营和金融决策方面和男性有一定的差异，有可能偏向保守，特别是金融服务产品往往与风险有关，她们对风险的偏好不一样。在解决“最后一公里”问题的时候，需要考虑性别差异。

**表4-1 金融服务边缘群体特征** 单位：%、人

| 特征 | 边缘群体 | 非边缘群体 | 差异 |
|---|---|---|---|
| 户主性别为男性比例 | 84.5 | 86.2 | −1.7 |
| 未婚比例 | 2.2 | 2.4 | −0.1 |
| 已婚有配偶比例 | 92.3 | 93.8 | −1.4 |
| 离婚比例 | 0.7 | 1.9 | −1.2 |
| 丧偶比例 | 4.3 | 1.7 | 2.6 |
| 子女数 | 1.48 | 1.33 | 0.14 |
| 户主是党员比例 | 8.3 | 16.2 | −7.9 |
| 家庭人口数 | 3.59 | 3.85 | −0.26 |
| 居住本地人口比例 | 95.0 | 93.2 | 1.8 |
| 家庭男性人口比例 | 53.0 | 52.6 | 0.4 |
| 家庭成年人比例 | 61.9 | 72.0 | −10.1 |
| 家庭60岁以上老年人比例 | 26.3 | 12.7 | 13.6 |
| 家庭初中以下人口比例 | 75.1 | 63.2 | 11.9 |
| 家庭就业成员人口比例 | 61.7 | 66.9 | −5.2 |
| 本县就业占就业人口比例 | 75.2 | 83.0 | −7.8 |

第二，劳动力供养人口比例比较高。边缘群体中，丧偶的比例高出了2.6%，也就是单亲家庭的比例比较高；平均子女人数比较多；成年人的比例低10个百分点；老年人的比例高13.6个百分点。这些指标表明，边缘人群家庭中劳动力供养人口比例比较高，经济负担比较重。

第三，教育程度偏低。边缘群体中，家庭初中以下教育程度的人口比例平均高出约12个百分点。低水平的教育，影响对金融知识的理解和金融产品的应用。

第四，边缘家庭中，就业成员人口比例和在本地就业人口比例都比较低，分别低了5.2个和7.8个百分点。就业人数少意味着人均收入比较低，同时由于边缘家庭的劳动力缺乏技能，主要以到外地打工维持生活，收入水平低。

2. 边缘家庭收入低

低收入是边缘人群最主要的表现，表4-2中边缘群体的家庭年人均收入为17400多元，比其他家庭减少40%。低收入自然会降低对金融服务的需求，影响信用额度。

**表4-2 边缘家庭收入来源**

单位：元、%

| 收入来源 | 边缘群体 | 非边缘群体 | 差异 |
|---|---|---|---|
| 家庭人均收入 | 26377.48 | 43789.73 | −17412.26 |
| 自用种植业收入 | 8234.19 | 12896.33 | −4662.15 |
| 对外销售种植业收入 | 5050.80 | 6627.22 | −1576.42 |
| 自用养殖业收入 | 1655.21 | 1694.25 | −39.04 |
| 对外销售养殖业收入 | 2957.76 | 8073.69 | −5115.93 |
| 其他经营性收入 | 21772.70 | 56893.92 | −35121.22 |
| 工资性收入 | 44760.59 | 61981.86 | −17221.28 |
| 财产性收入 | 2367.50 | 6309.35 | −3941.85 |
| 政府转移性收入 | 1643.14 | 1507.80 | 135.34 |
| 单位转移性收入 | 654.72 | 1144.50 | −489.78 |
| 家庭转移性收入 | 1423.89 | 2629.46 | −1205.57 |
| 务农为最高收入来源家庭比例 | 30.15 | 17.96 | 12.19 |
| 私营工商业为最高收入来源家庭比例 | 14.14 | 28.08 | −13.93 |
| 受雇于他人或单位为最高收入来源家庭比例 | 17.12 | 27.08 | −9.96 |
| 临时工为最高收入来源家庭比例 | 22.39 | 13.03 | 9.36 |
| 自由职业为最高收入来源家庭比例 | 9.62 | 10.38 | 0.77 |

在收入的构成中，边缘家庭和其他家庭似乎没有明显的区别，最主要的来源是工资性收入和经营收入。但是除了政府转移支付外，边缘家庭的其他来源获得的收入都是比较低的，尤其是工资性收入和经营收入，分别低了17221元和35121元。政府对低收入人群的扶持比较多，每户多出135元。

边缘家庭以就业和工商经营为主要收入的家庭比例分别低了14个和9个百分点。而以农业和临时工为主要收入来源的家庭比例分别高出13个和9个百分点。由于农业和临时工的收入不稳定，边缘家庭收入的稳定性不如其他家庭。

3. 边缘家庭的消费者支出比例大

与收入相对应，边缘家庭的人均总支出也少了1.6万元（见表4-3）。边缘家庭在支出数额比较小的情况下，将46%的支出用于消费，高出其他家庭约12个百分点，而在经营和住房支出方面明显低于其他家庭。在支出具体数额方面，边缘家庭几乎都低于其他家庭，特别是在消费、经营性和住房支出方面，分别低了1.47万元、1.77万元和1.74万元。高比例和低绝对值的消费模式，影响了家庭生活水平的提高以及扩大再生产，当然也影响了对金融消费的需求。

**表4-3　边缘家庭的支出**

| 支出 | 边缘群体 | | 非边缘群体 | | 差额（元） |
|---|---|---|---|---|---|
| | 金额（元） | 占总收入比例（%） | 金额（元） | 占总收入比例（%） | |
| 人均总支出 | 12603.99 | | 28686.54 | | −16082.55 |
| 种植业支出 | 3868.27 | 8.52 | 5855.14 | 5.55 | −1986.87 |
| 养殖业支出 | 2663.44 | 5.86 | 5575.63 | 5.28 | −2912.20 |
| 消费性支出 | 20901.14 | 46.02 | 35547.10 | 33.68 | −14645.96 |
| 经营性支出 | 5868.59 | 12.92 | 23544.07 | 22.31 | −17675.48 |
| 财产性支出 | 1458.45 | 3.21 | 3563.25 | 3.38 | −2104.80 |
| 转移性支出 | 521.32 | 1.15 | 1159.12 | 1.10 | −637.80 |
| 社会保障支出 | 1576.52 | 3.47 | 4323.57 | 4.10 | −2747.05 |
| 构建房支出 | 8563.89 | 18.85 | 25979.76 | 24.61 | −17415.85 |

4. 边缘家庭没有自信能够获得社会帮助

由于边缘人群的不利特征和收入低等情况，他们获得社会帮助的机会也比较少。在调查中（见表4-4），当问到在紧急情况下获得亲戚和朋友帮助的程度，边缘家庭认为“非常有帮助”的比非边缘家庭低了10个百分点，认为“挺有帮助”“有少量帮助”“完全没有帮助”的比例均高于其他家庭。对于在紧急情况下能否借到1万元以及能够借到的金额，边缘家庭也表现得很不自信。

**表4-4　边缘家庭获得帮助的自信程度**　　单位：%、万元

| 人际关系 | 边缘群体 | 非边缘群体 |
|---|---|---|
| 紧急情况下，亲人的帮助程度 | | |
| 非常有帮助 | 65.63 | 75.01 |
| 挺有帮助 | 28.04 | 20.32 |
| 少量帮助 | 4.78 | 4.18 |
| 完全无帮助 | 0.00 | 0.00 |
| 紧急情况下，朋友的帮助程度 | | |
| 非常有帮助 | 31.58 | 41.74 |
| 挺有帮助 | 50.56 | 47.23 |
| 少量帮助 | 14.64 | 10.23 |
| 完全无帮助 | 3.23 | 0.80 |
| 紧急情况下，邻居的帮助程度 | | |
| 非常有帮助 | 25.56 | 28.33 |
| 挺有帮助 | 40.01 | 37.47 |
| 少量帮助 | 26.99 | 29.67 |
| 完全无帮助 | 7.44 | 4.53 |
| 紧急情况下，筹到1万元现金的可能性 | | |
| 没问题，现在就有 | 48.45 | 74.02 |
| 很有可能 | 23.76 | 15.98 |
| 有一些可能 | 12.78 | 5.31 |
| 可能性不大 | 5.46 | 1.67 |
| 完全没有可能 | 9.55 | 3.01 |
| 紧急情况最多筹到资金的平均值 | 3702.47 | 14725.06 |

5. 边缘人群受到金融排斥的程度比较严重

我们所构建的普惠金融指数衡量的是金融的排斥程度。表4－5显示，边缘家庭受到的排斥程度大于其他家庭。如果用其他家庭的排斥作为基数，在可得性方面边缘家庭受到的排斥程度高出60%，在使用方面的排斥程度高出31%，在能力方面引起的排斥高出39%，在数字化方面受到的排斥高出40%。边缘家庭遇到的金融障碍也高于普通家庭。

**表4－5　边缘人群普惠金融综合指数**

| 指数 | 边缘群体 | | | 非边缘群体 | | | 差值 | | |
|---|---|---|---|---|---|---|---|---|---|
| | 均值 | 最小值 | 极大值 | 均值 | 最小值 | 极大值 | 均值 | 最小值 | 极大值 |
| 综合指数 | 0.5290 | 0.5000 | 0.6335 | 0.4050 | 0.1827 | 0.4999 | 0.1240 | 0.3173 | 0.1336 |
| 可得性 | 0.4478 | 0.0750 | 0.9583 | 0.2806 | 0.0084 | 0.8417 | 0.1673 | 0.0667 | 0.1166 |
| 使用情况 | 0.6397 | 0.2996 | 0.8091 | 0.4889 | 0.2002 | 0.7760 | 0.1508 | 0.0994 | 0.0331 |
| 质量 | 0.2475 | 0.0635 | 0.3894 | 0.2148 | 0.0295 | 0.6421 | 0.0327 | 0.0340 | －0.2527 |
| 满意度 | 0.4852 | 0.3114 | 0.6257 | 0.4467 | 0.1800 | 0.5971 | 0.0385 | 0.1314 | 0.0286 |
| 金融能力 | 0.8248 | 0.4104 | 1.0000 | 0.5940 | 0.0396 | 1.0000 | 0.2308 | 0.3708 | 0.0000 |
| 障碍 | 0.0522 | 0.0000 | 0.2328 | 0.0453 | 0.0000 | 0.3582 | 0.0069 | 0.0000 | －0.1254 |
| 数字化程度 | 0.2595 | 0.0130 | 0.5193 | 0.1859 | 0.0130 | 0.5772 | 0.0736 | 0.0000 | －0.0579 |
| 预期 | 0.5988 | 0.3143 | 0.8286 | 0.6215 | 0.3274 | 1.0000 | －0.0227 | －0.0131 | －0.1714 |

（二）“最后一公里”的边缘地区

“最后一公里”问题主要存在于什么地区？东西部的差距有多大？CAFI将东部沿海某市及西部某市的调研数据进行对比，从数据上证实了我国的东西部地区在普惠金融发展上的差异明显。利用CAFI的普惠金融指标与监测指数体系，我们测算了这两个市的村/社区指数，如表4－6及表4－7所示。指数的意义与上述的边缘人群的定义类似（0表示没有任何排斥，1表示完全被排斥，以0.5为阈值，大于等于0.5为受到排斥）。

表 4-6　西部某市村/社区普惠金融指数

| 村/社区 | 样本量 | 被排斥样本量 | 村/社区被排斥指数 | 被排斥率（%） |
|---|---|---|---|---|
| 红三村社区 | 20 | 14 | 0.509 | 70.0 |
| 李家庄村委会 | 20 | 12 | 0.513 | 60.0 |
| 新营村委会 | 20 | 13 | 0.513 | 65.0 |
| 五里铺社区 | 20 | 18 | 0.518 | 90.0 |
| 团结新村社区 | 22 | 15 | 0.522 | 68.2 |
| 王家湾村委会 | 20 | 14 | 0.522 | 70.0 |
| 夏官营村委会 | 22 | 15 | 0.524 | 68.2 |
| 清水村委会 | 23 | 14 | 0.527 | 60.9 |
| 定西二支路社区 | 20 | 17 | 0.529 | 85.0 |
| 西村村委会 | 21 | 19 | 0.529 | 90.5 |
| 上庄村委会 | 20 | 18 | 0.531 | 90.0 |
| 安定门社区 | 21 | 17 | 0.533 | 81.0 |
| 西城巷社区 | 26 | 22 | 0.533 | 84.6 |
| 三墩营村委会 | 20 | 17 | 0.534 | 85.0 |
| 砂河村委会 | 20 | 17 | 0.534 | 85.0 |
| 定西路社区 | 21 | 20 | 0.538 | 95.2 |
| 平凉路 | 21 | 19 | 0.54 | 90.5 |
| 五里铺东社区 | 20 | 18 | 0.541 | 90.0 |
| 徐家巷社区 | 20 | 20 | 0.543 | 100.0 |
| 和平新村 | 22 | 20 | 0.545 | 90.9 |
| 南河新村社区 | 20 | 17 | 0.547 | 85.0 |
| 雷坛河社区 | 22 | 22 | 0.553 | 100.0 |
| 牟东社区 | 23 | 23 | 0.554 | 100.0 |
| 金塔巷社区 | 20 | 20 | 0.558 | 100.0 |
| 滩尖子社区 | 20 | 18 | 0.565 | 90.0 |
| 金崖村委会 | 24 | 23 | 0.567 | 95.8 |
| 定远村委会 | 21 | 20 | 0.571 | 95.2 |

表 4-7　东部沿海某市村/社区普惠金融发展指数

| 村/社区 | 样本量 | 被排斥样本量 | 村/社区被排斥指数 | 被排斥率（%） |
|---|---|---|---|---|
| 黄桐村 | 20 | 0 | 0.304 | 0.0 |
| 渔滘村 | 23 | 0 | 0.322 | 0.0 |
| 茶林村 | 21 | 0 | 0.35 | 0.0 |
| 仁字坑村 | 20 | 1 | 0.358 | 5.0 |
| 扫口村 | 20 | 0 | 0.366 | 0.0 |
| 七里村 | 29 | 1 | 0.368 | 3.4 |
| 三石村 | 24 | 2 | 0.374 | 8.3 |
| 竹山村 | 20 | 1 | 0.387 | 5.0 |
| 高演村 | 21 | 4 | 0.396 | 19.0 |
| 大均村 | 20 | 2 | 0.397 | 10.0 |
| 驮垟村 | 20 | 5 | 0.398 | 25.0 |
| 章坑村 | 20 | 3 | 0.405 | 15.0 |
| 叶谢村 | 20 | 2 | 0.407 | 10.0 |
| 水溪村 | 22 | 4 | 0.408 | 18.2 |
| 东塘村 | 20 | 2 | 0.409 | 10.0 |
| 张庄村 | 21 | 6 | 0.415 | 28.6 |
| 枫林口村 | 21 | 2 | 0.417 | 9.5 |
| 金岱村 | 20 | 2 | 0.417 | 10.0 |
| 新塘垟村 | 24 | 3 | 0.427 | 12.5 |
| 马坑村 | 34 | 6 | 0.43 | 17.6 |
| 王山头村 | 23 | 6 | 0.434 | 26.1 |
| 库头村 | 20 | 4 | 0.435 | 20.0 |
| 坑垟口村 | 22 | 6 | 0.437 | 27.3 |
| 石梯村 | 22 | 6 | 0.439 | 27.3 |
| 芎岱村 | 21 | 7 | 0.448 | 33.3 |
| 隆下村 | 20 | 10 | 0.454 | 50.0 |
| 惠明寺 | 20 | 7 | 0.46 | 35.0 |
| 岗石村 | 23 | 9 | 0.461 | 39.1 |
| 白坦村 | 20 | 10 | 0.467 | 50.0 |
| 三枝树 | 20 | 7 | 0.471 | 35.0 |
| 半岭村 | 20 | 11 | 0.492 | 55.0 |

从表 4－6 与表 4－7 表格的对比中我们可以看到，从排斥指数看，东部沿海某市的村或社区均在 0.5 以下，而西部某市的村或社区取值均在 0.5 以上，发展水平差异非常大，从排斥率上看也是如此。当然，排斥度都是相对的，如果把阈值提高到 0.55，西部某市的村/社区被排斥率就会大大降低。

造成这种差距的主要因素是什么？通过对影响普惠金融发展的维度影响因素进行分析，我们有如下发现。

使用 CAFI 普惠金融发展指标体系对收集到的西部某市三县区 2488 份调研问卷数据进行整理分析后得出，西部某市的普惠金融综合排斥指数均值为 0.5268，其中被调查对象最大值为 0.6592，最小值为 0.3330。从图 4－1 中可以看到，除金融能力的维度外，西部某市普惠金融发展在可得性、使用情况、质量及满意度等方面均处于被排斥度最大的位置上。

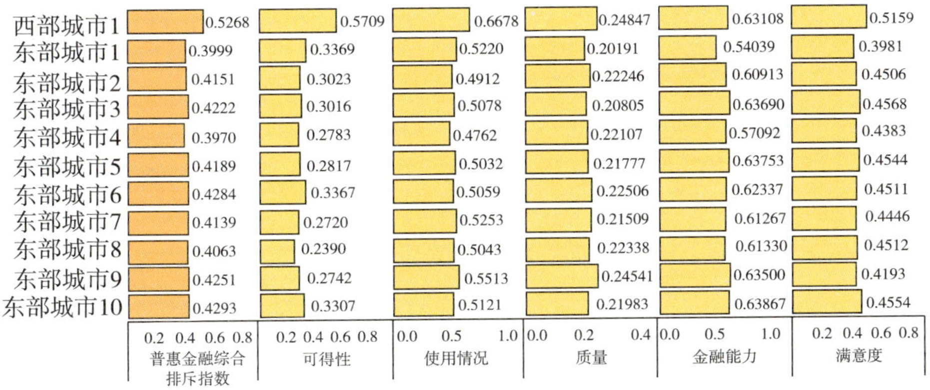


**图 4－1　西部部分市的普惠金融发展指数对比**

可得性维度反映金融服务的可触达性，该维度包括当地的基础设施、公共服务项目的数量、互联网、电信服务、银行服务网点等指标。基础设施及公务服务等之所以被包含在这个维度，是因为这些设施及服务往往是提供或使用金融服务的基础，如互联网是使用数字金融服务的基础，而智能手机等是使用移动金融服务的基础。如图 4－1 所示，西部某市在可得性维度的平均指数值为 0.5709，排斥率明显高于相对比的其他地区，说明西部某市的普惠金融可得性排斥度较高，作为普惠金融发展的短板需要提高。

使用情况指数反映各种金融服务及设施的使用现状，该维度主要包括需求方对银行账户、支付、理财、融资、保险、征信、ATM 及 POS 机等的使用情况，旨在全面度量被访者的金融服务使用状态。如图 4－1 所示，西部某市在使用维度的平均指数值为 0.5709，排斥度显著高于对比地区，有较大提升空间。

在质量维度上，虽然西部某市数据的排斥程度与其他地区差异不大，为 0.2485，但仍然是几个地区中最高的。质量维度通过银行、小额贷款公司、资金互助社或其他途径贷款的年化利率、除利息外的额外成本、贷款获批时间长短以及汇款成本，是否遭遇金融诈骗等标准进行衡量。而西部某市的调研对象如图4－2所示，仅有12%有贷款，其中大部分为子女的教育贷款。与其他城市数据相比，西部某市的消费贷款与经营性贷款数量非常少。由于调研对象大多未使用过银行贷款服务，所以西部某市被调研对象对贷款过程中存在的问题及体会到的困难较少，进而导致了普惠金融质量维度排斥率较低的情况。

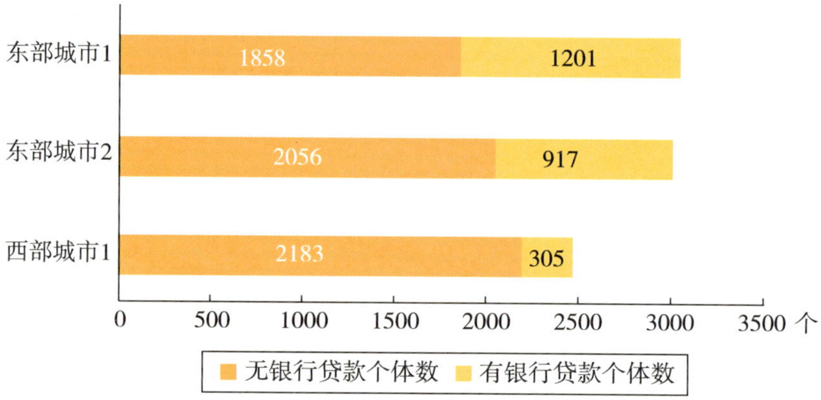


**图4－2　西部某市、东部沿海某市银行信贷个体户对比**

满意度指数主要从传统与数字两个方面反映客户对传统和数字金融服务的主观感受。传统金融服务包括银行柜台、ATM、POS机、便民金融服务站、资金互助社、定期存款、银行理财产品等客户主观感受指标；数字金融服务包括网上银行、手机银行、第三方支付、电商消费信贷等客户主观感受指标。结果显示，西部某市客户满意度排斥指数平均值为0.5159，高于其他城市，说明西部某市调研对象对金融服务的满意度较低。

金融能力指数反映客户自身金融素养、技能、金融行为、态度等方面的状态，主要包括对单利、复利计算、是否主动学习金融知识及向外界寻求帮助、对数字技术适应度、家庭财富管理自我评价等指标。西部某市金融能力指数的平均值为0.63108，与其他地区相比差异不大，说明全国地区的居民金融能力普遍不高①。

总体而言，我国的东西部地区普惠金融发展水平差异较大，未来发展与扶持政策重点应该向西部地区有一定程度的倾斜。

① 0.63距离上限1较近，因此排斥度较高。

### （三）金融服务的“最后一公里”问题

普惠金融服务包含支付、理财①、保险、信用、融资等内容。除金融业务外，需要强调的是金融教育/能力建设，因为只有金融能力提高了，才可以更加有效地选择金融工具，作出更好的金融决策。从地理分布上来说，金融服务的“最后一公里”问题往往出现在广袤的农村地区。

1. 农村是基础金融服务的薄弱地区

基础金融服务主要包含两类：一类是传统的金融服务，如地区的银行服务网点、金融机具、人均银行账户等的数量；另一类是互联网金融服务，随着互联网技术的发展，金融科技对居民的消费行为影响越来越大，尤其是在支付行为上。

就农村而言，提供传统基础金融服务的机构（见表 4－8）包含农村信用社、农村商业银行、农村合作银行、村镇银行和信贷公司。在 2011—2017 年，机构数略有增长，从 5369 家增长到了 5901 家，但其中的机构结构却发生了非常大的变化。首先，农信系统内部发生了结构性变化，农村信用社、农村合作银行家数大幅减少，多数正在向农村商业银行改制，完善法人治理结构；此外，作为新型农村金融机构，村镇银行数量呈现快速增长，由 635 家增长到 1562 家。

**表 4－8　农村中小金融机构法人机构数**　　单位：家

| 机构名称 | 2011 年 | 2012 年 | 2013 年 | 2014 年 | 2015 年 | 2016 年 | 2017 年 |
|---|---|---|---|---|---|---|---|
| 农村信用社 | 2265 | 1927 | 1803 | 1596 | 1373 | 1125 | 965 |
| 农村商业银行 | 212 | 337 | 468 | 665 | 859 | 1114 | 1263 |
| 农村合作银行 | 190 | 147 | 122 | 89 | 71 | 40 | 33 |
| 村镇银行 | 635 | 800 | 987 | 1153 | 1311 | 1443 | 1562 |
| 信贷公司 | 10 | 14 | 14 | 14 | 14 | 13 | 13 |
| 农村资金互助社 | 46 | 49 | 49 | 49 | 48 | 48 | 48 |
| 总计 | 5369 | 5286 | 5456 | 5580 | 5691 | 5799 | 5901 |

虽然机构数量增加，但是从表 4－9 中可以发现，金融机构在农村地区提供的基础金融服务，与全国的平均水平相比，还有一定差距。差距最明显体现在每万人拥有的 POS 机及人均信用卡数量上。POS 机的差距主要是由于城镇中的商业网点比较密集，而这些商业网点是 POS 机使用最为频繁的场所；信用卡的数量差距主要是由于农村地区的信用数据缺乏、征信体系建设较为滞后而形成的。

① 限于重要性及数据可得性原因，本书没有对理财作进一步的分析。

近年来，由于中央银行的推动，农村地区的助农服务取款点覆盖率已经达到了97.34%，基本已经实现全覆盖。这为农村地区的存、取款提供了极大的便利，同时也为农村居民降低了存、取款的成本。

**表4-9 2017年农村地区传统基础金融服务情况**

| 指标 | 农村地区 | 全国 | 全国/农村地区比率 |
|---|---|---|---|
| 每万人银行网点数量（个） | 1.30 | 1.65 | 1.27 |
| 每万人ATM数量（台） | 3.89 | 6.95 | 1.79 |
| 每万人POS机具（个） | 73.27 | 225.56 | 3.08 |
| 人均借记卡数量（张） | 2.77 | 4.42 | 1.60 |
| 人均信用卡数量（张） | 0.2 | 0.39 | 1.95 |
| 助农取款服务点覆盖率（%） | 97.34 | N/A | N/A |

资料来源：中国人民银行。

随着数字金融技术的不断发展，通过互联网向农村提供金融服务可以实现较低成本的覆盖，因此必然会成为传统及新型金融机构进一步挖掘农村市场的有力工具。如表4-10所示，农村地区的网上银行、手机银行账户数呈现了快速增长的趋势，尤其是移动端的手机银行业务，而电话银行服务则有回落的趋势。

**表4-10 农村地区电子银行账户数** 单位：亿个

| | 2017年 | 2016年 | 2015年 |
|---|---|---|---|
| 网上银行账户数 | 5.31 | 4.29 | 3.56 |
| 手机银行账户数 | 5.17 | 3.73 | 2.76 |
| 电话银行账户数 | 1.90 | 2.15 | 1.81 |

从网络支付情况看，如表4-11所示，农村地区与全国相比，差距也比较大。从银行业机构的网络支付①情况看，无论从支付笔数还是金额来看，农村地区的占比均很少，这种情况的发生，可能是由于主要的企业均集中于城市，而企业的业务结算基本上由银行业机构来负责。如果我们考察个人业务占比较多的农村地区，非银行业支付机构的网络支付（其中移动支付占多数）笔数及金额的占比均较大，这说明在数字金融时代，农村地区的网络支付使用基本与城市相差无几，这是一个非常令人欣喜的发现。因为支付作为其他金融服务的重要入口，如果农村地区能够在网络支付方面不落后，这说明其他金融服务也可以有非常大的发展空间。

① 网络支付包括互联网支付及移动支付两种情况。

**表 4-11　农村地区网络支付情况**

| | 农村地区网络支付笔数（亿笔） | 全国网络支付业务笔数（亿笔） | 农村网络支付笔数占比（%） | 农村地区网络支付金额（万亿元） | 全国网络支付业务金额（万亿元） | 农村网络支付金额占比（%） |
|---|---|---|---|---|---|---|
| 银行业机构 | 185.79 | 861.30 | 21.57 | 191.62 | 2278.02 | 8.41 |
| 非银行业支付机构 | 1417.82 | 2867.47 | 49.44 | 45.00 | 143.26 | 31.41 |

资料来源：中国人民银行。

从微观角度进行研究，CAFI 通过对东部沿海某市、西部某市调研发现关于支付习惯偏好、移动支付的使用频率方面存在一些有意思的现象。在普惠金融综合排斥指数较高的西部某市，其偏好使用大的第三方支付平台进行支付的比率，以及每天使用移动支付的比率①都高于东部沿海市。当然，从不使用移动支付的比率上看，西部市要稍高一些，但差距并不大。具体数据如表 4-12 所示。

**表 4-12　东部沿海某市、西部某市居民支付情况比较**　　单位：%

| | 东部沿海某市 | 西部某市 |
|---|---|---|
| 偏好现金支付比率 | 65.9 | 61.6 |
| 偏好大的第三方支付平台比率 | 10.7 | 18.5 |
| 每天使用移动支付比率 | 23.1 | 27.6 |
| 从不使用移动支付比率 | 27.7 | 30.4 |

这似乎预示着金融服务不是非常发达的地区在互联网时代其移动支付并没有落后，而且有一定的后发优势。

2. 保险

“三农”领域风险较高是既有的共识。但由于种种原因，农村的保险市场一直都没有大的发展，而在未来的乡村振兴过程中，可以预期资金会大规模涌入农村地区。因此作为投资过程中的一种风险分散的有效手段，相关“三农”保险产品可以预见会有较大的市场空间。

从市场发展来看，目前中国的“三农”保险总体上说以政府推动、保险公司配合、农民参与为主，市场化的力量还不是很强。农业保险经营主体从 2007 年的 6 家增加到 26 家，农业保险服务点乡镇覆盖率达 93%，村级覆盖率达 48%。

① 东部市调研样本为 3027 户，西部市样本量为 2488 户。

从农业保险的绝对规模上来讲，2007—2016年，我国农业保费收入从51.8亿元增长到了417.72①亿元，年均复合增长率为26%，同期内农业保险的风险保障额度从1720亿元增长到2.16万亿元②，年均增速32.5%，已经是位居亚洲第一、世界第二的农业保险市场。

但如果分别考察中国与北美国家的农业保险渗透率③，根据可获得的数据，2014年中国的农业保险渗透率为0.32%，北美为5.6%，全球平均水平为1.2%。直到2016年，中国的农业保险渗透率也只是0.37%。这之间的缺口我们不妨称为在保险服务方面的“最后一公里”缺口。

对比另外一个非常重要的农业保险指标——农业保险的保障水平④可以发现，中国与美国的差距也非常大，2015年中国农业保险保障水平为18%，美国为50%，缺口也非常大。

在农业生产日益向规模化发展的趋势下，“信贷服务+保险”这种保证保险的普惠金融服务模式也会催生巨大的保险业务需求。目前我国很多农村金融改革的试点地区⑤已经开始推出创新型的信贷保险产品，取得了良好的效果。如果未来可以在其他地区开展，这种农村保险服务中的“缺口”也将会变小。

除农业保险外，农村居民的“医疗、财产、人身”保险产品的潜在市场规模也是巨大的，初步预计2020年将有1万亿元左右的市场规模，在此不加以赘述。

从微观角度进行研究，CAFI通过对东部沿海某市、西部某市的调研活动数据进行分析，发现对于社会基本养老及医疗保险，东西部差距并不明显，因为这是政府在极力推动的基本社会保障。而在商业保险上则呈现了较大差距，东部沿海某市被调研对象的商业保险购买率要大于西部某市25个百分点，这说明东部沿海某市居民具有较强的风险防范意识。具体数据如表4-13所示。

**表4-13　东部沿海某市、西部某市居民保险购买情况比较**　　单位：%

| | 东部沿海某市 | 西部某市 |
|---|---|---|
| 购买了社会基本养老保险的比率 | 92.5 | 89.2 |
| 购买了社会基本医疗保险的比率 | 93.1 | 92.9 |
| 购买了除基本养老、医疗保险以外其他保险的比率 | 44.0 | 18.9 |

① 资料来源：麦肯锡：《中国保险业白皮书》，2018年5月。

② 资料来源：中国人民银行农村金融服务研究小组．中国农村金融服务报告2016［M］．北京：中国金融出版社，2017.

③ 农业保险保费收入占农业GDP的比率。

④ 农业保险保障水平=单位面积保额/单位面积产值。

⑤ 例如，浙江丽水开展了“银政保”以及小额贷款保证保险产品等金融服务。

3. 信用体系建设

信用体系建设最早是应信贷市场的需求而产生的，而农村市场的融资难与融资贵问题，一定程度上是与征信体系的不完备有关。

目前全球的征信体系主要有两种模式：一是以美国为代表的市场主导型的征信体系，征信机构基本都是以盈利为目的的企业，政府只是负责信用管理立法，监督信用管理法律的贯彻与执行；二是政府主导的征信体系，以中国为例，人民银行主导的征信中心是国内最大的信用基础数据库，而民间的 134 家①企业征信机构和 11 家②个人征信机构是完善、补充人民银行征信中心的重要组成部分。值得注意的是，中国人民银行于 2018 年 1 月正式批准了首家市场化个人征信机构——百行征信有限公司，该公司由芝麻信用、腾讯征信等 8 家市场机构联合中国互联网金融协会组建，旨在打破信息孤岛，为降低信息成本、控制风险提供更好的信用服务。

目前，我国农村整体的征信覆盖率与发达国家相比还有很大差距。以个人征信为例，截至 2016 年末，全国累计为 1.72 亿户农户建立了信用档案，其中有 9248③ 万户农户获得银行贷款，覆盖率为 53.7%。而美国在 2014 年，这一比率就高达 92%④，差距非常明显。

如果从农民自身的角度来看，CAFI 2017 年在浙江 14 个县域开展的普惠金融调研问卷的数据显示，只有 28.8%⑤的农村居民了解自己在人民银行的个人征信情况，个人信用意识薄弱现象突出。这种现象在某种程度上也可以视作“最后一公里”问题的一种缺口。

当然，随着数字金融技术的发展，数字化信用评分也开始逐步纳入农村居民，但在实践中由于农村的应用场景较少，必须与线下调查相结合，才能得出比较可靠的评分。

从微观角度进行研究，CAFI 通过对东部沿海某市、西部某市的调研活动数据进行分析，发现东部沿海某市居民对自身的信用状况较为关注，而且信用户比率较高。如表 4-14 中的数据所示，知道自己在人民银行征信中心信用状况的东部沿海某市居民比率比西部某市多了 40%，信用户的比率也多了 38.4%。

---

① 资料来源：征信宝。

② 资料来源：信用中国网站。

③ 资料来源：中国人民银行农村金融服务研究小组．中国农村金融服务报告 2016 [M]．北京：中国金融出版社，2017.

④ 资料来源：BCG 发布的《中国个人征信行业报告（2015）》，2016 年。

⑤ 总样本数为 13505 个，其中回答了解的样本数为 3898 个。

**表 4-14　东部沿海某市、西部某市居民信用情况比较**　　单位：%

| | 东部沿海某市 | 西部某市 |
|---|---|---|
| 知道在央行征信中心的信用状况比率 | 51.5 | 11.5 |
| 信用户比率 | 90.2 | 51.8 |

4. 融资

农村居民的融资难、融资贵似乎已经成为一个老调常谈的问题。之所以经常提起这个问题，是因为融资是解决农村产业发展从而提高农村居民收入的关键推动力。

融资难、融资贵的主要原因是什么？从金融机构的风险防控角度来讲，一方面是由于农村居民的平均资产存量低、年收入少而且不稳定，因此不能提供足额抵押或担保；另一方面是由于农村的信用体系建设还很不完备，信用生态不健全，农村居民的信用意识淡薄。

如果从农村居民的信贷可得性的角度来研究，CAFI 在浙江省的调研数据显示，28%①的受访人在 2016 年申请过银行信贷，在申请信贷的群体中有 96%最终获批了贷款，也就是说总样本中有 26.9%在银行有贷款。从全国来看，25%②左右的农户在银行有贷款。浙江省是中国经济较为发达的地区，很多农村地区都进行了金融改革，银行服务在农村地区的触达率已经非常高。

如果从量的方面看，农村的融资缺口到底有多大？《中国“三农”互联网金融发展报告（2016）》③ 测算了 2014 年的“三农”金融的资金缺口约为 3.05 万亿元。

如果从每年新增的涉农贷款增量的均值出发来测算这个缺口，我们可以得出 2011—2017 年的平均增量为 28787.4 亿元，如表 4-15 所示。两种计算方法得出的数值比较接近。当然，如果未来农村经济规模呈现较为快速的增长，这一缺口可能会加速扩大。

**表 4-15　2011—2017 年涉农贷款增量**　　单位：亿元

| | 2011 年 | 2012 年 | 2013 年 | 2014 年 | 2015 年 | 2016 年 | 2017 年 |
|---|---|---|---|---|---|---|---|
| 涉农贷款余额 | 146016 | 176310 | 208893 | 236002 | 263522 | 282336 | 309500 |
| 较上年增量 | 27271 | 30119 | 34024 | 29984 | 28803 | 24147 | 27164 |

资料来源：中国人民银行及中国银保监会。

① 总样本数为 13505 户，其中有 3810 户在 2017 年有融资需求。

② 数据来自中国银保监会普惠金融部主任李均锋在第十届陆家嘴论坛（2018）上的讲话。

③ 该报告由中国社会科学院编写。根据行业的资金投入构成，在工业或服务业领域，信贷资金占全部资金投入的比重约为 70%。如果“三农”领域的资金投入中信贷资金能够达到 65%，则 2014 年的贷款投入需求大约为 8.45 万亿元，而实际农户贷款余额约为 5.4 万亿元。因此，我国“三农”金融的缺口约为 3.05 万亿元。

如果从资金供给的机构结构来看，除农村贷款一项外，传统的农村金融机构依然在农业、农户贷款中发挥着主要作用，这一结论可以从表 4－16 中得出。而农村贷款可能涉及农村的基础设施等投资额较大的项目融资，大中型的金融机构占到了较大的比例。

**表 4－16　2016 年“三农”贷款机构余额及占比**

| | 农业贷款（亿元） | 占比（%） | 农村贷款（亿元） | 占比（%） | 农户贷款（亿元） | 占比（%） |
|---|---|---|---|---|---|---|
| 全国 | 36627 | 100 | 230092 | 100 | 70846 | 100 |
| 农村商业银行 | 12828 | 35.0 | 46107 | 20.0 | 23735 | 33.5 |
| 农村信用合作社 | 10920 | 29.8 | 24712 | 10.7 | 14092 | 19.9 |
| 村镇银行 | 1724 | 4.7 | 4953 | 2.2 | 3234 | 4.6 |
| 农村合作银行 | 730 | 2.0 | 1468 | 0.6 | 989 | 1.4 |
| 合计 | 62829 | 71.5 | 307332 | 33.6 | 112896 | 59.4 |

此外，虽然信贷额相对银行业金融机构较小，但小额贷款公司也是重要的农村金融机构。截至 2018 年 6 月末，全国共有小额贷款公司 8394 家[①]。贷款余额 9763 亿元，上半年增加 22 亿元。

值得指出的是，互联网金融向农村的不断扩展将为农村发展带来新的资金。互联网金融机构广义上应当包括银行业机构、网络小额贷款公司、P2P 网贷、众筹平台等。虽然目前除银行业金融机构外的互联网信贷业务规模较小，但随着农村金融市场的不断扩大以及金融基础设施的不断完善，在未来必然会成为一片“蓝海”市场。

据不完全统计，截至 2017 年末，业内至少有 77 家[②]正常运营的 P2P 网贷平台以农村金融为重要业务，占正常运营平台数量（1539 家）的 5.0%。P2P 涉农贷款历史累计交易规模约 1241 亿元，其中 2017 年信贷余额约 500 亿元，同比增长 11.1%。

从微观角度进行研究，CAFI 通过对东部沿海某市、西部某市的调研活动数据进行分析，发现两地居民在有无银行授信额度、上一年是否申请过贷款的比率上差距较大，但在贷款申请的获批比率上相差并不大（见表 4－17）。

**表 4－17　东部沿海某市、西部某市居民融资情况比较**　　单位：%

| | 东部沿海某市 | 西部某市 |
|---|---|---|
| 有银行授信额度的比率 | 42.8 | 15.5 |
| 上一年申请过银行贷款的比率 | 35.3 | 7.2 |
| 贷款申请获批比率 | 91.3 | 82.6 |

① 资料来源：中国人民银行。
② 资料来源：零壹智库。

## 二、农村金融聚合器的类型

农村金融中，聚合器在现阶段有其存在的必要性。前面我们剖析了农村金融中各种业务的现状，由于中国农村社会、经济、文化、人群的发展能力与城市差别非常大，导致农村金融服务与城市金融服务有很大的不同，很多金融服务必须要通过连接供给、需求双方的聚合器来完成（见图 4－3）。

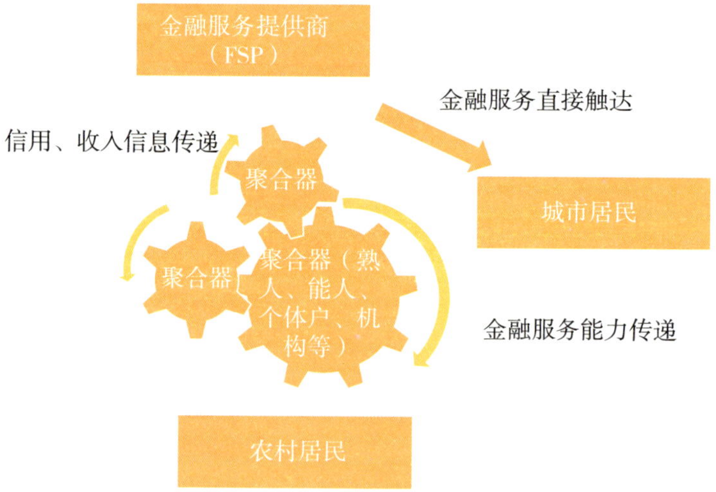


**图 4－3　农村金融聚合器作用**

无论是传统的还是新型的金融机构，通过物理网点的覆盖（平均成本较低）或数据风控能力（收集数据场景繁多），都可以比较有效地服务于城市居民（金融能力相对较高）。与城市居民相对而言，大部分的农村居民（金融能力相对较低）由于其生产、经营、收入、支出、信用状况等金融信息获取难度大（数据场景少），而且在农村地区直接设立服务网点成本高，导致传统及新型金融服务提供商（以下简称金融服务商）都无法有效地通过直接触达的方式为多数农村居民服务。因此，必须依赖金融服务的聚合器来赋能。一方面聚合器赋能于金融服务商，帮助其将服务能力传导到农村居民；另一方面聚合器也赋能于农村居民，在与金融服务商的沟通中获取更多、更好的金融服务。

### （一）村级金融服务站

村级金融服务站或助农取款服务点等农村支付服务是指在中国人民银行的推动下，由当地的金融机构在不适合直接设立综合营业网点的农村地区设立的服务站。

作为一种聚合器，服务站最初的服务内容主要是便利村民的现金存取、汇款，但目前很多的服务站也增添了电子商务的服务功能，帮助实现“工业品下乡，农产品进城”，甚至有些金融服务站与传统的线下零售企业相结合，打造“新零售”项目。浙江农村信用社（以下简称浙江农信社）的丰收驿站是其中的典型代表。

### 专栏 4-1 浙江农信社丰收驿站

丰收驿站事实上是农村金融服务站的“升级版”，是一种“线上线下”相结合的金融服务载体。在业务类型上，可以实现小额存取款、转账、查询及法院案款、非税缴款、电力电信缴费、城乡医保、城乡养老等中间业务签约、缴费的线上自助办理。同时，客户经理会定期在丰收驿站内提供知识普及、业务咨询、贷款受理、客户签约等“一站式”线下服务。

在金融服务之外，丰州驿站整合了其他的农村服务。一是在电商业务方面，挖掘了当地土特优产品的代购代销，助推“工业品进村、农产品进城”。截至 2016 年末，累计网上代购 20.03 万笔、4508 万元，为 1247 家农户网上代销 6.47 万笔、317.87 万元。二是在物流业务方面，与浙江顺丰速运签订战略协议，同期累计代收代发各类快递 23.48 万件。三是在社区服务方面，提供健康体检、电信代办、生鲜配送、信息咨询、社区公益活动等丰富的便民服务，并拓展推出代挂号、代购车票等新业务。四是在政务服务方面，深化政银合作，有效提供低保、落户、建房、办证等各类行政许可事项咨询、代办养老保险等多项综合服务，并与当地组织部、团委、供销社、志愿者联盟等合作，进一步延伸服务内涵。

### 专栏 4-2 丰收驿站·联华小店

浙江农信社与其他商业渠道进行合作，依托原有的“丰收驿站”，打造“新零售”项目，这是浙江农信社充分运用“丰收驿站”的金融服务功能，并拓展其业务范围的一次新尝试。

2017 年 6 月 30 日，浙江建德农商行下涯大洲丰收驿站·联华小店开业，这是浙江农信社丰收驿站与联华超市探索合作运营的首家小店。丰收驿站·联华小店是集金融、实体超市、便民服务于一体的全能型金融服务点，使社区居民、农户不仅在家门口就可以办理小额存取款、代理转账、生活缴费等业务，还享受安全、便捷、实惠的商超服务，有利于更好地推进“农产品进城、工业品进村”。

这种聚合器的优势在于服务站的设立成本较低，不需要依赖太多的技术设备及消耗很多人力成本，依托社区或村内的熟人圈，可以比较好地解决一些基础性的金融服务。但同时由于其架构较为简单，风险控制能力较弱，一些比较复杂的金融业务如贷款等不能直接实现，因而功能较为单一，而且在很多地区的利用率也不是非常高。

### （二）金融服务代理商

农村地区的金融服务代理商主要是与金融服务提供商合作开展支付及快递、电商等服务的个体工商户，如便利店或小超市等，事实上也是一种基础金融服务站，只是由个体工商户进行代理服务，收取少量的服务费。

作为聚合器，在合作过程中，金融服务提供商可以通过这些小型网点扩大其客户基数，如农村信用社或其他银行可以推广其“聚合支付”项目，阿里巴巴、京东等电商可以依托这些网点进行简单的电商服务等。

代理商这种聚合器的优势与劣势与金融服务站基本一致，区别在于其金融服务的规模可能更小一些，因为这些代理商的主营业务在于其零售业务，而非专注于金融及电商服务。

**专栏 4－3　聚合支付**

浙江农信社通过与农村的便利店、小超市合作，将自身的手机银行服务“丰收互联”支付与第三方支付机构（如支付宝支付、微信支付）进行整合，扫描一个二维码可以在多种支付渠道中进行选择，截至 2017 年 9 月底，这种支付方式已经介入医院、学校、交通、菜场、零售业、电商等领域，新型支付商户突破 50 万户。

### （三）农村合作组织

农村合作组织是一个比较广义的概念，包括农业专业合作社、综合合作社、互助资金社、互助担保组织等。

作为聚合器，这些组织本身就是农村居民的一个集合，因此对其区域内的成员信息掌握非常全面，甚至非常精确，这就会对金融服务商进行金融风险控制起到非常关键的作用，它们通过信用、信息传递，赋能于金融服务商及组织成员。但其能力上的薄弱之处主要在于其治理结构，这会限制其服务规模的扩大。

### （四）农村基层组织

农村基层组织主要是指行政村中的村委会、村支部等机构。

这些机构与农村合作组织类似，对农村居民的信息、信用掌握非常到位，但范围更广，可以扩大到全村的范围。另外，其作为村集体组织，更有一定的组织权威性。金融服务商或政府机构通过与其合作，可以极大限度地降低信息不透明及贷后风险。但其缺点与合作组织也是类似的，即治理结构的不完善很容易导致整体风险失控。

（五）农业龙头企业

龙头企业在本书中指的是从事农、林、牧、渔业及农产品加工的企业。农业企业作为聚合器，一方面通过供应链的上下游对农户的核心经营信息有充分的了解，而且在一定程度上对农户的经营有相当的影响力，因此开展供应链金融业务将非常有效；另一方面作为金融服务商向个体农户或合作社提供金融服务的传递者，在为农户或合作社向金融服务商争取更多、更优惠的服务上也能起到一定的作用。

目前，比较典型的农业龙头企业有蒙羊公司、北大荒、新希望集团等，通过与银行、保险公司、担保公司合作，为上下游的供应商及农户、合作社、小型农业公司等提供金融服务。

（六）农村平台企业

除淘宝、京东、苏宁、宜信等大型数字平台外，专业服务于农村的还有类似汇通达等平台企业。

这些农村平台企业的优势在于：通过其服务规模的扩大，可以产生一定的规模及品牌效应，同时积累大量的农业及农民数据，并通过与大的互联网平台合作进一步增强其服务农村金融的作用，起到了“聚合”农村资源与金融资源的作用。

**专栏 4－4　汇通达**

汇通达网络股份有限公司（以下简称汇通达），总部位于南京，成立于 2010 年。汇通达以会员制形式整合乡镇夫妻店，通过赋能乡镇夫妻店（会员店），使其成为“互联网化＋数据化＋服务化＋生态化”的本地化“店商＋电商”服务平台，构建全新的农村流通服务体系。让农民客户“买得好”、少花钱；帮助会员店高效经营农民家庭资源，让农民客户“卖得好”、多挣钱。

截至 2018 年 5 月，汇通达网络覆盖全国 19 个省、16000 多个乡镇，服务 92000 多家乡镇会员店，带动 50 多万名农民创业就业，服务网络惠及 7000 多万户农民家庭。2017 年实现销售 235 亿元（2016 年销售 160 亿元）[①]。

① 资料来源：汇通达网站。

### （七）金融监管机构搭建的平台

在一些普惠金融改革试验区内，当地的金融监管机构也在尝试搭建平台，为金融机构及金融服务需求方“牵线搭桥”，成为一种较为新颖的聚合器。

这种聚合器的优势在于其拥有一些需求方的“强关系”数据，同时对金融机构有很强的影响力，此外还有一定的政府影响力，因此其搭建的平台可使供需双方更快地达成交易。

典型的案例有河南省兰考县推出的“普惠金融一网通”（普惠通 APP），该平台是由人民银行郑州中心支行主导建设的具有普惠性质的公共平台，综合了农村居民的信用信息集金融机构的金融业务于一身，将完全实行市场化运营。我们将在下文中进行详细分析。

## 三、金融聚合器的应用模式

前面我们提到农村金融服务的实现形式大部分都要依赖于某种或几种聚合器。而在商业实践中，农村金融服务的实现形式或“触达”模式在不同地区、不同机构、不同人群中会各有不同，依赖的聚合器类型不同，会产生不同的商业模式。本书绪论中所提到的打通农村金融“最后一公里”的各种模式在实践中也并非绝对独立，多数机构采用几种模式综合提供金融服务。

### （一）直营（含金融服务站）+代理+数字模式

作为银行业机构中提供农村金融服务最直接也最多的机构，信用社系统积累了众多的服务“三农”的经验，同时也顺应金融技术的发展开展了数字金融服务，通过金融服务站、线下代理商、合作商户等聚合器，构建自身的服务生态，通过多种途径及模式触达客户，成为打通“最后一公里”服务的重要金融机构。

浙江农信社在不断的金融改革中逐步建立起服务于省域的金融服务生态系统，通过直营（银行网点+村级综合金融服务点）+代理（聚合支付）+数字（电商平台+手机银行）等多种途径触达客户，实施了“社区金融+互联网金融”的双轮驱动经营战略，可以用图 4-4 简要说明。

1. 直营

这是最传统的触及客户的方式。截至 2017 年 9 月底，浙江省农信联社共有 81 家[①]

① 资料来源：浙江农信社。

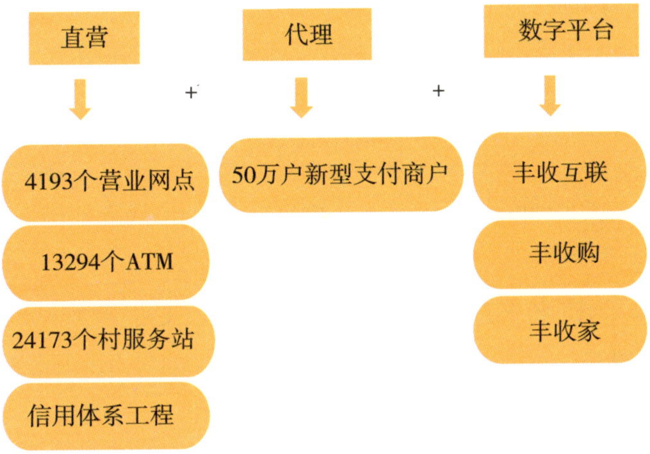


**图 4-4　浙江农信社"最后一公里"解决方案**

县级法人机构（其中农村信用联社 14 家、农村合作银行 5 家、农村商业银行 62 家）、4193 个营业网点。

在社区基础金融服务上，布设了 ATM 13294 台、村级金融服务点 24173 个，其中有 5785 家聚集了金融、电商、物流、公益、政务等综合服务于一体的"丰收驿站"；在信贷服务上，推出了"普惠快车""小微专车""企业直通车"等一系列产品；同时开展整村授信、移动办贷，发展农村小额信用贷款，余额达 2405 亿元，占同期总贷款余额的 20%（同期各项贷款余额 11878.30 亿元）；开展信用卡消费金融，余额 551 亿元。

浙江农信社依托农村金融服务体系，逐步构建农村的信用信息数据库，打造信用村、信用镇，营造良好的信用环境，有效降低信用风险。利用其庞大的农村金融服务员工群体（截至 2017 年 9 月底，浙江农信社有 5.35 万名员工），浙江农信社评定的信用户有 872 万户，占浙江全省农户的 74%；信用村（社区）1.79 万个，占全省行政村的 61%；信用乡（镇、街道）455 个，占全省乡镇的 34%，A 级以上农民专业合作社 2.1 万个。相比全国水平而言，信用体系建设是较为领先的。

2. 数字平台

浙江农信社在发展互联网金融上也是不遗余力，创新推出新一代手机银行"丰收互联"以及电商平台"丰收购""丰收家"。截至 2017 年 9 月底，手机银行用户达 920 万户，电商平台用户达 250 万户。此外，浙江农信社还积极利用大数据风控技术，推出了纯互联网信贷"浙里贷"。

**专栏 4－5 "丰收购""丰收家""浙里贷"**

"丰收购"是浙江农信社于 2015 年 6 月推出的以浙江本地名特优农副产品为主、实现销售、购买、支付结算、消费金融等功能为一体的金融电子商务平台。截至 2017 年 10 月底，"丰收购"电商平台共有注册用户 198.6 万人，完成交易笔数 237.9 万笔，交易金额 10018.8 万元。

"丰收家"于 2015 年 7 月上线试运营，是一个以支付（收单）为基础、以商户为主要服务对象的综合商户服务平台。截至 2017 年 10 月 31 日，注册客户数 68.74 万人，交易笔数 105.79 万笔，交易金额 9757.81 万元。

"浙里贷"是浙江农信社一款线上信用贷款，客户无须抵押担保、无须到银行网点当面签约，只需在手机上进行操作，贷款就能"秒级"到账，最高额度为 50 万元。

3. 与其他超级平台链接的可能性

目前浙江农信社金融服务已经初步在浙江省内形成了一个生态系统。当然在很多服务上，也许还可以与外部大平台进行合作，共享各方的信息与技术资源。例如，在信用体系建设方面，浙江农信社目前接入了国家发展改革委牵头建设的"信用中国"数据平台；在数字化信贷技术上，也许可以探索与其他更加成熟的互联网金融平台进行合作。例如，输入根据大数据模型建设的风控能力，共享信用信息，从而提高服务能力、降低风险、扩大信贷服务范围等。

### （二）依托数据化能力，塑造平台化的农村金融新模式

一些互联网平台企业在农村金融市场的渗透实践过程中，由于农村与城市在市场、社会关系的区别非常大，新型的互联网企业正在从最早的纯线上、大数据模型风控向线下数据采集、与农村金融服务各类聚合器合作的方向发展。在这个过程中，借助农村各类机构的优势，实现了双方的资源优化配置，即"线上＋线下"的信息互补，风险控制措施互补，这可能是解决农村金融的一个重要方向。这种依托数据化能力、以平台化角色与农村机构合作，为农村家庭及小微经营者服务的模式我们可以用图 4－5 进行简单描述。

这种模式的典型代表是蚂蚁金服。作为农村金融市场的积极参与者，蚂蚁金服正在通过多种途径向农村市场进行渗透。为缓解农村金融中的风险防控和客群触达两大难题，蚂蚁金服等金融科技企业积极探索依托数据化能力、打造平台化的农村金融新

**图 4-5　互联网平台企业的农村金融“最后一公里”解决方案**

模式。其中，数据化能力运用科技创新有效解决信息不对称问题，有效增强风险管理能力，并可进一步下探授信准入人群；平台化模式则整合各方数据优势，打通农村价值链，进一步增强风险甄别能力，并且与涉农龙头企业、农村金融机构、县域政府、其他农村机构等合作拓宽服务群体，形成合力共同推动普惠金融发展。主要的模式我们可以用图 4-6 简要说明。

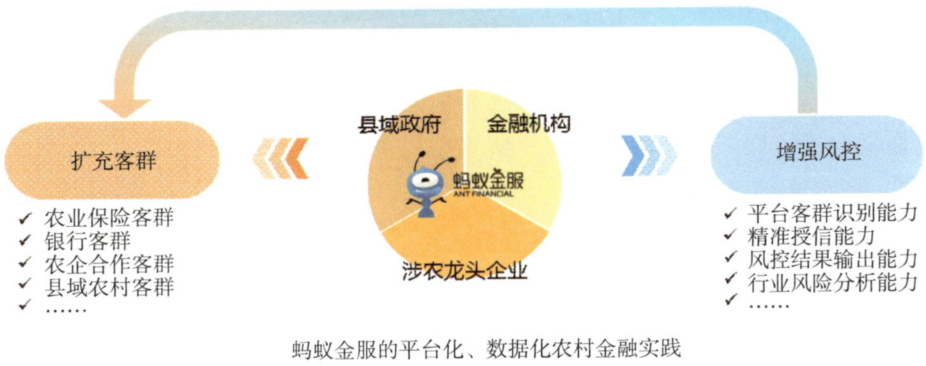


**图 4-6　蚂蚁金服的农村金融实践**

具体而言，蚂蚁金服及网商银行在数据化、平台化方面的实践如下。

1. 通过数据化能力有效管理信贷风险，并进一步下探客群，满足农村消费者和小型经营者的碎片化信贷需求

2016 年，蚂蚁金服针对农村消费者和小型经营者提供基于数据化预授信模式的信贷服务。这一群体客户基数大，单笔资金需求小，数据化预授信模式将大数据技术运用于风险授信决策，为这类客户提供无须抵押物担保的“310”信贷服务（客户花 3 分钟在线申请，1 秒钟资金到账，全程 0 人工干预）。

在贷前阶段，蚂蚁金服通过大数据技术建立含有农户多层风险分级的授信模型；在贷后阶段，蚂蚁金服对风控策略进行有效性追踪分析，并及时收集和反馈农户的支用和还款信息，实现贷后有效管理的同时，根据实际业务数据修正预授信模型，进一步下探授信准入人群。

通过这种方式，蚂蚁金服可以直接触达农村家庭及小微型经营者，为其提供支付、理财、信贷、保险等各种金融服务。

2. 通过平台化开放大数据风控能力，整合蚂蚁金服与聚合器的数据优势，在风险防控中产生互补价值，拓宽信贷服务客群

蚂蚁金服在农村金融过程中，逐步积累大数据风险防控能力，从自营逐步走向平台化模式，与涉农龙头企业、金融机构和县域政府、其他农村机构（如农村淘宝服务站的合伙人）等这些农村金融服务的聚合器合作，极大地提升信贷风险防控能力，并拓宽平台的信贷服务客群。

（1）通过平台化与涉农龙头企业合作。

从 2016 年开始，蚂蚁金服联合农业龙头企业，为其上游种植、养殖户提供产融信贷服务和销售渠道。

在贷前阶段，蚂蚁金服联合农业龙头企业采用多维度数据分析上游种植、养殖户的经营状况和信用状况，并根据其偿债能力实现智能化的授信额度决策；在贷中阶段，蚂蚁金服打造贷款资金定向支付系统，不直接发放现金，而是将贷款打入支付账户并用于电商平台上定向购买农资农具，确保贷款资金的“专款专用”；在贷后阶段，蚂蚁金服不仅通过大数据跟踪养殖户经营状况和风险状况，同时由龙头企业收购农产品并利用电商平台进行推广销售，锁定客户销售渠道的同时控制还款来源，为资金回笼提供保障。

**案例：蚂蚁金服与安徽强英鸭业集团合作服务上游养殖户**

安徽强英鸭业集团是我国第三大肉鸭龙头企业，是“周黑鸭”和“绝味”等品牌供货商。蚂蚁金服通过“数据化产融模式”在一个月内，向强英鸭业上游 142 户肉鸭养殖户发放用于购买鸭苗、饲料等农资的专项贷款近 3000 万元贷款。

2018年3月，安徽省宿州市泗县瓦房乡吴宅村的周道菊就收到蚂蚁金服发放的21万元贷款。周道菊是强英集团的合作养殖户。目前的养殖规模是一年出栏量90000只鸭子，可以赚20万～30万元，同时家里还种了6亩小麦，有一定的收入来源。为了扩建鸭棚和修缮周围的路面，周道菊在银行贷过款，但手续较为烦琐，需要别人帮忙。而目前只要在手机上就可以申请到蚂蚁金服的贷款，从而满足生产生活需要。

（2）通过平台化与金融机构合作。

不少中小金融机构，尤其是在农村地区的金融机构，在服务“三农”金融服务方面有丰富的经验，并且有线下触达优势，但受制于传统手段，效率低、成本高、风控难，只能服务农村市场的少数大客户，客户群体不能有效扩大。而蚂蚁金服作为科技公司，有较强的大数据风险防控技术和经验。正是这样的双方对互补性资源的需求，才使得传统金融机构与数字金融机构开展了合作。蚂蚁金服为金融机构提供了账户体系、风控能力、数据处理能力；金融机构发挥自己线下优势，帮助农户接触和了解互联网，实现在线数据积累，完善用户画像，以便得到更合理的授信服务，让农户轻松享受到信用贷款服务。

**案例：蚂蚁金服与桂林银行合作“线上＋线下”信贷模式**

目前，桂林银行与蚂蚁金服已经探索出一条“线上＋线下”优势结合的道路，利用数据风控的农业信贷新模式，设计以小额、批量、信用、线上为特点的融资产品，借助各级政府、农资供应商、核心企业，精准对特定区域、产业、人群进行信贷投入，实现了规模化授信，助力政府实现农业产业政策和精准扶贫，帮助更多农户高效、便捷地获得现代化的金融服务。目前，桂林银行和蚂蚁金服合作的“旺农贷”产品已经累计放款超过3.5亿元，服务农户超过2万户。

**案例：蚂蚁金服与中和农信合作“线上＋线下”信贷模式**

2016年6月，蚂蚁金服宣布与中国扶贫基金会下的中和农信达成战略合作意向，开展“互联网＋保险＋小额信贷”模式。双方的合作把农村贷款搬到了“网上”，让村民像城里人一样拥有了享受金融服务的基础——信用画像。此后，有借有还、再借不难。同时，利用蚂蚁的大数据AI（人工智能）能力、安全保护机制和互联网思维，帮助中和农信提升线上运营能力和安全风控能力。

中和农信一贯专注农村，而农村人口的数据相对匮乏。针对这种情况，蚂蚁特别为其定制研发了配套算法，能在小数据样本上完成算法训练，比较精准地预测贷款风险。这套算法在前期测试阶段将风控效果提升了整整一倍。虽然蚂蚁的AI能力在中和农信的实际业务运用上刚刚起步，但也取得了不错的效果，成为其重要的风控依据。

与此同时，蚂蚁金服的互联网思维，也在影响和帮助中和农信逐步完成互联网化改造，一个重要的标志就是获客和运营方式从线下走向线上，在降低成本的同时风险也得到了更有效控制。比如，蚂蚁金服的大数据 AI 能力，不仅可以帮助中和农信建立预测模型和甄别真实的线上申请，还能最大限度地提高授信的自动化程度。

（3）通过平台化支持县域政府推进普惠金融发展。

蚂蚁金服旗下网商银行运用长期积累的技术和经验，协助县域政府建立“区域专属授信模型”，基于政府在行政行为和公共服务过程中产生的数据，为农户提供无抵押、免担保的纯信用贷款，支持农户生产经营，同样实现了“310”信贷模式，人均贷款额度 1000～200000 元不等。

**案例：蚂蚁金服支持内乡县普惠金融发展**

河南省内乡县是网商银行落地县域普惠金融模式的第一个县。随着当地农业经济的发展，传统模式下的金融服务越来越难以覆盖农户“额小、高频、快速”的资金需求。面对此类需求，内乡县政府希望金融机构能够推出一款“覆盖面广、纯信用无抵押、即时放款、可多次循环”的信贷产品，解决县政府面临的农村金融供给侧难题。

2017 年 12 月，网商银行与内乡县政府合作，推出了面向内乡县农户的“县域大数贷”产品。农户在申贷授权后，网商银行通过对土地确权、农业补贴等涉农数据的调用，结合网商银行体系内的大数据，实现对农户的精确识别、精准画像、自动授信。大数贷产品，由于农户信贷申请、支用和还款全部在支付宝 APP 上完成，无须提供任何纸质材料，真正实现了农民足不出户即能享受的“7×24 小时”贴身信贷服务。自上线至今，已经有数千名内乡农户通过该产品得到资金支持，用于农业生产生活。

内乡县当地农民杨冠军回乡后准备扩大家中的果园生产规模，为此需要一笔资金。他曾多次申请贷款，却由于没有抵押担保被拒绝。当县域普惠金融服务在当地上线后，他通过支付宝在线申请，马上就获得了贷款。

截至 2018 年 2 月底，蚂蚁金服为全国 9161 万户“三农”用户提供信贷支持，其中包括 303.3 万名涉农经营者，经营类贷款累放金额达到 2673.5 亿元，经营类贷款余额达到 238.6 亿元。

这种数据化、平台化的“线上＋线下”相结合的模式，通过互联网自身的能力与农村金融服务的聚合器进行合作，使普通农户和小微涉农企业都能获得较为平等、便捷的信贷支持，这可能代表着农村金融发展的一个趋势性方向。

### （三）互联网金融＋公益小额贷款机构/农村信用社＋农户

基于互联网平台的金融公益模式在国内比较少见。作为互联网金融的代表机构之一，宜信集团在 2009 年推出了宜农贷这一公益助农平台。这一平台的基本模式可以用图 4－7 简要说明。

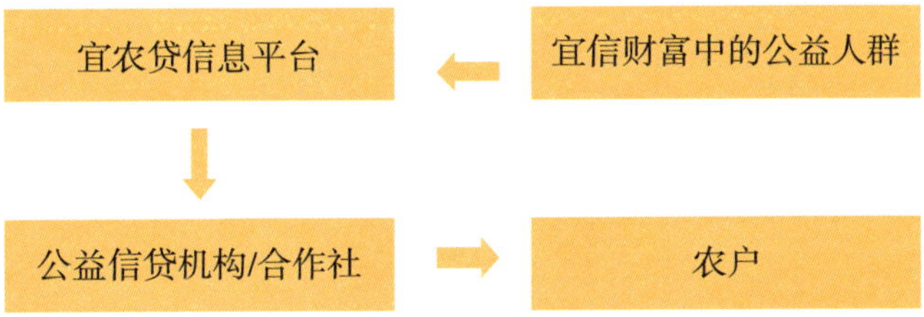


**图 4-7　宜信农村金融“最后一公里”的公益解决方案**

宜信通过其体系内的两大平台：宜信财富与宜信普惠，同时与农村的公益性小额贷款机构或合作社（聚合器）进行合作，通过宜农贷这个信息平台，具有公益意愿的高净值人群可以帮助农户。在这个过程中，宜信财富的公益人士只收取2%的回报，宜农贷平台收取1%的服务费，公益性小额贷款机构或合作社收取少量服务费，承担放款及收款的责任，因此到达农户的信贷资金的成本很低，是一种纯公益性质的信贷产品。

通过宜农贷平台，目前共有172435位公益人士资助了26022户农户，资助金额超过3亿元，基本没有出现过坏账。这种公益与互联网金融相结合的方式，比较好地实现了助农金融服务的目的。

### （四）G2B2C数字模式（监管机构与金融机构合作为农村居民提供服务）

河南省兰考县作为国家级的普惠金融服务试验区，目前正在探索综合金融服务体系的建设，助力乡村发展。目前，兰考探索出了通过互联网金融的模式，结合金融机构与政府掌握的农户信息数据，开展综合性的金融服务。

从模式上看，这是一种政府监管机构发起的普惠金融服务模式，通过聚合金融机构，最终触达客户。该服务模式主要是通过互联网或移动平台“普惠通”完成的（见图4-8）。

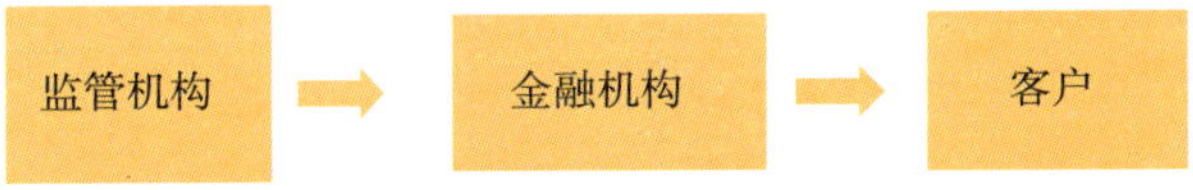


**图 4-8　兰考普惠金融试验区的“最后一公里”解决方案**

“普惠通”手机应用软件是依托于由中国人民银行郑州中心支行发起的“普惠金融一网通”项目。该项目于2017年10月上线，致力于为农民、小镇居民、个体工商户等弱势群体提供相关服务的移动信息服务产品，旨在为用户提供普惠授信、账户管家、金融超市等一系列信息技术服务，并通过协助用户在线申请“普惠授信”等产品，生成完整的个人数据，以最终实现信用体系建设的目标。

截至 2017 年 12 月底，河南省普惠金融一网通平台注册用户量接近 100 万户①，兰考县近 4.5 万户，“普惠通” APP 兰考县下载量超过 1 万户；平台上可以支付近 300 个生活缴费项目，涵盖水、电、气、暖、通信等民生领域，累计办理各类业务 13 万笔，交易金额超过 1 亿元。

目前服务过程中存在的问题包括基础信用体系建设问题、金融机构的积极性问题、APP 的用户体验问题等，都需要进一步的改进。

### （五）互助模式

农村居民可以通过互助形式在一定范围内实现生产、信贷、担保等目的，从而有效降低风险，进而获得外部金融机构的资金支持。在实践中有很多互助模式。

1. 村民互助资金会

村民互助资金会是农村居民通过互助形式，将原先的个人资金转换为“集体资金”，调剂给有资金需求的农户，从而达到资金配置的目的，我们也可以称为线下的 C2C 模式。

2. 村民互助担保

村级互助担保组织，我们也可以称为线下的 C2C2B 模式。农村居民通过互助担保，将个体信用转换为“集体信用”，这样就可以降低融资风险，借此达到有效吸引银行或其他外部资本进行融资的目的。在这个过程中，互助担保组织就是一种金融聚合器。这种担保除了以村民间的信用担保外，在一些农村产权制度改革的试验地区，还推出了“互助担保 + 反担保”模式，反担保就是获得贷款的村民以其土地经营权、房屋财产权向村级组织进行担保，进而获得村级组织向银行等机构进行担保的权利。

这两种模式在进行农村金融改革的浙江东部沿海某市都有具体的表现形式，我们做如下简要介绍。

**案例：东部沿海某市村民资金互助与担保互助**

第一，村民互助资金会。东部沿海某市选择产业基础较好、村两委组织能力较强、村民信用较好的村组建资金互助会，为农户提供资金互助服务，满足农村多样化融资需求，填补商业金融、政策性金融的服务空间。截至 2017 年末，东部沿海某市共有 408 个扶贫重点村组建了资金互助会，数量居浙江省第一位，占全市扶贫重点村总数的 26%，累计有入会农户 2.85 万户，其中低收入农户 1.05 万户，占比为 36.8%；互助会共有资金本 8390 万元，累计发放借款 2.2 亿元，借款农户 1.2 万户次，其中低收入农户占 1/3，呆账坏账率为零。

---

① 资料来源：河南省人民政府印发的《河南省兰考县普惠金融改革试验区运行报告（2017）》，2017 年。

第二，村级互助担保组织。该组织是为本村农户提供贷款担保服务的非营利性组织，坚持“担保自组、入社自由、借款自主、用款自律、服务自助、守信自励”的发展理念，由具备一定经济条件的村民委员会或村经济合作社牵头设立，担保基金一般由农户（社员）、村集体出资以及政府拨入的引导资金共同构成并存入合作的金融机构，合作的金融机构按最高不超过担保金的10倍向农户发放贷款。村级互助担保组织，为农户贷款提供担保，同时农户以林权、农房、土地流转经营权等提供反担保。贷款农户一旦出现逾期未还的情况，由合作的金融机构和担保组织共同追索，如追索无果，则由担保组织先行代偿债务，并在一定区域内处置、流转贷款农户的反担保资产。

通过设立村级担保组织，以“产权+村级担保”形式开展农村产权抵押贷款，有效发挥村集体资产可在村内流转、村干部对抵押物资产价值信息对称的优势，在规避农村产权抵押贷款法律障碍、解决不良贷款处置难问题方面取得了积极成效。这种做法既有效拓宽了农户融资渠道，还较好地解决了农村产权抵押特别是农房和土地经营权“两权”抵押贷款过程中的确权发证、价值评估、流转处置、风险管控四大难题。对银行来说，农村产权的“资产专用性”较高，流动性较差，价值较低，而对于村内的村民或者合作社而言，农村产权就是其经营的同质产品，因此有较高的价值，从而会提升农村资产的流动性。

截至2017年末，全市已建成村级互助担保组织202家，累计为农户提供担保11.49亿元。

3. 村两委主导的扶贫资金+互助资金协会

在农村的社会组织中，村委、村党委成员一般是村里的能人，有较强的组织与协调能力。在农村金融的实践中，这些村里的精英人员会根据与当地政府的政策，结合本村实际，创造性地推出一些符合本村的措施。

西部某市就根据村民实践，推出了“支部+协会”的扶贫滚动至今，最近距离地服务于村民。在这种模式中，“支部”事实上是一种聚合器。

**案例：兰州市榆中县的“支部+协会”村级发展互助资金**

兰州市最初的“支部+协会”的做法出自榆中县中连川乡中连川村。村支书白元智说起当初成立互助资金的缘由：2007年的时候甘肃省扶贫办给村里奖励10万元，县财政给了10万元扶贫款，但这些资金应当如何使用才能更加有效？白元智认为，与其把这些钱一次性发给村民，不如将其滚动起来，有需求的村民可以借款，这样钱就多起来了，就可以办更多的事，于是村党支部研究决定把这20万元作为全村发展资金，让其有效运转起来。

之后，中连川村注册成立了具有独立法人资格的“村级发展互助资金协会”，制定了协会章程，规定以“五户联保”的方式为有需要的村民借钱，为致富好项目提供资金支持。如今，中连川村的互助资金已经累计发放借款 168.5 万元，累计收回借款本金 103.5 万元，切实解决了农户发展生产资金短缺的问题。

榆中县贫困村“村级发展互助资金”试点项目自 2008 年启动以来，截至 2017 年 12 月，已在 23 个乡镇、263 个行政村注册成立了扶贫互助社，资金总规模达到 10396.7 万元，资金机构如下：财政专项扶贫资金 5155 万元，市级配套资金 710 万元，县级财政配套 1410 万元，农户缴纳 189 万元，占用费补充本金 115 万元，其他 2817 万元，每个协会都成立了理事会和监事会。入社农户达到 19519 户，借款余额 5310 万元，有 5084 户借款，户均 1 万元左右。

4. 农村综合性合作社的内部信用合作模式

农村的专业合作社随着其生产规模的扩大，在社员内部会自然产生融资需求与供给。在一些自下而上发展起来的农村合作组织中，社员内的信用互助有显著不同于纯资金互助的资金会的特点。在这种合作模式中，山西的蒲韩乡村社区具有典型的代表意义。

**案例：综合合作基础上的信用互助**

蒲韩乡村社区位于山西省永济市，目前覆盖蒲州、韩阳两个镇，43 个自然村，社区共有 3865 个农户，提供的服务触达近 26000 人，占到两个乡镇人口的 58%左右。其主要方案如图 4－9 所示。

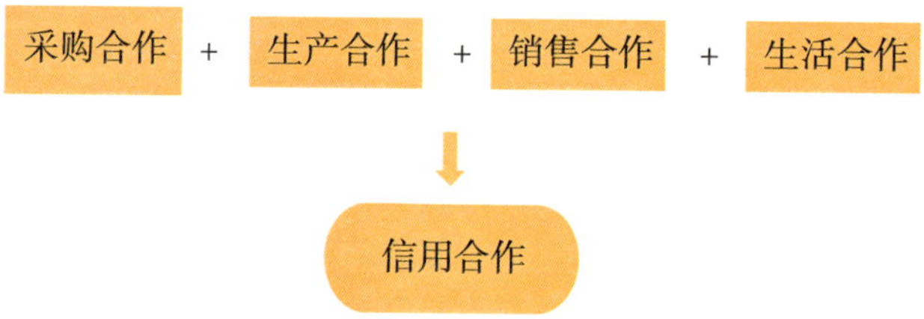


**图 4－9　兰考普惠金融试验区的“最后一公里”解决方案**

蒲韩乡村社区的承载主体是“蒲韩种植（养殖）专业合作联合社”，联合社有九大业务板块，分别是农业技术培训、土壤生态转化、农资统购、日用品统购、城乡互动、资金互助、手工艺、老人服务、儿童服务，已经是一种集于经济和社会生活于一身的综合服务组织。

这九大业务板块可以再次区分为采购合作（农资、日用品统购）、生产合作（土壤生态转化）、销售合作（城乡互动）、生活合作（农业技术培训、手工艺、老人及儿童服务），在所有这些生产、生活服务的基础上，自然衍生出了信用合作服务。

这种信用合作服务一般会比较稳固，风险相对较低，因为信用合作基于综合性的互助，这种互助模式对身处其中的社员会产生综合性的收益，因此信用违约带来的成本就不仅仅是单笔的资金损失，还会给生活的各个环节带来不可低估的损失，是一种综合性的成本。

截至2016年末，社区信用互助的贷款余额约为4200万元。其资金来源主要是：土地股金750万元，流动股金900万元，其他社会资本3000万元左右。在这里，合作社就作为一种金融服务的聚合器而存在。

社区内的资金互助具有明显的普惠性质，这主要体现在以下几个方面：纯信用贷款，无须抵押和担保；提前还款不需要缴纳违约金；借贷成本低。社区借贷额度利率的具体级别划分，如表4-18所示。

**表4-18　蒲韩乡村社区信用互助贷款额度及利率**

| 月利率 | 0 | 0.5% | 0.81% | 1.3% | 1.5% | 1.5% | 1.5% |
|---|---|---|---|---|---|---|---|
| 期限 | 3个月 | 1年 | 1年 | 1年 | 1年 | 1年 | 1年 |
| 额度 | 2000元 | 2000～5000元 | 5000～10000元 | 10000～20000元 | 20000～30000元 | 30000～50000元 | 50000～100000元 |

相比于其他很多农村金融机构的单一利率，这种梯度设计的利率及期限结构也显示了很大的普惠性。可以看出，该设计倾向于对小额短期贷款的社员进行利率优惠甚至免息。

此外，资金互助社的大部分利润会返还社区。资金互助部门及其他经济业务部门的利润将按照如下方式进行分配：60%在三年内返还给社员，30%提为公益金，10%作为社区团队的激励。利润返还一般不以现金形式，而是用于引导社员的消费，比如有的社员修了很好的房子，却不注重卫生，返还款就用于给他家修厕所①。30%比例的公益金多用于为老人、为儿童启蒙教育、为农业技术培训学校提供公共服务。

5. 容易出现的问题及与其他平台合作的潜力

合作社内部的信用合作、村民的互助资金、互助担保在信用合作及互相担保过程中，由于其组织较为松散、治理结构不完善、规模较小、风险控制技术较为薄弱等原因，可能会出现种种问题。而这些问题，通过与外部的机构与平台合作，可以得到消除或缓解。如通过与银行签订资金的托管协议，可以监测资金的流动，与银行或其他平台合作开展信用信息、生产信息等，可以有效地缓解信用信息、产业链信息不透明带来的融资困难问题。此外，与规范的机构进行合作事实上也是一种金融教育的过程。

① 根据蒲韩社区调研访谈资料整理。

## 四、问题及建议

我们总结了目前农村中各种金融服务的具体模式，可以看到，聚合器在其中发挥了重要的“桥梁”作用，金融服务提供商依据地区及自身掌握的资源，通过对农村金融需求者的分析，对资源进行优化组合，形成了各自的比较优势，但同时也存在着各自的局限性。

### （一）传统农村金融服务机构

传统的农村金融服务机构主要是指农信系统、合作社、村民互助组织等。这些机构扎根于农村，熟悉农业、农村、农户，掌握很多“三农”的信息，但这些机构存在着如下的局限性。

第一，治理结构相对较弱。机构的治理结构在经营、风险控制上会起到非常重要的作用，如果没有较好的治理结构，其经营业绩及风控都会受到影响。

第二，资金规模较小，服务范围相对较窄。除信用社系统外，无论是合作社，还是村民互助机构，在资金规模以及服务人群方面范围都是较小的。

第三，数据风控能力较弱。传统的信用社系统具有线下的风控能力，但其基于农村居民生活数据的风控能力较弱，而其他合作性质的机构则在线上、线下的风控能力都比较薄弱。

### （二）新型农村金融服务机构

新型的农村金融服务机构，一般是指互联网金融机构，它们具有触达面广、成本较低、数据风控能力较强的特点，但在农村金融的实践中，相应地也有一些薄弱之处。

第一，农村市场不同于城市，仅仅有客户的线上数据并不能产生较好的数据风控模型，而线下数据的获得则比较困难。

第二，农村的社会关系与城市不同，没有当地机构的合作，金融服务的风险较大。

第三，新型机构在农村市场的触角较少，因此产生的线上数据也比较少，进一步限制了其金融服务的能力。

### （三）利用聚合器的“桥梁”作用，金融服务提供商之间的融合合作是解决农村地区“最后一公里”的有效途径

事实上，从前面分析中我们已经可以看到，线上的金融服务机构已经开始与一些农村机构开展合作，线下的金融机构也开始寻求线上的客户，但双方都是有能力局限

性的，而通过具体分析其能力结构，双方存在着潜在的、多方面的合作可能性，在支付、信用体系建设、信贷、保险、理财业务上都可以通过合作达到共赢。比如，如何打通信息孤岛，共同服务于当地的农村居民，这是需要政府、机构、金融服务需求者共同协作才能完成的任务。而从根本上来说，金融服务应当依托于具体产业，真正使金融服务在乡村振兴过程中服务于当地的农民，而非被其他社会资本利用造成进一步的分化与农民的资源被剥夺。这也是需要政府引导、市场主导、农村居民的能力提升等多方努力才能实现的局面。总之，线上与线下融合，新型与传统机构融合，利用各种聚合器进行合作，这是解决农村金融“最后一公里”问题的必经之路。

# 案　例　善用金融聚合器<br>锻造多方共赢普惠金融服务

虽然金融聚合器是国际上近年才延伸运用到金融领域的新概念，但宜信早在2009年就开始尝试探索金融聚合器的雏形，用于连接“最后一公里”的“中小微弱”群体。目前，针对“最后一公里”的贫困地区或农村地区的妇女、农业经营主体、牧场等几类典型的“中小微弱”群体，宜信进行了公益性和商业性两种数字金融服务的尝试，积累了攻坚“最后一公里”的宝贵经验。

宜信专注于贫困地区或农村地区的业务平台主要有两个：一是公益型的宜农贷平台；二是商业型的宜信租赁平台。

## 一、小额贷款业务的金融聚合器工作模式与成效

宜农贷的定位是公益助农平台。出借人都是社会爱心人士，他们提供借款并不是为了获取高额利息，而是支持借款人发展生产、改善生活；宜农贷的目标客户则是贫困地区或农村地区的20～60岁的妇女，她们大多有很强的家庭责任感，渴望改善家庭生活，且具备一定的生产技能。出借人的助贫助困目标，以及借款人的脱贫脱困目标，在宜农贷平台上得以实现。

在宜农贷的产品或服务链条中，很好地引入小额信贷机构（小贷公司、扶贫协会、合作社）作为金融聚合器，它们大多扎根贫困地区或农村地区，对乡土人情、目标客户都比较了解。如图1所示，从出借人、宜农贷平台、小额信贷机构到借款人之间形成了一条纽带，他们各取所需、各自获益。

第一，出借人出于公益目标，为借款人提供资金，在借款人按期还款之后，还能获得一笔2%的利息。

第二，作为金融信息服务中介的宜农贷平台，其主要工作职责是专心为出借人和借款人提供撮合服务、改进风控模式，以及维护平台的可持续运营等，仅收取1%的

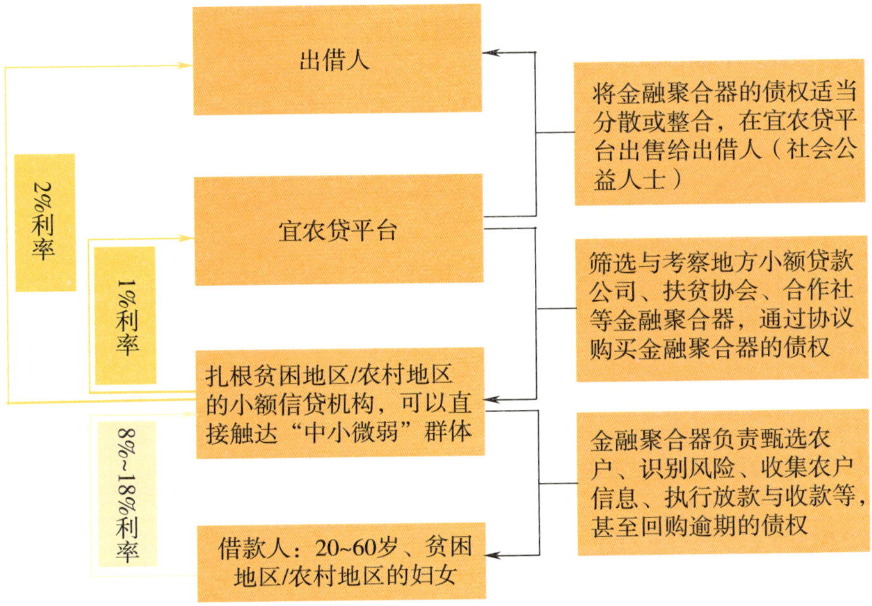


**图1　农村小额信贷机构作为金融聚合器的工作模式**

利息作为服务费。

第三，作为金融聚合器的小额信贷机构，其主要工作职责是充分利用自身的在地资源，负责甄选农户、识别风险、收集农户信息、执行放款与收款，甚至还要承担回购逾期债权等。在借款人按期还款之后，小额信贷机构可以获得5%～15%的利息，用于维持机构运营。借款人和宜农贷平台把大部分利息留在了小额信贷机构，除了入户服务成本高的原因之外，还有意帮助小额信贷机构实现同步发展。

第四，借款人获得借款后，通过劳动、生产、经营，获得一定收益，按期还款之后，还能有盈余用于改善生活。

可见，将宜农贷平台的小额贷款业务引入农村小额信贷机构作为金融聚合器的工作模式，实现了四方共赢的局面：出借人在实现公益目标的同时，还能获得小笔利息；宜农贷平台既实现风险可控，又节约了触达目标客户的成本；小额信贷机构通过与宜农贷平台的合作，可以赢得机构财务可持续的机会；借款人在获得最急需的贷款之后，也获得改善家庭生活状况的机会。

自2009年起，被宜农贷平台选为金融聚合器的小额信贷机构共22家；有爱心助农人士172481位，为26093名农户提供307359300.63元资助；出于对出借人爱心款的保护，宜农贷平台和小额信贷机构对于借款人的筛选比较严格，因此，宜农贷平台一直保持零逾期。从扩大受益面的角度来看，宜农贷平台的风控模式还可以进一步放开，面向更多的农村妇女。

## 二、租赁业务的金融聚合器工作模式与成效

宜信租赁平台于2012年创立，研发了农机租赁（农租宝）和活体租赁（宜定牛）两款符合“最后一公里”农业生产需求的普惠金融产品。其中，农机种类包括田间到餐桌，覆盖耕、种、管、收、烘干、储藏、加工全产业链的各种设备；活体种类目前主要以奶牛为主，还在论证奶羊、果树的租赁可能性。

在农租宝的产品链条中，宜信租赁平台引入农机经销商作为金融聚合器，而宜定牛则引入了奶业协会、畜牧局、饲料厂等作为金融聚合器。这些金融聚合器与有承租需求的农民、农业经营主体，或者符合一定条件的牧场之间，有着比较紧密的联系，如买卖关系。因此，金融聚合器对承租人的需求、还款意愿、还款能力等比较了解。如图2所示，金融聚合器把宜信租赁平台与承租人连接起来，他们各自承担责任，也相应地获益。

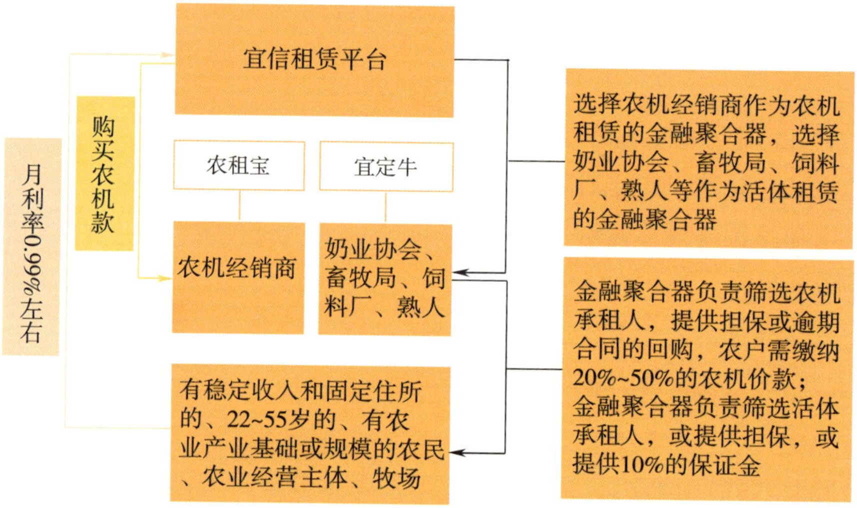


**图2　农机经销商、奶业协会、畜牧局、饲料厂等作为金融聚合器的工作模式**

第一，宜信租赁平台为承租人提供融资租赁服务，先将农机或活体购买下来，再租给承租人。承租人只需支付少部分首付，就可以先行使用农机或养殖活体，并获得收益。待承租人按期还款之后，宜信租赁平台再将农机或活体的所有权转让给承租人。

第二，作为金融聚合器的农机经销商，与宜信租赁平台建立合作之后，之前赊销给承租人的资金可以立刻回款；在整个链条中，农机经销商要承担筛选农户、提供担保的责任；如果遇到逾期情况发生，还要回购农机，进行二次销售。作为金融聚合器的奶业协会、畜牧局、饲料厂，甚至是熟人，可以为宜信租赁平台推荐有需求的承租

人；发生买卖关系时，如饲料厂，还会为承租人提供保证金。

第三，有承租需求的农民、农业经营主体、牧场通过与宜信租赁平台的合作，通过租赁的形式，得到获取收益的机会，收益用于还款之后，还能有盈余用于改善生活或扩大生产。

此外，值得一提的是，宜信租赁平台的风控模式比较特殊，承租人获得的融资有非常明确的用途，即场景明确。尤其是活体租赁的目标客户——牧场，其风险指标比较规范，如奶款账户、出库入库、饲料用量，只要数据真实，风控模型给出的评分都比较可信。据宜信租赁平台累积的风控经验来看，评分在680分以上的牧场，基本上没有坏账；500分以下的，坏账率就要高一些。实际上，好的风控模式，也是对宜信租赁平台可持续运营的重要保障之一。

总的来说，将宜信租赁平台的租赁业务引入农机经销商、奶业协会、畜牧局、饲料厂等作为金融聚合器，同样实现多方共赢的局面：宜信租赁平台的农租宝和宜定牛是商业型业务，虽然目前还未实现很好的盈利，但面对远未满足的农机租赁市场，以及创新型的活体租赁市场，农租宝和宜定牛已然成熟的业务模式只待扩张；对于农机经销商来说，与宜信租赁平台的合作，其最大好处是解决了赊销的问题，有利于资金回笼；对于饲料厂来说，与宜信租赁平台和牧场合作，对饲料直销有很大的帮助，免去了饲料销售的中间环节，形成稳定的饲料供应关系，而且同样有利于解决赊销的问题；对于有承租需求的农民、农业经营主体、牧场来说，不仅解决了资金的时间错配问题，而且他们还有可能获得更优惠的农机、饲料等。

自2014年起，宜信租赁平台的农机租赁业务已累计放款10亿元，合作经销商500多个，已发出过万台农机，涉及农机设备约14大类、180种，目前已覆盖中国的粮食主产区黑龙江、吉林、内蒙古、辽宁、山东、河南、河北等20多个省（自治区、直辖市），涉农融资租赁客户遍及全国196个县（市、区）。自2015年7月第一单活体租赁业务以来，该业务已累计放款3亿元，范围覆盖14个省、48个县市、300家牧场、6万头牛。

# 第五章　超级数字金融平台与“最后一公里”

【摘要】超级数字金融平台已比较常见，具备综合化、数字化、平台化、客户群规模化等特征。超级数字金融平台触达“最后一公里”的难点在于解决与“不触网客户”链接的问题，金融聚合器作为可以直接接触“最后一公里”的“中小微弱”群体的个人或机构，正好在这个链接链条中起到代理作用。目前，超级数字金融平台参与解决金融“最后一公里”问题仍面临不少难题，如超级数字金融平台的合规发展、金融聚合器的发展程度、“中小微弱”群体的金融能力等。

## 一、超级数字金融平台的发展现状

### （一）超级数字平台的类型

“互联网+金融”逐步发展成新型产业，其融合形式、服务与产品、工作原理等展现出多样性与创新性的特征。现如今，我们把一个协调多元数字生态系统的实体机构称为超级数字金融平台（Superplatform），既能为目标客户提供电商、消费、物流、社交、生活、数字技术、人工智能、大数据、云计算、物联网、区块链等在线平台服务，还能提供支付、转账、信贷、理财、保险、众筹等数字金融服务。

以超级数字金融平台的主营业务为划分依据，如表 5－1 所示，电商、消费、物流、供应链、产业链与金融服务的综合平台，生活、社交与金融服务的综合平台，数字技术、人工智能、大数据、云计算、物联网、区块链与金融服务的综合平台，纯金融技术与金融服务的综合平台，传统大型金融机构升级的综合性金融服务平台等几类大型平台已然是比较常见的。当然，并不是说这些超级数字金融平台就泾渭分明地固守单个或几个业务板块，大多数超级数字金融平台都会根据自身优势，选择性进行跨业务、跨领域的战略布局。

表 5-1 中国超级数字金融平台分类

| 类型 | 服务与工作原理 |
| --- | --- |
| 电商、消费、物流、供应链、产业链与金融服务的综合平台 | ◇ 服务：围绕“商品”，综合平台主要为客户提供电商、消费、物流等服务，逐步形成“供应链”“产业链”的生态圈，在此基础上加载支付、转账、信贷、理财、保险、众筹等数字金融服务<br>◇ 客户群体：综合平台积累了海量的客户群，有个人/家庭客户，也有中小微企业客户 |
| 生活、社交与金融服务的综合平台 | ◇ 服务：围绕“生活化需求”，综合平台为客户提供社交、健康、社保、出行、天气、政务、便民等多种服务，在此基础上加载支付、转账、信贷、理财、保险等数字金融服务<br>◇ 客户群体：综合平台积累了海量的客户群，以个人为点，形成一张“生活化需求”或“社交”的网络 |
| 数字技术、人工智能、大数据、云计算、物联网、区块链与金融服务的综合平台 | ◇ 服务：围绕“技术”，为客户提供数字技术、人工智能、大数据、云计算、物联网、区块链等技术服务，在此基础上加载支付、转账、信贷、理财、保险、众筹等数字金融服务<br>◇ 客户群体：综合平台积累了海量的客户群，可以是个人/家庭客户，也可以是中小微企业客户，还可以是金融机构客户 |
| 纯金融技术与金融服务的综合平台 | ◇ 服务：围绕“金融技术”，既为客户提供各类数字金融服务，又为客户提供金融技术服务<br>◇ 客户群体：综合平台积累了海量的客户群，可以是个人/家庭客户，也可以是中小微企业客户，还可以是金融机构客户 |
| 传统大型金融机构升级的综合性金融服务平台 | ◇ 服务：传统大型金融机构通过数字化升级后打造了自己的综合性平台，既能为客户提供各类线上的数字金融服务，也延伸出其他非金融服务<br>◇ 客户群体：传统大型金融机构本身累积了海量的客户群，可以是个人/家庭客户，也可以是中小微企业客户 |

可见，超级数字金融平台具备综合化、数字化、平台化、客户群规模化等特征。综合化是指超级数字金融平台是一个巨型综合体，既是业务的多元综合，也是技术的复杂综合，可承载或提供多元而复杂的服务；数字化是指超级数字金融平台是互联网时代的产物，其基本载体是互联网；平台化是指超级数字金融平台可为数量庞大的市场主体提供服务，包括线上服务与线下服务，从而形成独特的数字生态系统；客户群

规模化是指超级数字金融平台通过互联网技术，实现客户的跨时间、跨地域连接，去除时间限制与地域限制之后，平台的客户群可实现指数级增长。

### （二）超级数字金融平台触达“最后一公里”的难点与两种路径

对于超级数字金融平台来说，他们的客户可分为“触网客户”和“不触网客户”。“触网客户”即那些熟悉并使用互联网与智能设备的客户，“不触网客户”则是那些对互联网与智能设备不熟悉或有使用障碍的客户。

在中国，目前仍有众多“最后一公里”的“中小微弱”群体并未触网，或者仍有触网的困难，如基础设施建设不足，或因生活贫困而无法负担触网的费用等。这也就是超级数字金融平台触达“最后一公里”的困难所在。

如图5-1所示，超级数字金融平台与触网的“中小微弱”群体基本实现了链接的闭环，其链接路径不外乎是通过互联网与智能设备实现平台与客户的直接联系。但超级数字金融平台的服务到输送给不触网的“中小微弱”群体，只能暂时通过可直接接触到不触网的“中小微弱”群体的中介，以实现平台与客户的间接联系，如金融聚合器。

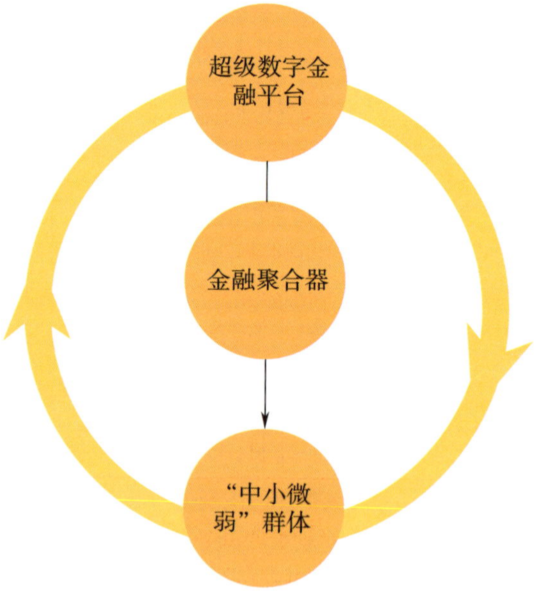


**图5-1　超级数字金融平台触达“最后一公里”的两种路径**

我们把金融聚合器（Aggregator）称为，为超级数字金融平台和目标客户（“中小微弱”群体）提供链接服务的金融代理，他们可以是一个个体，也可以是一个实体机构。金融聚合器一般具有扎根“中小微弱”群体聚集的村/社区或乡镇，持续为“中小微弱”群体提供各类服务，可直接触达“中小微弱”群体，以及可有效使用互联网与智能设备等特点。

表5-2列举了金融聚合器的分类与实例。根据金融聚合器的规模，可以将它们划分为家庭类型、社区类型、公共组织类型和经济组织类型。根据金融聚合器的机构类型，可以将它们划分为村民或农户、农村基层组织、农村金融机构、农业服务中心和农村中小微企业主体。

**表5-2 金融聚合器分类**

| 按机构类型分类 | 按规模分类 | 实例 |
| --- | --- | --- |
| 村民或农户 | 家庭类型 | 家庭农场 |
| 农村基层组织 | 社区类型 | 村两委、农业服务中心、文化卫生服务中心等 |
| 农业服务中心 | 公共组织类型 | 农业技术推广中心、农民专业合作社、农业协会等 |
| 农村金融机构 | 经济组织类型 | 农村资金互助社、农信社、小额贷款公司等 |
| 农村中小微企业主体 | 经济组织类型 | 小商店、电子商务中心、物流中心、饲料厂、农机经销商等 |

### （三）超级数字金融平台与金融聚合器的合作方式

超级数字金融平台带着触达“中小微弱”群体的难题与金融聚合器建立合作，看中的正是金融聚合器与“中小微弱”群体的紧密关系，包括对乡土人情的了解。从“双赢”的角度来说，金融聚合器为超级数字金融平台分享了自身的在地资源，则一定也期望在合作中能获得回报。

从这个角度来看，为了解决金融“最后一公里”的问题，超级数字金融平台与金融聚合器的合作方式包括业务加载形式、业务混合形式和业务拓展形式。

第一种是业务加载形式，即指定金融服务加载到金融聚合器原有的业务之上。例如，由中国人民银行推广建立的农村金融服务站，就是把指定的金融服务（存取款、查账、支付、汇兑等），通过铺设POS机、ATM等电子设备到小商店、电子商务中心、物流中心等金融聚合器上，使附近村民可以享受到金融服务。

第二种是业务混合形式，即超级数字金融平台与金融聚合器从事的业务有相关性，可以进行金融业务的混合经营。这种形式的合作，一般发生在超级数字金融平台与农村资金互助社、农村信用社、小额贷款公司等金融聚合器之间。实际运作中，这也是常见的线上业务与线下业务的融合，如蚂蚁金服与中和农信的合作。

第三种是业务拓展形式，即通过与超级数字金融平台的合作，金融聚合器的业务得以更好的发展。例如，饲料厂为超级数字金融平台推荐农场客户，农场客户从超级数字金融平台上获得贷款之后，就可以提前付清对饲料厂的赊账，而饲料厂除了可以及时回笼资金之外，还有利于与更多农场客户开展良性合作。

## 二、超级数字金融平台解决“最后一公里”问题的难点与建议

### （一）难点

第一，兼顾解决“最后一公里”问题和合规发展是难点。对于互联网金融企业来说，监管政策风险是进入“互联网金融监管元年”之后不得不面对的一个难题。随着互联网金融监管细则逐见眉目，一些不合规型互联网金融企业逐渐被淘汰，互联网金融的产品与服务也将更加规范。经历过严监管的冲击，现存的超级数字金融平台基本上在各类金融牌照基础上经营金融产品与服务，这是合规发展的必然。虽然超级数字金融平台早就开始探索解决金融“最后一公里”问题的方法，也确实形成了各式各样的渠道、产品，但仍未达到规模化、精细化、标准化、可持续发展等标准，仍有市场淘汰的压力。

第二，金融聚合器的发展程度参差不齐、规模不一。作为深入村/社区或乡镇的金融聚合器，理论上可以形成链接全国农村的服务点。理想的状态是，这些金融聚合器的服务点通过互联网串联起来，形成一张为农村地区提供金融服务的巨大的网，有效解决金融“最后一公里”问题。现实情况是，受限于金融聚合器的自身，金融聚合器的服务点可能只提供有限的金融服务，这张由“点”及“面”的“网”还未发挥出最大的效率。

第三，“最后一公里”的“中小微弱”群体的金融能力并不乐观。原则上来说，如果“最后一公里”的“中小微弱”群体可以顺利触网，那么超级数字金融平台就可以直接为他们提供金融服务，而无须通过金融聚合器这个代理来实现金融服务的触达。现实情况是，除了农村地区基础设施建设的问题外，“中小微弱”群体本身不具备触网的能力，是影响农村地区触网率的重要原因。此外，“中小微弱”群体对金融产品的认知、对风险的认识、对个人与家庭发展需求的认识、对个人与家庭财务平衡的能力等，都是影响“中小微弱”群体是否获得金融服务，并能否有效利用金融服务的重要原因。

### （二）建议

第一，随着互联网金融的政策法规与业务准则逐渐明晰，超级数字金融平台需在合规的基础上摸索并打造成熟而可持续的业务模式，真正发挥互联网金融的数字技术、

大数据、人工智能等方面的优势，有效解决金融“最后一公里”问题。

第二，创新超级数字金融平台与金融聚合器的合作模式。合作不稳定的原因在于金融聚合器自身机构发展困难，平台与金融聚合器之间的合作协议时间短，金融聚合器转变业务或退出金融服务，金融聚合器服务人员能力不足等。可见，超级数字金融平台和金融聚合器的合作机制需要有所突破，“双赢”策略是最佳选择，最终才能形成共同繁荣的整体生态。

第三，无论是金融聚合器，还是“中小微弱”群体，金融能力都需进一步提升。除了超级数字金融平台尽可能提供易懂、易用、易操作的产品与服务之外，金融聚合器需要提升自身机构可持续发展的能力，包括业务能力、经营能力、财务能力、管理能力等，而“中小微弱”群体则需要提升自身适应互联网时代的能力，包括互联网金融知识、触网能力、个人与家庭财务能力等。

第四，超级数字金融平台可为“最后一公里”的“中小微弱”群体提供更多元、更丰富的产品与服务。超级数字金融平台与金融聚合器建立长效合作机制，动态监测“中小微弱”群体需求的变化，使产品与服务的设计尽可能贴合“中小微弱”群体的需求。

第五，超级数字金融平台应积极融入国家信用体系建设。对于超级数字金融平台来说，与国家信用体系建立有效联系，形成信用信息共享机制，既有利于超级数字金融平台控制风险，又有利于形成良好的社会信用环境，起到相互促进的作用。

## 三、超级数字金融平台的业务发展逻辑、优势与趋势

国际上，超级数字金融平台概念最早多用于数字技术领域。随着数字金融的兴起，尤其是大型互联网平台加载金融业务之后，超级数字金融平台的概念也随之用于金融领域。无论是业务模式，还是客户规模，美团金服都称得上是超级数字金融平台。按照前面所述的分类来看，美团金服属于典型的“生活服务 + 金融服务”的超级综合平台。

### （一）业务发展逻辑

如图 5－2 所示，美团金服的业务发展经历了四个步骤，包括搭建平台基础、积累客户基础、加载数字金融服务、形成多元数字生态系统。

第一步是搭建平台基础。美团点评集团最早的业务是团购，逐渐延伸出酒店旅游、点评、外卖、打车、民宿、餐饮智能服务等各类生活服务，其每一个小平台的产品或服务，都是基于满足消费者某个痛点需求而设计的。通过一个个小平台的聚合，美团

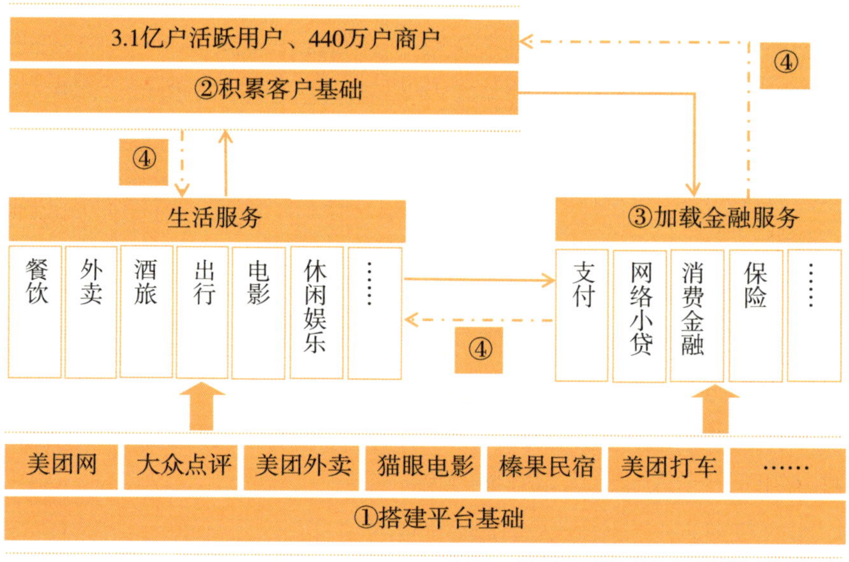


**图 5-2 美团金服业务发展逻辑**

点评集团的综合平台雏形渐次显现，每个平台在客户转化和业务促进方面，逐步形成良好的效能。美团点评集团的服务涵盖 200 多个品类，业务覆盖全国 2800 个县（区、市），2017 年全平台交易额（GMV）3570 亿元，日订单量峰值超过 2700 万个。

第二步是积累客户基础。基于美团点评集团的精准服务与综合平台效应，美团全平台迅速积累了海量客户，这是平台基础上最宝贵的资源。截至 2017 年，美团全平台的年度交易用户数达到 3.1 亿人，年度活跃商家达 440 万户商户。

第三步是加载数字金融服务。基于平台基础和客户基础，美团点评集团逐步加载第三方支付（北京钱袋宝支付技术有限公司）、网络小贷（重庆三快小额贷款有限公司）、消费金融（吉林亿联银行股份有限公司）、保险（重庆金诚互诺保险经纪有限公司）等数字金融服务，正好满足个人消费者和商户的金融需求。2016 年至今，美团金服获得了民营银行、第三方支付、保险经纪、互联网小贷、商业保理等牌照，如此“生活服务 + 金融服务”的超级综合平台基本搭建完成。

第四步是形成多元数字生态系统。美团金服形成了前台、中台、后台三个层次的数字生态系统：前台直接面对各类客户的需求；中台是各类生活服务平台和金融服务平台；后台是数字技术支撑体系，包括分布式系统、大数据处理挖掘系统、人工智能系统、实时风控系统等。一旦多元数字生态系统找到最佳运行方案，美团金服也会形成良性供需平衡，从而实现稳步与可持续的发展。

### （二）业务优势

从美团金服的整体业务来看，超级数字金融平台提供金融服务的优势主要体现在：

渠道优势、精准服务优势、风险管理优势。

第一，渠道优势。实际上，个人消费者和商户的金融需求是在美团点评集团各个业务场景基础上衍生出来的。以美团智能支付为例，它结合了支付、外卖、团购、卡券营销等功能，让个人消费者和商户无缝连接，形成“买—支付—卖”的互联网闭环，体现了数字金融服务的方便、快捷、高效、智能等基本特征。因此，每一个业务场景就成为美团金服加载金融服务的最佳渠道。

第二，精准服务优势。美团金服的金融产品主要围绕场景业务和消费服务展开。以美团保险为例，其服务对象是3.1亿户活跃用户、440万户商户和日均53.1万名活跃的配送骑手，险种主要涉及众包骑手、加盟代理骑手、外卖延误，另外还包括航空意外、门票意外、打车承运人责任、火车意外、住宿意外等。可见，美团保险充分结合业务特性，利用大数据大幅提高对客户需求及风险的把握能力，推出定制化、个性化的保险产品，优化服务流程，为客户提供精细化、专业化、差别化的配套保险服务。

第三，风险管理优势。超级数字金融平台在做风控设计时，最突出的特点是沉淀数据的使用。以美团生意贷为例，它形成了三位一体的组合式风险管理机制：基于内部数据的客户信用评价体系、结合外部数据的欺诈风险管理、与合作金融机构的联合风控模式。美团生意贷的主要服务对象是美团点评集团的440万户商户，主要满足他们企业经营过程中产生的资金需求，如开新店、老店装修、购买新设备、原材料采购等。这些商户在美团点评集团的平台上留存了丰富的交易数据，包括经营资质数据、交易数据、消费者评价数据等，而这些交易数据正是美团风控设计的基础。

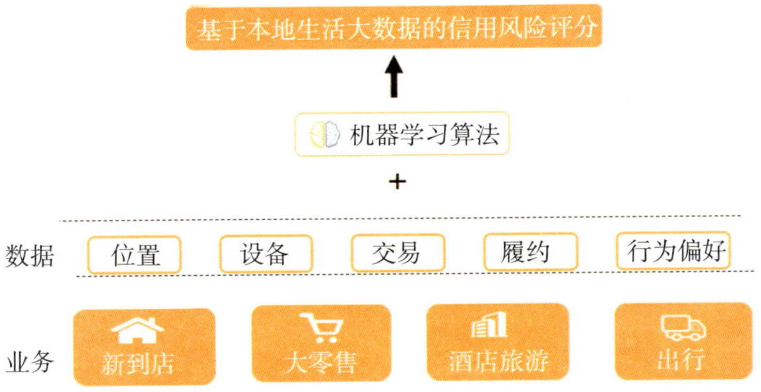


资料来源：美团金服。

**图5-3 风险管理1——基于内部数据的客户信用评价体系**

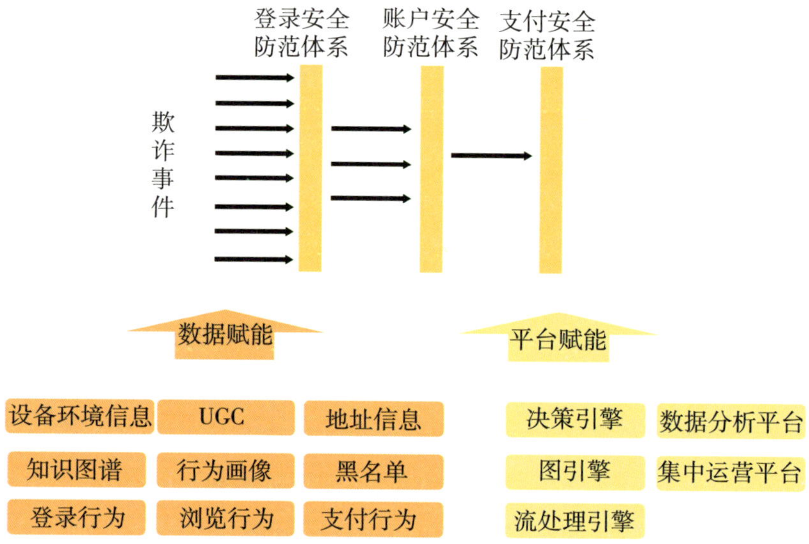


资料来源：美团金服。

**图 5-4　风险管理 2——结合外部数据的欺诈风险管理**

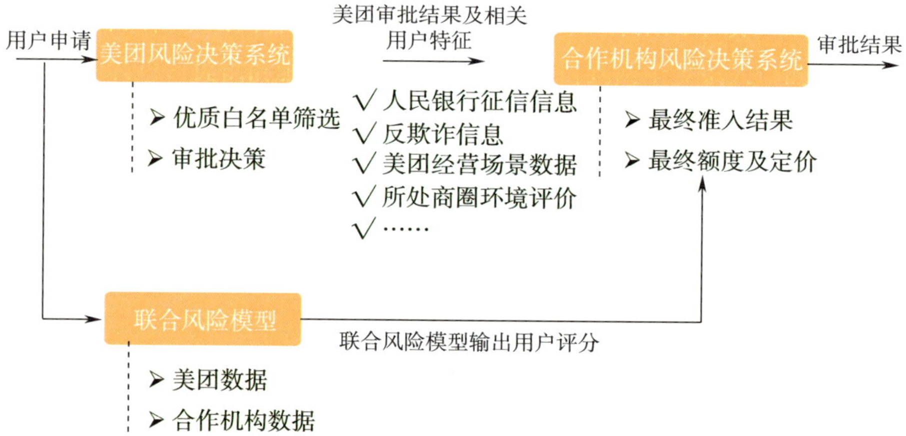


资料来源：美团金服。

**图 5-5　风险管理 3——与合作金融机构的联合风控模式**

## （三）业务趋势

美团点评集团从 2010 年创建，到发展成现在的超级数字金融平台，仅用了不到 8 年的时间。可见，未来金融业务的趋势如下。

第一，数字化趋势。数字化为金融服务提高了效率、降低了成本、增强了风控，其优点已经过反复验证。超级数字金融平台发展金融业务也将围绕数字化进行迭代更新。

第二，平台聚势化趋势。如前所述，一旦超级数字金融平台找到多元数字生态系统的最佳运行方案，其势能就会愈发强大。无论是平台与平台的合作、平台与金融聚合器的合作，还是平台与“中小微弱”群体的合作，也多会更加强调强强联合与强势赋能。

第三，服务融合化趋势。超级数字金融平台上提供的服务，其界限会逐渐淡化。对于超级数字金融平台而言，多元业务的融合对其服务能力提出了更高的要求。

# 第三部分

# 穿越"最后一公里"的环境条件

“最后一公里”问题的存在与金融环境密不可分。为了解决这个问题，需要建立良好的金融环境。科技进步为解决金融“最后一公里”问题提供了技术手段。基础设施和监管环境可以为解决“最后一公里”问题提供良好的条件。

# 第六章　金融科技与“最后一公里”

**【摘要】**本章主要讨论金融科技（Fintech）与普惠金融“最后一公里”问题的相关内容，主要介绍了目前在金融科技中常使用的关键技术、金融科技在解决“最后一公里”问题中的应用、金融科技在降低成本和风险控制中的具体作用，以及金融科技在解决“最后一公里”问题实践中仍存在的问题。金融科技使用云计算、大数据、人工智能等技术大大降低了交易和风险控制的成本，但仍存在数据安全、数字鸿沟与排斥等问题。

## 一、金融科技中的关键技术

金融科技的发展离不开硬件设备的快速发展。无论是服务器的计算能力，还是存储资源和网络资源，随着工业技术的成熟度越来越高，硬件设备的成本逐渐降低，这保证了云计算平台实现时间与空间灵活度的可能性，同时为后续的大数据、人工智能等技术打下基础。

在软件方面，虚拟机技术不断发展，VMware、Xen、KVM 等虚拟化平台不断成熟，云平台开源软件 OpenStack 得到广泛应用，大大降低了云计算平台的成本。

在服务器方面，随着英特尔 X86 架构的不断成熟发展，与 RISC 和 IA 架构的处理器的性能差距不断缩小，使工业标准服务器抢占了不少本该属于商业关键服务器的份额。服务器计算性能密度不断提升，更易于管理，更加节能，与虚拟化技术和调度算法的结合也更加紧密，使得云计算真正实现了时间与空间的灵活性。全新的服务器架构如惠普企业的 The Machine[①]、IBM 的量子计算机等也正在崭露头角，为服务器性能质变飞跃做好准备。

在存储方面，固态硬盘成本不断降低，纯闪存和混合存储技术将传统存储阵列的

① https://www.labs.hpe.com/the-machine。

性能提高了成百上千倍，为大数据应用打下了良好的基础。得益于服务器性能的提升，软件定义存储[①]也越来越流行，对于多数中小企业来说，软件定义存储可以最大化利用硬件资源，降低IT成本，同时使得存储设备更易于管理。

### （一）云计算

云计算实际上是对IT资源的统一管理，并在此基础上提供三种服务模式：在IAAS层管理的主要是计算资源、网络资源和存储资源，同时实现时间和空间的灵活性。它还使用到了虚拟化技术、调度算法等技术。在PAAS层解决了应用层的弹性问题，提供通用的应用服务，例如，提供应用开发和生产运行环境，包括运行环境、操作系统、开发API、开发工具、数据库、服务和应用部署、资源监控与管理、扩容、网络等。在SAAS层提供的是完整的软件服务，只需调用相应的服务即可。

由于部署完整云计算平台的成本非常高，且金融信息化建设的发展并不平衡，所以越来越多的云计算平台推出针对金融的服务平台。这使得金融企业能够以更低的成本获取更强的计算能力和服务能力，降低中小微金融机构的金融服务门槛。

在国外，云计算在金融领域已经有了相对成熟的应用。如Inovance[②]是一家基于云计算的金融数据管理平台，通过大数据分析和人工智能技术的应用，普通人也可以在平台进行投资分析和金融市场研究。它们开发的SAAS软件“TRAIDE”已经推出市场，能够同时容纳1800万用户和上千家金融机构同时在线。据Gartner报告，2016年全球云计算市场规模是2066亿美元，金融云占其中超过20%的份额，且在不断扩大中[③]。

金融领域是当前中国云计算应用需求最为迫切的领域之一，大量金融机构正在开始应用自建私有云或与第三方公有云合作的方式来承载应用和处理高并发业务。但由于金融行业涉及资金、交易、客户身份等大量敏感信息，对信息安全提出很高要求，导致目前金融云的渗透率不高[④]。

### （二）大数据技术

大数据技术是云计算PAAS层上非常重要的通用应用之一，通常指在海量结构化、非结构化数据的基础上所形成的一种新型数据存储及处理模式，也就是通过清理数据，得到有用的信息，将信息进行总结和归纳，发现其中的内在联系，进而得到知

① Wikibon-Server SAN 2012—2026。
② 百度金融和埃森哲发布的《与AI共进 智胜未来——智能金融联合报告》，2018年。
③ 方正证券：《计算机行业：互联网巨头携手银行IT龙头，金融云市场蓄势待发》，2018年。
④ 中国产业信息：《2018年中国金融云行业发展规模及未来成长空间分析预测报告》，2018年。

识，再将得到的知识用于实践，形成对于实际业务产生促进作用或者为决策提供支持的智慧。

整个大数据处理过程包括数据的收集、传输、存储、处理和分析、检索与挖掘等环节，且在各个阶段都有相应的技术支持。例如在大数据采集阶段，最亟须解决的问题就是高并发数，要在采集端部署大量数据库，并在其之间进行负载均衡以实现有效管理。将大量数据导入分布式数据库后进行统计和分析，一些实时性需求会用到 Oracle 的 Exadata[①]、Infobright[②] 等软件，而一些批量并行处理就要使用 Hadoop 架构。大量的数据分析产生很高的 I/O 吞吐量。在数据挖掘时使用的比较典型算法包括用于聚类的 Kmeans[③]、用于统计学习的 SVM 和用于分类的 NaiveBayes，主要使用的工具有 Hadoop 的 Mahout 等[④]。

大数据在金融中的应用，主要是将金融活动转化为数据处理活动。利用数据分析与挖掘的结果为用户画像，为核心的金融风控提供了全新的风险定价模式，极大地降低了人为因素的干扰，有效提高了风险的评估、分析和预警能力，提升了金融的资源配置效率。

### （三）人工智能

人工智能（Artificial Intelligence，AI）是研究使用计算机来模拟人的某些思维过程和智能行为的技术，即希望计算机能够像人类一样思考。比如，通过自然语言处理，能够正确理解人类向计算机传达的信息，并通过自动推理，像人类一样去学习，能够表达人类理性思维的同时又具有感性的意识，实现让计算机成为人类大脑的延伸扩展。如图 6－1 所示，从 2017 年 Gartner 新兴技术成熟曲线中人工智能的位置来看[⑤]，最重要的技术深度学习和机器学习已经进入期望膨胀期的顶端，接下来需要在期望膨胀之后，让泡沫破裂，真正将技术与实际需求融合，才能进入生产成熟期。

对于普惠金融来说，人工智能与金融服务的结合是符合发展需要的。传统金融受人力成本和资源的制约，金融机构只为高净值顾客提供定制化服务，而对绝大多数普通客户只提供一般通用型服务。人工智能能够改变这种格局，极大地降低业务的人力成本。在前台可显著提升客户体验，使普通客户也能享受更加便捷且个性化的服务，即智能获客；在中台辅助交易的预测和执行，使分析决策更加智能化，即智能投顾；在后台用于风险控制和识别，提升风控质量，即智能风控。

---

① https://www.oracle.com/cn/engineered-systems/exadata/database-machine-x7/index.html。

② http://www.ignitetech.com/solutions/information-technology/infobrightdb。

③ https://www.cnblogs.com/bourneli/p/3645049.html kmeans 聚类理论篇。

④ https://blog.csdn.net/ZcwJeff/article/details/76862128 大数据学习。

⑤ 百度金融和埃森哲发布的《与 AI 共进　智胜未来——智能金融联合报告》，2018 年。

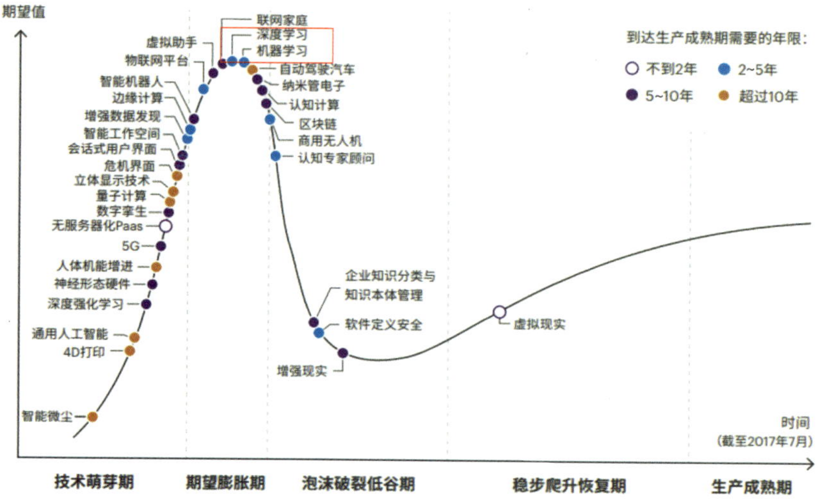


**图 6-1　2017 年 Gartner 新兴技术成熟曲线**

智能投资顾问则是利用人工智能技术，为每一位客户生成个性化的投资组合并提供交易执行与追踪等服务。当然，在做资产配置组合之前要先了解用户画像和风险偏好。这其中包括客户的人生阶段、消费习惯、信用情况、资产情况、投资偏好、流动性要求、风险承受能力等因素，以此类信息为基础才能配置出合理的投资组合，达到客户的预期收益，提高客户满意度。这要求所有的投资组合不再是为了某些特定客户而设计，必须针对每个客户动态设计，实现产品的个性化特点。不仅如此，智能投顾还必须依据客户情况变化和反馈及时进行自我学习，不断完善推荐投资组合模型。

智能投顾可以让原先对于投资和理财知识匮乏的客户得到适合个人情况的投资组合，这大大降低了投资门槛，无疑会扩展投资理财的用户边界，也就做到了“普”。而“惠”本身就是一个因人而异的概念，不同的人对于是否“惠”的判断需视自身情况而定，智能投顾根据用户不同风险偏好和收益预期进行投资组合管理，这也就达到了“惠”的要求。同理，人工智能还可以和贷款、保险组合，制定个性化的贷款利率和保险费率等，这种产品设计的灵活性无疑可以让更多的人享受到更优质的金融服务，对于解决普惠金融“最后一公里”问题有着积极的作用。

### （四）区块链

区块链本质上是去中心化的分布式记账技术，它有三个核心的技术，即分布式存储、密码学和共识机制。分布式存储保证了区块链中的账本采用分布式的核算和存储，可由多节点共同维护，且其中的数据对于任何一个节点均可查询。相比传统的中心数据库有更低的成本。密码学和共识机制保证了区块链的安全性，加入区块链中的数据必须通过加密算法同时验证各节点的计算结果相同，才允许加入区块链，如果某节点的运算结果不匹配，也会被其他节点纠正，这也就保证所有节点安全一致性。区块链依据使用范围可分为公有链、私有链和联盟链。①

区块链概念虽然炒得火热，但真正落地的应用场景一直在摸索中，各家机构也在纷纷试水区块链项目。从区块链的概念和特点来说，它的安全、低成本与普惠金融有较高的契合度。在支付清算、资产证券化、供应链金融等领域均有应用的可能性。在支付清算领域，尤其是跨境支付领域，利用区块链技术可以大大缩短清算时间，减少成本。在资产证券化方面，可将多家中小企业的资产打包组合成一个资产证券化产品，同时使用区块链管理整个资产包，各家中小企业可随时动态管理资产包内的资产变化②。这种做法对于投资方、中介机构和监管机构来说，可随时了解资产证券化产品内底部资产的变化，做到合理的评级和监管；同时对于中小企业来说可以盘活资产，成为融资的新途径。在与供应链金融结合方面也有多种模式可以进行探索，例如，对于生产农作物的小企业，如果从收购、物流、仓库、零售、购买每一步都得到相应的质量保证认证并记录在区块链内，消费者拿到农产品后，通过扫描二维码或条形码，就能追根溯源查询到商品生产、运输信息以及品质认证等信息，则可以较大提升商品附加价值、增加企业收益。

目前，蚂蚁金服推出的全球首个基于区块链的电子钱包跨境汇款服务已在中国香港上线③。港版支付宝的用户可以通过区块链技术向菲律宾钱包 Gcash 汇款。第一笔跨境汇款耗时仅 3 秒，而在以前这需要 10 分钟到几天不等。在区块链技术的支持下，跨境汇款从此能做到像本地转账一样，实时到账、省钱、省事、安全、透明。这也是继公益捐款、食品溯源、租房管理之后，蚂蚁金服在区块链应用场景的又一次创新探索。

## 二、金融科技的应用

《G20 数字普惠金融高级原则》指出，数字技术能够为无法获得金融服务的群体（其大多数为妇女）以可负担的方式提供教育储蓄、支付、获取小额商业贷款、汇款以及购买保险等④金融服务。金融科技之所以成为解决普惠金融“最后一公里”问题的一个重要工具，主要是因为金融科技利用数字技术大幅降低交易成本和获客成本、提

---

① 高盛公司发布的《区块链：从理论走向实践》，2016 年 5 月。

② 中国通信院．区块链在金融领域的应用［J/OL］．网经社，2018－04－28．

③ https://www.sohu.com/a/237709281_99940985。

④ 中国人民银行发布的《G20 数字普惠金融高级原则》，2016 年 9 月。

高征信覆盖范围，提升风险控制的质量，缓解商业可持续与普惠金融定价之间的矛盾。而这个矛盾正是普惠金融"最后一公里"问题的核心所在。

目前已较成熟的数字普惠金融服务，其服务类型可分为支付服务、征信服务、融资服务、理财服务及保险服务。其中，融资服务包含 P2P、小额贷款、众筹等形式。这些服务均是金融科技将传统的银行、证券、保险等业务进行分解，并提供更加精准高效的金融服务。目前用到的金融技术主要为云计算、大数据及人工智能。

## （一）数字支付服务

支付服务虽然只是数字普惠金融体系中的基础服务之一，但却是解决普惠金融"最后一公里"问题的重要一环。金融科技带来的数字支付服务，有着高效、便捷、易使用等特点。依托于智能手机的大量普及，支付服务可以满足普惠金融高覆盖性的需求。人民银行发布的《2017 年支付体系运行总体情况》显示，2017 年非银行支付机构发生网络支付业务 2867.47 亿笔，总金额 143.26 万亿元，同比增长 74.95% 和 44.32%。支付业务的快速增长也使得数字普惠金融的触角进一步延伸到欠发达地区。如图 6－2 所示，2017 年地级市、乡镇、农村使用支付业务的比例增幅最大，分别为 37.24%、47.15%、51.52%。

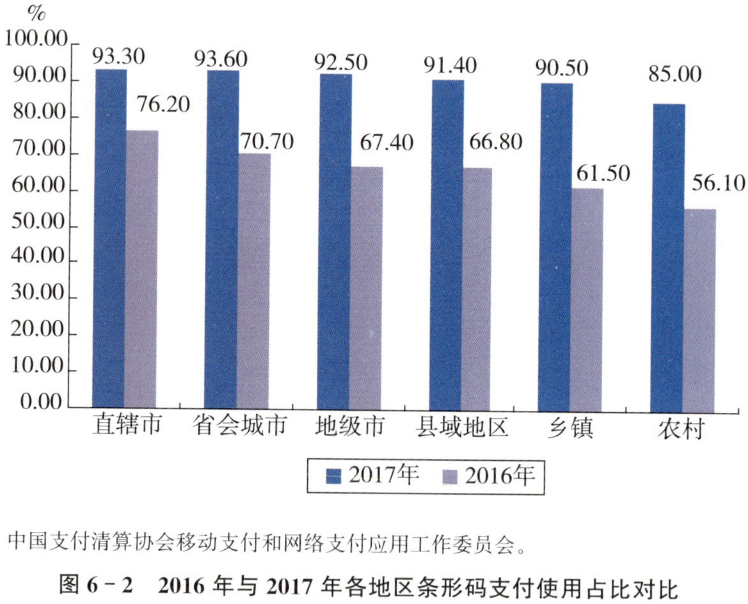


资料来源：中国支付清算协会移动支付和网络支付应用工作委员会。

**图 6－2　2016 年与 2017 年各地区条形码支付使用占比对比**

数字支付服务拓展了大量不发达地区的市场，同时，第三方支付平台也在不断改善支付服务的业务体验。首先，将多种支付场景进行整合，除常用消费以外，生活支出、投资理财等多种支付场景越来越集中，使得用户对于数字支付平台有了更强的依赖性。其次，技术不断发展，无论是指纹、面部识别等人工智能技术对于支付服务的安全性有更强的保障，还是 QR 码、NFC 的广泛使用，使得支付的方式与场景结合越来越紧密。正因以上特点，数字支付成为了用户一种新的生活方式和潮流，进一步增强了其广泛性和普适性。

数字支付服务所使用的技术虽然并不高深和前沿，但却对数据的交互、准确性和安全性有很高的要求，因此更需要支付服务商保持后台系统的高效性和稳定性。同时，数字支付服务所产生的数据流也是大数据征信服务的数据来源之一，这为进一步拓展普惠金融服务打下了基础。

### （二）大数据信用服务

从普惠金融的角度看征信服务，大数据信用服务是解决普惠金融“最后一公里”问题的重要工具之一。

金融活动中存在大量对资源使用权的让渡。借用者与所有者之间信息不对称导致信用风险，因此，金融活动的核心是信用风险管理，而信用风险管理的核心是征信。这个原理在普惠金融中也同样适用，大量普惠金融所服务的目标客户均是没有征信记录的客户群，因此存在更加严重的信息不对称和信用风险。要想真正解决普惠金融“最后一公里”问题的同时保持商业可持续性，就必须要有一套完善的征信体系。

目前，我国的征信体系是以人民银行征信中心为核心，民营机构为补充，即形成政府主导、市场共同推动的格局。2015 年末，人民银行征信中心收录自然人规模 8.8 亿人，有信用记录人群规模 3.8 亿人，预计 2017 年末收录的自然人规模有 9.2 亿人，信贷记录人数达到 4.4 亿人。即便如此，我国征信人口覆盖率与美国相比依然存在较大差距，美国 2015 年征信人口覆盖率已经达到 92%①。

正是因为人民银行征信中心的征信覆盖率无法满足普惠金融定义的客户群体，同时大量的数据被广泛留存于互联网平台上且能成为反映个人信用状况的补充信息，尤其是部分互联网金融数据还能成为判断用户整体负债和偿还能力的强数据。因此，大数据信用服务应运而生。

在数据来源方面，大数据信用机构普遍采用多维度的信息来源。这些信息来源包括：（1）客户的标识信息，包括姓名、证件类型和号码、身份信息、居住信息等；（2）信贷信息，包括借贷记录、信用卡和担保信息等；（3）履行义务的信息，包括社会保险参保缴费信息、住房公积金缴存信息、车辆抵押交易信息等；（4）非金融负债信息，例如，电信等公用事业缴费信息，以及公共部门的相关信息，包括获得资质信

① 宜人智库：《个人征信行业研究报告 2017》，2017 年。

息、行政许可信息、行政处罚信息、获得奖励信息、执业资格信息、法院判决和执行信息、欠税信息、低保救助信息、上市公司监管信息等；（5）互联网原始数据源，包括互联网公开数据、电信运营商数据、移动 APP 安装及活跃数据、用户的互联网深度行为或者社交数据、网上金融行为数据等。虽然个人或者中小企业可能没有全部的信息来源，但是大数据信用服务可通过多维度的信息来对客户进行相对准确的用户画像，以提高征信服务的真实性和客观性。

除了金融征信之外，随着大数据技术的发展，信用与场景的结合也越来越密切，个人信用的好坏不仅仅影响到借贷等金融行为，同时会切实影响到生活，如需要押金服务的场景中，可充分发挥芝麻信用分数的作用，免共享单车押金、免酒店押金等，甚至可以在办理某些国家签证时免去资产证明等。截至 2017 年末，芝麻信用已累计为 4150 万户用户免押金超过 400 亿元①。这种方式对于帮助个人实现诚信价值、推进诚信社会建设、提高信用服务的社会价值具有重要意义，也是补充完善和解决普惠金融“最后一公里”问题的有效途径。

大数据信用服务使用到了多项金融科技技术，海量的数据存储和计算需要云计算平台和大数据技术的支持，同时大量平台之间的信息交互对于信息的传递和数据安全提出了更高的要求。

### （三）互联网理财服务

传统理财投资产品往往针对富裕人群，并设置一定的门槛和规则。例如，银行理财产品通常需要 3 万元人民币起投，信托产品则要 100 万元人民币起投。同时也为客户设置了线下风险评估、T+1 或 T+2 赎回等一系列规则。自 2013 年以来，以余额宝为代表的互联网基金的出现则彻底打破了这些门槛和规则，实现了理财投资零门槛、零网点、T+0 赎回、可用于生活消费等一系列突破。而这些突破正是解决理财服务在“最后一公里”问题中的关键。

截至 2018 年 6 月底，余额宝已经为超过 3 亿户用户累计创造收益近 1500 亿元，其中农村地区余额宝用户数超过 1 亿户。从 2018 年 5 月起，余额宝正式宣布开放。到 6 月底，除天弘基金之外，余额宝平台已经接入了博时基金、中欧基金、华安基金、国泰基金等 5 家基金公司的货币基金。余额宝分流成效显著，天弘基金单只基金规模下降超过 2000 亿元。

互联网理财服务提高了大众对于理财的认识。高流动性、操作的便捷性、用途的广泛性都使得理财成为了全民参与的金融服务，这正实现了普惠金融的高覆盖性，用

① 资料来源：支付宝“2017 年全民账单”。

户的可负担性。从金融技术的角度，理财服务所用到的技术不多，更多的是支付服务与基金公司的数据对接，所以同样强调系统的稳定性和数据的安全性。此外，理财服务是征信数据来源中的一环，同时也是丰富普惠金融产品体系的重要组成部分。

### （四）融资服务

在普惠金融各产品中，融资服务最具综合性，同时也是最能体现普惠金融“最后一公里”问题的服务。它不仅需要支付系统和征信业务的支持，还需要机构在此基础之上制定合理的利率、额度等关键因素，因此完善的风险控制体系是融资服务的核心。无论是个人通过融资用于消费或者资金周转，还是中小微企业用于生产经营，只要是被银行类金融机构排斥的客户需要资金，那么就应该有相应的服务帮助客户快速、便捷、在可负担成本的条件下获得资金。在这种理想情况下，才算真正解决了普惠金融“最后一公里”问题。

金融科技在这其中起到了至关重要的工具作用——风险定价。要想为用户提供可负担的成本和合理的融资额度，就需要充分了解用户信息，测算其还款能力和意愿，了解用户的信用资质，对其发生违约的概率进行预测，做好相应的风险防范措施。这其中使用到的金融科技主要是云计算和大数据技术。与征信服务不同的是，在信贷业务的模型中，征信信息只是用户画像的一部分，反欺诈模型、信用风险模型才是业务的核心。这就对数据挖掘有了更深的要求，所有信息都可用于描绘用户的行为习惯，同时大量多维度的信息需要人工智能中的深度学习、无监督学习等技术的支持，以便快速发现数据异常，保证业务稳定性。

### （五）互联网保险服务

在保险产品方面，通过金融科技技术的运用，保险公司提升了自身的风险识别、定价和产品管理能力，使保障对象从健康人群扩展到特定人群，使过去的一些不可保风险变为了可保风险，进一步提升了保险对风险的覆盖，如 UBI 车险、正品险、手机碎屏险、癌情预测险、航空延误险等，进一步扩展了保险产品范围的边界。比如，网络购物场景下的退货运费险，以平均不到一元钱的保费为用户退换货产生的快递费用提供经济补偿，这在传统保险的定价逻辑下是难以完成的，运营成本都很难覆盖。又如，近年来出现的高额消费型医疗保险，不限社保用药、不限疾病种类，只是通过适当提高免赔额的设计，让消费者以较低的保费享受更丰富的医疗保障，使健康险的保障功能更全面。

在保险可获得性方面，互联网保险产品消除了物理网点和营业时间的限制，降低了保险服务的门槛和成本。丰富的保险产品，方便快捷的保险服务，使得“中小微弱”

群体也可以获得合适的风险保障。例如，一些保险产品专门针对电子商务小微商户，为其提供卖家拖欠货物履约保险和服务履约保险，小微商家选择这两款产品后，无须再按以往方式缴纳数额较大的保证金，只需缴纳1000元左右的保费就可释放50万元的资金。市场上还开始出现面向慢性病患者、残疾人群、老年人等传统意义上高风险人群的专属保险产品。

因此，互联网保险服务通过云计算、大数据、人工智能技术的运用，无论是在保险产品的多样性，还是在保险的可获得性、易用性方面，甚至是价格方面都作出了重大的改善，从多角度解决了普惠金融“最后一公里”问题，使保险成为数字普惠金融体系中重要的一环，也使得保险日渐成为人们生活不可缺少的金融产品。

再保险产品定价方面，对于消费者行为习惯等非结构化数据的挖掘和分析，显著提升了保险精算和产品定价的能力，使量身定制个性化的保险方案成为了主流。金融科技改变了传统保险对于大量同质风险的聚合方式，原有的精算假设和概念面临重新定义。基于互联网思维设计的保险产品，将会更加通俗化、人性化，同时产品价格也更加便宜。以腾讯保险平台推出的普惠型健康险产品“微医保”为例，针对有社保的被保险人，21周岁一年保费216元、26周岁276元、31周岁372元、36周岁456元，价格大大低于同类的传统保险产品①。

综上所述，可以发现整个数字普惠金融体系中各个产品均集中于解决普惠金融“最后一公里”问题。根据不同需求，解决方式不同，所使用到的金融科技技术也不尽相同。以支付服务为基础，大数据征信服务作为其他业务的依据和支撑，信贷业务作为提供普惠金融服务的有效手段，配合理财和保险服务，达到为用户提供全方位的金融服务。而金融科技在其中扮演重要的工具角色，帮助服务提供商降低获客成本，提高风控和定价能力，降低金融服务的门槛，真正体现了普惠金融高可得性、可负担、产品丰富、商业可持续的特点。

其他服务均使用到了云计算和大数据技术。而人工智能技术与各种服务的融合也能产生新的产品或业务模式。人工智能与普惠金融相结合比较紧密的技术有机器学习和生物识别技术。机器学习中的集中学习、监督学习、深度学习等衍生算法主要用于风险评估，可以得到更加精准且层次多样化的风控结果以用于融资业务。生物识别技术主要包括指纹识别、人脸识别、虹膜识别等技术，这些技术主要用于支付业务和身份验证。对于老年人来说，指纹与人脸识别等技术使用起来更加简便，也降低了传统密码被盗用的风险。

---

① http://tech.sina.com.cn/i/2017-11-02/doc-ifynmvuq8084893.shtml。

## 三、金融科技在降低成本中的作用

### （一）降低运营成本，提高效率

交易成本过高是阻碍传统金融服务于“中小微弱”群体的最主要因素。完成小而分散的金融服务交易，双方都要付出较高的成本。金融机构提供小额的金融服务的边际成本比较高。由于传统金融机构服务网点都布局在人口比较密集的地方，客户需要花时间和附加费用才能获得这种小额的金融服务。这使得小额交易难以发生。

数字化可以大幅度降低获客成本。一是数字化服务可以大幅度减少一线服务人员数量，减少人员费用的开支。数字普惠金融通过互联网和手机连接客户，金融机构从自己的渠道和其他服务渠道获得大量的客户信息，通过大数据建模对客户进行数字画像，对客户的需求进行细分，提供个性化的金融服务。二是数字化服务特别是手机银行不需要建设许多物理网点，因此减少了大量的租赁及装修费用，同时也减少了与物理网点相关的物业水电、装修折旧、安保支出、运钞等日常运营成本。根据 McQuinn（2016），专用 IT 基础设施的建设成本和维护成本分别是传统银行的 60%～80%和 30%～59%，人头数只是传统银行的 10%～15%。

提高效率是数字普惠金融降低成本的主要途径。中国普惠金融研究院对中和农信数字化项目的调查发现（贝多广、李焰、莫秀根，2017），有 85.13%的员工认为数字化以后可以让他们腾出更多的时间进行营销；有 65.1%的员工认为他们的贷款业务量由此提升。与此同时，如图 6－3 所示，80%以上的受访信贷员认为数字化服务节约了交通工具的油耗，减少了上门放收款的时间；超过 90%的受访信贷员认为数字化服务减少了其去银行存取款的时间；信贷员同时更关注现金放收款带来的安全问题，90%以上的信贷员认为集中代付避免了保管大额现金、降低了自己收到假币的风险。

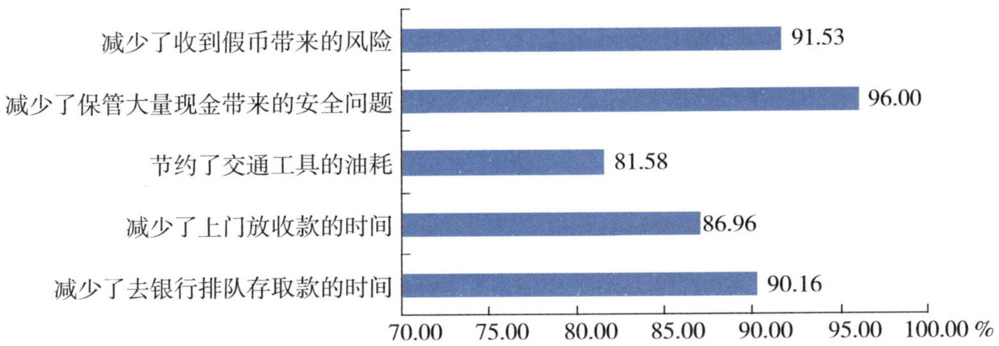


**图 6－3　信贷员对集中代付提高效率情况的感受**

### （二）降低风险管理成本

风险管理是金融服务的中心内容，获客、放贷和贷后管理等环节都要围绕风险管理来开展。在信用体系不健全的情况下，金融机构根据客户的个人信用来评估客户是否具有违约风险，并采取合适措施防范金融风险。金融机构之间的信息壁垒，形成的信息孤岛，使恶意欺诈等问题经常发生。为了避免风险，金融机构只能投入更多的人力，层层把关，严格审批程序。成本增加和风险降低是一种负相关关系。综合起来风险管理成本在金融服务成本中占据了主要部分。

大数据应用的核心是金融风控。大数据技术使金融机构对客户信用情况更加了解。大数据不仅能够了解客户的信贷情况，也了解客户与信贷相关的经济活动、社交活动和生活消费行为等，依托丰富的数据，金融机构可以建立比较完善的征信体系。例如，由中国人民银行主导建立的征信体系已经在全国范围防范金融风险中起到重要作用。

大数据风险管理体系对成本的影响有两个方面，一方面是减少风险管理中的人工成本。大数据技术能够收集和存储金融业务当中的各种数据，经过建模技术进行智能化的风险管理决策，因此减少人工成本。另一方面是提高了效率，由于大数据风险管理可以在几秒钟内作出决策，极大地提高决策的效率。综合起来大幅度地降低了风险管理的成本。

由于成本是企业非常重要的机密信息，很难获得数字技术造成的风险成本降低的实操数据。IIF 和麦肯锡（2017）采用模拟的办法，推算成本下降的幅度，采用机器人和自动化的风险控制，可以提高信用风险管理和风险预警功能的效率达 10%～20%；由于模型能够更好地对不良进行预判，可以减少信用风险损失 5%～10%；由于自动化减少了人为错误，改善了对员工不适当行为的监督，运营和罚款损失下降 8%～10%；由于资本配置效率增加，储备率降低，资本成本降低 4%～8%；信贷和风险加权资产的比例降低 5%～9%；随着数据管理的优化，用于风险管理的 IT 的效率可以提高 10%～20%。

## 四、金融科技在风险控制中的作用

金融最重要的核心就是风控。风控能力直接决定了普惠金融业务的成本和可持续性，也是解决普惠金融“最后一公里”问题中的重要一环。在具体风控模型中，云计算和大数据技术的组合使得风控模型层次多样，更能准确反映用户真实的风险承受能力。这其中最核心的技术就是利用大数据解决反欺诈问题和用户信用风险测评。

## （一）反欺诈模型

反欺诈问题的模型设计贯穿整个信贷业务过程且不同机构的反欺诈模型均不相同。各机构结合自己业务及获取的数据来源特点进行模型和流程设计。以移动端为例，从获客注册开始就要考虑虚假注册或身份冒用的风险，即考虑人与设备的关系。因此，需要使用成熟的指纹或人脸识别等活体检测技术与公安部权威的后台信息进行比对，再通过第三方信息确定用户真实性，同时也需要银行信息以确定人与银行卡的关系。无论何种校验方式，身份验证最终目的就是要确认人、设备和银行卡三者之间一对一或者一对多的真实关系。

接下来要校验客户填写信息的真实性，即通过数据对客户填写信息进行核实，查看可能潜在的风险点。这涉及钩稽对比和交叉检验等方法，其目的就是利用多维度数据对用户填写的信息进行逻辑检验，从而判断其真实性和可靠性。例如，用户填写的收入信息、工作地址、家庭住址和自动检测 IP 地址所属区域这些代表用户属性的信息若存在较大的差异，则有欺诈的风险或表示信息真实性有待考量。又如，检测到用户申请业务时设备 IP 地址所在区域频繁更换且与工作地址和家庭住址均不匹配，那么就要考虑有恶意欺诈的风险，需进一步核实用户信息。

在反欺诈模型中，“羊毛党”和“黑中介”同样是必须考虑的问题。“羊毛党”利用大量终端设备迅速注册参加服务商的活动，从中获益后再迅速退出；“黑中介”则是通过社交网站等平台获取急需贷款的客户，然后收取高额利息，甚至直接盗用他人身份信息骗贷，这都将大大增加平台的不良率。这两种恶意行为都利用同一 GPS 位置或者 IP 地址、利用同一部电脑设备或手机设备提交多笔借贷申请。这需要反欺诈系统对于此类恶意申请行为进行识别和阻拦，同时也需要不断完善机构黑名单制度，以便后续对用户进行信用风险管理做好铺垫。

另外，在反欺诈业务中，用户异常流量同样是一个重要的考量因素。例如，用户在短时间内 GPS 位置大范围移动或者 IP 地址的所在区域与 GPS 定位差异过大；又如，用户设备的机器 IMEI 值（国际移动设备识别码，International Mobile Equipment Identity）在较短时间内有多次变化，或同一个位置信息短时间内出现大量贷款申请等，这些都是异常情况的流量体现，需要反欺诈模块能及时发现并将风险隔离在外。总之，反欺诈模型中需要用到人工智能技术的活体识别、OCR（光学字符识别）技术、黑名单制度、多维度信息核实、地理位置校验、多头防控识别等多个角度对用户信息和行为进行追踪，并贯穿整个信贷业务过程。

## （二）信用风险管理

信用风险管理同样需要多数据来源进行综合测评。尤其是很多普惠金融服务对象未在人民银行的征信系统覆盖范围内，就更需要使用其他维度数据来对客户进行信用风险评估。对于个人评估，一般评价来自五个维度，分别是身份特质、履约能力、信用历史、人脉关系和行为偏好。这五个维度的数据来源除了机构自身所拥有的之外，还需要第三方征信机构提供的数据、电信或网络运营商的数据、银行交易信息的数据、电商消费行为偏好、社交网络数据等。

信用风险管理除了使用多种维度的数据，同时还会与反欺诈模块结合。例如，在社交关系中如果某用户与黑名单上的用户有密切联系或与多名黑名单上用户有交叉关系网，那么其信用风险相对较高。又如，用户行为触发了反欺诈规则但未超过阈值，此种情况同样会影响用户的信用风险评价。

除了利用大量的数据来源作为信用风险控制系统的基础之外，为了提高信用风险评估的准确度和风险区分度，还需要利用集成学习、深度学习等技术构建多变量的信用评估模型。例如，Zest finance 利用 10 个预测分析模型进行集成学习或多角度学习，对数据进行挖掘并应用模糊算法和神经网络最终形成一个独立的信用评分。百度的大数据风控系统"般若"则通过集成学习梯度增强决策树算法聚合大数据高维特征，将 3000 多种基础行为特征聚合成 200 棵以上的决策树，相对于传统的风险控制技术能够提升 10%的风险区分度。

## 五、金融科技当前的问题所在

### （一）数据安全问题

金融科技在解决普惠金融"最后一公里"问题中发挥着至关重要的作用，随着智能手机在农村的普及，农村地区及弱势群体享受普惠金融产品的成本大大降低的好处，但对金融知识了解普遍较少，对法律格式的合同文本理解不够透彻。如果同村威望较高的人被金融诈骗分子收买，其他村民很容易跟风行动，造成经济损失。所以数据安全，即保护普惠金融用户的个人信息具有非常重要的意义。一旦数据安全出现问题，涉及的人群与覆盖面更加广泛，最终甚至造成难以挽回的巨大损失。

现有的数据平台多基于 Hadoop 生态框架的 Hbase/Hive、Cassandra/Spark 等，这些平台在设计之初并没有重点考虑数据安全问题，但这种分布式的计算和存储架构造成了数据安全的外延扩展，这也就不再是单纯的数据库安全即可解决的问题。同时，数据的生命周期管理由于共享、调用等频繁使用也由原来的单链条变成了复杂的多链条形态，使数据的应用场景以及使用角色变得多样化，从而带来的大量访问控制也造成了新的安全挑战。

不仅如此，大量的数据共享与调用也对个人隐私构成了严重威胁。其实大数据的共享开放与用户的个人隐私保护存在天然的矛盾关系。正如上所述，为了能够更好地描绘用户画像，全方位对用户进行风险评估，个人信息在多家机构之间交叉互换几乎是不可避免的，甚至用户的社交媒体、行为偏好等侧面信息均被广泛滥用。这也对数据安全提出了更高的要求。另外，大数据快速发展的同时也伴随着多种攻击方式的诞生，如分布式拒绝服务（DDoS）攻击，包含 SYN Flood①、ACK Flood、ICMP Flood 等多种攻击方式，还有针对大数据平台的高级持续性威胁（APT）攻击，甚至基于数据挖掘的新型攻击手段等都对金融科技安全造成了新的冲击。

在政策法规方面，我国近几年也开始重视数据安全，出台了一系列的政策法规（见表 6-1）。

**表 6-1　我国与数据安全相关的政策法规**

| 时间 | 政策法规 | 内容 |
|---|---|---|
| 2012 年 12 月 | 第十一届全国人大常务委员会通过了《全国人大常委会关于加强网络信息保护的决定》 | 国家保护能够识别公民个人身份和涉及公民个人隐私的电子信息；网络服务提供者和其他企业事业单位及其工作人员对在业务活动中收集的公民个人电子信息必须严格保密，不得泄露、篡改、毁损，不得出售或者非法向他人提供等共十一条规定 |
| 2013 年 7 月 | 工业和信息化部公布《电信与互联网用户个人信息保护规定》 | 电信业务经营者、互联网信息服务提供者及其工作人员对在提供服务过程中收集、使用的用户个人信息应当严格保密，不得泄露、篡改或者毁损，不得出售或者非法向他人提供等共二十五条规定 |
| 2014 年 3 月 | 《消费者权益保护法》 | 第二十九条经营者及其工作人员对收集的消费者个人信息必须严格保密，不得泄露、出售或者非法向他人提供。经营者应当采取技术措施和其他必要措施，确保信息安全，防止消费者个人信息泄露、丢失。在发生或者可能发生信息泄露、丢失的情况时，应当立即采取补救措施 |
| 2015 年 8 月 | 国务院《促进大数据发展行动纲要》 | 指导思想里要完善法规制度和标准体系，科学规范利用大数据，切实保障数据安全；要在法律许可和确保安全的前提下，加强对社会治理相关领域数据的归集、发掘及关联分析，强化对妥善应对和处理重大突发公共事件的数据支持，提高公共安全保障能力，推动构建智能防控、综合治理的公共安全体系，维护国家安全和社会安定 |

① https://blog.csdn.net/hxx78/article/details/32093601。

续表

| 时间 | 政策法规 | 内容 |
|---|---|---|
| 2016 年 3 月 | 《关于国民经济与社会发展第十三个五年规划纲要》 | 其中第二十七章为实施国家大数据战略，第二十八章为强化信息安全保障 |
| 2016 年 12 月 | 国家互联网信息办公室《国家网络空间安全战略》 | 实施国家大数据战略，建立大数据安全管理制度，支持大数据、云计算等新一代信息技术创新和应用。建立完善国家网络安全技术支撑体系。加强网络安全基础理论和重大问题研究。加强网络安全标准化和认证认可工作，更多地利用标准规范网络空间行为。做好等级保护、风险评估、漏洞发现等基础性工作，完善网络安全监测预警和网络安全重大事件应急处置机制 |
| 2017 年 5 月 | 国家标准《信息安全技术 大数据安全管理指南》征求意见稿 | 对于大数据安全管理做了术语和定义，从大数据安全管理原则、大数据安全管理基本原则、制定大数据安全目标与策略、明确大数据安全管理的角色预测人、管理大数据安全风险及大数据平台运行安全等方面阐述了大数据安全管理的标准与原则 |
| 2017 年 6 月开始实施 | 《中华人民共和国网络安全法》 | 建设、运营网络或者通过网络提供服务，应当依照法律、行政法规的规定和国家标准的强制性要求，采取技术措施和其他必要措施，保障网络安全、稳定运行，有效应对网络安全事件，防范网络违法犯罪活动，维护网络数据的完整性、保密性和可用性等共七十九条 |
| 2018 年 5 月开始实施 | 国家标准《信息安全技术 个人信息安全规范》GB/T 35273—2017 | 对于个人信息安全做了术语和定义，从个人信息的收集、保存、使用、委托处理、共享与转让、安全事件处置等各方面均做了原则与标准的说明。提出了个人信息安全基本原则：权责一致原则、目的明确原则、选择同意原则、最少够用原则、公开透明原则、确保安全原则、主体参与原则 |

随着数据安全行业规范不断完善，数据安全架构也越来越成熟。各种安全技术例如 HTTPS 加密、防 DDos 攻击、APP 加固等技术层出不穷。阿里云、IBM、华为、浪潮等云平台均在不断完善自己的数据安全保护机制，从数据加密、访问控制、身份验证及审计方面，再加上根据生命周期管理和分类以及异地数据容灾，形成一整套数据安全解决方案。

### （二）数字鸿沟与排斥问题

数字技术极大地拓展了普惠金融的服务边界，使更多人可以享受普惠金融服务，同时显著降低了普惠金融的成本，成为实现普惠金融可持续发展的重要工具，一定程度上解决了传统金融对于低净值人群的排斥问题。但是知识鸿沟、数字鸿沟等因素导致在实施数字普惠金融时又出现了新的排斥。普惠金融产品不断推陈出新，但能否服务到真正需要的人群却仍是个未知数。这也就产生了数字鸿沟及排斥问题。这种排斥可以分为地域、信用评估、价格、营销、工具和自我六个方面[①]。

中国的4G基站数已达到315万个，城市范围已实现了4G网络全覆盖，行政村4G网络覆盖比例也超过了92%。在基站网络覆盖方面已经比较完善。根据浙江报告中数据显示（见图6-4和图6-5），农村地区目前拥有智能手机比例达到了77%，每天使用互联网比例达到53%，每周至少使用1次的比例达到72%。说明工具的排斥还是存在的[②]。

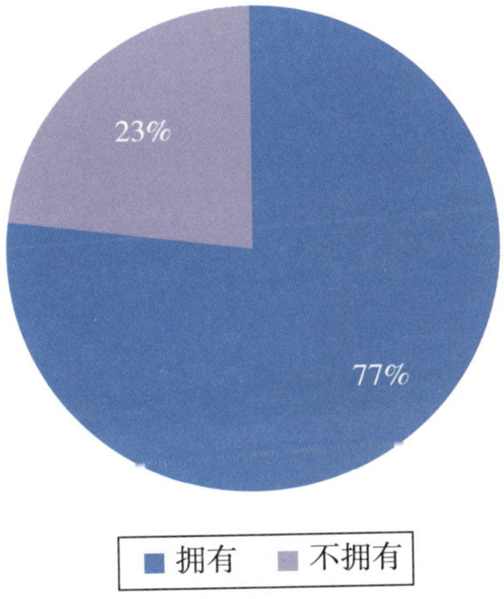


**图6-4　浙江省农村地区智能手机拥有比例**

在自我排斥方面，存在多种因素。自我排斥可分为能力排斥和意愿排斥。

在能力排斥方面，除了前面提到的工具排斥，还有其他排斥因素，如农村地区用户教育程度偏低、金融素养不高、对金融服务的理解力较差等。对金融服务理解能力的匮乏会进一步演变成意愿排斥，即对于金融服务缺乏信任感，这就导致了有能力但是不愿意去使用金融服务的情形。这需要普惠金融能力建设和营销推广能够落到实处。

① 中国普惠金融研究院发布的《中国普惠金融发展报告——普惠金融能力建设》，2017年9月。
② 中国普惠金融研究院发布的《中国普惠金融发展检测报告——浙江》，2018年6月。

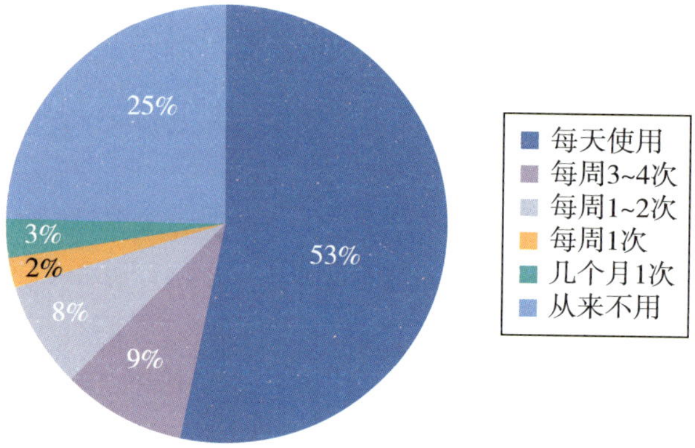


**图 6－5　浙江省农村地区互联网使用频率**

营销排斥即数字普惠金融的推广方法老套，以及频频发生的互联网金融诈骗案件造成农村地区居民对普惠金融营销产生排斥，尤其在农村地区用户厌恶损失的心态更为敏感的情况下，此种情况更为突出。不仅如此，农村地区用户重视熟人情面，习惯跟随村内德高望重者的选择，这也容易导致营销排斥的产生。

对数字鸿沟与排斥问题进行分析可以发现，金融科技的推进产生了大量新的普惠金融服务，但是服务推进过程并没有将欠发达地区用户对于产品的适应程度考虑在内。这种适应程度可以分为用户本身的金融能力，以及对于数字金融使用度及满意度来分析。

《中国普惠金融发展监测报告》显示，低收入者和高龄人群受金融排斥的可能性较大，且数字化排斥与金融排斥呈现正相关关系，也就是说金融教育和能力建设是有效解决数字鸿沟的手段之一，而金融科技公司应该在易用性和使用引导方面更加简洁和有效，不断改善用户体验，使服务的包容性得以不断完善。

### （三）金融科技机构的监管问题

金融科技机构快速发展也给监管带来了难题。其原因之一是金融科技的快速发展使得金融交易的数量和规模快速增长，大量的金融科技公司在推动普惠金融的同时也导致数据流量和风险的急剧上升。这就对监管机构的技术水平提出更高要求。原因之二在于，金融科技机构具有跨市场、跨行业的特性，服务的人群众多且更加多元化，这也对监管范围和方式提出了挑战。

2016 年可以被称为"互联网金融监管元年"。在互联网金融被写入"十三五"规划之后，伴随着互联网行业的快速发展，一系列监管办法相继出台。《互联网金融风险专项整治工作实施方案》（国办发〔2016〕21 号）的公布开启了对互联网金融风险专项整治工作的全面部署，深入并稳妥地推进金融监管体制的改革，构建了以技术为驱动的监管体系新范式。

随着金融技术的不断发展，监管也将利用机器学习、人工智能、数字加密以及云计算等新技术，以互联网思维应对互联网金融的监管需要。综合利用银行、媒体、税务、公安等各种渠道的信息与数据，搭建预警监测平台和监管指标体系，通过人工智能等技术实现监管能力的提升，帮助金融机构满足监管与合规要求。一方面，监管机构要发挥引领作用，由监管机构建立数字金融行业监管标准，制定相关的监管计划和技术标准，开发国内的 RegTech 科技监管系统，有效规范市场进出准则，为行业提供公平有序的竞争环境。另一方面，RegTech 也牵扯金融机构和金融科技公司的行为，因此整个数字金融领域也要积极配合监管部门，遵守并推动 RegTech 的可持续发展。

# 第七章　穿越金融“最后一公里”的基础设施

【摘要】改革开放四十年后，穿越“最后一公里”的普惠金融基础设施建设得到稳步发展，支付结算系统、征信系统、评估系统、支持性系统的建设不断提升了普惠金融的可得性和可负担性。但是，目前农村地区的支付结算系统整体建设水平仍低于城镇地区，征信系统仍存在城乡差距大、失信惩戒效用低、信息安全等问题，评估系统尚未实现高效的行业预测和风险预警，也未形成普惠金融全行业的支持系统。下一轮普惠金融的发展浪潮在于大力发展代理商、互联网和其他无网点银行渠道。在这样的趋势与背景之下，中国农村地区金融基础设施建设更多地从“中小微弱”群体的需求与习惯出发。

改革开放四十年，中国普惠金融行业的发展得益于政府投入、民间参与、金融科技掘金等动力支持。目前，穿越“最后一公里”的基础设施，包括支付结算系统、征信系统、评估系统、支持性系统等各方面得到稳定提升。此外，随着金融科技应用的下沉，金融“最后一公里”的“中小微弱”群体对基础设施的需求发生了明显改变，对互联网与移动设备的依赖增强。

## 一、建设现状

国内农村地区金融基础设施建设稳步发展，金融科技在一定程度上改变了传统金融基础设施的需求与覆盖情况。

## （一）支付结算系统

截至2017年末，农村地区[①]银行网点数量12.61万个；每万人拥有的银行网点数量为1.30个，县均银行网点55.99个，乡均银行网点3.93个，村均银行网点0.24个。[②]

1. 结算账户覆盖情况

银行机构在农村地区结算账户覆盖稳定增长（见表7-1），单位银行结算账户和个人银行结算账户的户数都有所增长，电子银行开通户数增长较快。

第一，单位银行结算账户方面，截至2017年末，农村地区累计开立单位银行结算账户1966.51万户；第二，个人银行结算账户与银行卡方面，农村地区个人银行结算账户39.66亿户，其中，借记卡26.91亿张、信用卡1.75亿张；第三，农村电子银行账户方面，截至2017年末，农村地区网上银行开通数累计5.31亿户，发生网银支付业务笔数94.69亿笔，金额152.73万亿元；手机银行开通数累计5.17亿户，发生手机银行支付业务笔数91.10亿笔，金额38.89万亿元；电话银行开通数累计1.9亿户，发生电话银行支付业务笔数9788.24万笔，金额1214.71亿元。[③]

**表7-1 农村地区结算账户统计**

| 年份 | 单位银行结算账户（万户） | 个人银行结算账户（亿户） | 借记卡（亿张） | 信用卡（亿张） | 网上银行开通数（亿户） | 手机银行开通数（亿户） | 电话银行开通数（亿户） |
|---|---|---|---|---|---|---|---|
| 2015年 | 1630.3 | 33.04 | 20.85 | 1.36 | 3.56 | 2.76 | 1.81 |
| 2016年 | 1823.07 | 35.61 | 23.87 | 1.65 | 4.29 | 3.73 | 2.15 |
| 2017年 | 1966.51 | 39.66 | 26.91 | 1.75 | 5.31 | 5.17 | 1.9 |

资料来源：历年中国人民银行发布的《中国支付体系发展报告》。

随着移动数据网络以及固定宽带等网络基础设施建设的不断完善，中国农村网民数量稳定增长。截至2017年末，农村网民达2.09亿人（见图7-1），占比为27%。对比农村地区电子银行业务数据可知（见表7-2），电话银行交易和网上银行交易呈下降趋势，手机银行交易增长快速。

① 《2017年农村地区支付业务发展总体情况》指出，截至2017年末，所统计农村地区拥有县级行政区2252个，乡级行政区3.21万个，村级行政区52.97万个，农村地区人口数量9.71亿人。

② 资料来源：中国人民银行发布的《2017年农村地区支付业务发展总体情况》，2018年4月。

③ 资料来源：中国人民银行官网。

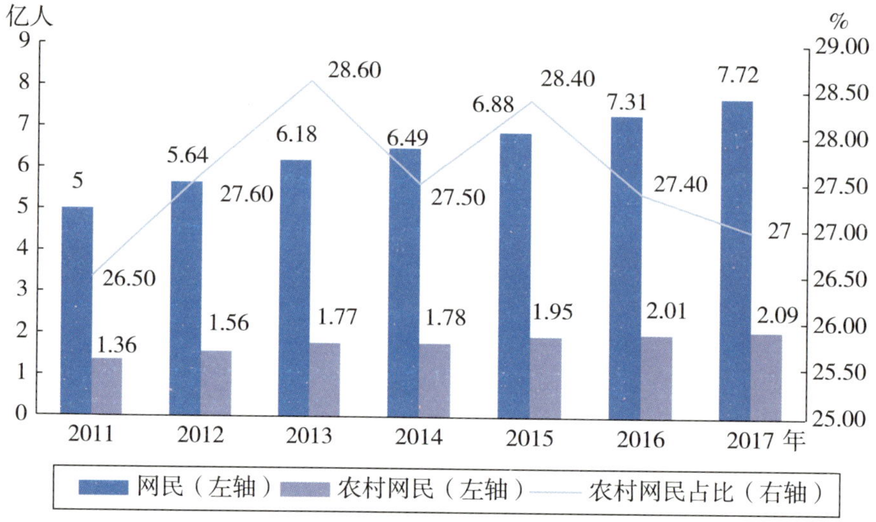


资料来源：中国互联网络信息中心发布的历次《中国互联网络发展状况统计报告》。

**图 7-1　2011—2017 年中国网民规模**

**表 7-2　农村地区电子银行业务统计**

| 年份 | 网上银行业务 | | 手机银行业务 | | 电话银行业务 | |
|---|---|---|---|---|---|---|
| | 笔数（亿笔） | 金额（万亿元） | 笔数（亿笔） | 金额（万亿元） | 笔数（亿笔） | 金额（万亿元） |
| 2015 年 | 105.46 | 150.44 | 31.49 | 13.68 | 2.49 | 0.44 |
| 2016 年 | 98.29 | 152.06 | 50.86 | 23.4 | 1.82 | 0.27 |
| 2017 年 | 94.69 | 152.73 | 91.1 | 38.89 | 0.98 | 0.12 |

资料来源：历年中国人民银行发布的《中国支付体系发展报告》。

除银行机构之外，非银行支付机构为农村地区提供支付服务增长迅速。2017 年，非银行支付机构为农村地区提供网络支付业务共计 1417.82 亿笔，金额 45 万亿元；其中，互联网支付 122.73 亿笔，金额 2.1 万亿元，单笔金额 171.11 元；移动支付 1295.09 亿笔，金额 42.9 万亿元，单笔金额 331.25 元。①

此外，银行机构和非银行机构都积极支持农村电商发展。2017 年，银行业金融机构为农村地区电子商务共提供收款服务 4.60 亿笔，金额 5543.13 亿元；非银行支付机构为农村地区网络商户提供收款 2.77 亿笔，金额 1791.68 亿元，单笔金额

① 资料来源：中国人民银行官网。

646.82 元。[①]

2. 支付系统覆盖情况

农村地区的支付系统覆盖继续稳固，人民银行支付系统的网点覆盖到乡级行政区，还未实现村级行政区全覆盖，农信银支付清算系统业务增长迅速。

人民银行支付系统方面，截至 2017 年末（见表 7-3），农村地区接入人民银行支付系统的银行网点 9.49 万个，代理银行网点 2.72 万个；农信银支付清算系统方面，截至 2017 年末，以参与者身份接入农信银支付清算系统的银行网点 4.41 万个，基本覆盖农信社等合作金融机构营业网点，通过农信银支付清算系统办理业务 33.49 亿笔，金额 6.68 万亿元（见图 7-2）。[②]

**表 7-3 农村地区支付系统网点与业务统计**

| 年份 | 农村地区接入人民银行大小额支付系统的银行网点（万个） | 农村地区接入人民银行大小额支付系统的代理银行网点（万个） | 以参与者身份接入农信银支付清算系统的银行网点（万个） |
|---|---|---|---|
| 2015 年 | 8.31 | 3.23 | 4.10 |
| 2016 年 | 8.41 | 3.43 | 4.34 |
| 2017 年 | 9.49 | 2.72 | 4.41 |

资料来源：中国人民银行发布的历年《中国支付体系发展报告》《2016 年农村地区支付业务发展总体情况》。

截至 2017 年末，虽然农村地区人民银行支付系统的银行和代理银行网点覆盖率超过了 96.83%[③]，但农村地区支付系统办理业务的笔数和金额占人民银行支付系统整体业务的比例都相对较低（见图 7-3 和图 7-4），占比分别为 4.33%和 0.12%。因此，仍需加大力度推进农村地区支付系统的使用效率。

3. 无网点银行[④]与设备覆盖情况

农村地区无网点银行与设备的覆盖稳步发展，尤其助农取款服务点实现了村级行政区的覆盖，并且随着金融科技的发展，使支付结算业务对网点的依赖下降。

截至 2017 年末（见图 7-5），农村地区特约商户 526.33 万户、ATM 37.74 万台、POS 机 711.49 万台（含转账电话 235.23 万台），以及除 ATM、POS 机之外的其他自

---

① 资料来源：中国人民银行官网。

② 资料来源：中国人民银行官网。

③ 资料来源：中国人民银行发布的《2017 年农村地区支付业务发展总体情况》，2018 年 4 月。

④ CGAP 发表的《中国：无网点银行发展的新模式》中指出，无网点银行业务是指在传统的银行网点之外提供金融服务，它利用代理商或其他第三方中介机构作为与客户接触的主要渠道，依靠相关技术（如读卡 POS 机和手机）传输交易情况来。

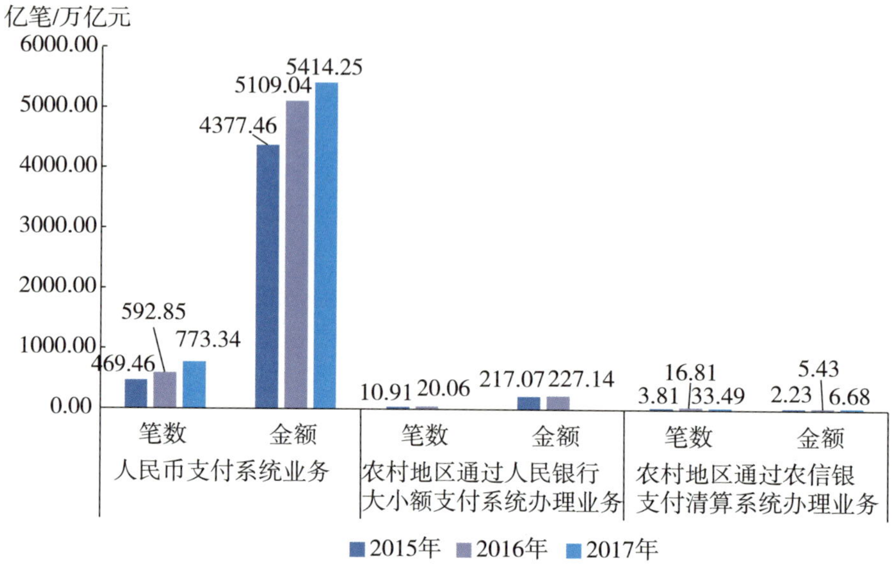


资料来源：中国人民银行发布的历年《中国支付体系发展报告》《2016 年农村地区支付业务发展总体情况》。

**图 7－2　2015—2017 年农村地区支付系统业务统计**

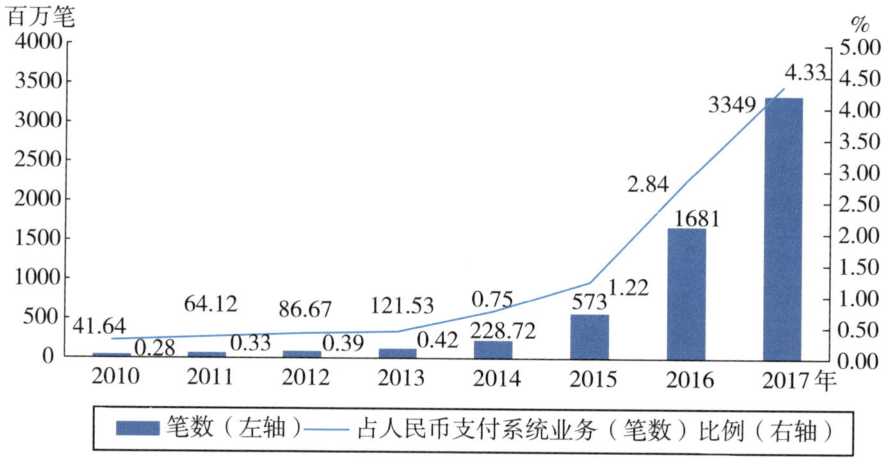


资料来源：中国人民银行官网。

**图 7－3　2010—2017 年农信银支付清算系统业务（笔数）情况**

助服务终端（如多媒体终端等）18.24 万台。另外，截至 2017 年末，农村地区拥有助农取款服务点 91.4 万个（其中，加载电商功能的有 13.98 万个），覆盖村级行政区 51.56 万个，村级行政区覆盖率达 97.34%，村均拥有量为 1.73 个。①

此外，农村地区互联网普及率逐年增高，农村网民数量也逐年增加，农村网民使

① 资料来源：中国人民银行发布的《2016 年农村地区支付业务发展总体情况》，2017 年 3 月。

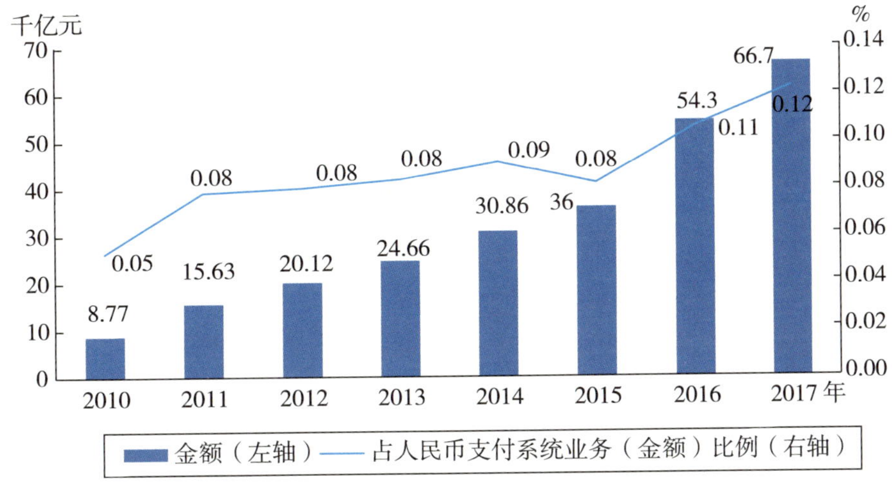


资料来源：中国人民银行官网。

**图7-4　2010—2017年农信银支付清算系统业务（金额）情况**

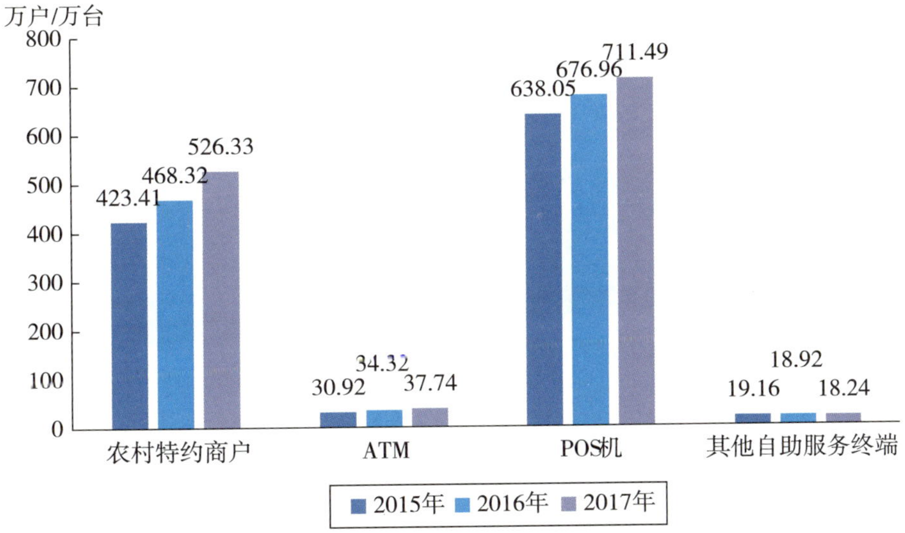


资料来源：中国人民银行发布的《2016年农村地区支付业务发展总体情况》，2017年3月。

**图7-5　2015—2017年农村地区银行卡受理服务终端的统计**

用手机上网的比例最高。截至2015年末（见图7-7），我国农村手机网民1.7亿人，占所有手机网民总数的27.4%。截至2017年末（见图7-6），我国农村地区互联网普及率是35.4%，低于城镇地区的71%。

从业务量来看，随着银行电子渠道、助农取款服务、非银行支付机构业务在县域的快速发展，银行卡在POS机的交易业务、农民工银行卡特色服务业务都呈现萎缩状态（见图7-8）；值得注意的是，手机银行支付业务增长迅速（见图7-9）。

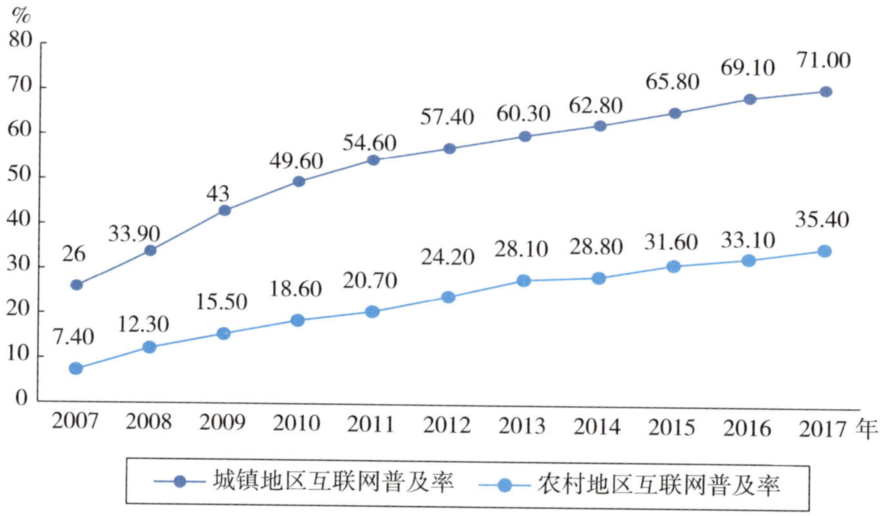


资料来源：中国互联网络信息中心发布的历次《中国互联网络发展状况统计报告》。

**图 7－6　2007—2017 年城乡互联网普及率**

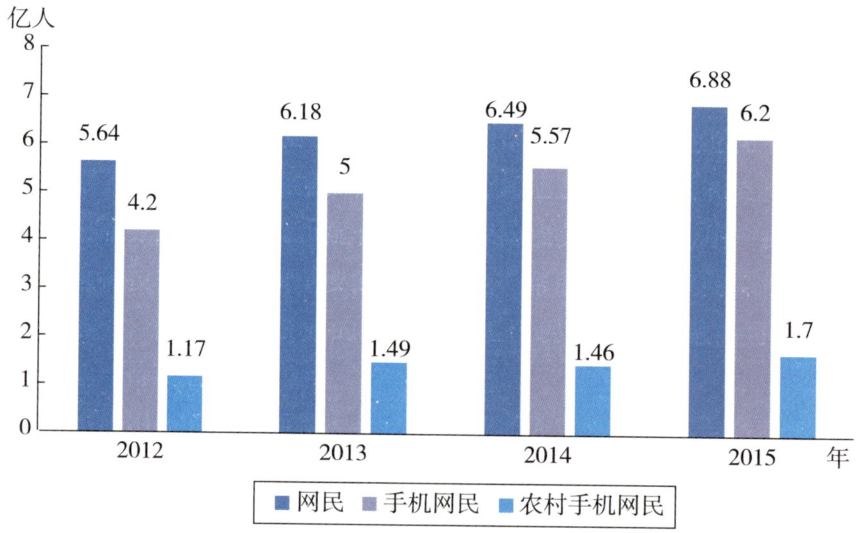


资料来源：中国互联网络信息中心发布的《2015 年农村互联网发展状况研究报告》，2016 年 8 月。

**图 7－7　2012—2015 年农村手机网民人数**

可见，打通“最后一公里”金融服务的基础设施日益多元。除了银行网点之外，无网点银行和互联网金融基础设施与设备的普及，可以有效解决银行网点覆盖村级行政区带来的成本过高与机构可持续能力不足的问题，有助于农村地区居民获得更多样化、更便捷的金融服务。

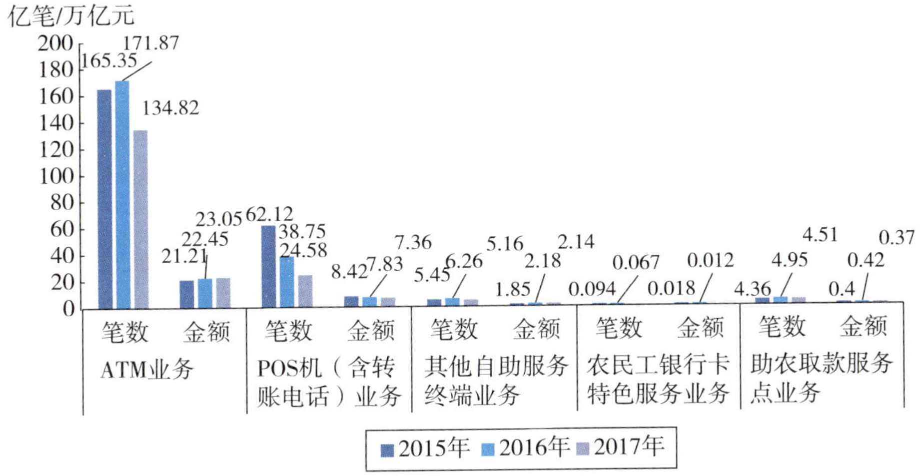


资料来源：中国人民银行发布的《2016年农村地区支付业务发展总体情况》，2017年3月。

**图7-8　2015—2017年农村地区银行卡受理服务终端发生交易业务统计**

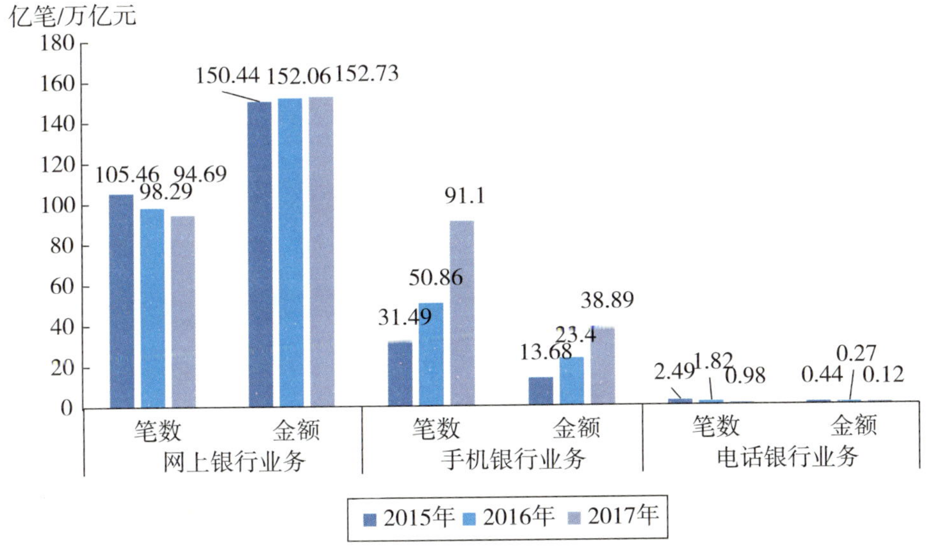


资料来源：中国人民银行发布的《2016年农村地区支付业务发展总体情况》，2017年3月。

**图7-9　2015—2017年农村地区电子银行支付业务统计**

### （二）征信系统

目前，我国基本形成了传统征信与大数据征信并存，且以公共征信为主、商业征信为辅的征信系统。

传统征信方面，以人民银行征信中心为主导，建立收录全国企业与个人信用档案的数据库。中国人民银行征信中心已建成全球规模最大的征信系统，但有信用记录的人数仅为3.8亿人，只占收录自然人总数的44%。

大数据征信方面，以互联网经济为基础，是基于大数据和数据处理技术的新型征信手段。2015年初获批的8家个人征信试点机构，2016年9月初获批准备案的135家企业征信机构，多数有互联网背景。目前，大数据征信机构在数据源上对传统征信进行了有益补充，而商业征信的引入，势必通过竞争提高服务质量和服务效率。百行征信的筹建，正是打通传统征信与大数据征信、公共征信与商业征信壁垒的一次尝试。

1. 传统征信

企业征信系统方面，截至2016年9月初，共有2828家接入机构①，包括农村合作金融机构、小额贷款公司、村镇银行等普惠金融供应方。截至2016年末，全国累计补充完善中小企业信息261.14万户（见图7-10），占所有建立档案的企业及其他组织数的11.81%，累计已有47.16万户中小企业获得银行贷款，贷款余额10.5万亿元。②

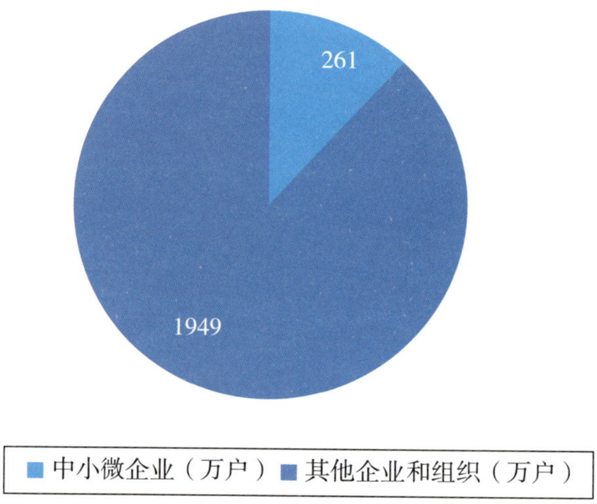


资料来源：中国人民银行金融稳定分析小组．中国金融稳定报告2017［M］．北京：中国金融出版社，2017.

**图7-10　2016年末，人民银行征信中心建立中小微企业信用档案情况**

个人征信系统方面，截至2016年9月初，共有2927家接入机构（见图7-11），包括小额贷款公司、村镇银行、农村信用社/农村商业银行等普惠金融供应方。截至2016年末，人民银行征信中心为全国累计1.72亿农户（见图7-12）建立信用档案，

① 资料来源：瞭望智库和财经国家周刊联合发布的《中国社会信用体系发展报告2017》，2016年10月15日。

② 资料来源：中国人民银行金融稳定分析小组．中国金融稳定报告2017［M］．北京：中国金融出版社，2017.

占所有建立信用档案自然人人数的 18.9%，有近 9248 万户农户获得银行贷款，贷款余额 2.7 万亿元。①

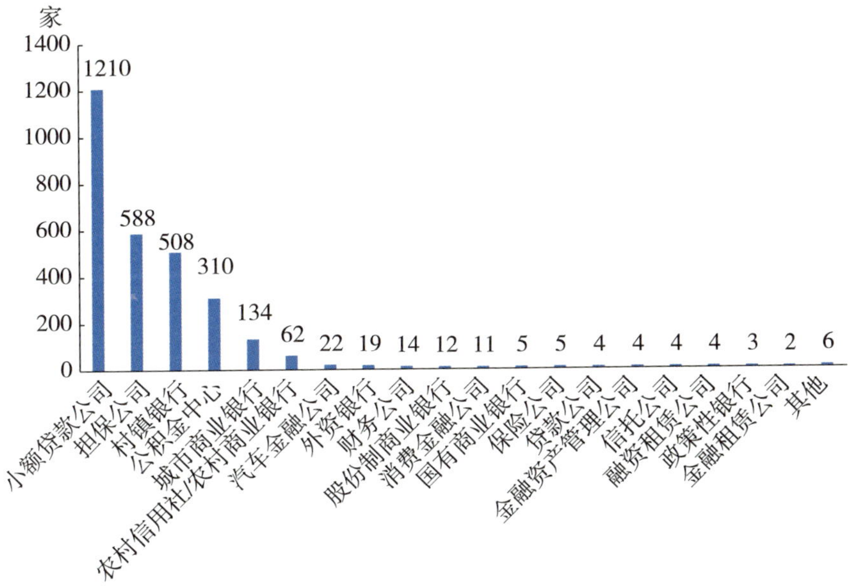


资料来源：瞭望智库和财经国家周刊联合发布的《中国社会信用体系发展报告 2017》，2016 年 10 月 15 日。

**图 7-11　2016 年 9 月初，中国人民银行个人征信系统机构接入数**

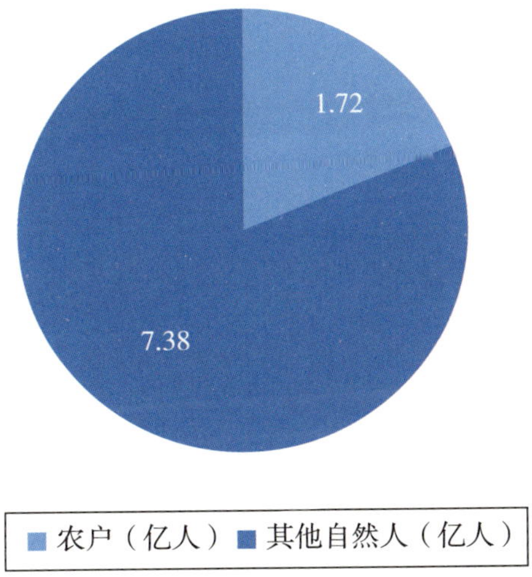


资料来源：中国人民银行金融稳定分析小组．中国金融稳定报告 2017［M］．北京：中国金融出版社，2017.

**图 7-12　2016 年末，人民银行征信中心建立农户信用档案情况**

① 资料来源：中国人民银行金融稳定分析小组．中国金融稳定报告 2017［M］．北京：中国金融出版社，2017.

2. 大数据征信

易观智库根据征信产品数据源、数据处理方式、数据服务对象等的不同，可以把大数据征信机构分成三类：第一类是传统大数据征信机构，如中智诚征信、中诚信征信和鹏元征信；第二类是互联网大数据征信机构，如芝麻信用、腾讯征信、前海征信、考拉征信和华道征信等；第三类是第三方数据服务商，如百融至信、91 征信、安融征信和聚信立等。

截至 2017 年末，中国网民达到 7.72 亿人。用户在网络上发生的购物、社交、搜索、交通出行、金融服务、民生服务、浏览网页等行为产生了海量的数据，为大数据征信提供了数据基础，是传统征信数据源的重要补充。如表 7－4 所示，芝麻信用、腾讯征信等互联网大数据征信机构从各自的主营业务中获得多元且海量的互联网金融数据。

**表 7－4　国内领先大数据征信机构的农村地区与中小企业数据源**

| 机构名称 | 数据源 | 农村地区与中小企业覆盖情况 | 应用场景 |
| --- | --- | --- | --- |
| 芝麻信用 | 阿里系内部电商、蚂蚁金服；外部如公安、法院、政府以及商户回流的数据；用户自我提交的信用数据 | 蚂蚁金服提供支付、保险、信贷服务的 1.63 亿名农村消费者，175.7 万家农村小企业、个体工商户和种植、养殖户①；3700 多万家中小微企业；4000 多万户使用收银数字化服务的小商家 | 交易场景、消费金融、酒店、租车、婚恋、公共事业服务 |
| 腾讯征信 | 社交网络、电商、支付、视频、旅游、地图、餐饮、浏览器、ID | 全国 9.63 亿户微信用户、1 亿户腾讯理财平台用户、8.5 亿户移动 QQ 用户中的农村用户和中小企业用户 | 反欺诈；银行、证券、保险、消费、金融、P2P 等商业机构；生活领域和人脸识别 |

① 资料来源：蚂蚁金服对外公布截至 2017 年 3 月底的数据。

续表

| 机构名称 | 数据源 | 农村地区与中小企业覆盖情况 | 应用场景 |
| --- | --- | --- | --- |
| 深圳前海征信 | 平安各子公司数据、合作机构数据（电信公司、公安机构、银联等、50 多家小额贷款公司和 P2P 公司） | 近 2000 家机构客户中的农村客户和中小企业客户 | 反欺诈产品、信用风险产品、数据开放平台、综合报告等产品，用于租赁、借贷、购物、酒店、餐饮、交通、公益事业等领域 |
| 拉卡拉（考拉征信） | 个体工商户、手机商户信用卡还款、转账、水电煤气、火车票机票信息、理财、信贷 | 百万个体工商户 | 金融、民生、购物、租车租房、交友等 |
| 北京华道 | 信贷、公安司法、运营商数据、公共事业数据、网络痕迹数据 | | 租房情景中，租房者信用情况，帮助房主降低风险 |
| 百融至信 | 电商、社交、媒体、购物、金融 | | 反欺诈产品、信用风险产品、数据开放平台、综合分析报告，主要服务于银行信贷风险控制 |
| 鹏元征信 | 从外部的传统金融机构和 P2P 互联网金融平台获取数据 | 13.3 亿人中的农村用户 | 反欺诈 |
| 中智诚 | 从外部的传统金融机构和 P2P 互联网金融平台获取欺诈数据、信用卡逾期信息 | | 征信报告、风险信息查询、互联网身份验证 |
| 中诚信 | 从外部的传统金融机构和 P2P 互联网金融平台获取数据 | | |

资料来源：部分数据摘自中国普惠金融研究院历年发布的《中国数字普惠金融发展报告》。

以芝麻信用为例，其企业数据源来自提供过电子商务、贷款等服务的3700多万名中小微企业客户，占我国小微企业总数[①]的50%以上；其农村地区个人数据源来自提供过支付、保险、信贷服务的1.63亿名农村消费者，占全国网民总数的20%以上，占农村网民总数的比例超过75%。

### （三）评估系统

普惠金融的评估系统主要包括行业发展指标体系、机构评估与评级等用以评价行业、机构、风险环境的一整套系统。由于社会影响力投资概念的兴起，国内也开始讨论普惠金融社会影响力评估指标的建设，以期形成财务绩效和社会影响力绩效两套指标。

1. 行业发展指标

相对于普惠金融行业的发展进程而言，国内外对普惠金融指标体系研究与实践的起步较晚，国际组织的普惠金融指标体系建设先于中国。

国际上，国际组织开发的与普惠金融相关的指标体系主要包括：全球普惠金融合作伙伴（CPFI）的G20普惠金融指标体系、世界银行普惠金融方面的8项调查（全球普惠调查、企业调查、金融能力调查、生活水平评估调查、全球支付系统调查、全球普惠金融责任调查、经商调查、农业经营调查）、国际货币基金组织的金融服务可获得性调查、经合组织普惠金融相关的3项调查（国际金融教育调查、中小企业计分板、国际学生评估项目）、普惠金融联盟的普惠金融核心指标。

在中国，如表7-5所示，人民银行早在2014年就选取四川、陕西、吉林、浙江、福建、贵州6个省份作试点，开始了普惠金融指标体系的建设工作。中国人民银行济宁市中心支行率先在2014年6月发布的普惠金融指数包含5大类、26个分析指标。2016年12月，中国人民银行正式下发《中国普惠金融指标体系填报制度（试行）》及《中国普惠金融指标体系》。《中国普惠金融指标体系》涵盖了3个维度、20类51项指标。此外，还有台州市政府在2015年11月发布的小微金融指数（台州样本），以及北京大学和蚂蚁金服在2016年7月发布了《北京大学数字普惠金融指数》，包含3个维度、24个指标。

---

① 资料来源：国家工商总局代表在小微企业创新发展高层论坛上的发言，截至2017年7月底，我国小微企业名录收录的小微企业达7328.1万户。其中，企业2327.8万户，占企业总数的82.5%；个体工商户5000.3万户，占个体工商户总数的80.9%。

表 7－5　国内普惠金融指标体系建设情况

| 时间 | 机构 | 指标 |
| --- | --- | --- |
| — | 中国人民银行研究局、国家开发银行、世界银行、中国金融教育发展基金会等 | 中国小微金融标准委员会 |
| 2014 年 | 中国人民银行 | 普惠金融指标体系建设试点工作：四川、陕西、吉林、浙江、福建、贵州 6 个省份 |
| 2014 年 6 月 | 中国人民银行济宁市中心支行 | 普惠金融指数：5 大类、26 个分析指标 |
| 2015 年 11 月 | 台州市政府、台州市政府金融办公室、浙江（台州）小微金融研究院、浙江工商大学 | 小微金融指数（台州样本） |
| 2016 年 7 月 | 北京大学、蚂蚁金服 | 北京大学数字普惠金融指数：3 个维度、24 个指标 |
| 2016 年 7 月 | 中国人民银行 | G20 普惠金融指标体系（2016 版）：提出用于衡量数字金融服务发展的新指标 |
| 2016 年 12 月 | 中国人民银行 | 《中国普惠金融指标体系填报制度（试行）》及《中国普惠金融指标体系》：涵盖金融服务的可得性、使用情况和质量 3 个维度，包含 20 类、51 项指标，其中使用情况维度包含 11 类共 28 项指标，可得性维度包含 4 类共 9 项指标，质量维度包含 5 类共 14 项指标 |
| 2016 年 12 月 | 中国人民大学中国普惠金融研究院 | CAFI 数字普惠金融指标与监测体系：59 个指标，以及包含 8 个维度的中国普惠金融排斥指数以及综合排斥指数，2018 年 5 月发布的《中国普惠金融发展监测报告·2017 浙江》 |

在综合了国际组织及各国专家学者等研究经验的基础上，结合中国的实际情况，中国普惠金融研究院启动“数字普惠金融指标与监测体系项目”，建立了包含 8 个维度的中国普惠金融排斥指数以及综合排斥指数，并于 2018 年 5 月发布了《中国普惠金融发展监测报告·2017 浙江》。

目前，多数普惠金融行业发展指标体系多基于金融服务的可获得性、产品质量、使用情况等几个维度进行指标建设，与普惠金融的“普及”与“惠及”目标高度吻合。不过，普惠金融的服务对象就是“最后一公里”的“中小微弱”群体，其社会意义不仅仅是金融行业的，还具有全面的社会性。在指标设置方面，新兴的社会影响力评估体系，包括影响力报告与投资标准（IRIS）、社会投资回报率（SROI）、社会企业的B影响力评估（B Impact Assessment）等，在诸如可持续社区、生态环境能源、性别平等、科教文卫等基于可持续发展目标的指标设计值得普惠金融借鉴。

2. 机构评估与评级

普惠金融机构的评估与评级目前还集中于对小额信贷机构的评级，主要是对机构财务绩效和社会绩效的评价，帮助识别小额信贷机构本身的运营情况和社会目标实现情况，也可以满足小额信贷机构的融资需求。

国际上，小额信贷机构的评级主要进展包括：世界银行扶贫协商小组组建了社会绩效工作组，目标在于创建社会绩效的标准与评估工具；目前比较知名的评级机构有印度的M-CRIL、意大利的Microfinanza Rating、美国的MicroRate等；提供市场分析和机构评估的在线数据平台Mixmarket。

在中国，小额贷款机构评级的主要进展包括：为了满足监管需求，各省金融办推进的小额贷款公司评级分类管理试点；中国小额信贷机构联席会发布《小额贷款公司分类评级体系（征求意见稿）》；网贷之家、网贷天眼等在线数据平台对P2P网贷平台进行相关指标的排序。

不过，无论国内外，目前都还没有形成针对普惠金融机构的完整评估与评级体系。

### （四）支持系统

支持系统包括农村地区通信基础设施的建设、合作网络平台的搭建以及智库研究的投入，为攻坚“最后一公里”的普惠金融服务提供发展环境、资源拓展、人才培养等各种支持。

1. 农村地区通信基础设施

农村地区通信基础设施建设方面，截至2017年末（见图7-13），电信业完成3.2万个行政村通光纤的电信普遍服务任务部署①，农村宽带用户达到9377万户，在固定宽带接入用户中占26.9%；从2015年城乡互联网络接入设备使用情况来看（见图7-14），农村地区使用手机上网的比例高达87.1%，远高于台式电脑、笔记本电脑、平板电脑、电视等设备；2013—2017年（见图7-15），由于移动电话的普及，农村地区固定电话用户数逐年减少。

---

① 资料来源：工业和信息化部发布的《2017年通信业统计公报》，2018年。

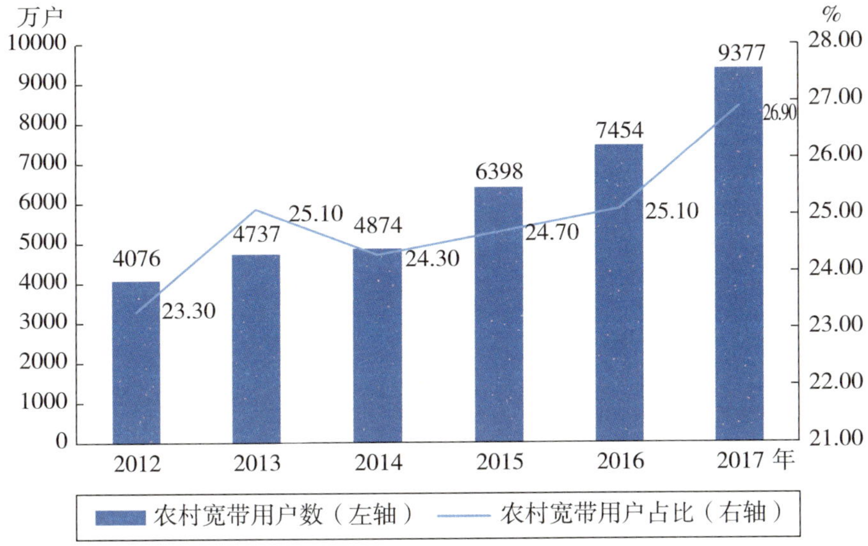


资料来源：工业和信息化部发布的《2017 年通信业统计公报》，2018 年。

**图 7-13　2012—2017 年农村宽带用户情况**

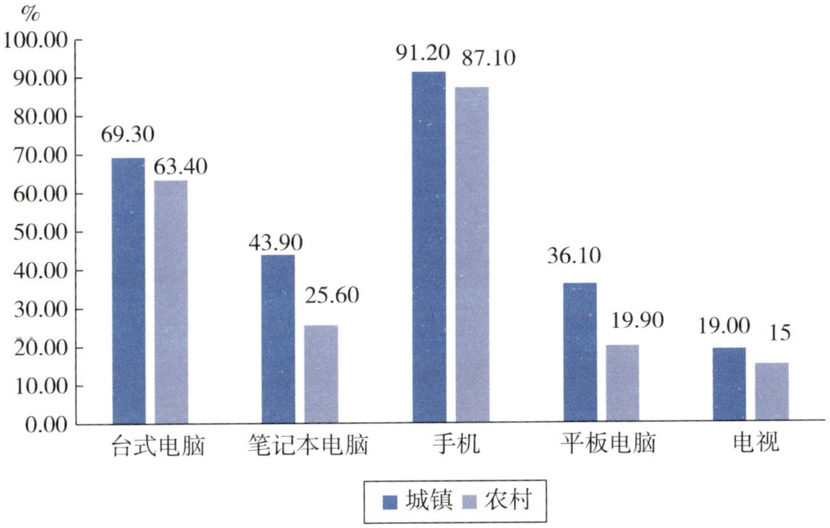


资料来源：中国互联网络信息中心发布的《2015 年农村互联网发展状况研究报告》，2016 年 8 月。

**图 7-14　2015 年城乡互联网络接入设备使用情况**

2. 合作网络平台

合作网络平台搭建方面，成立于 2005 年的中国小额信贷联盟是国内最早的全国性合作平台，其会员机构包括提供普惠金融服务的非政府组织和农村资金互助社、商业银行、小额贷款公司、中介机构、P2P 平台、协会组织等；多数地方性小额贷款公司协会集中在 2009—2013 年成立；2015 年 4 月成立的中国小额贷款公司协会是银监会

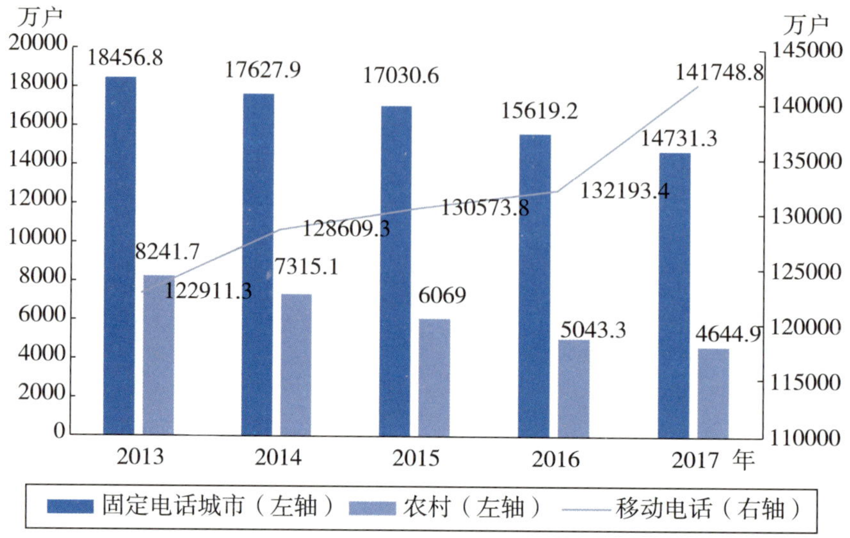


资料来源：工业和信息化部的电话用户分省统计。

**图 7－15　2013—2017 年电话用户情况**

主管的全国性小额贷款公司的行业性协会；2016 年 11 月，广州市成立全国首个普惠金融协会。国际性的合作网络中，银监会和人民银行是普惠金融联盟的会员机构，中国也加入了全球普惠金融伙伴关系组织。

3. 智库研究

智库研究投入方面，最早在中国推进普惠金融研究和实践的是中国社会科学院农村发展研究所。进入 21 世纪后，各类普惠金融相关的智库研究机构逐渐多起来，包括清华大学五道口金融学院互联网金融实验室、中国小微金融研究院、中国人民大学小微金融研究中心、中国普惠金融研究院等。目前，北京、浙江、江苏、福建、山东等地都已成立普惠金融研究机构。其中，中国普惠金融研究院历年发布的《中国普惠金融发展报告》和《中国数字普惠金融发展报告》，都比较全面地反映了近年中国普惠金融的整体发展情况。

## 二、仍然存在的问题

农村地区金融基础设施建设在支付结算系统、征信系统、评估系统、支持系统等方面取得了一定成就，但仍面临不少问题。

第一，支付结算系统方面，农村地区金融基础设施建设水平仍低于全国或城镇地区水平。随着移动数据网络、固定宽带等基础设施不断完善，以及互联网技术的发展与应用，我国农村地区的支付系统、无网点银行与设备等的覆盖情况取得了较大进展。

但是，对比全国或城镇地区的数据，农村地区金融基础设施的覆盖率、支付结算的笔数与金额、支付结算系统的使用效率等都远低于城镇地区的水平。

第二，征信系统方面，农村地区存在信用数据远未实现全覆盖、失信惩戒机制效用较低、城乡信用体系建设差距明显、信息安全隐患等问题。在传统征信手段下，在农村地区，尤其是边远或欠发达地区，对“中小微弱”群体的征信工作面临成本高、数据较缺乏、信用意识较弱等问题。借助大数据征信手段之后，可以大大提升“中小微弱”群体数据源的覆盖面和质量的问题，但大数据征信机构本身的市场化倾向过重，信息安全隐患问题比公共征信系统高。此外，虽然百行征信有限公司已经筹建完成，但传统征信与大数据征信之间的数据壁垒并未彻底破除，公共征信与商业征信、传统征信与大数据征信如何实现有效合作，还有待探索。

第三，评估系统方面，行业评估和机构评估远未能全面保障普惠金融行业生态的可持续性与安全性。由于中国已经加入普惠金融联盟和 G20 全球普惠金融合作伙伴关系，因此行业发展指标体系建设与世界比较同步，但国内还没有行业普遍认可的机构评估与评级指标体系。

第四，支持性系统方面，随着国内小额信贷、小微金融、互联网金融的实践发展，虽然通信基础设施、合作网络平台与智库研究都有及时跟进这些变化并发挥对普惠金融行业发展的促进作用，但还未形成普惠金融全行业的支持系统，金融创新力还不足。从农村地区通信基础设施建设方面来说，随着金融科技的发展，对通信基础设施建设提出更高要求，设备的更新与迭代需求不断升级。从合作网络平台方面来说，全国性和地方性的合作网络平台发展迅速，为行业发展提供了必要的支持，但地方性合作网络平台远未能在全国性合作网络平台上实现合力。从智库研究方面来说，中央与北京、浙江、江苏、福建、山东等地，依托政府、高校、科研机构的力量，对行业基础研究、发展预测、人才培养等有一定投入，但金融创新能力仍有待挖掘。

## 三、改善建议

下一轮的普惠金融发展浪潮将主要是代理商、互联网和其他无网点银行渠道的发展。[①] 在这样的趋势与背景之下，中国农村地区金融基础设施建设需要更多地从“中小微弱”群体的需求与习惯出发，使支付结算系统、征信系统、评估系统、支持性系统等与普惠金融的目标相匹配。

第一，要实现支付结算系统的村级行政区全覆盖，并提高支付结算系统的使用

① LEESA SHRADER，ERIC DUFLOS. 中国：无网点银行发展的新模式［M］. CGAP，2014.

效率。

一是充分结合金融科技的优势，继续布局结算账户、支付系统、无网点银行与设备的建设，以实现对“最后一公里”的“中小微弱”群体的全覆盖。

二是从需求出发，继续提高“最后一公里”的“中小微弱”群体的能力建设，以提高金融基础设施的使用效率。

三是除金融基础设施之外，电信、互联网、物流等配套基础设施建设也要同步跟上，以全面提高“最后一公里”的“中小微弱”群体的生活质量。

第二，探索传统征信与大数据征信的合作机制，提升“最后一公里”的“中小微弱”群体的征信数据覆盖面，并提高失信成本以塑造更良好的信用环境。

一是做好传统征信与大数据征信的合作探索，打通数据壁垒，提高数据质量，形成更完整的“最后一公里”的“中小微弱”群体画像。

二是完善失信惩罚机制，行政性惩罚、监管性惩罚、市场性惩罚、社会性惩罚、司法性惩罚等多管齐下，提高失信成本，还市场风清气正。

三是提高“最后一公里”的“中小微弱”群体的信用意识，充分了解失信的危害。

四是借助金融科技的优势，以实现“最后一公里”的“中小微弱”群体的征信全覆盖。

五是继续完善信息安全制度建设，全面预防数据泄露、安全漏洞、恶意攻击等信息安全事故。

六是提高征信机构的能力建设，从源头控制信息安全事故，以保证征信机构的可靠性与社会信誉。

第三，形成可供市场参考的行业评估、机构评估，从行业预测与风险预警的角度为普惠金融行业发展提供支持与保障。

一是在原有的行业发展指标系统和机构评估与评级指标系统中，增加社会影响力指标，一方面可以更全面评估普惠金融行业与供应方的经济效益和社会效益；另一方面有助于引导资本流向有利于实现社会可持续发展目标的行业，提升全社会福利。

二是提高普惠金融供应方的能力建设，更好地借助行业评估和机构评估，既完成普惠金融目标与社会目标，又实现机构可持续发展。

第四，形成普惠金融全行业的支持系统，打通小额信贷、微型金融、互联网金融等普惠金融业态的服务界限。

一是继续完善农村地区的通信基础设施建设，在全覆盖的基础上，充分考虑“最后一公里”的“中小微弱”群体的需求，甚至是对金融与技术的发展进行前瞻研究，从而更好地布局通信基础设施的排布。

二是继续发展全国性与地方性合作网络平台，提高平台间的凝聚力，合力为普惠金融触达“最后一公里”的“中小微弱”群体而服务。

三是着眼于行业发展需求，政府、高校、科研机构继续投入智库研究的建设，在行业预测、能力建设、金融创新等方面为行业发展提供智力支持。

四是提升金融创新能力，从供应模式、产品开发、技术研发等方面，不断提高普惠金融服务的质量，形成更强的“2CC”（“to China Copy”的简称，意为“到中国复制”）能力。

# 第八章　打通“最后一公里”问题的适度监管

【摘要】我国当前普惠金融监管中存在着农村金融监管资源不足、个别监管政策过于刚性和粗糙、过于严苛的利率管制导致资金价格扭曲、对农村普惠金融消费者保护有待提高以及部分监管指标过于理想化等诸多问题，本章在适度监管原则指导下，提出许多建设性的普惠金融监管新举措和新方法，对于进一步打通“最后一公里”的监管问题具有一定理论指导价值。

## 一、当前金融监管对“最后一公里”问题造成实际影响

### （一）金融监管体系尚未成熟，农村金融监管资源不足

目前，绝大多数农村中小金融机构都设在县（市）、乡（镇）和行政村，各地银监办（局）在这些地方只设有办事处，这些办事处并不具有独立的监管主体资格，工作人员也只有1～2人，应对辖区内农村中小金融机构就已经相当困难，监管更是难以为继。①

与此同时，大量非正规农村金融机构游离于监管之外，难以形成有效监管。例如，近年来日趋活跃的小额贷款公司是由省政府指定各地金融办（局）负责监督，实际情况是，各地金融办（局）把监管权限再次下放到县政府，真正负责小额贷款公司日常监督的是当地工商局，但工商局并不熟悉金融业务和普惠金融政策，对小额贷款业务中许多问题无法形成有效监管，而各地银监局又管不着，总体上小额贷款公司处于监管真空状态。于是，追逐商业利润成为很多小贷公司的第一选择，而不是为农村最贫困人群提供及时、可得和负担得起的小额贷款，产生“最后一公里”问题在所难免。

① 刘牧晗．完善我国农村金融监管的法律分析［J］．经济研究导刊，2009（2）．

### （二）个别监管政策过于刚性和粗糙

目前我国普惠金融机构类型、数量偏少，大型商业银行、股份制银行网点主要分布在县域以上经济发达的城市地区，欠发达地区普惠金融机构网点明显偏少，普惠金融服务供给不足。[①]中国普惠金融研究院于2018年2月在甘肃兰州榆中县、永登县进行调研时发现，即便是村镇银行，其经营主体大都设在县城，仅在小部分乡镇设有分支机构，大多数乡镇基本处于空白状态。究其原因，与目前对普惠金融监管政策密切关联。我国监管机构规定村镇银行的设立必须有一家大型商业银行做第一大股东，监管门槛提高了不少，越来越多的村镇银行望而却步，直接导致村镇银行长期发展受阻，对农村普惠金融的支持自然有限。而大多数大型商业银行、股份制银行并不热衷于下乡开展普惠金融，其网点主要分布在县域以上经济发达地区，县域及以下农村地区人均金融网点占有率很低，金融服务资源难以覆盖到乡镇一级的广大农村地区，普惠金融资源有效供给明显不足，产生“最后一公里”问题也就不足为奇了。

又如，现行监管对抵押担保方式监管过严，要求必须提供实物抵押担保。而银行机构出于自身金融风险防控的目的，对抵押物尽调、审查都很严格，流程烦琐冗长。在农户缺乏足够的抵押品的情况下，农村金融机构无法放贷，严重影响农村普惠金融落地。

### （三）过于严苛的利率管制导致资金价格扭曲

目前，我国金融资源配置不甚合理，尤其是利率管理过于严苛，直接影响普惠金融的推广落实。为此，我们建议监管部门对当前利率监管政策进行调整，完善利率结构，适当放松利率管制，允许小额信贷机构在政策允许的范围内，加大小额信贷利率上浮空间，与市场利率相互匹配。

### （四）对农村普惠金融消费者保护有待提高

我国普惠金融真正开始实施也就三年时间，政府、金融机构、社会对普惠金融的认识既不全面也不深入，没有真正将普惠金融提升至国家战略层面来部署和推动，农村普惠金融知识教育尚在初创阶段，对农村金融消费者的保护有待提高。在广大农村和边远地区，农民金融知识匮乏、自我保护意识淡薄，普惠金融专项教育基本没有开展，真正成功保护普惠金融消费者的案例并不多见。

与此同时，不少农村地区依然存在各类侵害普惠金融的行为，非法集资、非法吸

---

① 白振华．当前普惠金融存在的问题与建议 [J]. 时代金融，2015 (21).

储、非法经营等违法活动较为常见，地下黑钱庄、高利贷等非法融资也日渐猖獗，给创业创新、小微企业、贫困人口等薄弱环节和特殊群体带来不少侵害。

### （五）部分监管指标过于理想化

目前，对农村金融机构信贷监管指标上过于理想化，有可能陷入了“质量与效益共存”“商业信贷与政策业务共赢”的误区。例如，监管部门提出“两个不低于”指标，即涉农贷款增量不低于上年、增速不低于各项贷款平均增速。又如，行管部门提出“两个不低于”，即当年到期贷款本金和利息收回率不低于98%。

但问题是，当前农村小额信贷及农民信贷需求发生了巨大变化，小额农贷需求量大大减少，涉农贷款增量明显降低。加之农民长年外出务工，劳动力严重匮乏，贷款本息很难按期收回。在这种情况下，上述过于理性化的监管指标会让农村金融机构在信贷管理中因为很难达到监管指标而面临两难选择：要么干脆不放贷款，小心翼翼坚守监管红线，最后造成信贷经营的困境，直接影响农村地区普惠金融服务成效；要么不把监管红线当回事，弄虚作假，最后可能受到严厉的监管处罚。

## 二、解决“最后一公里”问题适度监管原则调整

我国长期以来一直传承分业监管模式，金融领域按照银行、保险和证券业务的不同，分别设立不同的监管机构。各个监管机构之间分工明确、权责清楚、互不干涉。由于证监会、银监会、保监会（注：银监会、保监会现已合并为银保监会）彼此地位平等，没有从属关系，在这种格局下，监管者对本部门管辖市场稳定考虑较多，对金融市场整体协调发展关注较少。于是，2013年8月成立了由人民银行牵头的金融监管协调部际联席会议制度，目的就是为协调解决交叉金融业务的法律（法规）冲突问题，但这种会议机制更多地是协调部门之间利益平衡和关系，执行具体监管措施并不多见。

自2017年以后，经济规制成了指导性主张，穿透式监管逐渐成为我国金融监管部门的首选，主要是因为穿透式监管能带来行政管理权限的扩张性解释，并以此制定出各种严厉的监管规则、监管方式，进而达到控制金融市场的“监管目的”。于是，越来越多的地方监管部门使用这一概念。对此，有学者忧心忡忡，认为穿透式监管完全有“可能僭越既有法律的框架、原则和方向”，引发“概念滥用、过度解释”等新问题。①

其实，目前我国穿透式监管原则并不符合国际通行的金融自由化理论（Financial liberalization或Financial deregulation，两者的意思都是“解除金融束缚”），容易产

① 邓峰．“一人生病，全家吃药”穿透式监管或概念乱用［J］．财经杂志，2018（1）．

生“金融抑制”问题，不利于普惠金融的健康发展。[①]

早在20世纪70年代初，罗纳德·麦金农（Ronald I. Mckinnon）和爱德华·肖（Edward S. Shaw）就发现发展中国家普遍存在“金融抑制”现象，严重制约金融市场的快速发展。于是，爱德华·肖在《经济发展中的金融深化》（*Financial Deepening in Economic Development*）中提出了“金融深化理论”，认为发展中国家普遍存在着利率限制、信贷管制、高储蓄率以及各种对金融中介歧视性监管措施，直接导致“金融抑制”的发生。由此，他们认为通过金融自由化可以增加投资总量，利率和汇率自由化可以提高投资效率，金融市场准入自由化可以促进金融业务快速发展，进而消除“金融抑制”现象。而金融自由化最根本的措施就是政府减少对金融产品价格、市场模式和经营行为的干预，使金融部门运行由政府管制逐步转由市场力量决定。[②]

显然，罗纳德·麦金农（Ronald I. Mckinnon）和爱德华·肖（Edward S. Shaw）在五十年前提出的金融必然由分业经营走向混业经营的理念，在互联网金融监管趋于严格的今天，依然具有现实意义：虽然全世界没有统一的监管模式，但有一个共同理念，就是采取最合适行业发展的监管方式。结合我国实际情况，采取更为宽松、包容的监管政策最适合我国普惠金融的初创阶段。可以在原有金融监管原则基础上，对审慎监管原则审慎使用，增加“适度性监管原则”“包容性监管原则”和“差异性监管原则”，有效避免穿透式监管、机构监管对普惠金融带来的负面影响，有利于促进普惠金融行业有效竞争和公平发展。

### （一）适度性监管原则

近几年，综观监管部门的每一次监管松绑都给金融市场带来了积极的反应。例如，取消存贷比考核，为大幅降低高成本表外融资规模创造了条件。[③]从监管的角度来看，既要在以往的监管过程中保持动态的调整和完善，又要在不同时期根据市场发展需要有不同的监管侧重点。现阶段，最需要修改的一个硬性监管法规，就是小微企业必须先还本付息才能重新续贷的硬性规定。

---

① 金融自由化，最初源于美国经济学家罗纳德·麦金农（Ronald I. Mckinnon）和爱德华·肖（Edward S. Shaw）的金融深化理论，与其相对的一个概念则是“金融抑制”（Financial Repression），意思就是阻碍了一国的金融市场的健康、快速发展。

② ［美］爱德华·肖．经济发展中的金融深化［M］．北京：中国社会科学出版社，1989.

③ 存贷比考核在我国已经实行了很长的一段时间。但随着我国经济、金融的市场化发展，存贷比监管已不适应当前商业银行资产负债多元化和业务创新发展的需要。全国人大常委会2015年8月29日果断修改《中华人民共和国商业银行法》，删除了实施已有20年之久的商业银行75%存贷比监管指标，并自2015年10月1日起施行。此次银行监管政策的调整顺应市场发展规律，果断取消存贷比监管指标，不仅是支持银行业的创新改革，有利于增强商业银行服务实体经济的能力，更好地支持实体经济的发展需要，在经济下行压力较大情况下稳增长的一项措施，也完全符合国际惯例，受到了我国银行业的广泛欢迎和支持。

对于这些资金流紧张的小微企业，如果一时无法实现先还款再借款，就只能从社会融资机构借入短期、高成本的过桥资金，或者干脆借入高利贷。这实际上加重了小微企业的负担，流动性接近干涸，直接导致中小企业难以为继。一些没有抵押物的小微企业无法获得授信，只能求助于融资担保公司甚至“地下钱庄”，而高昂的资金成本有可能压得小微企业更加无法解脱困境。显然，如果继续坚持“先还后续”的监管政策，融资难、融资贵的“最后一公里”问题就没法真正解决，最后倒霉的是那些真正需要帮助的小微企业。

所以，普惠金融领域监管必须要和时代的发展相吻合、和金融市场相匹配，不能单纯为稳定金融秩序而采取过于严厉的监管模式。我们要敢于打破那些以加强监管为名、实则画地为牢的监管门槛，更多地鼓励金融产品创新和市场发展。

### （二）包容性监管原则

金融监管模式不是一成不变的，不存在一种监管模式适合于所有金融领域的情况。监管模式的选择、调整和完善是一个动态的转换过程，不能用单一的、固化的监管模式应对日新月异的普惠金融市场。因此，我们既然鼓励依法合规创新，就应该允许市场主体在一定规则下创新产品，并伴随着金融市场的发展而适时调整和不断完善。例如，现阶段对农村信用社的监管长期秉持单一、固化的监管模式，缺乏包容性。监管部门只要求省级联社、市级联社在管理上去行政化，并没有给省市联社规划未来。难怪有人比喻农信社作为推进改革的主体是进行一场没有最好归属的“自我革命”。①

确实如此。监管层是否应该包容农联社在其使命结束时，以一个全新的、以资本为纽带的农业金融投资控股集团面目出现呢？监管层是否采取包容性监管原则支持各省农联社成立农业金融投资控股公司，让这个公司成为推动县域农信社改制农商行的积极力量？毫无疑问，我们不仅应该跟上对互联网金融等新兴业态的监管步伐，更要保证金融体系安全有效运行，防范系统性金融风险的发生，实现自我更新，实现新旧体制顺利转换。

### （三）差异性监管原则

普惠金融涉及领域宽泛，各市场之间发展速度差异较大。例如网络支付、互联网货币基金已是发展数年的成熟业务，业务形态逐渐固化，风险基本可控。而网络借贷、小额贷款公司、网络私募众筹等新兴业务各方面尚未成熟，正在探索阶段，有待进一步规范。因此，对不同普惠金融业务不能采取一刀切的监管策略，应该采取差异化监

① 王一楠．一个副省长的金融见识［J/OL］．凤凰财经，2018－02－05.

管措施。监管部门可以根据不同类型、不同特点的普惠金融实行差异化监管。例如，城市与农村、传统业务与创新模式之间的新型普惠金融监管，使得普惠金融监管更趋合理和有效，用差异性监管引导普惠金融个别化发展，使用差异化监管方式。又如，目前设立村镇银行要求必须有一家商业银行做第一大股东，这当然有助于防控风险，但问题是，大多数大型商业银行并不热衷于此，它们主要聚焦国有大中型企业的存贷款业务。于是，尽管国家长期鼓励村镇银行进入普惠金融领域，尽管有这一条硬性监管规定，但是普惠金融领域最接地气的农村金融机构开展普惠金融业务并不顺利。很难想象，缺少了村镇银行大力支持，贫穷落后地区农村普惠金融会有怎样的起色？

除此之外，村镇银行是否可以不再承担小微企业的政治扶贫任务，与大银行实行错位发展？国家是否应该放开地方城市商业银行和农村商业银行的网点设置监管限制？监管机构能否解禁小微企业抵（质）押物的法律限制？希望在不远的将来，监管机构真正实行不同层面、不同地区和不同机构的差异性监管，让那些熟悉当地的小微企业情况的地方金融机构更多地承担小微企业的金融支持。

## 三、解决“最后一公里”问题适度监管若干建议

### （一）对现行抵押担保监管方式进行调整

根据《物权法》关于动产抵押担保的规定，建议在农村金融市场，农户和农村企业在向银行申请贷款时候可以用动产做抵押，从事传统农业产业的农户可以用农产品和养殖品或者以产品的未来收入作为抵押向银行申请贷款。当然，这种方式还需要很多细则组织和配套设施，但在法理上是可行的。对农村担保抵押形式作出灵活变动，创新担保形式，符合《物权法》有关动产抵押担保的规定。

### （二）加强普惠金融教育

2015 年国务院办公厅印发的《关于加强金融消费者权益保护工作的指导意见》明确规定我国金融消费者拥有知情权、受教育权。政府可以充分利用电视广播、书刊杂志、数字媒体等官方媒体或平台，通过在线查询、法制案例，多层面、广角度宣传普惠金融，利用“3·15 消费者权益保护日”“5·15 打击和防范经济犯罪宣传日”等主要宣传节点，重点针对城镇低收入人群、农村贫困人口、创业农民、残疾劳动者、老年人等特殊群体，解读当前互联网金融政策，以便农村社员、城镇居民能够全面、客观和及时地了解普惠金融。例如，针对城市年轻市民喜欢尝试新鲜事物的特点，重点提示“校园贷”“手机贷”、虚拟货币、消费返利、高利众筹等的金融风险，通过播放警示教育短片、解读典型案例等方式，提高青年对相关行为的警惕性以及金融工具的

运用能力和金融风险防范能力，从源头上远离金融风险和诈骗。

在深入推进普惠金融知识普及教育方面，印度经验值得我们借鉴和学习。在今天的印度，文盲率高达 27.8%，较低的文化水平明显不利于普惠金融知识和金融消费理念的传播，这是造成印度普惠金融“最后一公里”问题的重要原因。为此，印度一直在强调“消除贫困，保证公平”的概念，从早年的农业贷款的强制性额度到最近的“PMJDY 计划”（Pradhan Mantri Jan Dhan Yojana）无不体现出政府推进普惠金融的决心。[①] 2008 年，印度中央银行还通过金融启蒙小组（TGFIL）成立金融素养中心，提供免费的普惠金融课程和信贷咨询服务，积极推广普惠金融运动。至今为止，该中心已对 200 多万人提供相关培训，极大地推广了农村普惠金融的应用。[②]

值得一提的是，印度中央银行网站还下设有金融消费者培训与保护板块，提供的内容主要包括获得电子支付与清算许可的银行、代理商、实时转移支付和电子平台转移支付等。虽然它的实效性还有待进一步验证，但对提高老百姓金融意识、帮助偏远地区文化程度低的人群及时维护自身权益还是有价值的。

这一点对我国有所启发。我国与印度有一定相似性，两国都是幅员辽阔的国家，农村人口文化程度都不高，文盲也较多，物理网点的推进在中国和印度农村地区同样面临障碍，都存在“最后一公里”的传播障碍。也许，借助电子平台能够更好地宣传相应的知识，坚持自律与他律相结合，进行相关培训，发挥好普惠金融市场主体自治、行业自律、社会监督的作用，最大限度地帮助农村地区普及金融知识和维护自身权利。

### （三）对当前利率监管政策适度调整

目前农村小额信贷风险较大，利率较低，我们建议适当放宽利率管制，放宽利率浮动的范围，对农村小额信贷实行灵活的利率，由农村小额信贷机构根据农户的收入状况、信用记录以及风险情况来确定不同的贷款利率水平，可以将风险水平和贷款利率水平挂钩，以贷款利率来补偿风险损失，扩大小额信贷资金来源渠道，引导农村资金回流。

同时，在资金来源渠道上，可以将非正规金融纳入正规金融的监管范围，合理利用民间闲散资金，扩大小额信贷的资金来源，允许经营良好的小额信贷机构进入资本市场，可以在同业拆借市场、再贷款融资。可以借鉴孟加拉国模式，资金来源于成员存款、经营收入和批发资金。

---

① 纪晓晴，欧明刚．印度的普惠金融政策及效果［J/OL］．和讯评论，2017－10－11.
② 戈松雪．印度农村信息化建设的经验［N］．学习时报，2010－10－09.

### （四）完善普惠金融消费者保护体系

随着金融在国民经济中地位的不断提升，世界各国都需要在金融消费者保护方面加强能力建设。以美国次贷危机为例，在危机发生前，很多家庭都可以轻易获得信贷，信贷普及率极高，看似实现了高水平的普惠金融服务，但由于缺失金融消费者保护，使消费者承受了过高的风险，损失惨重。危机波及银行、证券和保险机构等整个金融行业，最终损害了整个宏观经济。危机发生后，美国迅速制定法律，提出了“负责任金融”（Responsible Finance）理念，要求对消费者的风险承受能力开展尽职调查，而不是盲目扩张金融服务。①

我国普惠金融目前的实际情况是业态众多、模式各异，市场呈现复杂性、多样性的风险特征，给现有监管资源和技术带来挑战，仅靠政府一个或两个部门管理是很困难的，需要建立普惠金融消费者权益保护体系，有效打击普惠金融领域违法犯罪行为。因此，政府及相关部门携手共进，探索出一批可复制、可推广的消费者权益保护模式。

第一层面，建立健全县域普惠金融消费权益保护工作机制，让所有阶层能够以平等的机会、合理的价格获得及时的服务，畅通投诉、审理渠道，查处侵害金融消费者权益的行为，防止欺诈和不公正交易，切实维护普惠金融消费者合法权益。

第二层面，加强金融监管协调机制建设，落实地方金融监管和风险处置责任，及时开展重点领域金融风险专项整治，切实保障小微企业、创业创新、贫困人口等薄弱环节和特殊群体少受、免受非法行为侵害，严厉打击非法集资、非法吸储、非法证券业务等违法违规金融活动，加大各类风险隐患排查和化解力度，妥善处置金融风险事件，守住不发生系统性金融风险的底线。

第三层面，加强与金融消费者权益有关的信息披露和风险提示，利用手机移动客户端，加大网上宣传力度，定期在本地有较大影响力的微信号上剖析互联网金融诈骗典型案例，揭示互联网金融诈骗的特征和常见手段，让农村社员、城镇老年人树立正确合理的理财观念，增强群众的风险防范意识，切实提升公众风险防范能力，引导金融消费者根据自身风险承受能力进行理性投资与金融消费，最大限度地保障普惠金融消费者权益。

第四层面，强化金融机构受理、处理普惠金融消费纠纷的主体责任，不断完善普惠金融消费者保护机制，改进处理纠纷的工作效率和服务质量，打击普惠金融领域违法犯罪问题，切实保护金融消费者合法权益。

---

① 易纲．普惠金融可在宏观经济中发挥重要作用［J/OL］．搜狐财经，2017－09－23．

### （五）用科技创新驱动普惠金融快速发展

未来几年，应该更多、更安全地运用科技创新解决农村地区的支付交易不便、网点奇缺、人手紧缺等难题，有效降低单位融资的成本，提升农村普惠金融服务能力。①

第一，鉴于大数据在互联网银行、互联网保险和互联网支付领域的广泛应用，可以利用大数据统计分析和数据挖掘技术，诸如用户画像、精准营销、风险管控、运营优化和市场预测等，建立风险预测模型，及时识别流动性风险，帮助普惠金融领域有效规避流动性风险。

第二，鉴于云计算能够使金融机构的 IT 资源具备更高的可扩展性，可以在普惠金融领域布置多个不同物理位置的 IT 资源，有效规避普惠金融机构内部 IT 资源配置不足或普惠金融机构可能丢失重要交易数据的风险，以系统架构、资源整合等方面的优势，在满足长尾客户多样化服务方面发挥重要作用，降低普惠金融机构的风险损失。

第三，鉴于人工智能应用到互联网金融领域中能够有效缓解金融服务智能化不足的问题，可以利用人工智能从用户提供和搜索到的大量信息中提取有用部分，对该部分信息进行分析并反馈给互联网金融机构，并利用生物识别技术在身份验证、支付等场景的应用，降低了交易双方的信息不对称性，降低了道德风险，有效驱动普惠金融行业的智能化发展。

第四，区块链技术已开始为互联网金融的发展带来裨益，区块链技术的安全性、可追溯性、不可篡改性、透明性以及智能合约实现的协议自动执行，可以有效地解决信用创造问题、提高信息披露透明度，实现更好地保护隐私，提高整个金融系统的安全性，进一步减轻政府的监管负担。

## 四、穿越“最后一公里”宏观制度环境与政策支持

### （一）穿越“最后一公里”体制机制保证

1. 穿越“最后一公里”宏观体制保证

2017 年全国银行业监督管理工作会议进一步提出，要以互联网金融为依托，不断将普惠金融发展引向深入，具体措施之一是协同建设线上线下渠道，加快构建县、乡、村三级服务网络体系，最大限度打通金融服务“最后一公里”，在宏观体制上确保普惠金融全方位为社会所有阶层和群体提供服务。

---

① 徐林．现代经济体系需改革和完善现代金融服务与监管［J/OL］．财新网，2017－12－06．

2. 穿越“最后一公里”运行机制保证

为了确保穿越“最后一公里”的顺畅运行，积极推进普惠金融机构、农村省联社运行机制转换，提高农村商业银行、农村合作银行、农村信用联社服务小微企业和“三农”的职能，重点布局中西部和老少边穷地区、粮食主产区、小微企业聚集地区，实现广大人民群众获得普惠金融服务的共同愿望。

3. 穿越“最后一公里”政策法规制定

随着我国经济不断发展，我们应该逐步制定和完善普惠金融相关法律法规，形成系统性的法律框架，明确普惠金融服务供给、需求主体的权利义务，确保普惠金融服务有法可依、有章可循。同时，在健全完善现有“三农”金融政策基础上，研究论证相关综合性法律制度，对土地经营权、宅基地使用权、技术专利权、设备财产使用权和场地使用权等财产权益，开展确权、登记、颁证、流转等方面的规章制度建设。

### （二）穿越“最后一公里”金融制度安排与保障

1. 推动下沉式金融管理体制建设

根据 2015 年《政府工作报告》提出的大力发展普惠金融的要求，积极倡导金融行政管理的优化模式，坚持政府引导与市场主导相结合、完善基础金融服务与改进重点领域金融服务相结合，不断提高金融服务的覆盖率、可得性和满意度，增强所有市场主体对金融服务的获得感。

虽然 2017 年我国增设了 3300 多家金融机构，其中农村信用社 69 家、村镇银行 584 家，但是，我国目前只仅限到县一级，乡级以下的金融机构缺失严重，亟待规划建立。因此，有必要要求所有商业银行设立普惠金融事业部，下到农村基层，承担起普惠金融业务的政策研究、规则制定、产品研发、风险管理等职责，采用信用联保等模式，突破制约农村金融、农业贷款的层层坚冰，为急需资金的农民雪中送炭，解决燃眉之急。

2. 构建多层次金融信用管理体系

多层次组织体系是普惠金融体系的基础，它涵盖了大型国有银行的普惠金融事业部、中小银行、农村商业银行和农信社，以及与“三农”“小微”关系密切的非银行金融机构，其中金融信用管理体系建设是普惠金融体系的重点。传统金融机构将“金融弱势群体”拒之门外，原因之一是银行和贷款者之间的信息不对称可能引发道德风险，银行拒贷也是在审慎原则下不得已而为之。可见，完善征信体系、健全信用管理机制就是解决这一矛盾的关键，也是打通“最后一公里”问题的关键之一。

## （三）穿越"最后一公里"金融生态环境建设

1. 货币政策及配套措施

根据经营环境和货币政策调控意图要求，采用不同的准备金比率。在货币政策意图紧缩银根的情况下，对经营环境好、规模大的对象，要求以较高的准备金比率缴纳准备金。而对经营环境差、规模小的对象，其存款派生或信用创造能力弱，诸如主要经营网点在农村经济欠发达地区的分支机构或农业银行和农村信用合作社，实施较低的准备金比率要求，采取控制力度小一些的货币政策，否则可能会因为受到的调控力度过大而导致贷款的刚性收缩或发生流动性危机。

2. 信贷、财政政策及配套措施

我国政府积极采取货币信贷政策、税收政策以及监管政策等一系列政策措施，促进普惠金融"最后一公里"的贯通。其中，货币信贷政策包括近年来中国人民银行通过差别存款准备金率、再贷款、再贴现等一系列政策，鼓励金融机构加大对"三农"和小微企业的信贷支持力度。

财税政策则包括政府通过市场化途径作用于不同的金融产品和服务：（1）农业贷款和小微企业贷款风险补偿基金；（2）支持地方普惠金融发展的专项资金；（3）鼓励和支持政府担保机构发展；（4）农业保险；（5）税收政策；（6）各类惠农政策包括支农补贴、新型农村社会养老保险补助、新型农村合作医疗保险补助。

3. 金融人力资源政策及配套措施

近年来，金融业的创新与互联网技术的融合，使金融人才培养与管理面临新挑战。然而，普惠金融特殊性导致人们对其认知与社会对普惠金融实际需求并不匹配，更使普惠金融人才培养与管理面临新的问题与挑战，其人才缺口不断扩大。

目前全国范围内真正拥有正规金融从业背景或金融（经济/财务）专业的员工非常少，大约只有30%。因此，未来必须打造普惠金融人才孵化体系，培养普惠金融人才。全国高等院校、普惠金融培训机构应该为社会提供更多的宝贵的实践机会，培养更多的普惠金融人才。我国普惠金融教育模式亟须从以下几个方面调整，建立既符合本土需求，才能适应经济全球化的普惠金融人才培养机制。

首先，课程设置应该体现普惠金融特征，在微观金融方面进一步细分课程，避免课程的交叉重复，形成一个完整的课程体系设置，在普惠金融专业开设互联网金融课程，侧重数字普惠金融与贷款模式、数字普惠金融与筹资模式、大数据与普惠金融等方面的教育，以期培养具有金融业务操作能力、战略规划能力以及基于互联网发展开展金融业创新能力的高端人才。

其次，金融课程的教材在引进西方经典的金融理念与文化理念的基础上，融入大量符合我国国情和时代特征的经典金融案例，引发学生思考与讨论，改变传统的输入输出式教学法，充分利用先进的多媒体技术和网络技术，采取“慕课”“翻转课堂”等先进的教学方法，将枯燥的理论制作成生动的教学课件，或者根据所要授课内容提前到相应的金融机构录制视频，在课堂上向学生播放，给学生直观的视觉、听觉的刺激，充分调动学生的学习兴趣，使学生充分理解并在实际情况中加以应用。

最后，注重专业师资队伍建设。职业院校应实施“走出去”和“请进来”的办法建设普惠金融师资队伍，即鼓励教师走出校园，将经验丰富的金融人才和先进的金融理论引入校园，请各行业专家来学校就最新发展动态进行讲座，与世界名校合作，为教师提供定期培训的机会，以此完善教师的综合知识体系，同时，在校内组织金融机构业务模拟课程，引导学生体验金融产品与服务，进一步加强学生对普惠金融知识的运用。

# 第四部分

# 决胜“最后一公里”的社会效果

“最后一公里”问题，不仅仅是金融问题，也是社会问题。基于大量的问卷数据建立的普惠金融指数，使我们能够验证金融改革的有效性，分析金融服务的经济意义和社会意义。

# 第九章　指标监测结果对解决“最后一公里”问题的启示

【摘要】从客户角度出发理解普惠金融发展的障碍，是解决普惠金融“最后一公里”问题的正确逻辑。在收集到大量客户的普惠金融相关数据的基础上，我们制作了中国普惠金融发展指标体系（简称CAFI指标体系）。该体系不仅可以量化一个地区的普惠金融整体发展程度，也可以通过不同地区之间的对比，发现影响地区普惠金融发展的具体因素。

我们应用该体系对浙江省的普惠金融发展作出了较为全面的评估，得出了浙江省的普惠金融发展已经走在了世界前列的结论，同时我们也对存在的不足提出了政策建议。此外，我们还使用该体系对丽水市金融改革效果做了一个全面的评估，得出的结论为金融改革对丽水市的普惠金融整体发展起到了积极推动的作用。

## 一、中国普惠金融发展指数的构建

作为普惠金融发展的重要基础设施建设之一，指标与监测体系可以精准度量、动态监测、适时评估其发展程度。在普惠金融已成为国家发展战略的背景下，在我国建立一个科学、可信的指标与监测体系以指导普惠金融的发展实践已迫在眉睫。

本着这一宗旨，中国普惠金融研究院（CAFI）正式启动了“数字普惠金融指标与监测体系建设”项目。2017年，CAFI正式开始了具体项目的实施，首个实施点选在浙江，由CAFI与浙江省农村信用社联合社合作共同开展。为了数据采集的准确性与科学性，项目实施分为预调研与正式调研两个阶段。预调研在浙江省乐清市开展，正式调研在浙江省的14个县区同步进行。采用随机抽样的方法，在每个县/区抽取50个行政村或社区，共1000户家庭、200家小微企业进行调研。数据收集采用手机答题、现场录入的方式进行。最终收到了 13505 份家庭/个人答卷，2730 份企业问卷及 677 份村/社区总体情况问卷。

CAFI 在收集到的浙江省数据基础上建立了一套普惠金融指标体系。该体系包含 59 个指标。在这些指标的基础上，建立了包含 8 个维度的中国普惠金融排斥指数以及综合排斥指数（简称 CAFI 指数）。指数反映的是排斥程度，指数值区间为［0，1］，指数值越高，受到的排斥程度越大。由于普惠金融发展受到各种因素的制约，度量中心障碍因素有利于采取相应对策，解除障碍因素的阻碍作用。为此我们筛选出 17 个障碍因素进行衡量。

CAFI 指数的 8 个维度分别是金融服务的可得性、使用、质量、满意度、金融能力、障碍、预期、数字化程度。可得性指数反映金融服务的可触达性。浙江在可得性维度的平均指数值为 0.3009，而且在分布上呈现较小趋势，说明浙江地区的排斥度很低，可得性高。使用情况指数反映各种金融服务及设施的使用现状，旨在全面度量被访者的金融服务运用状态。浙江省在使用维度的平均指数值为 0.5065，而且在分布上基本呈现正态分布，排斥度较高，在分布上比较均匀。质量指数包括汇款成本、贷款年化利率、除利息外的额外成本、贷款获批时间长度、遭受金融诈骗等。浙江省的普惠金融质量指数的平均值为 0.2189，而且在分布上呈现集中度高的特点，说明浙江省金融服务质量较高。满意度指数主要从传统与数字两个方面反映客户对传统和数字金融服务的主观感受。浙江省客户满意度指数平均值为 0.4512，虽然在分布上呈现右偏，但不满意程度大多数低于 0.5 的中间水平，总体满意度比较高。金融能力指数反映客户自身金融素养、技能、金融行为、态度等方面的状态。浙江金融能力指数的平均值为 0.6215，是所有指数中平均值最高的维度，说明金融能力是普惠金融发展的主要短板，需要加大力度解决。障碍指数反映阻碍客户使用金融服务的因素。浙江省普惠金融的障碍指数并不高。预期指数反映客户对未来的信心和展望。普惠金融预期指数是一种前瞻性指数，政府和企业可以根据这个指数采取相应的行动。图 9－1 显示，浙江地区的预期指数相对较高，表示受访者对未来信心较高。数字化程度指数反映传

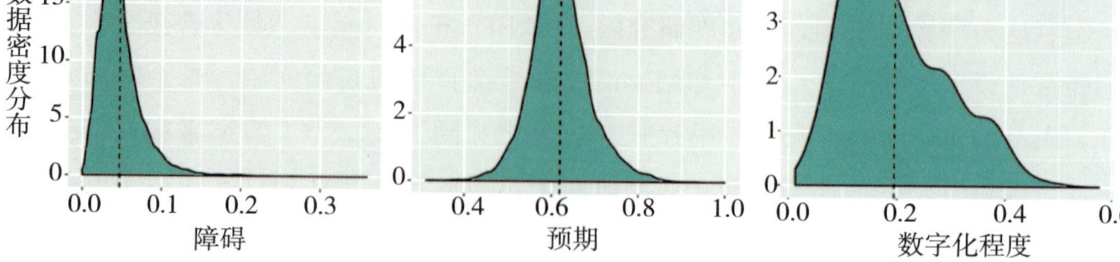


**图 9－1　普惠金融发展障碍，预期与数字化指数分布情况**

统与数字化金融服务比值，体现的是数字技术的渗透程度。从图 9－1 可以看到，浙江的数字化程度较高。

以上 8 个维度中，可得性、使用、质量、满意度和能力 5 个维度反映普惠金融发展的程度。这 5 个维度的指数综合起来形成普惠金融综合指数。根据本研究建立的普惠金融指标体系及综合指数进行计算，浙江省样本地区个人指数最大值为 0.6335，最小值为 0.1827，均值为 0.4198，中位数为 0.4204。图 9－2 所示为浙江省普惠金融综合指数分布直方图，横轴代表指数大小，纵轴代表分布在各指数值上的受访样本频率。总体而言，浙江省的普惠金融服务水平较高，受排斥程度较低，从分布上来讲，也较为均匀。

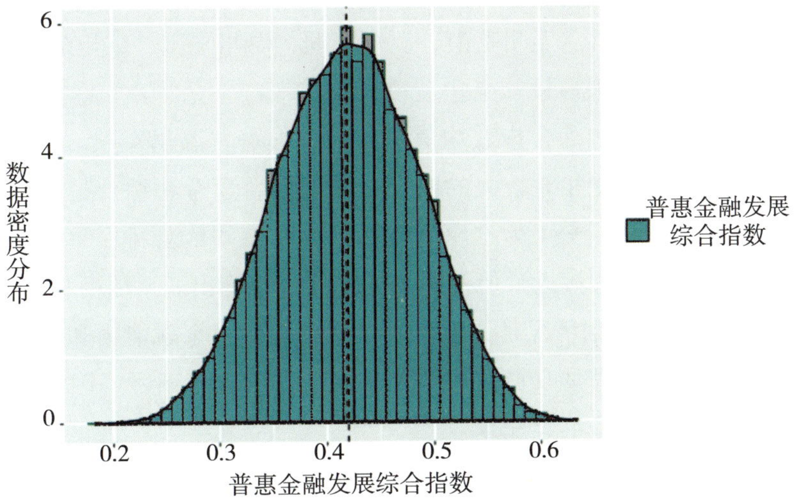


**图 9－2　中国普惠金融发展综合指数**

## 二、指数应用之一：浙江省普惠金融发展现状分析

### （一）浙江省普惠金融指数监测结果的分析

1. 浙江省普惠金融发展达到国际先进水平

第一，浙江省成年人银行及移动支付账户渗透率为 92.9%，显著高于我国平均水平并逼近高收入国家水平，银行及移动支付账户的高渗透率为浙江省活跃的经济金融活动铺就了坚实的根基。第二，浙江省成年人信用卡持有率为 31%，显著高于我国 20.8%的平均水平。持有信用卡既是良好资信水平的证明，也意味着可以长期地、持续地获得银行信用服务。相应地，个人和家庭也就能够更为灵活地调剂生活资金余缺。第三，2017 年浙江省获得金融机构贷款批准的家庭比例为 29.1%，而从民间渠道获取

借款的家庭比例约为1.8%，远低于从金融机构获取贷款的比例。这一方面体现了浙江发达活跃的经济活动所产生的贷款需求大，另一方面也反映了浙江省金融机构在家庭贷款服务中的突出表现。第四，根据2017年世界银行Global Findex数据，高收入国家通过手机或互联网渠道使用账户的成年人比例为51.8%，而浙江省通过手机或互联网渠道使用账户的成年人比例为74.2%，不仅接近我国平均水平的两倍，也显著高于高收入国家水平。基于上述分析可以发现，以账户渗透率、贷款使用率、信用卡持有率、移动支付使用率等常用指标来对浙江省和国际数据进行比较，浙江省普惠金融发展已经走在了中国甚至世界前列。

2. 浙江省普惠金融发展水平高，体现为普惠金融服务水平较高，受排斥程度较低，从分布上来讲，也较为均匀

具体到每一个样本区县（温州苍南、温州泰顺、温州平阳、杭州余杭、嘉兴海盐、舟山岱山、绍兴诸暨、绍兴柯桥、金华兰溪、金华浦江、金华市区、宁波象山、湖州南浔等）的情况，普惠金融综合指数均值差异并不显著。温州泰顺、绍兴诸暨、宁波象山和金华市区是内部分化相对较大的四个区县。以普惠金融综合指数从低到高累计分布80%位置的指数值0.4784为排斥线，可以计算不同区县排斥率的差异。虽然各区县平均金融排斥程度较为接近，但按照上述排斥线计算出的排斥率具有显著差异。

3. 浙江金融能力和使用情况是普惠金融发展的短板，金融能力和使用情况维度的排斥程度最高，是浙江省最具改善空间的两个维度，这也与国际、国内普惠金融发展现状相符合

第一，在整体排斥程度最高的金融能力维度中，杭州余杭的金融能力排斥程度明显低于其他地区，代表该地区受访人的平均金融能力在所有样本区县中是最高的。第二，虽然提高金融能力是所有样本区县都需要努力的方向，温州苍南和温州平阳两地区尤其需要重视居民金融能力提升。第三，金融能力维度的排斥度来自金融教育指标的贡献率最高。观察其下具体指标可以发现，在金融教育培训经历、主动学习金融知识的经历及未来金融学习计划三个具体指标中，均只有不到20%的受访样本具有相应经历或学习计划，表明浙江省亟须加强面对更广泛群体的金融教育。第四，金融态度指标和金融行为指标也是非常值得重视的金融能力指标。第五，数据表明受访样本在基础金融知识的理解和计算等方面表现相对较好但仍然有相当的提升空间。

4. 低收入跟高年龄受金融排斥的可能性较大，提高受教育程度可以减少排斥度的特征

比如，从指数在不同学历的分布来看，受访人所在家庭户主学历越高，其所受金融排斥的程度越低。结果反映了所在家庭高学历家庭成员尤其是通常掌握着家庭经济决策权的户主的学历水平对受访人所受金融排斥的影响。虽然学历并不完全决定个人

能力，但更丰富的教育经历确会增强阅读、计算和信息处理等参与金融活动所需的基本技能。与此同时，更高学历者所在的社交圈层也可能为其带来更多高质量的信息和行为影响。

5. 除了可得性、使用情况等构成指数的维度和指标外，受访人年龄、所在家庭户主学历、所在家庭人均收入、金融服务使用障碍以及数字化程度指标均对普惠金融综合指数具有显著影响

结果验证了普惠金融不仅仅意味着更加包容的金融体系，教育、收入、数字技术等方面都需要齐头并进，同时减少使用金融服务的障碍，才能更好地实现“好金融”所应归属的“好社会”。进一步地，我们对障碍维度中贡献率较高的指标及其子指标进行了分析，可以作为致力于减少障碍的政策参考。

6. 数据显示更低金融排斥程度对应更好未来预期

比如，在“对明年中国经济表现预期”问题上，超过八成的受访人认为2018年中国经济会变好；在“对周围金融服务情况预期”问题上，68.9%的受访人表示会变好。相关度结果也表明，个人CAFI普惠金融综合指数越低（所受金融排斥越低），其预期越好，即个人普惠金融水平越好，其对个人、金融环境及经济发展的预期都会更加乐观。

### （二）浙江省普惠金融指数监测结果的启示

根据对浙江省普惠金融发展现状的分析，我们对浙江省普惠金融的未来发展提出如下两个方面的主要建议。

1. 要构建具有持续更新机制的金融能力提升体系

这要求充分认识经济、技术和人文形态变迁中的金融能力挑战，其主要体现在人口老龄化和技术影响下的人文变迁两个方面。上面分析结果显示，受访人年龄与其所受金融服务排斥显著正相关，年轻人更可能以更低的成本和更高的效率获取信息这种金融活动的重要生产资料。人口老龄化趋势中的金融能力挑战将是一个不容忽视的动态问题，如果技术进步的速度继续提升，那么老龄化群体受到的金融排斥就有可能会进一步强化。此外，在充分认识到经济、技术和人文形态变迁中的金融能力挑战的基础上，明确提升金融能力在普惠金融发展战略中的重要地位。例如，探索恰当的干预方式以提升不同群体的金融能力，调研锁定目标群体及需要改善的具体方面，从金融知识、技能、态度和行为全方位入手设计干预方式，以及设计一个对干预方式进行影响评估的体系。

识别和改善金融能力的外部约束条件要求政策制定者需要识别不同外部约束条件下所需金融能力的区别。外部条件的改善可以让内部能力更好地发挥，进而更容易地

实现政策目标。相关研究发现改变消费者作出金融决策的环境可能比改变消费者金融能力更为高效。比如，从个人或家庭所拥有的资源来看，相较拥有中等或较多资产的消费者，为实现相同金融目标，拥有极少资产的消费者所需的技能是大不相同的，因此，贫困群体与非贫困群体的金融能力具有不同特征，要分开讨论，并且从个人或家庭所处经济金融环境来看，相较经济繁荣向好阶段，在经济下行波动时期要实现一定的金融目标将更加困难。此外，随着社会信用不断扩张、个人退休金压力不断增大，以及高等教育的资金压力越来越多地由学生负担，个人金融能力的缺乏将会带来更加严重的后果。

就金融环境而言，形成约束的主要包括三个方面：一是金融基础设施，二是多样化金融产品的可得性，三是客户保护机制。以客户保护机制为例，如果金融服务信息披露的规则和监管是有效的，金融机构以可触达、易懂得的方式对关键风险进行信息披露，那么对个人投资者的金融知识和技能要求就会降低；另外，从所需遵循和履行的社会规范和责任来看，这一类约束条件直接关乎个人从事金融事务的目标。

综合上述分析，我们建议在对个人金融能力进行干预的同时，要明确其所面临的外部约束条件，避免模糊地对约束条件相差甚远的目标群体施以同样的干预。我们特别强调要设置金融能力提升体系的持续更新机制，持续地对金融知识与技能、金融态度和金融行为等层面的具体内容、模式、方法进行更新，充分考虑数字技术和社会人文的变迁，以及相应的金融服务、金融行业变迁。除此之外，还应不断将心理学、行为学等领域的最新研究成果运用于金融能力干预效率的提升。

2. 优化以客户为中心的“最后一公里”金融服务

虽然浙江省普惠金融发展已经走在世界前列，但作为我国经济金融最为活跃发达的地区之一，浙江省应该进一步关注如何优化以客户为中心的“最后一公里”金融服务。

首先，要提升“最后一公里”基础金融服务的质量和效率。经过多年的普惠金融战略推进，浙江省银行业金融机构目前已经通过流动银行、金融服务站等形式覆盖偏远地区，实现了基础金融服务全覆盖。然而，调研数据显示，受访样本对金融服务站的不满意程度在总体不满意度中贡献了相对较高比例；受访样本对银行业金融机构柜台服务的改进期待，仍然有高达72.8%的受访人期待银行柜台服务简化手续、41.6%的受访人期待银行增加柜台网点。可见，“最后一公里”基础金融服务还有相当大的提升空间。未来，应该在尽可能兼顾商业可持续的情况下，探索逐渐减少低效率服务网点，完善代理模式的服务体系和支持体系，不断提升“最后一公里”基础金融服务的质量和效率。

其次，要丰富“最后一公里”金融产品种类。普惠金融服务不止于存贷汇服务，在提升基础金融服务质量和效率的同时，还应不断丰富“最后一公里”金融产品的种类，让更多群体享受到全面、多样化的金融服务，能够根据生产生活需要更加自由、便利地调整资产负债组合。在“使用情况”维度排斥指数中的，可以看出理财、保险等服务的使用排斥度还相对较高。反观近年来曝出的互联网金融欺诈、“跑路”事件，许多试图对财富进行管理的人群遭受欺骗和损失，这也反映出受监管的理财服务并未很好地满足市场需求。在相对富裕的浙江省，由受监管的供应商提供更多样化理财服务的需求更为迫切。此外，调查还显示浙江省受访样本保险服务的使用排斥度也相对较高，而合适的保险服务是平滑意外冲击的重要工具，因此，未来浙江省还需着重推进保险服务的深化。需要注意的是，理财和保险只是2017年调研中反映出来的“使用情况”排斥度最高的两种服务。在推进“最后一公里”金融服务发展的进程中，丰富金融产品的目标应该是为“最后一公里”客户提供可持续、负责任、功能全面的金融服务。

最后，要减少“最后一公里”金融服务障碍。基于浙江省数据的相关性分析表明，受访人在各类金融服务中遇到的障碍越多，其在可得性、使用情况、质量、满意度、金融能力各维度受到的排斥都更大。相应地，障碍越多，普惠金融综合指数所示的整体金融排斥度也越大。因此，减少“最后一公里”金融服务障碍应该是未来浙江省普惠金融发展需要持续关注的领域。据此，作为数字金融服务的入口，我们在调研中特别关注了网上银行、手机银行和第三方支付使用中的障碍。如上文分析所示，“不信任”选项在三种服务中占比都是较低的，也就是说，这三种数字金融服务都已经基本取得了绝大部分群体的信任。相较而言，操作的复杂性、使用传统服务方式的行为惯性，以及对网络/电信欺诈的恐惧成为了阻碍数字金融服务使用的重要原因，在未来的数字金融相关政策中，浙江省监管当局可以从上述障碍程度较高的方面着手进行政策干预，金融部门也应积极改善障碍程度较高的服务。

综上所述，CAFI建立的普惠金融指标体系可以用于衡量个人以及任何区域或群体金融排斥度的普惠金融综合指数，并将其用于衡量浙江省普惠金融发展现状，对浙江省普惠金融的未来发展提出了建议。有利于普惠金融政策制定和实施，可以作为金融机构决策的参考并具有对普惠金融发展持续监测的意义。

## 三、指数应用之二：浙江丽水市金融改革效果分析

### （一）丽水市普惠金融指数的分析

丽水市是一个典型山区，位于浙江省西南部，是浙江省面积最大的地级市①。一

① 资料来源：http://www.lishui.gov.cn/xsls/xsqjs/201703/t20170306_2016498.html。

方面，丽水农村金融服务供给不足问题在改革之前普遍存在。改革之初，仍有41个乡镇的农户因为没有固定的金融机构网点而无法获得基础金融服务；同时因为农户缺乏有效的抵押担保物、农村信用体系不健全、金融机构与农户间的信息不对称等问题的存在，长期以来当地金融机构提供的农业信贷不足以满足农户的需求。另一方面，当地农村金融服务需求旺盛。第一，丽水市形成了香菇、茶叶等多个有全国影响力的农业产业，乡村旅游、农家乐、民宿经济等新型乡村经济发展迅速，经济的快速发展产生了大量的金融需求；第二，在浙江省城市化快速发展的过程中，失地农民在建房、搬迁、缴纳城镇职工养老保险等方面也有迫切的资金需求。

丽水金融改革的最终目标是要提高金融的包容性，也就是提高金融服务的可得性、使用率和满意度。丽水市农村金融改革经历了两个阶段，第一个阶段是自发探索阶段（2006—2011年），第二个阶段是全国农村金融改革综合试验区（2011—2017年）。第一个阶段主要做法包括实施了以破解农村抵押担保物缺失问题为目标、以林权抵押贷款为重点的“信贷支农”工程；以破解银农信息不对称问题为目标、以农村信用体系建设为重点的“信用惠农”工程；以破解农民取现难问题为目标、以助农取款服务为重点的“支付便农”工程，开始探索农村金融改革。第二个阶段主要做法包括以“三权”抵押贷款为重点，大力推进农村产权融资服务体系；以优化农村金融生态环境为主线，加快完善农村金融信用体系建设；以改善投融资环境为目标，健全农村“四级”融资担保体系；以提升农村金融服务便利性为中心，探索和深化农村基础金融服务体系；以培育农村金融服务主体为导向，多形式推动农村金融组织体系建设；以健全政策保障为支撑，强化多元化的金融惠农政策体系；以拓宽农村金融服务渠道为着力点，建立健全农村金融市场体系；以完善农业风险分担机制为切入点，积极推进农村保险服务民生体系①。

我们使用CAFI指数对收集到的丽水市三县区（莲都区、景宁畲族自治县、云和县）3027份调研问卷数据进行了整理分析，通过定量分析方法，从可得性、使用率、质量、满意度、能力、障碍、数字化程度和预期8个维度，评估丽水市农村金融改革的普惠金融综合效果。丽水普惠金融发展指数与浙江其他地区的平均指数对比如图9－3所示。该观测结果表明丽水市与浙江其他地区均表现出了较高的普惠金融发展水平，在综合指数与各分维度上没有体现出较大的差异。

如图9－4所示，在普惠金融数字化排斥指数维度上，丽水市表现出了比其他浙江地区更小的值，这说明了丽水的平均普惠金融数字化程度较高。与之相对应的，丽水市的受访者表达了对普惠金融发展最好的平均期望值。

① 资料来源：人民银行丽水市中心支行。

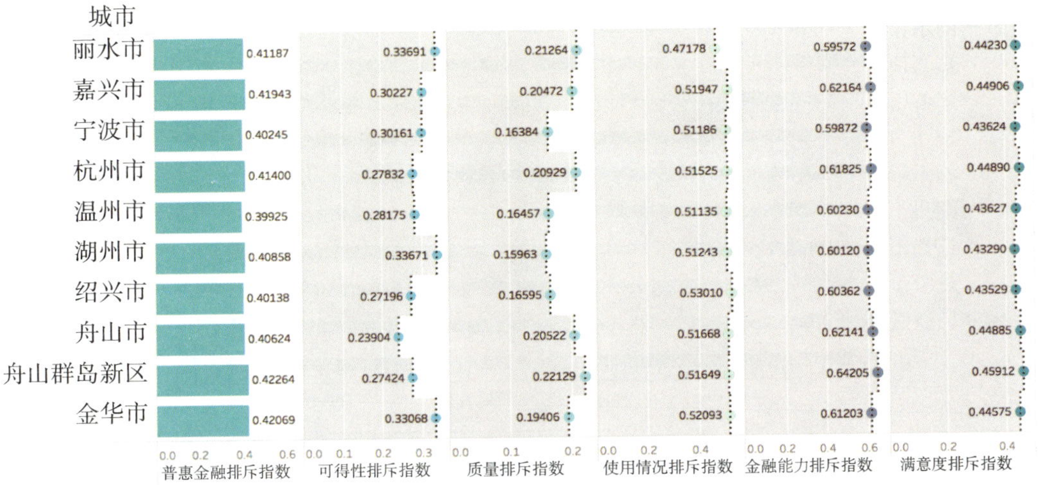

图 9-3　丽水与浙江其他地区普惠金融排斥指数及子维度指数

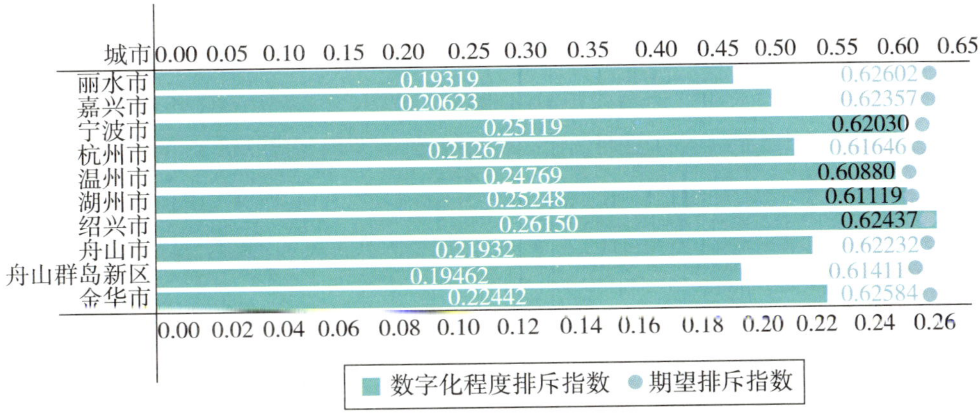

图 9-4　丽水与浙江其他地区普惠金融数字化排斥指数与期望值指数

如图 9-5 所示，在普惠金融障碍排斥指数上，丽水市的数据体现了最低的平均排斥度。这表明了丽水民众在普惠金融的推广过程中感受到的障碍最少。

## （二）丽水市农村金融改革对普惠金融发展的影响

我们使用倾向评分匹配方法来检测丽水金融改革对普惠金融发展各指标的影响。倾向评分匹配（Propensity Score Matching，PSM）是一种处理观察研究数据的统计学方法。在观察研究中，倾向评分匹配的方法可以减少数据偏差和混杂变量对于分析结果的影响，以便对丽水金融改革组和其他非金融改革组数据进行更合理的比较。这种方法最早由 Paul Rosenbaum 和 Donald Rubin 在 1983 年提出并用于社会学、经济学等

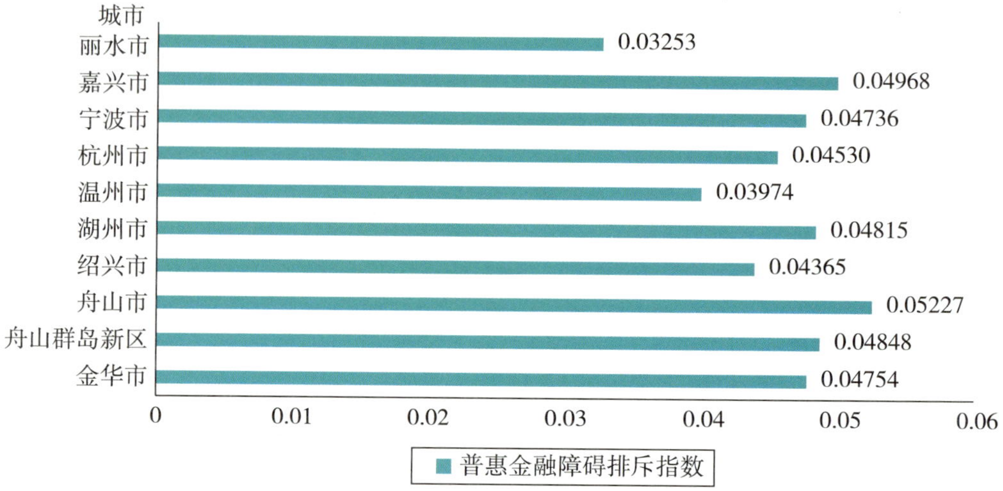


**图 9－5　丽水与浙江其他地区普惠金融障碍排斥指数**

研究①。我们通过构建倾向评分匹配逻辑回归模型来量化丽水市金融改革对衡量普惠金融发展的各指标产生的影响。

在此观察研究建模分析中，结果变量为是否有金融改革，实验组为进行了金融改革的丽水数据，对照组为未进行金融改革的其他浙江数据。模型中的代码如表 9－1 所示。为了构建倾向评分匹配模型，我们使用了包含性别、婚姻、收入、年龄、家庭成员数、拥有的资产等 22 项特征变量作为控制变量来寻找改革组与非改革组的匹配样本来进行改革对各指标影响的分析。匹配后每个丽水样本都从其他浙江样本中找到了 1～5 个匹配样本来比对。以下分别体现了匹配前与匹配后的金融改革组与非金融改革组数据。

**表 9－1　普惠金融综合指数匹配模型分析结果**

| 指标 | 代码 | 非改革样本平均值 | 改革效果 | T value | 显著水平 |
|---|---|---|---|---|---|
| 普惠金融综合排斥指数 | Exclusion. Index | 0.4562 | －0.0463 | －45.651 | *** |
| 可得性排斥指数 | Avai | 0.2990 | 0.0303 | 5.8331 | *** |
| 使用情况排斥指数 | Util | 0.5460 | －0.0573 | －33.005 | *** |
| 质量排斥指数 | Qual | 0.2015 | 0.0133 | 10.336 | *** |
| 金融能力排斥指数 | Fcap | 0.6664 | －0.0573 | －21.905 | *** |
| 满意度排斥指数 | Safy | 0.4514 | －0.0036 | －3.6887 | *** |
| 障碍排斥指数 | Barr | 0.0453 | 0.0037 | 7.8064 | *** |
| 数字化程度排斥指数 | Digi | 0.2362 | －0.0405 | －21.402 | *** |
| 期望指数 | Expe | 0.6132 | 0.0120 | 9.6982 | *** |

① ROSENBAUM, PAUL R., and DONALD B. RUBIN. The Central Role of the Propensity Score in Observational Studies for Causal Effects [J]. Biometrika 70.1, 1983: 41－55.

第一，通过倾向评分匹配及数据分析结果上表显示，丽水市的普惠金融综合指数，以及可得性、使用率、质量、满意度、金融能力、金融障碍、数字化程度和预期八个子维度的指数差异，均达到统计学上的显著水平，说明它们之间的差异是真实可靠的。本结果反映了丽水金融改革显著降低了丽水普惠金融服务的排斥率并显著提高金融服务的总体包容性。如表 9－1 所示，丽水普惠金融综合排斥指数的差异值为－0.0463。这说明丽水农村金融改革有效地降低了金融服务的排斥程度。反过来说，改革确实增加了金融服务的包容性，也就是有效促进普惠金融的发展。普惠金融综合排斥指数由可得性、使用率、质量、满意度和金融能力五个维度组成，虽然总体上，改革促进了普惠金融的发展，但是改革在不同维度上的表现有所不同。

第二，丽水金融改革显著降低与客户体验直接相关维度的金融排斥。与客户体验直接相关的使用率、满意度、金融能力三个子维度差值为负值，也就是说，改革在这三个方面降低了金融排斥程度，增加了金融的包容性。这显然与改革的内容紧密相关。改革在金融组织、金融产品、惠农政策、金融市场、信用、服务平台、支付服务、金融生态八大体系着力，最主要的目的就是改善客户端的体验。显然，改革对客户端产生显著的良好效果。

第三，结果显示丽水金融服务的可得性和质量两个维度的指数差值均为正值，表明丽水市在金融服务的包容性落后于其他地区。这两个维度和丽水市的一些客观原因有关，例如，可得性方面的排斥程度与人口的分散度有关，金融服务的质量与获得服务的成本有关。因此我们认为，这种差异并不能够反映金融改革没有产生效果，而是由于丽水市客观条件明显落后于其他地区，改革产生的效果还没有能够将这种客观条件的差异填平，换言之，如果没有改革，差异的程度可能还会更大。

第四，丽水的金融服务数字化在降低金融排斥方面产生了显著效果。如表 9－1 可知，数字化金融服务在丽水市排斥程度显著低于其他地区的客户。改革提高了消费者金融服务的使用率、满意度、金融能力，这些方面都有助于客户使用数字化的产品获得金融服务。通过改革，丽水市金融消费者对未来的预期显著提高。获得良好的金融服务，使人们以更加积极的态度面对未来，对未来更加有信心，更加自信。

第五，需要注意的是丽水市普惠金融障碍的地区差异还没有完全消除。虽然丽水市总体金融障碍程度不高，但是从个体匹配的结果来看，个人面对的金融障碍显著高于其他地区。改革还没有能够完全消除金融障碍的地区差异。

总的来说，丽水市的金融改革对提高普惠金融使用、可得性、满意度、数字化程度与预期，降低普惠金融的排斥度上起到了积极显著的效果，改善了金融客户体验。虽然在客观因素上，丽水市农村金融改革试图消除恶劣的自然条件造成自然金融排斥，但是从结果上来看，还没有能够完全消除这种差距。改革对客户产生的影响足以抵消客观因素造成的差异，最终成功降低金融服务的综合排斥程度，显著提高金融的包容性，促进普惠金融发展。

### （三）对丽水市发展普惠金融的建议

通过 CAFI 指数对丽水金融改革的成效分析，我们对丽水市发展普惠金融有以下几点建议。

首先，要坚持结合乡村振兴战略建设社会化的信用环境。丽水市的农村金融改革，县乡村的信用体系建设、信用信息平台的建设、担保抵押的改革创新，都是打造信用社会与振兴乡村的过程。

其次，要加强数字化金融科技的应用。从村级服务站的业务量逐步减少的迹象表明，数字化是未来金融服务的方向，也是解决普惠金融“最后一公里”问题的重要手段。数字技术可以大幅度地降低金融服务的成本，提高客户的体验，为客户提供个性化的金融服务。

再次，要挖掘金融综合信息平台的潜力。金融综合信息平台是数字化技术应用的重要基础设施。金融的复杂性和多维性，要求综合信用信息平台掌握的信息也是综合性的。如何打破各部门的信息孤岛，整合各部门的信息资源，形成一种安全的全面的保护个人权益的信用信息平台，是发展普惠金融的关键。金融综合信息平台，对于了解客户的需求，分析金融的发展趋势和障碍，以及对整个经济发展，都具有非常重要的作用，应该投入更多的资源挖掘其更大的潜在作用。

最后，要着力农村居民的金融能力建设。农村居民是主要的普惠金融客户。他们的金融能力决定着他们的金融需求，也决定整个社会的信用。金融能力建设，不仅要求客户积极主动提高自身的能力，也需要金融机构承担一定的责任。当然，政府在整个社会的金融能力建设中，应当发挥重要的作用。

# 第十章　银行服务促进小微企业发展

**【摘要】**“从好金融到好社会”是普惠金融发展的重要论述，但是目前很少有实证研究证明“好金融”与“好社会”之间的关系，困难在于两者都难以观察和度量。通常做法是用两个指标集合来分别反映“好金融”与“好社会”。如果能够证明两个指标结合之间的逻辑关系，就可以证明“好金融”与“好社会”的关系。例如，用银行账户的有无代表普惠金融发展，用低收入人群的就业机会和工资收入增长来代表好社会。本章通过实证发现，小微企业银行账户数（隐含获得多家金融服务）与合同工人数及其员工工资水平具有显著的相关，由此证明推动和发展“好金融”可以形成建设“好社会”的效果。

## 一、引言

是否拥有一个银行账户是目前国际、国内衡量一个人或者一个企业是否被银行服务排除在外的一个重要指标，但是人们很少分析拥有一个银行账户对于企业能够产生什么样的影响？这种影响是否能促进社会的公平发展？也就是说，拥有银行账户具有哪些普惠金融的意义？

普惠金融强调要为中小微企业提供银行服务，促进社会的均衡发展，是基于一种假设：中小微企业的发展可以为中低收入阶层提供大量就业机会，增加他们的收入水平，改善他们的生活。这就是为中小微企业提供金融服务的社会效果。

这种从为小微企业提供金融服务到提高中低收入人群的收入水平的因果关系，在现阶段只是一种逻辑推理出来的假设，如果这种假设是真实的，应该可以看到，代表普惠金融发展的银行账户拥有情况应该与小微企业的就业人数和员工收入水平具有某种关联。据我们了解，目前还没有文献能够证明这种关联的存在，本书将试图通过实证研究，证明这种关联的存在。

分析发现，银行账户的多少与小微企业的合同工人数[①]以及员工工资有显著的关系。由于银行账户开立是在企业发展历史中形成的，与去年的合同工人数和员工工资水平具有时间差，因而推断它们之间存在因果关系。

在多家银行开立账户，可能主观上只是为了方便财务管理，但是客观上增加了企业资金的流动性，增加获得信贷资金从而增加流动资金总量的机会，增加了企业生产服务的稳定性，提高了企业的效率，促进企业的可持续发展。具体表现为增加企业的合同制员工人数和员工工资。

通过改善小微企业账户服务，提高服务的便利性，可以促进小微企业发展，增加就业机会，改善低端就业人群的收入水平，促进社会均衡发展。

## 二、银行账户超越财务管理功能

在浙江调查 2729 个小微企业发现，每一个企业至少有两个以上银行账户。如图 10－1 所示，有 85％的企业开设有两个银行账户。近 15％的企业开立 3 个以上的银行账户。从财务和会计的角度看，企业有基本银行账户已经满足了所有业务的需要，为什么所有的企业都要开立两个以上的银行账户呢？分析发现，银行账户的功能已经超越了财务管理功能，尤其对于小微企业来说更是如此。

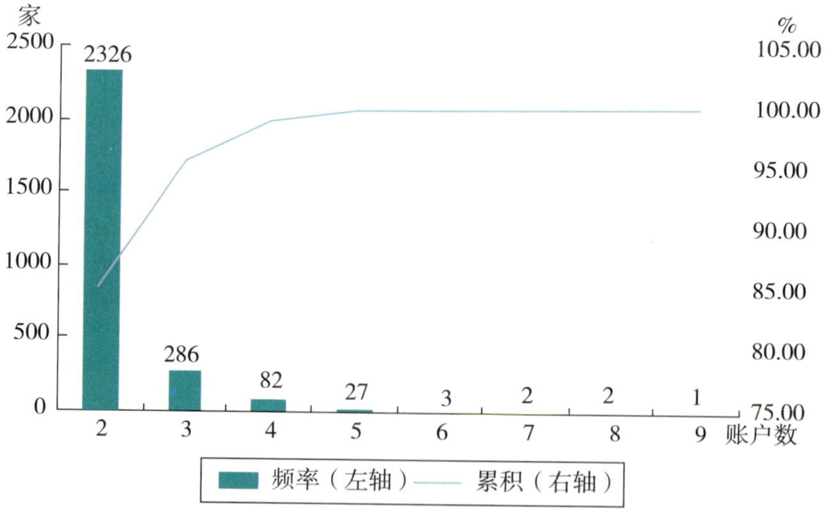


图 10－1　小微企业银行账户统计

### （一）增加财务管理的便利性

一般而言，凡是在工商部门登记的企业，都必须有一个基本银行账户，这是有关

① 在临时工人数模型中，企业银行账户数与临时工人数没有显著相关。

部门的一项基本要求（中国人民银行，2003）。企业在登记过程中，首先要在一家银行开立一个临时账户，注入注册资本金进行验资，当企业完成登记注册以后，该账户会转成企业的基本存款账户。个体工商户在申请经营许可的过程中，也要求开设基本存款账户。

基本存款账户是一个企业的主办账户，只能开立一个，企业可以通过它办理银行结算、转账和现金收付等。按规定，企业日常经营活动的资金收付及其工资、奖金和现金的支取等必须通过基本账户。开立基本账户后，企业因借款或其他结算需要，在基本存款账户开立行以外的金融机构开立一般存款账户，可以开立多个，用于企业办理借款转存、归还和其他结算的资金收付。一般存款账户可办理现金缴存，不得办理现金支取。

在财务实际管理工作中，除了发放工资和奖金外，企业一般使用基本账户提现以满足公司日常运转所需的现金，同时也进行小额资金的流转；对于大笔资金往来，一般选择通过其他账户进行。在不同银行开立多个账号，最主要的是为了方便财务管理，同时还有规避风险的考虑，如果公司不幸涉及法律纠纷被冻结账户，所冻结的只是基本户，其他账户的资金不受任何影响。

### （二）提高企业资金的使用效率

银行账户是企业存放资金的金库，同时也是资金流通的通道。每一家银行提供的转账服务，都有内外之别。与同一家银行内部转账相比，跨行转账需要支付更高的手续费，时间延迟比较长。由于企业的客户可能在不同的银行开户，在交易过程中，如果出现大量的跨行交易现象，必然导致交易成本增加，资金归集的时间延后。由此可见，在不同银行开设多个银行账户，可以以更低的成本和更快的速度把客户的资金归集到公司账户下；同时也便于以更低成本把资金支付给供货方。因此，在不同银行开设多个银行账户增加了企业资金的周转率，提高企业资金的流动性和使用效率。

### （三）增加企业信用

银行账户的使用也是一个建立企业信用的过程。在现有的体制下，虽然人民银行有统一的征信体系，每一家银行都有自己的客户信用记录，特别是在大数据和金融科技被广泛使用的时代，银行往往根据自己的记录对客户进行信用评价，授予不同的信用额度。在不同的银行开设账户，意味着在不同的银行都有一个信用额度，扩大了信用贷款的来源，增加企业流动资金供给的稳定性。

### （四）保持价值链的稳定发展

由于资金来源的稳定和使用效率的提高，在多家银行开立账户的企业，通过应付账和应收账的有效管理，能够和供货方以及客户端建立更稳定的相互信赖的财务关系，有利于提高企业在供应链中的信誉，保持其价值链的稳定发展，提高可持续发展能力。

### （五）增加企业人才储备

一个企业的可持续发展能力，体现在企业的效率以及人才储备。拥有多家银行账户，有利于提高企业资金的使用效率，扩大信用资金的来源，维持价值链的稳定，必然增加企业的人才储备能力。小微企业主要是通过吸纳合同制员工的方式进行人才储备，通过增加合同制员工人数保证生产的稳定性。相比之下，临时工流动性比较大。大量使用临时工体现了企业生产的波动性。

## 三、银行账户的普惠金融价值

普惠金融的发展需要改善对小微企业的金融服务，解决融资难、融资贵的问题。归根结底是提高小微企业的生产效率，增加小微企业的可持续发展能力。图 10－2 归纳了银行账户如何在提高小微企业的生产效率和可持续发展方面发挥作用。这种作用应该体现为银行账户数与合同制员工数量的关联。

如果这种关联存在，为小微企业提供银行账户服务具有重大普惠金融意义。一方面是增加就业机会。合同制员工数量的增加意味着为社会提供更多的稳定的工作机会。由于小微企业提供的工作机会往往是针对低收入人群的，因此具有促进社会均衡发展的意义。另一方面是增加收入。如果银行账户服务能够提高小微企业的生产效率，提高的企业的收益能力必然会转化为员工的工资收入增加。也就是说，通过增加小微企业的银行账户服务，可以增加低收入人群的就业机会，提高他们的收入水平。

图 10－2 也说明，银行账户服务、小微企业合同工人数及工资水平之间的关系，不是一种直接的关系，而是一种间接的关系。这意味着，银行账户通过中间变量，例如，应收账款和应付账款，来影响合同工人数和工资水平。银行账户和这些中间变量也应该有关联性。需要指出的是，这些中间变量都是生产体系中的环节之一，而银行账户服务与合同工人数和工资收入之间的关系，是一种综合的关系，是各种中间生产环节的综合体现。银行账户服务对每一个中间生产环节的影响可能是微弱的，但是综合起来可能是显著的。

上述分析认为，银行账户服务具有重要的普惠金融意义。但是这种意义是否现实存在，要通过实证分析来证明。只有当银行账户服务与小微企业的合同工人数以及工资水平之间的关联的假设被实证分析所验证，银行账户服务的普惠金融意义才能够被证实。下文将分析问卷数据，通过计量经济建模来证明这种关联的存在。

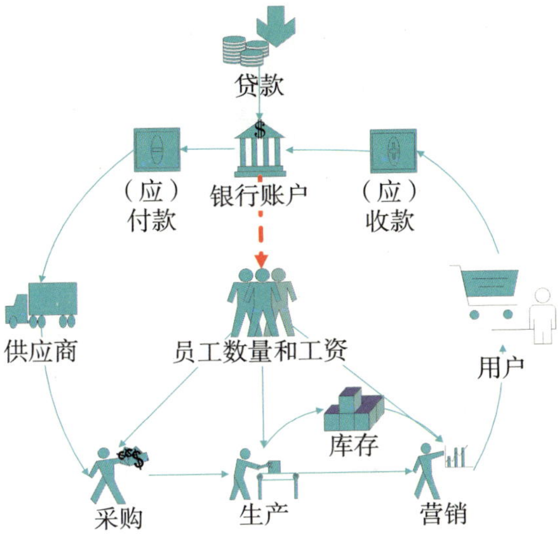


图 10－2　银行账户在企业经营中的作用

## 四、员工收入水平偏低

中国普惠金融研究院在当地政府、金融办、信用社的协助下，对浙江省 14 个县的 2729 个企业进行了调查。按类型对样本企业进行分类（见表 10－1）：个体工商户占 44%，有限责任公司占 30%，个人独资企业占 15%。有限责任公司往往也是以个人和家庭成员为中心登记注册的，可见小微企业以个人和家庭经营为主的特点非常明显。调查样本涵盖了我国统计部门分类的 30 个行业中的 27 个（见表 10－2），其中最集中的是制造业和批发零售业，两者合计约占 45%。

表 10－1　企业类型统计表

| 企业类型 | 企业数（家） | 平均合同工人数（人） | 平均临时工人数（人） | 员工平均工资（元） |
|---|---|---|---|---|
| 国有企业 | 13 | 42 | 17 | 4269 |
| 集体企业 | 16 | 18 | 7 | 4080 |
| 个人独资企业 | 406 | 16 | 9 | 3873 |
| 有限合伙企业 | 43 | 16 | 6 | 4059 |
| 有限责任公司 | 807 | 33 | 8 | 4362 |
| 合作社 | 84 | 5 | 7 | 3124 |
| 个体工商户 | 1191 | 3 | 3 | 3882 |
| 家庭农场 | 53 | 3 | 5 | 3257 |
| 股份有限公司 | 33 | 43 | 13 | 3916 |
| 其他 | 83 | 10 | 3 | 3651 |

**表 10-2 企业行业分布统计表**

| 行业 | 企业数（家） | 合同工 | | 临时工 | |
|---|---|---|---|---|---|
| | | 总人数（人） | 企业平均（人） | 总人数（人） | 企业平均（人） |
| 制造业 | 642 | 17607 | 27 | 4238 | 7 |
| 批发/零售 | 576 | 2029 | 4 | 1061 | 2 |
| 服装/纺织/皮革 | 320 | 7224 | 23 | 2216 | 7 |
| 农业/渔业/林业 | 213 | 1224 | 6 | 1460 | 7 |
| 餐饮/娱乐/旅游/酒店/生活服务 | 181 | 814 | 4 | 493 | 3 |
| 快速消费品（食品/饮料/化妆品） | 175 | 350 | 2 | 559 | 3 |
| 其他行业 | 142 | 2162 | 15 | 1161 | 8 |
| 汽车及零配件 | 79 | 1799 | 23 | 492 | 6 |
| 房地产开发/建筑工程/装潢/设计 | 66 | 2152 | 33 | 1559 | 24 |
| 家具/工艺品/玩具 | 65 | 964 | 15 | 492 | 8 |
| 机械/设备/重工 | 43 | 942 | 22 | 239 | 6 |
| 出版/印刷/包装 | 39 | 538 | 14 | 168 | 4 |
| 交通/运输/物流 | 35 | 788 | 23 | 276 | 8 |
| IT/软硬件服务/电子商务/因特网运营 | 34 | 505 | 15 | 169 | 5 |
| 医疗/护理/保健/卫生 | 18 | 14 | 1 | 22 | 1 |
| 通信/电信运营/网络设备/增值服务 | 16 | 204 | 13 | 66 | 4 |
| 家电 | 15 | 133 | 9 | 38 | 3 |
| 电子技术/半导体/集成电路 | 12 | 243 | 20 | 80 | 7 |
| 广告/公关/媒体/艺术 | 11 | 72 | 7 | 21 | 2 |
| 航天/航空/能源/化工 | 10 | 117 | 12 | 21 | 2 |
| 教育/培训/科研/院校 | 8 | 87 | 11 | 24 | 3 |
| 办公用品及设备 | 7 | 39 | 6 | 4 | 1 |
| 贸易/进出口 | 6 | 54 | 9 | 18 | 3 |
| 制药/生物工程/医疗设备/器械 | 6 | 268 | 45 | 71 | 12 |
| 中介/咨询/猎头/认证 | 4 | 54 | 14 | 1 | 0 |
| 仪器仪表/工业自动化 | 4 | 82 | 21 | 66 | 17 |
| 物业管理/商业中心 | 3 | 105 | 35 | 4 | 1 |
| 会计/审计 | | | | | |
| 法律 | | | | | |
| 银行/保险/证券/投资银行/风险基金 | | | | | |

（一）企业规模小

雇用人员的数量常常是衡量企业规模的重要指标。按照我国的统计标准，21～100名员工以下的企业都属于小型企业；20名员工以下的属于微型企业。图10－3显示，我们所调查的企业中，15％属于小型企业，83％属于微型企业。微型企业中有29％没有聘用合同制员工。图10－4显示，小微企业聘用临时工的现象非常普遍，54％小微企业聘用有不同数量的临时工。

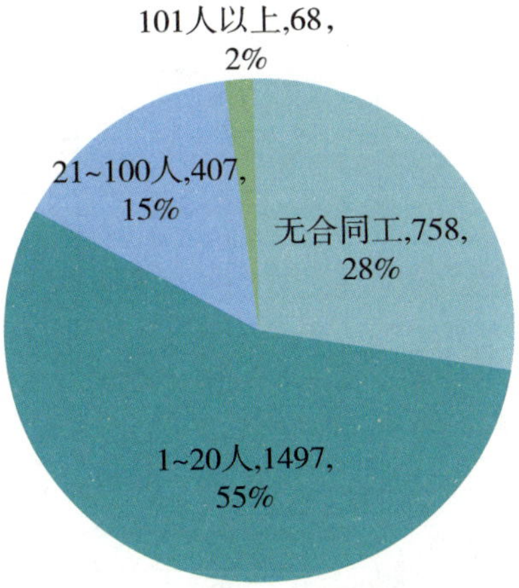


**图10－3　合同工雇用情况**

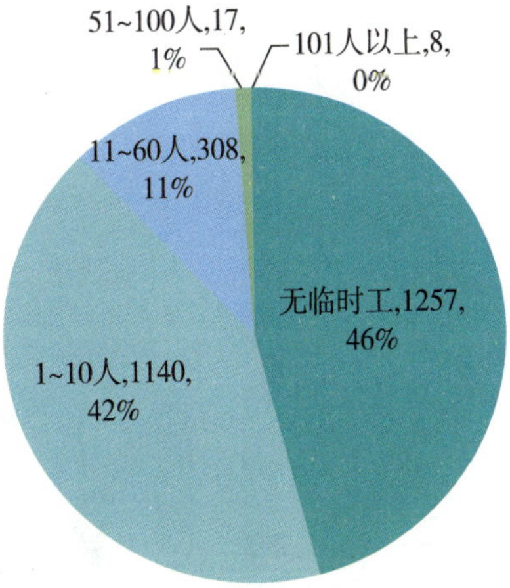


**图10－4　临时雇用情况**

（二）工资收入偏低

在有聘用员工的企业当中，平均月工资4004元，相当于2016年浙江省全社会单位就业人员月平均工资（4012 元）水平。工资水平和企业的类型和行业有关。其中，占份额比较大的个体户企业，其员工的月平均工资水平为 3884 元，个人独资企业为 3873 元，有限责任公司 4362 元。

图 10－5 显示，企业规模与公司水平具有正相关关系，企业规模越小，工资收入水平越低。由于大部分是比较小的小微企业，大多数企业的工资水平低于当地的平均收入水平。图 10－6 更加清楚地说明，有 58%的企业开出的平均工资低于平均工资水平。

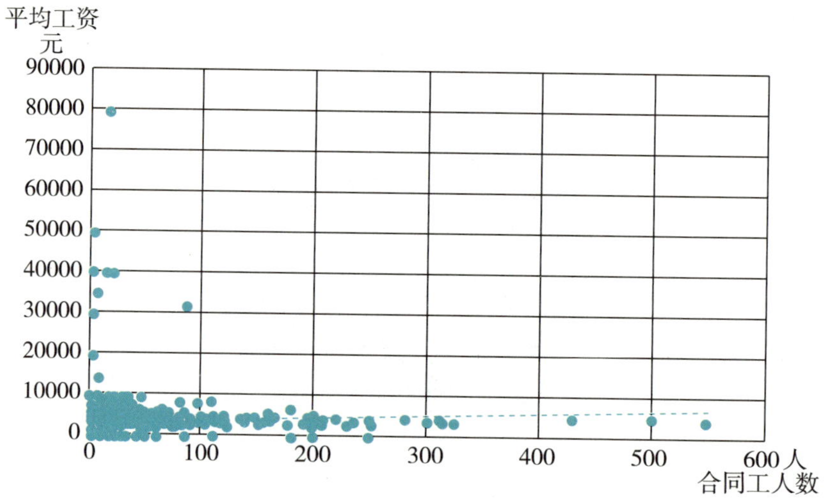


**图 10－5　工资水平与员工数量的关系**

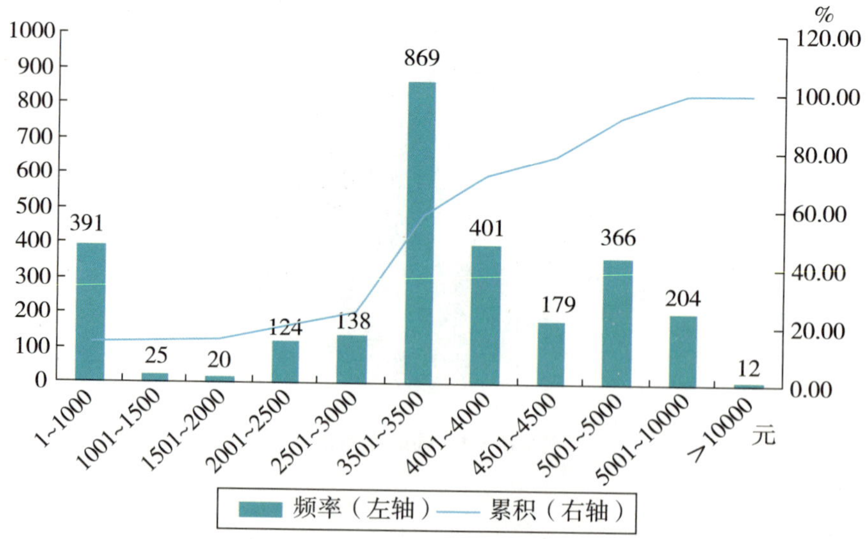


**图 10－6　企业平均工资水平分布**

## 五、证实模型

要证明银行账户与员工数量及工资水平的关系，需要借助计量经济模型，在大量的问卷调查数据的基础上，验证其是否相关。虽然要建立计量经济模型，是一个非常复杂的技术过程，但是其原理却非常简单，也就是检验其时间的关系系数是否为零。

两个变量时间的关系受到诸多因素的影响，为了获得比较可靠的结果，需要对其他的因素进行控制，以获得同等条件下的结论。由于我们的调查涵盖了诸多因素，使我们有机会在模型中加入地理位置、行业、企业类型、资产规模、法人特征等因素。也就是说，银行账户服务与企业合同制员工数量以及工资收入关系，是在上述因素同等条件下的关系。

### （一）银行账户与用工数量和员工工资成正比关系

表 10－3 中的“银行账户数”一行的系数是 2.996，意思是当企业增加一个银行账户时，企业可以增加 3 名合同制员工；对这个系数进行统计学 T 检验，验证它是否等于 0。表中对应的 t 值为 3.414，显著水平为三个星号（＊＊＊）。这个检验结果告诉我们，有 99％的把握认为这个系数不等于 0。这个结果证明小微企业的银行账户数量与合同制员工数量具有显著相关，而且这是一个正相关。结合图 10－2 进行分析认为，在表 10－3 中所列的其他因素相同的条件下，增加银行账户，可以提高企业的效率，增加就业岗位，扩大企业规模，促进企业的可持续发展。

**表 10－3　合同工模型**

| 自变量 | 系数 | 标准误差 | t 值 | 显著水平 |
|---|---|---|---|---|
| （常量） | 8.540 | 10.120 | .844 | |
| 银行账户数 | 2.996 | .878 | 3.414 | ＊＊＊ |
| 上年最大 2 笔贷款 | 7.959E－06 | .000 | 0.594 | |
| 上年最大 2 笔贷款利率 | －1.960E－02 | .137 | －0.143 | |
| 存货 | 2.226E－04 | .000 | 9.907 | ＊＊＊ |
| 应收账款 | －4.623E－06 | .000 | －0.170 | |
| 应付账款 | 8.637E－06 | .000 | 2.137 | ＊＊ |
| 每月水电费 | 8.903E－05 | .000 | 15.108 | ＊＊＊ |
| 上年营业收入 | 3.449E－06 | .000 | 0.755 | |
| 上年纳税额 | 1.870E－04 | .000 | 17.691 | ＊＊＊ |
| 上年净利润 | －7.380E－05 | .000 | －5.159 | ＊＊＊ |

续表

| 自变量 | 系数 | 标准误差 | t值 | 显著水平 |
|---|---|---|---|---|
| 净资产 | 4.282E−05 | .000 | 2.007 | ** |
| 经营年限 | .599 | .095 | 6.291 | *** |
| 注册商标 | .023 | .170 | 0.134 | |
| 当前注册资金 | 2.024E−07 | .000 | 0.627 | |
| 股金来源：自有资金 | −8.316E−06 | .000 | −0.446 | |
| 股金来源：银行贷款 | 1.255E−05 | .000 | 0.470 | |
| 股金来源：亲朋好友借款 | −4.996E−05 | .000 | −0.300 | |
| 总资产 | −2.077E−07 | .000 | −0.196 | |
| 经营场所面积 | 1.067E−05 | .000 | 0.946 | |
| 主要设备购买时价格 | −5.548E−06 | .000 | −0.701 | |
| 专利数 | .598 | .115 | 5.199 | *** |
| 是否财务记账 | 1.741 | 1.485 | 1.172 | |
| 独立财务 | 9.053 | 1.592 | 5.686 | *** |
| 代理记账 | −8.194 | 1.302 | −6.294 | *** |
| 使用财务软件 | 3.951 | 1.488 | 2.656 | *** |
| 法人年龄 | .249 | .067 | 3.691 | *** |
| 男法人 | 2.273 | 1.269 | 1.791 | * |
| 高中法人 | 2.417 | 1.262 | 1.914 | * |
| 本科法人 | 6.689 | 2.686 | 2.491 | ** |
| 专科法人 | 7.128 | 1.842 | 3.869 | *** |
| 研究生法人 | 93.142 | 10.173 | 9.155 | *** |
| 未知学历法人 | 2.983 | 2.718 | 1.098 | |
| 湖州市 | −11.280 | 2.984 | −3.781 | *** |
| 嘉兴市 | −9.116 | 2.769 | −3.292 | *** |
| 金华市 | −10.941 | 2.417 | −4.527 | *** |
| 宁波市 | −6.987 | 2.869 | −2.436 | ** |
| 绍兴市 | −14.793 | 2.494 | −5.930 | *** |
| 温州市 | −13.320 | 2.560 | −5.203 | *** |
| 舟山市 | −14.221 | 2.830 | −5.026 | *** |
| 其他 | −10.312 | 3.195 | −3.227 | *** |
| 快速消费品（食品/饮料/化妆品） | 1.827 | 5.073 | .360 | |
| 批发/零售 | .899 | 4.777 | .188 | |
| 服装/纺织/皮革 | 12.579 | 4.870 | 2.583 | *** |

续表

| 自变量 | 系数 | 标准误差 | t 值 | 显著水平 |
| --- | --- | --- | --- | --- |
| 家具/工艺品/玩具 | 9.163 | 5.665 | 1.617 | * |
| 教育/培训/科研/院校 | .431 | 10.267 | .042 | |
| 家电 | −1.519 | 8.150 | −.186 | |
| 通信/电信运营/网络设备/增值服务 | 5.126 | 7.952 | .645 | |
| 制造业 | 8.295 | 4.766 | 1.740 | * |
| 汽车及零配件 | 10.849 | 5.489 | 1.977 | ** |
| 餐饮/娱乐/旅游/酒店/生活服务 | 3.689 | 5.032 | .733 | |
| 办公用品及设备 | −6.852 | 10.826 | −.633 | |
| 电子技术/半导体/集成电路 | .964 | 9.076 | .106 | |
| 仪器仪表/工业自动化 | −19.180 | 13.916 | −1.378 | |
| 贸易/进出口 | −7.137 | 11.576 | −.616 | |
| 机械/设备/重工 | 8.560 | 6.131 | 1.396 | |
| 制药/生物工程/医疗设备/器械 | 20.263 | 11.619 | 1.744 | * |
| 医疗/护理/保健/卫生 | −3.021 | 7.695 | −.393 | |
| 广告/公关/媒体/艺术 | .431 | 9.046 | .048 | |
| 出版/印刷/包装 | −1.481 | 6.208 | −.239 | |
| 房地产开发/建筑工程/装潢/设计 | 11.250 | 5.590 | 2.013 | ** |
| 物业管理/商业中心 | 9.238 | 15.699 | .588 | |
| 中介/咨询/猎头/认证 | 14.927 | 13.802 | 1.082 | |
| 交通/运输/物流 | 4.151 | 6.416 | .647 | |
| 航天/航空/能源/化工 | −1.760 | 9.457 | −.186 | |
| 农业/渔业/林业 | .710 | 5.190 | .137 | |
| 其他行业 | 2.786 | 5.128 | .543 | |
| 集体企业 | −16.342 | 9.963 | −1.640 | * |
| 个人独资企业 | −20.868 | 7.825 | −2.667 | *** |
| 有限合伙企业 | −23.770 | 8.691 | −2.735 | *** |
| 有限责任公司 | −14.657 | 7.709 | −1.901 | * |
| 合作社 | −19.962 | 8.414 | −2.372 | ** |
| 个体工商户 | −23.664 | 7.798 | −3.035 | *** |
| 家庭农场 | −19.787 | 8.754 | −2.260 | ** |
| 股份有限公司 | −5.362 | 8.967 | −.598 | |
| 其他 | −19.517 | 8.238 | −2.369 | ** |

贷款常常被认为是银行为小微企业发展提供的至关重要的服务。但是，我们的实证模型没有证明给小微企业提供贷款可以增加小微企业就业机会。无论是上年企业的贷款总额，还是企业支付的贷款利率，都没有对合同制员工的数量产生显著的影响。这可能是因为企业上年的贷款，主要是解决流动资金的问题，没有从根本上扩大企业的规模。

另外，企业股本的来源，包括自有资金和银行贷款，都没有显著地增加小微企业合同制员工规模。当然，就业机会只是小微企业为社会提供的诸多利好中的一种。银行贷款可能在提供收入等方面发挥作用。

表 10-4 显示，银行账户数量与员工工资水平成正比关系，其相关系数达到统计学显著水平。这再一次证明了银行账户在提高企业效率方面发挥了作用。

**表 10-4　员工工资模型**

| 自变量 | 系数 | 标准误差 | t 值 | 显著水平 |
|---|---|---|---|---|
| （常量） | 2958.264 | 1149.073 | 2.574 | *** |
| 银行账户数 | 283.535 | 101.466 | 2.794 | *** |
| 上年最大 2 笔贷款 | .000 | .002 | −.253 | |
| 上年最大 2 笔贷款利率 | 53.633 | 15.856 | 3.383 | *** |
| 存货 | .000 | .003 | −.071 | |
| 应收账款 | .000 | .003 | −.076 | |
| 专利数 | −11.803 | 13.321 | −.886 | |
| 总资产 | −1.754E−05 | .000 | −.143 | |
| 上年净利润 | −.001 | .002 | −.631 | |
| 净资产 | .003 | .002 | 1.128 | |
| 应付账款 | .000 | .000 | −.461 | |
| 每月水电费 | .000 | .001 | −.442 | |
| 是否财务记账 | 491.372 | 171.794 | 2.860 | *** |
| 独立财务 | −173.007 | 184.181 | −.939 | |
| 代理记账 | 247.317 | 150.637 | 1.642 | * |
| 使用财务软件 | 148.826 | 172.127 | .865 | |
| 经营年限 | −19.409 | 11.010 | −1.763 | * |
| 注册商标 | −15.518 | 19.636 | −.790 | |
| 当前注册资金 | 2.669E−06 | .000 | .071 | |
| 股金来源：自有资金 | −6.813E−05 | .002 | −.032 | |

续表

| 自变量 | 系数 | 标准误差 | t值 | 显著水平 |
|---|---|---|---|---|
| 股金来源：银行贷款 | .000 | .003 | .075 | |
| 股金来源：亲朋好友借款 | −.017 | .019 | −.898 | |
| 法人年龄 | 5.412 | 7.798 | .694 | |
| 男法人 | 149.492 | 146.895 | 1.018 | |
| 高中法人 | 387.522 | 146.064 | 2.653 | *** |
| 本科法人 | 566.960 | 310.670 | 1.825 | * |
| 专科法人 | 484.100 | 213.144 | 2.271 | ** |
| 研究生法人 | 1294.562 | 1177.366 | 1.100 | |
| 未知学历法人 | −773.558 | 314.613 | −2.459 | ** |
| 湖州市 | 424.961 | 345.194 | 1.231 | |
| 嘉兴市 | −288.564 | 320.508 | −.900 | |
| 金华市 | −218.892 | 279.594 | −.783 | |
| 宁波市 | −279.742 | 332.016 | −.843 | |
| 绍兴市 | 35.172 | 288.532 | .122 | |
| 温州市 | −438.738 | 296.254 | −1.481 | |
| 舟山市 | −1085.584 | 326.651 | −3.323 | *** |
| 其他 | −892.752 | 369.666 | −2.415 | ** |
| 快速消费品（食品/饮料/化妆品） | −934.707 | 587.211 | −1.592 | |
| 批发/零售 | −359.970 | 552.930 | −.651 | |
| 服装/纺织/皮革 | −27.351 | 563.672 | −.049 | |
| 家具/工艺品/玩具 | −96.478 | 655.753 | −.147 | |
| 教育/培训/科研/院校 | 4198.158 | 1188.475 | 3.532 | *** |
| 家电 | −433.267 | 943.272 | −.459 | |
| 通信/电信运营/网络设备/增值服务 | −491.727 | 920.440 | −.534 | |
| 制造业 | 317.330 | 551.702 | .575 | |
| 汽车及零配件 | −64.102 | 635.310 | −.101 | |
| 餐饮/娱乐/旅游/酒店/生活服务 | −95.354 | 582.374 | −.164 | |
| 办公用品及设备 | 342.884 | 1253.140 | .274 | |
| 电子技术/半导体/集成电路 | −165.320 | 1050.304 | −.157 | |
| 仪器仪表/工业自动化 | −577.252 | 1609.984 | −.359 | |

续表

| 自变量 | 系数 | 标准误差 | t值 | 显著水平 |
|---|---|---|---|---|
| 贸易/进出口 | 81.648 | 1339.973 | .061 | |
| 机械/设备/重工 | 26.003 | 709.535 | .037 | |
| 制药/生物工程/医疗设备/器械 | 84.969 | 1344.953 | .063 | |
| 医疗/护理/保健/卫生 | −930.308 | 890.715 | −1.044 | |
| 广告/公关/媒体/艺术 | 285.327 | 1047.117 | .272 | |
| 出版/印刷/包装 | −314.693 | 718.589 | −.438 | |
| 房地产开发/建筑工程/装潢/设计 | 590.405 | 645.900 | .914 | |
| 物业管理/商业中心 | −522.366 | 1817.259 | −.287 | |
| 中介/咨询/猎头/认证 | 421.252 | 1597.617 | .264 | |
| 交通/运输/物流 | 2060.923 | 742.606 | 2.775 | *** |
| 航天/航空/能源/化工 | −779.616 | 1094.642 | −.712 | |
| 农业/渔业/林业 | 193.047 | 599.937 | .322 | |
| 其他行业 | 220.082 | 593.528 | .371 | |
| 集体企业 | −229.057 | 1138.804 | −.201 | |
| 个人独资企业 | −844.645 | 879.696 | −.960 | |
| 有限合伙企业 | −638.692 | 983.379 | −.649 | |
| 有限责任公司 | −471.333 | 866.347 | −.544 | |
| 合作社 | −1338.408 | 949.873 | −1.409 | |
| 个体工商户 | −696.210 | 875.837 | −.795 | |
| 家庭农场 | −1352.145 | 986.709 | −1.370 | |
| 股份有限公司 | −1098.037 | 1016.061 | −1.081 | |
| 其他 | −1104.030 | 928.398 | −1.189 | |

也许读者会质疑银行账户的多少与企业规模和工资水平之间的逻辑关系，也可能是由于企业规模比较大，所以需要在多家金融机构开立多个银行账户。但是，我们认为企业开立账户的多少是在企业发展历史中产生，在时间上与上年的用工人数和去年的员工工资具有时间差，即开立账户在先，员工人数和员工工资发生在后。而且我们在模型中对企业资产总额、销售额等反映企业规模的变量进行了控制。也就是说，在规模相同的条件下，开立账户越多，员工人数越多，工资水平越高。因此，我们推断，银行账户数与员工人数和工资水平具有因果关系。

### （二）银行贷款利率与员工工资成正比关系

解决小微企业“融资贵、融资难”常常被当作发展普惠金融的重要目的，其中“融资贵”被认为是由于供应不足造成的。为了解决“融资贵”的问题，提供利率补贴或者对利率进行限制是政府用以发展小微企业的主要手段。这种手段常常存在争议，被认为扭曲了市场的作用，妨碍了市场的自由发展，导致了市场供给不足。

表 10－3 和表 10－4 显示，小微企业所支付的利率并没有和合同制员工人数显著相关，但与员工工资有显著相关。这个结果可能与人们的常规认识有些差异，它们基于“零和游戏”的角度，认为高利息必将减少用工，降低工资。但是，模型所反映的是企业支付能力，即支付高利息的企业，就能支付更高的工资。这综合反映了企业的效率。

### （三）银行服务不是小微企业发展的唯一因素

我们已经在图 10－2 中描述了银行服务只是提高小微企业可持续发展能力的主要因素之一，还有许多因素也可能在企业发展中发挥重要作用。实证模型验证了财务管理水平、法人的经历和教育、企业所在的地理位置、不同的行业和企业类型等，对企业合同制员工数量和工资水平都有显著的关联。尤其是企业法人的教育程度和规范的财务管理，与员工数量和员工工资都有显著相关。

不同的调查发现，小微企业在财务管理方面很不规范，这将伤害企业的信用，减少从金融机构获得金融支持的机会，阻碍了企业的可持续发展。提高小微企业的财务管理能力和水平，应该被列为国家促进小微企业发展、增加社会就业的一个重要措施。

## 六、结论

发展普惠金融的目的是要促进社会的均衡发展。就促进小微企业的金融服务而言，目的是通过促进小微企业的发展增加全社会的就业机会，增加雇员的收入。银行账户被列为衡量普惠金融的一个重要指标，但是还没有研究证明银行账户与小微企业所创造的就业机会和员工收入水平具有必然的联系。

本章试图从理论上解释银行账户与小微企业发展带来的社会效果之间的关系，在问卷调查的基础上建立实证模型，验证银行账户与小微企业的合同工人数和员工工资之间的关系是否达到显著水平。

分析发现，银行账户的多少与小微企业的合同工人数以及员工工资有显著的关系。由于银行账户开立是在企业发展的历史中形成的，与去年的合同工人数和员工工资水平具有时间差，推断它们之间具有因果关系。

在多家银行开立账户，可能在主观上只是为了财务管理的方便，但是实际上增加企业资金的流动性，增加获得信贷资金从而增加流动资金总量的机会，增加了企业生产服务的稳定性，提高了企业的效率，促进企业的可持续发展，具体表现为增加企业的合同制员工人数和员工工资。

# 参考文献


[1] ARABEHETY, P. G., C. MCKAY, and P. ZETTERLI. Proximity Matters: Five Case Studies in Closing the CICO Gap [M]. CGAP Publication, 2018.

[2] BURRITT, K., and G., COETZEE. Customer centricity and financial inclusion: lessons from other industries [M]. CGAP Publications, 2016.

[3] COLLINS, D., J. MORDUCH, S. RUTHERFORD, and O. RUTHVEN. Portfolios of the Poor: How the World's Poor Live on \$2 a Day [M]. Princeton University Press, 2009.

[4] DERCON, S., T. BOLD, and C. CALVO. Insurance for the Poor: Social Protection for the Poor and Poorest [M]. Palgrave Macmillan UK, 2008.

[5] DERMISH, A., C. KNEIDING, P. LEISHMAN, and I. MAS. Branchless and mobile banking solutions for the poor: a survey of the literature [J]. Innovations Technology Governance Globalization, 2011, 6 (4), 81-98.

[6] MUDALIAR A., H. SCHIFF, R. BASS, and H. DITHRICH. Annual Impact Investor Survey 2017 [M]. Global Impact Investing Network, 2017.

[7] HANOUCH, M., and G. CHEN. Promoting Competition in Mobile Payments: The Role of USSD [M]. CGAP Publications, 2015.

[8] MAS, I. The economics of branchless banking [J]. Social Science Electronic Publishing, 2009, 4 (4), 57-75.

[9] MAZER, R., and K. MCKEE. Consumer Protection in Digital Credit [M]. CGAP Publications, 2017.

[10] MAZER, R., and P. ROWAN. Competition in Mobile Financial Services: Lessons from Kenya and Tanzania [M]. CGAP Publications, 2016.

[11] MAZER, R., J. VANCEL, and A. KEYMAN. Finding "Win-Win" in Digitally Delivered Consumer Credit [M]. CGAP Publications, 2016.

[12] MCKAY, C. Proximity Matters: Improving the Viability of Frontier Agents [M]. CGAP Publication, 2018.

[13] Planet Finance, the Micro-finance Platform. China Country Overview, 2004.

[14] Planet Finance，the Micro-finance Platform. China Country Overview，2008.

[15] World Investment Report 2017：Investment and Digital Economy. United Nations，2017.

[16] 贝多广，李焰. 好金融　好社会——中国普惠金融发展报告 [M]. 北京：经济管理出版社，2016.

[17] 程恩江，徐忠. 中国小额信贷发展报告 [J]. 财经杂志，2006 (10).

[18] 杜晓山. 我国小额信贷发展报告 [J]. 农村金融研究，2009 (2)，37-44.

[19] 盖永和，夏志琼. 农村金融服务站运行缺陷亟待改进——以辽宁凤城市为例 [J]. 银行家，2016 (12)，103-104.

[20] 焦瑾璞，黄亭亭，汪天都，张韶华，王瑱. 中国普惠金融发展进程及实证研究 [D]. 北京：中国人民银行工作论文，No. 2015/2.

[21] 皮特·斯帕布姆，艾瑞克·迪弗罗，世界银行扶贫协商小组（CGAP）和中国普惠金融工作组. 中华人民共和国的金融普惠状况——对现有研究和公开数据的分析 [D]. 中国普惠金融第7号论文，2012.

[22] 深圳国际公益学院公益金融与社会创新中心. 植根农村与服务低收入农户的小微金融典范——中和农信小额信贷案例研究 [D].

[23] 吴国宝. 小额信贷在中国——艰难前行的公益小额信贷 [M]. 北京：中国财政经济出版社，2013.

[24] 王云魁. 国际农业发展基金（IFAD）中国农村金融项目转贷模式研究 [D]. 乌鲁木齐：新疆农业大学，2009.

[25] 中国财政科学研究院，联合国开发计划署驻华代表处. 中国扶贫可持续筹资报告 [R]. 2016.

[26] 中国发展研究基金会，友成企业家扶贫基金会. 中国社会价值投资报告 [R]. 2016.

## 在本书编写过程中得到了以下单位的支持和协助

(排名不分先后):

中国人民银行丽水市中心支行

兰州市金融办

兰州银行

飞贷金融科技

京东金融

蚂蚁金服